SB
Shojo Beat

Tail of the Moon

8

Story & Art by
Rinko Ueda

Tail of the Moon

Volume 8

CONTENTS

Story Thus Far...

It is the Era of the Warring States. Usagi is a failure as a ninja, but she is a skilled herbalist. She is working hard to qualify as a ninja so she can be the bride of Hattori Hanzo (aka "Shimo no Hanzo")!

Usagi sets out to Azuchi to meet Oda Nobunaga. Hanzo accompanies her in disguise as her husband Hanbei, a samurai from Okazaki. On the way, the two share their feelings and finally feel connected to one another.

As it turns out, Usagi does not get to meet Nobunaga after all. However, she does remember seeing Nobunaga's page, Ranmaru, back in Kouga. Unfortunately, Ranmaru discovers that Usagi is wearing a wig! Usagi is worried that Ranmaru will remember her as a ninja, but he does not seem to notice. Afraid that her engagement to Hanzo will become null again due to her incompetence, Usagi decides to keep this matter a secret from Hanzo.

Just when Usagi and Hanzo decide to go back to Iga, Ranmaru suddenly says, "I'll accompany you to Okazaki"...!

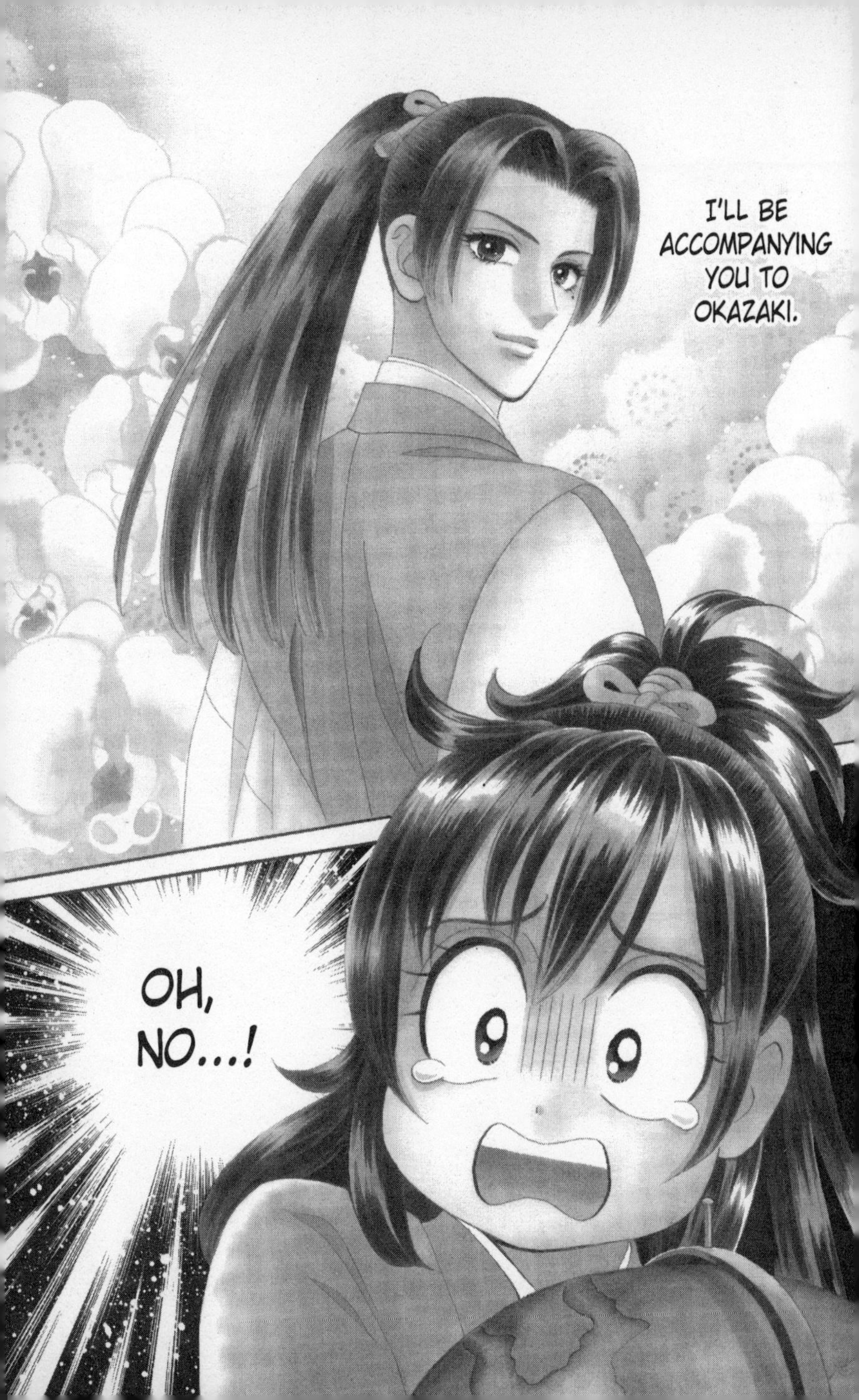
I'LL BE ACCOMPANYING YOU TO OKAZAKI.
OH, NO...!

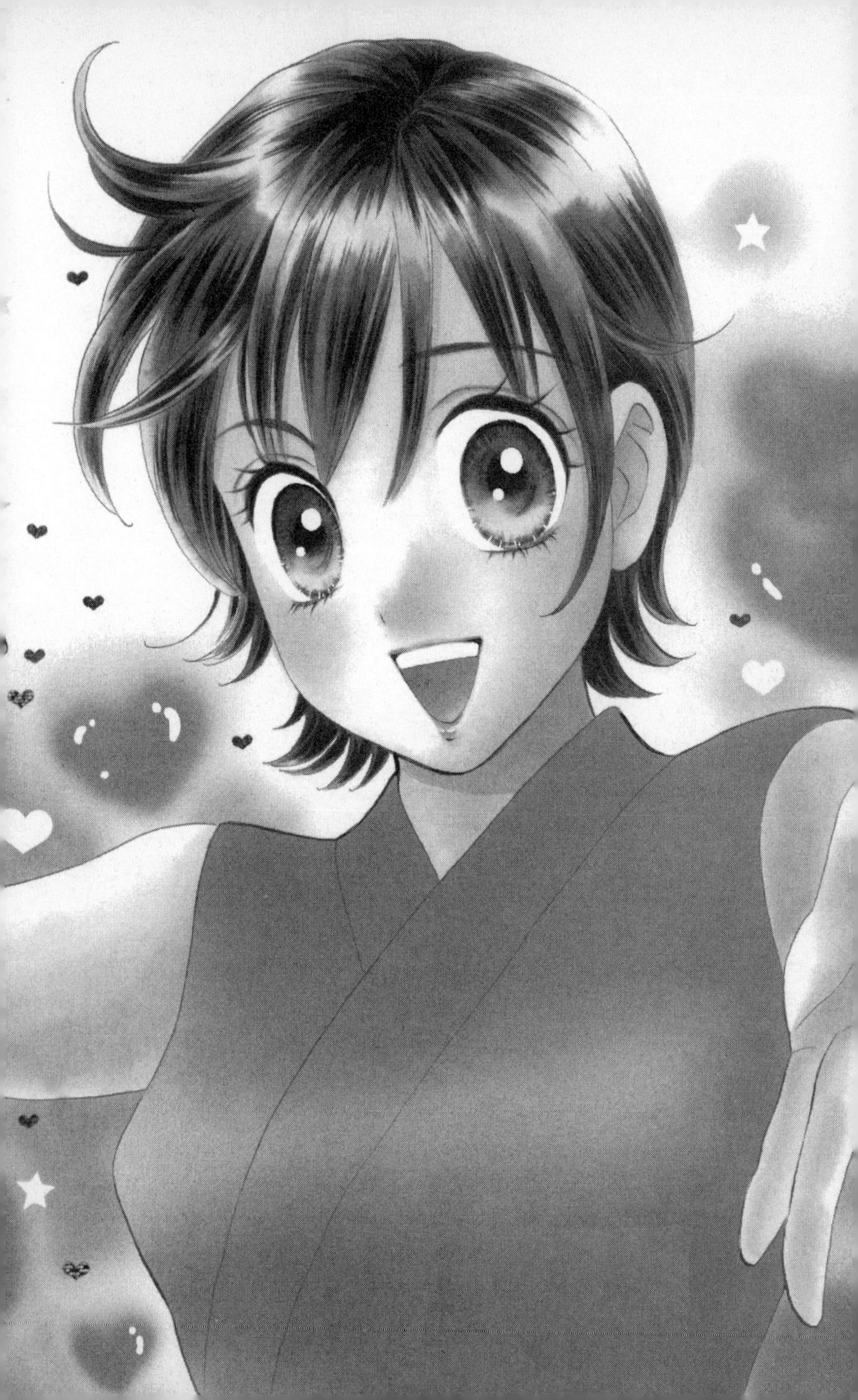

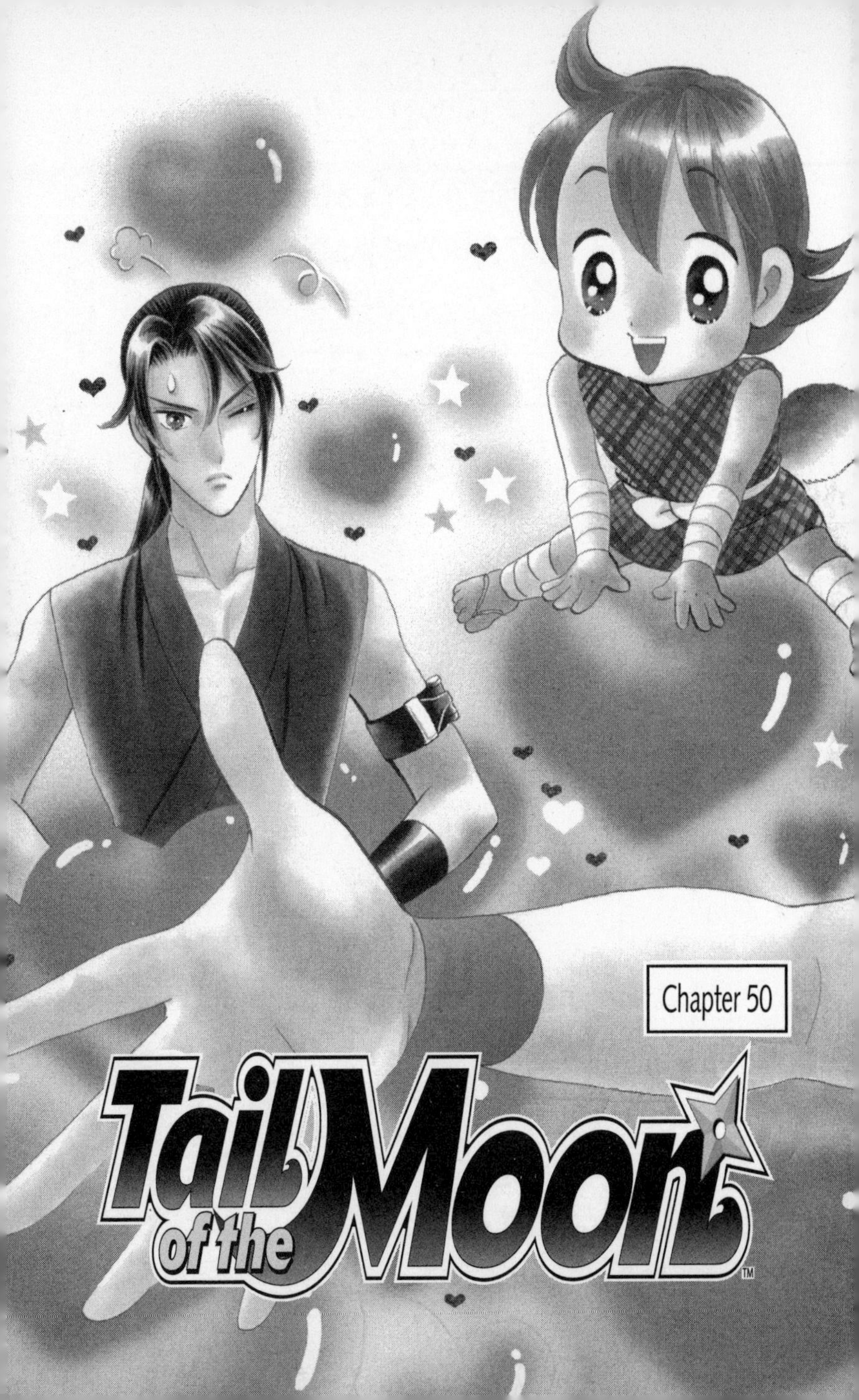
Chapter 50
Tail of the Moon™

TAIL OF THE MOON EXTRA: TODAY'S MISSION
"I WANT TO SEE HANZO DOING MATSUKEN SAMBA!"
-ABARENBO SHOGUN, TOKYO

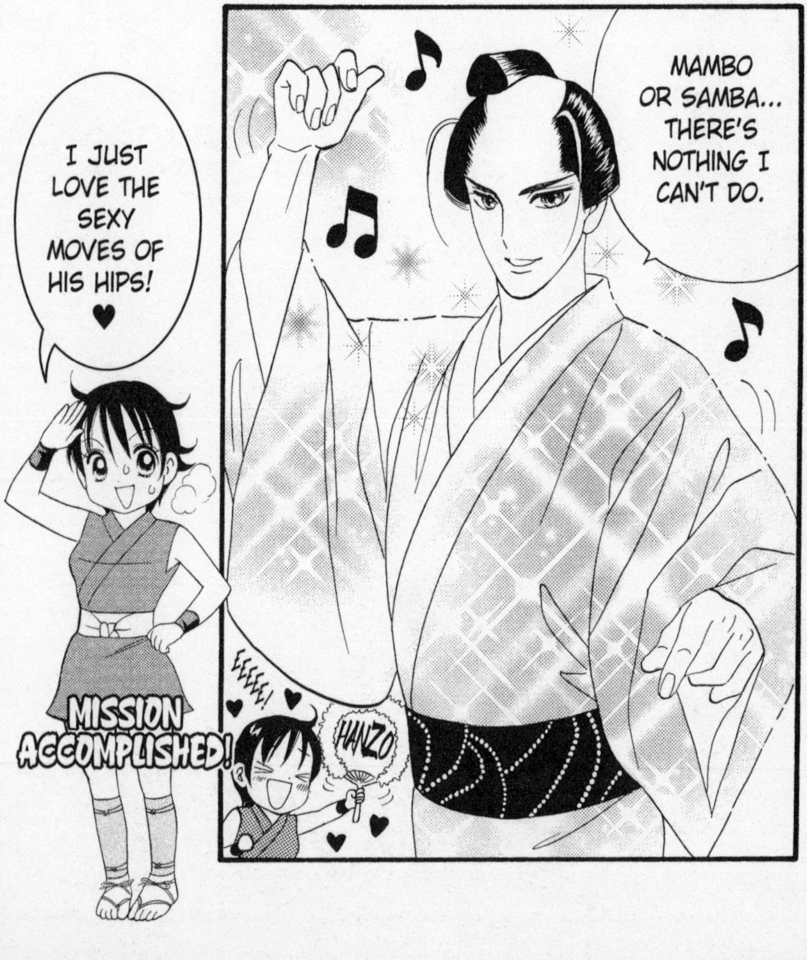

MAMBO OR SAMBA... THERE'S NOTHING I CAN'T DO.
I JUST LOVE THE SEXY MOVES OF HIS HIPS! ♥
HANZO
EEEEE!
MISSION ACCOMPLISHED!

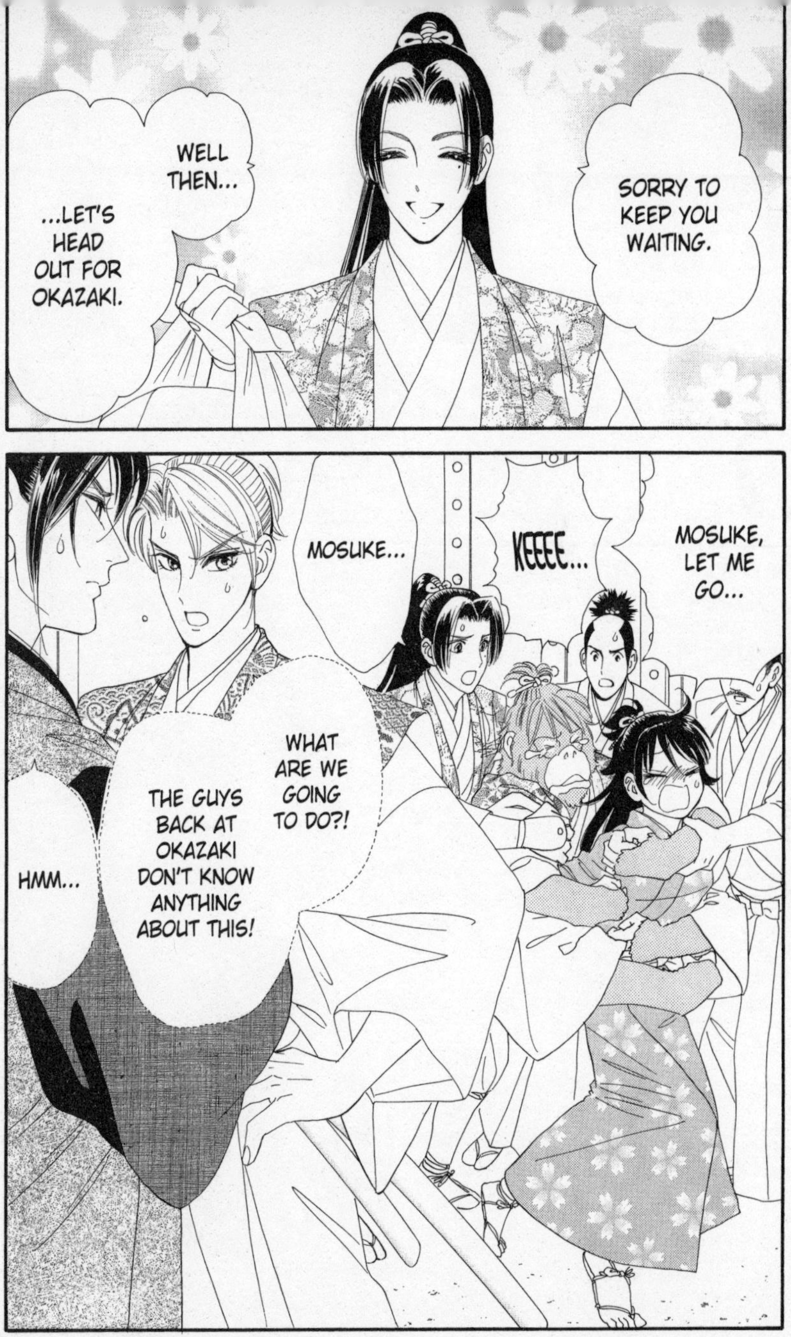
SORRY TO KEEP YOU WAITING.
WELL THEN...
...LET'S HEAD OUT FOR OKAZAKI.
MOSUKE, LET ME GO...
KEEEE...
MOSUKE...
WHAT ARE WE GOING TO DO?!
THE GUYS BACK AT OKAZAKI DON'T KNOW ANYTHING ABOUT THIS!
HMM...

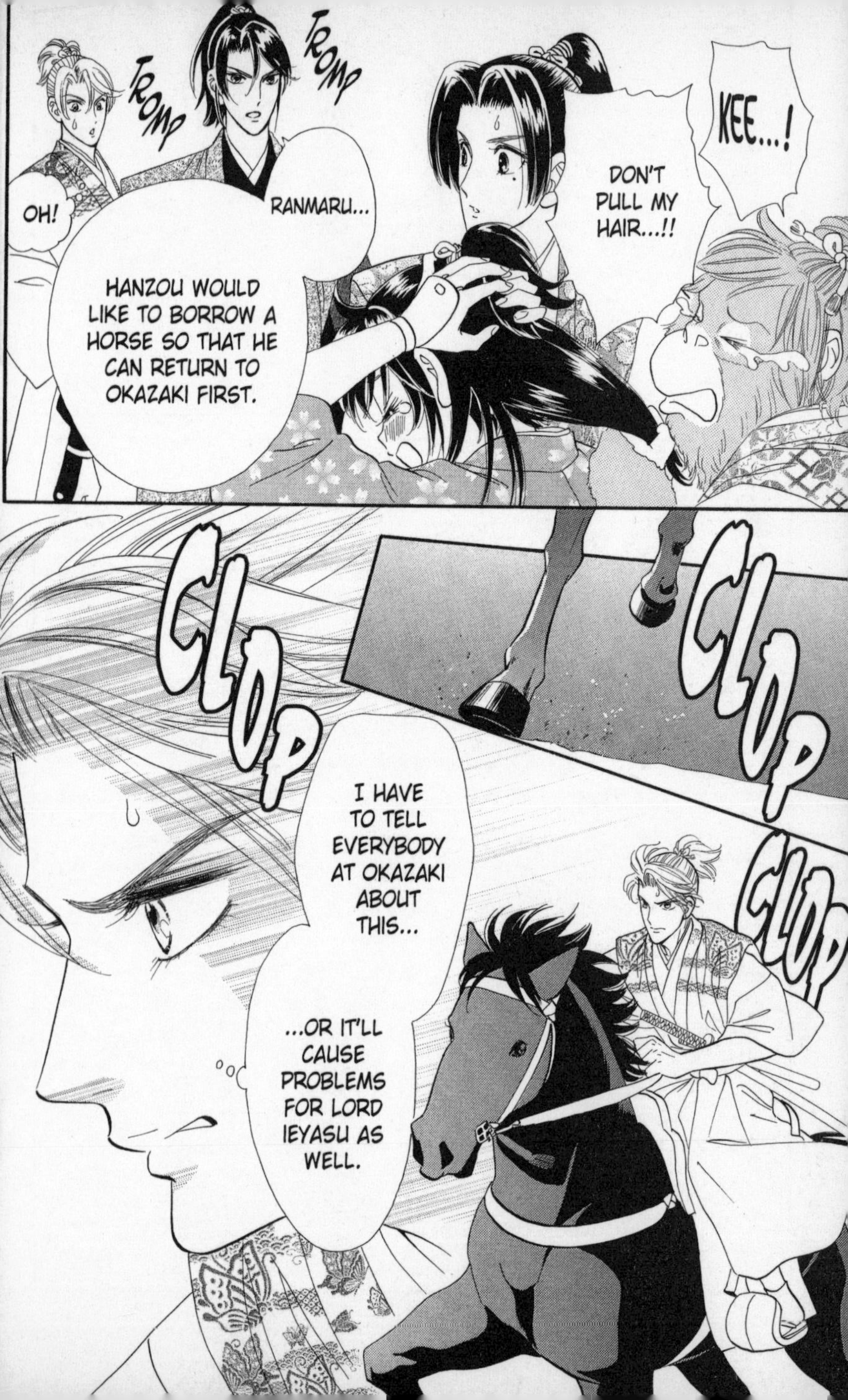
KEE...!
DON'T PULL MY HAIR...!!
TROMP
RANMARU...
TROMP
OH!
HANZOU WOULD LIKE TO BORROW A HORSE SO THAT HE CAN RETURN TO OKAZAKI FIRST.
CLOP
CLOP
I HAVE TO TELL EVERYBODY AT OKAZAKI ABOUT THIS...
CLOP
...OR IT'LL CAUSE PROBLEMS FOR LORD IEYASU AS WELL.

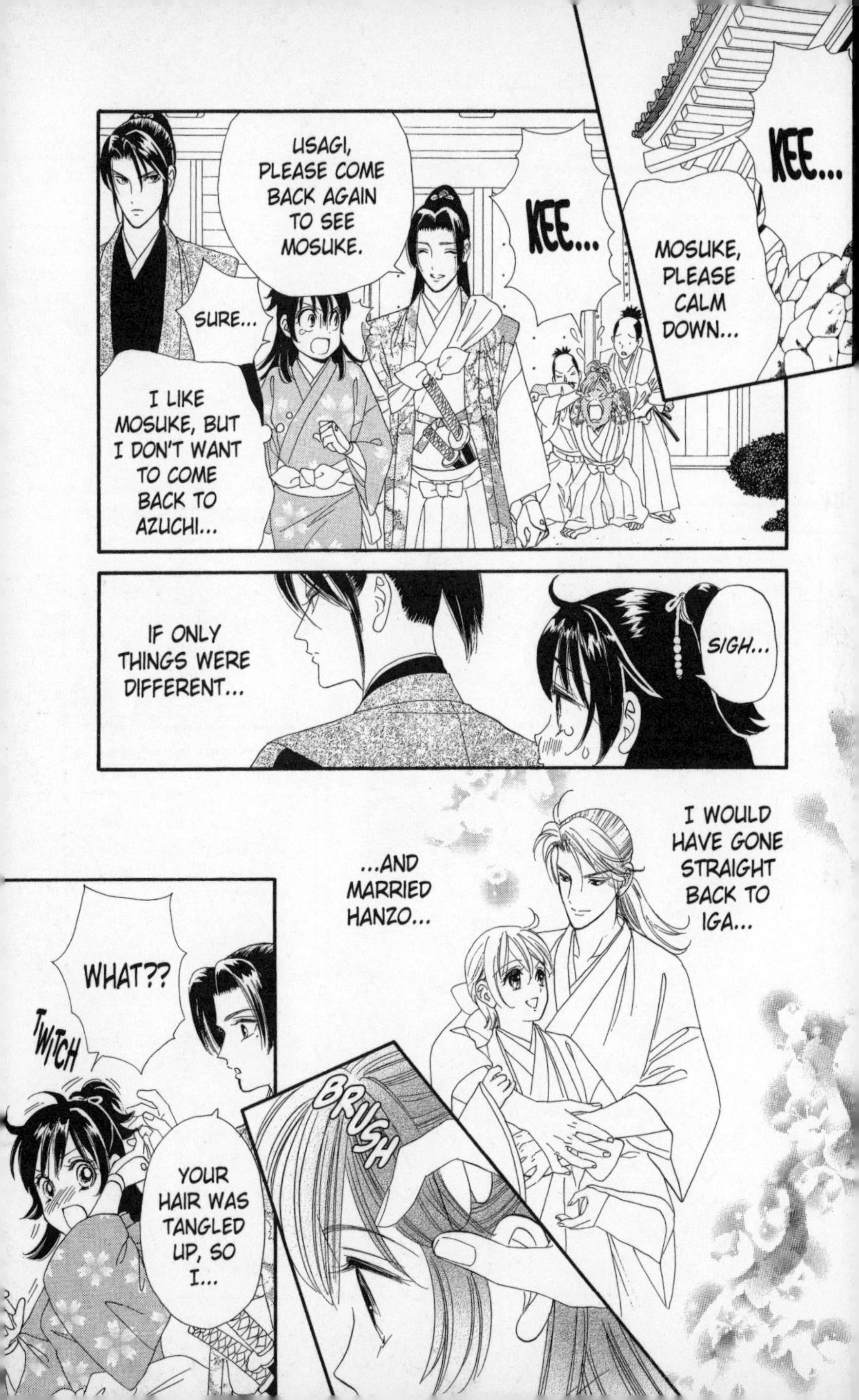
KEE...
MOSUKE, PLEASE CALM DOWN...
KEE...
USAGI, PLEASE COME BACK AGAIN TO SEE MOSUKE.
SURE...
I LIKE MOSUKE, BUT I DON'T WANT TO COME BACK TO AZUCHI...
SIGH...
IF ONLY THINGS WERE DIFFERENT...
I WOULD HAVE GONE STRAIGHT BACK TO IGA...
...AND MARRIED HANZO...
BRUSH
WHAT??
TWITCH
YOUR HAIR WAS TANGLED UP, SO I...

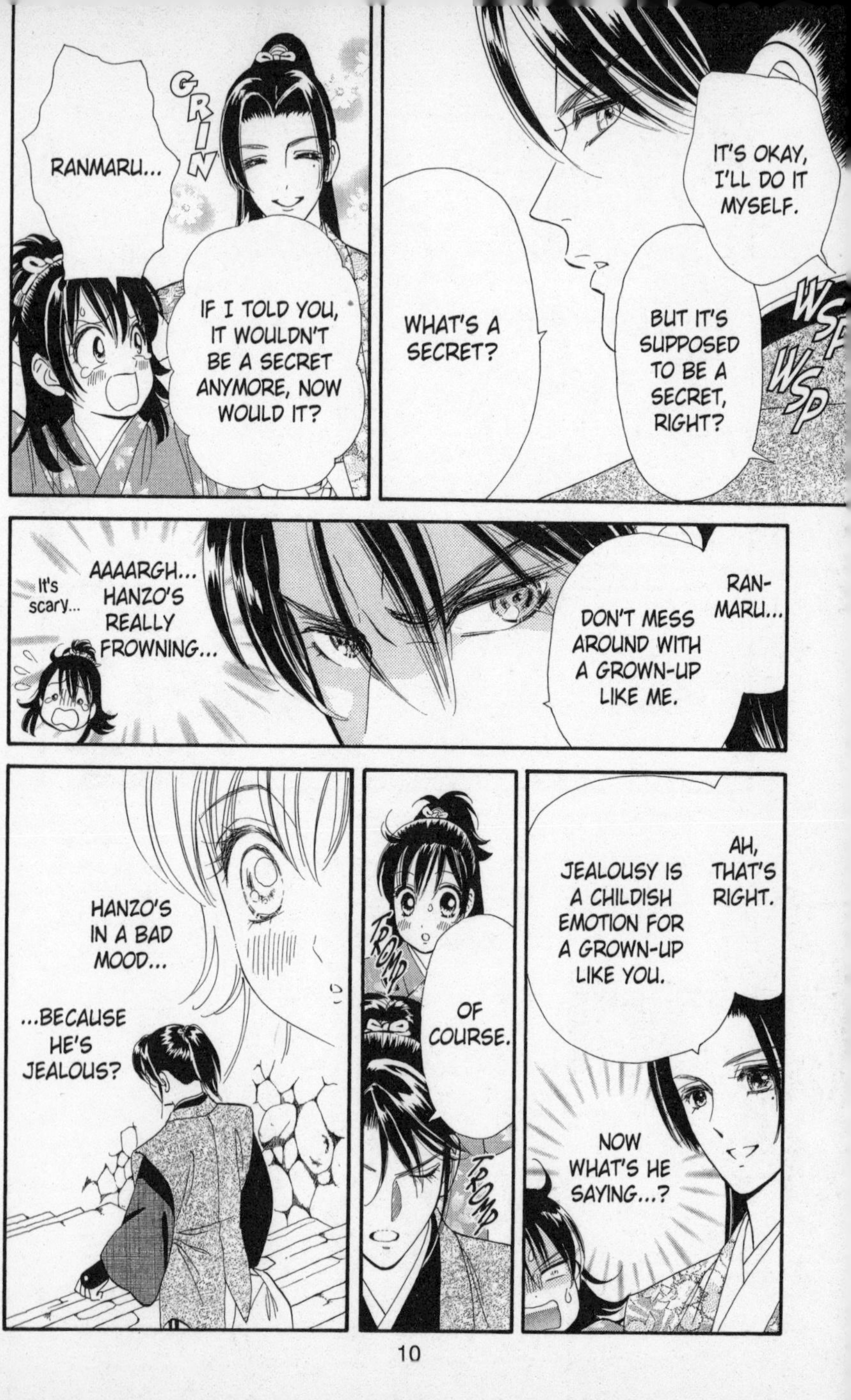
IT'S OKAY, I'LL DO IT MYSELF.
BUT IT'S SUPPOSED TO BE A SECRET, RIGHT?
WSP WSP
WHAT'S A SECRET?
GRIN
RANMARU...
IF I TOLD YOU, IT WOULDN'T BE A SECRET ANYMORE, NOW WOULD IT?
RAN-MARU...
DON'T MESS AROUND WITH A GROWN-UP LIKE ME.
AAAARGH... HANZO'S REALLY FROWNING...
It's scary...
AH, THAT'S RIGHT.
JEALOUSY IS A CHILDISH EMOTION FOR A GROWN-UP LIKE YOU.
NOW WHAT'S HE SAYING...?
TROMP
OF COURSE.
TROMP
HANZO'S IN A BAD MOOD...
...BECAUSE HE'S JEALOUS?

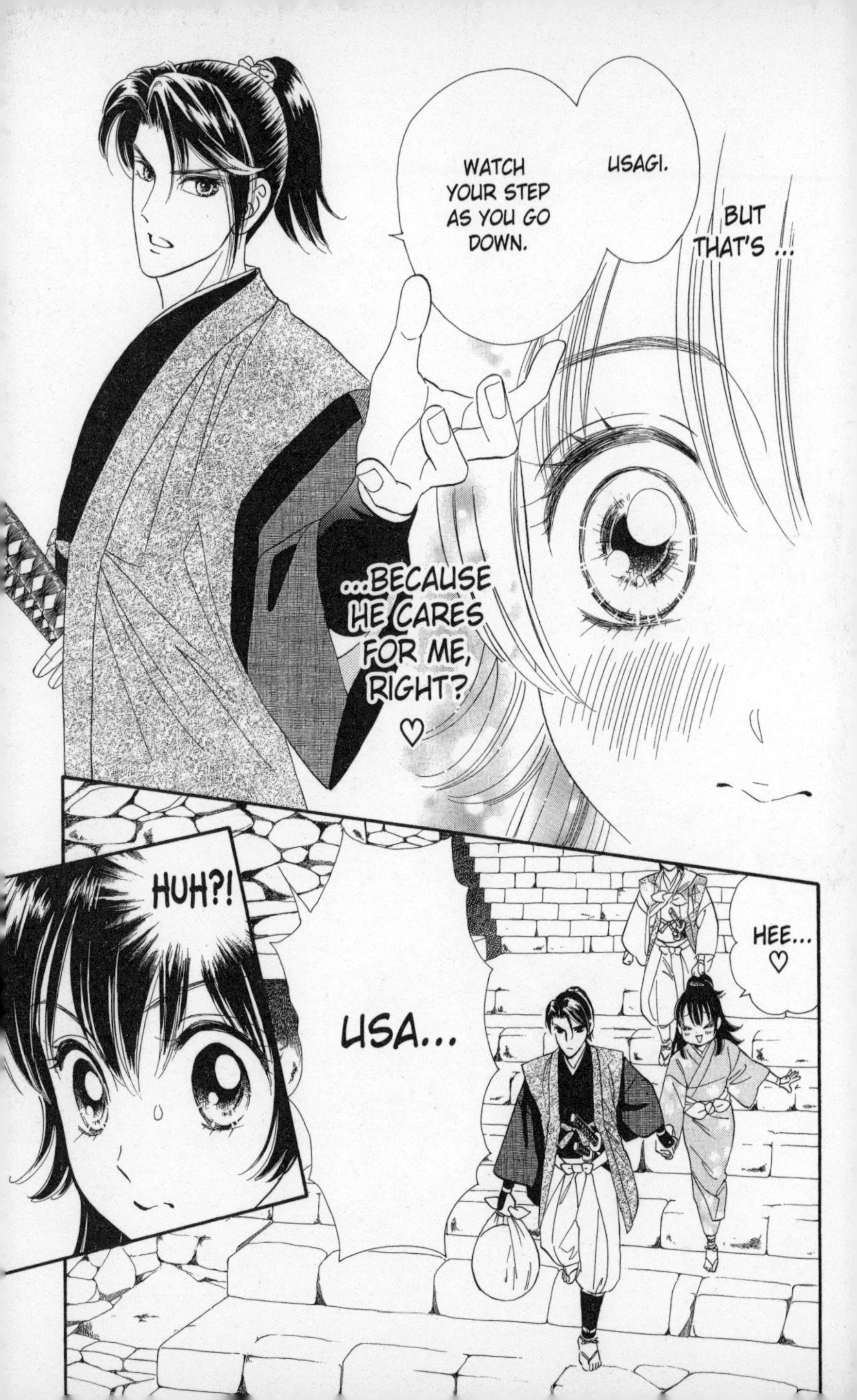
WATCH YOUR STEP AS YOU GO DOWN. USAGI.
BUT THAT'S ...
...BECAUSE HE CARES FOR ME, RIGHT? ♡
HEE... ♡
USA...
HUH?!

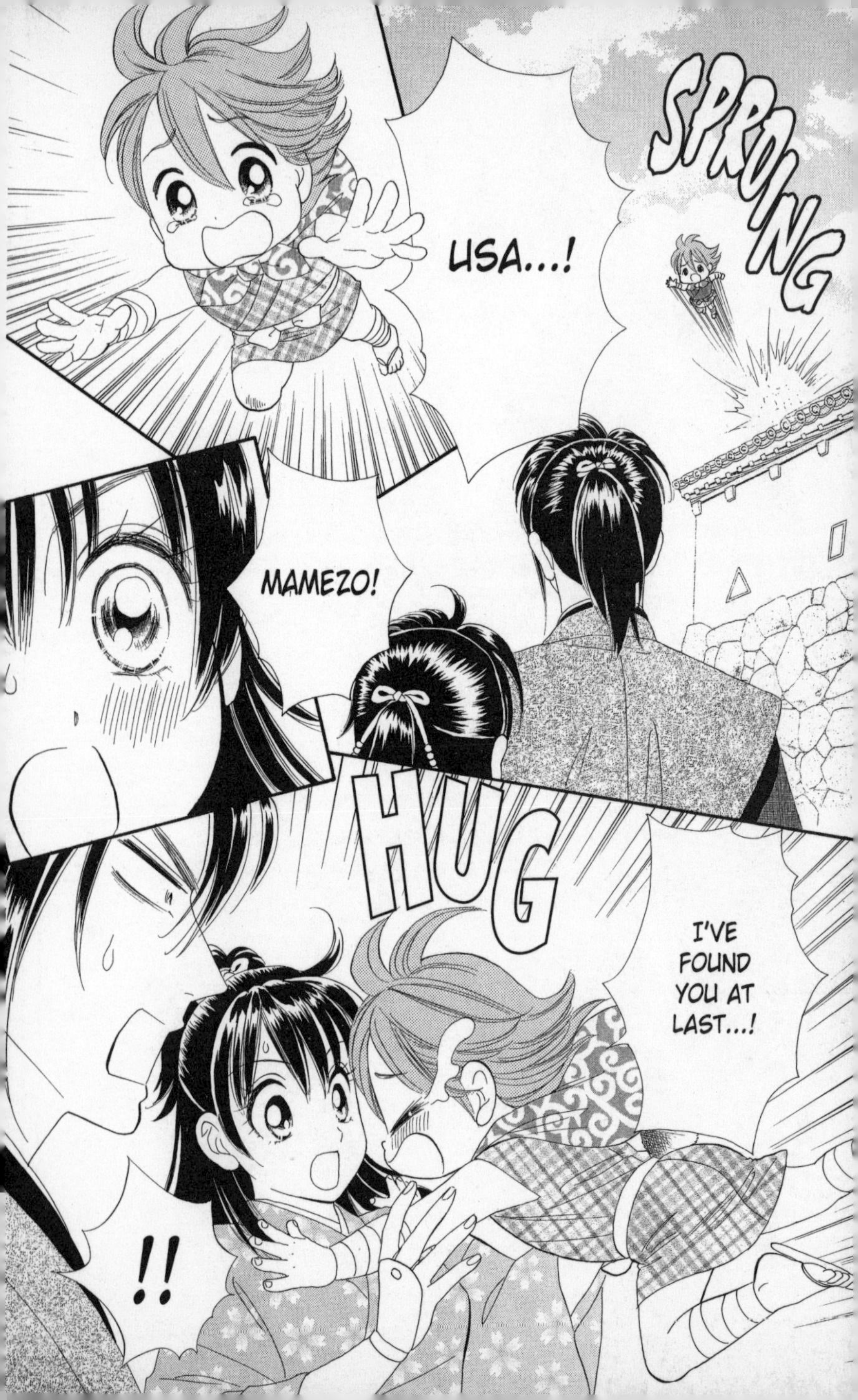
SPROING
USA...!
MAMEZO!
HUG
I'VE FOUND YOU AT LAST...!
!!

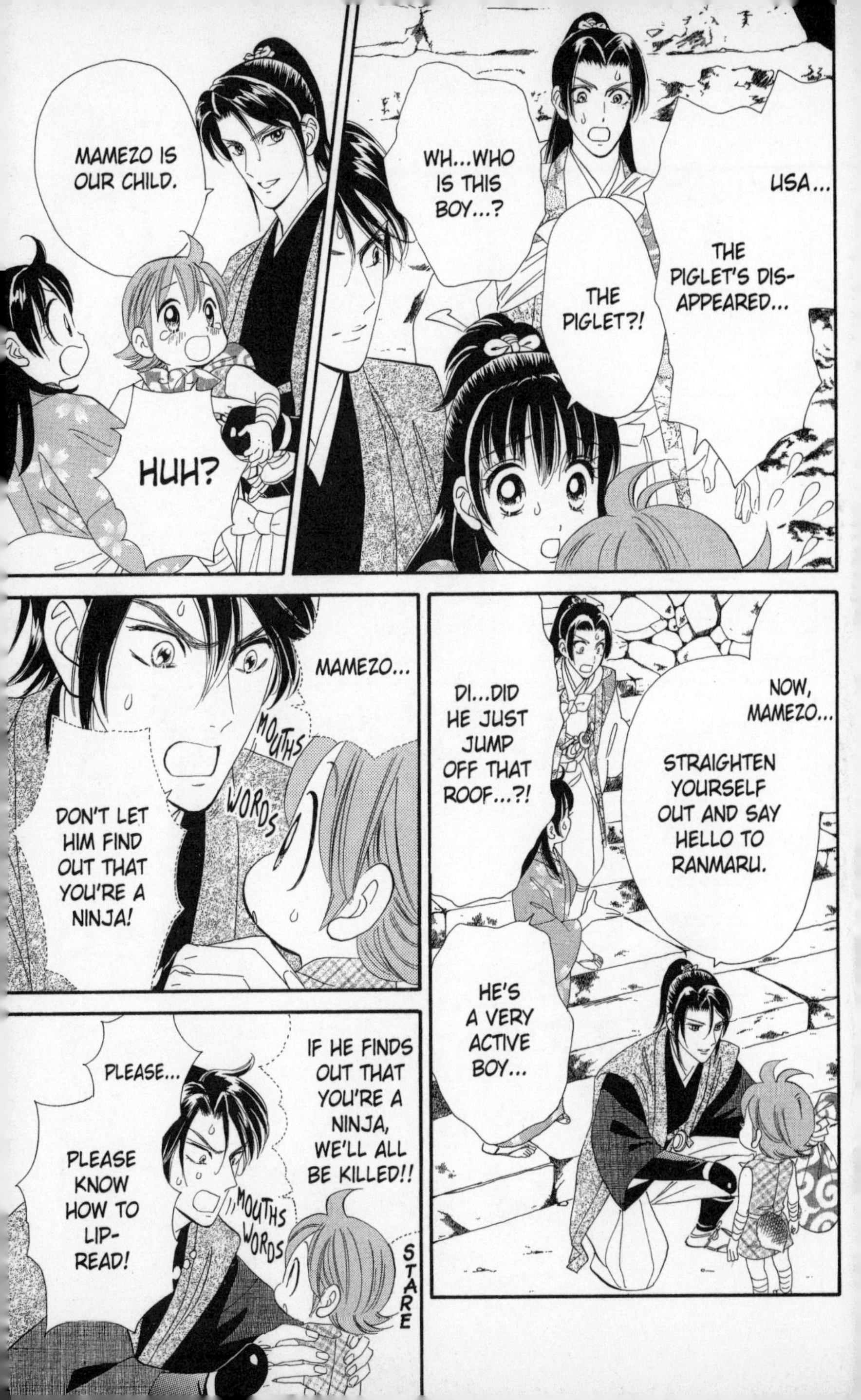
USA...
THE PIGLET'S DIS-APPEARED...
THE PIGLET?!
WH...WHO IS THIS BOY...?
MAMEZO IS OUR CHILD.
HUH?
NOW, MAMEZO...
STRAIGHTEN YOURSELF OUT AND SAY HELLO TO RANMARU.
DI...DID HE JUST JUMP OFF THAT ROOF...?!
HE'S A VERY ACTIVE BOY...
MAMEZO...
MOUTHS WORDS
DON'T LET HIM FIND OUT THAT YOU'RE A NINJA!
IF HE FINDS OUT THAT YOU'RE A NINJA, WE'LL ALL BE KILLED!!
STARE
MOUTHS WORDS
PLEASE...
PLEASE KNOW HOW TO LIP-READ!

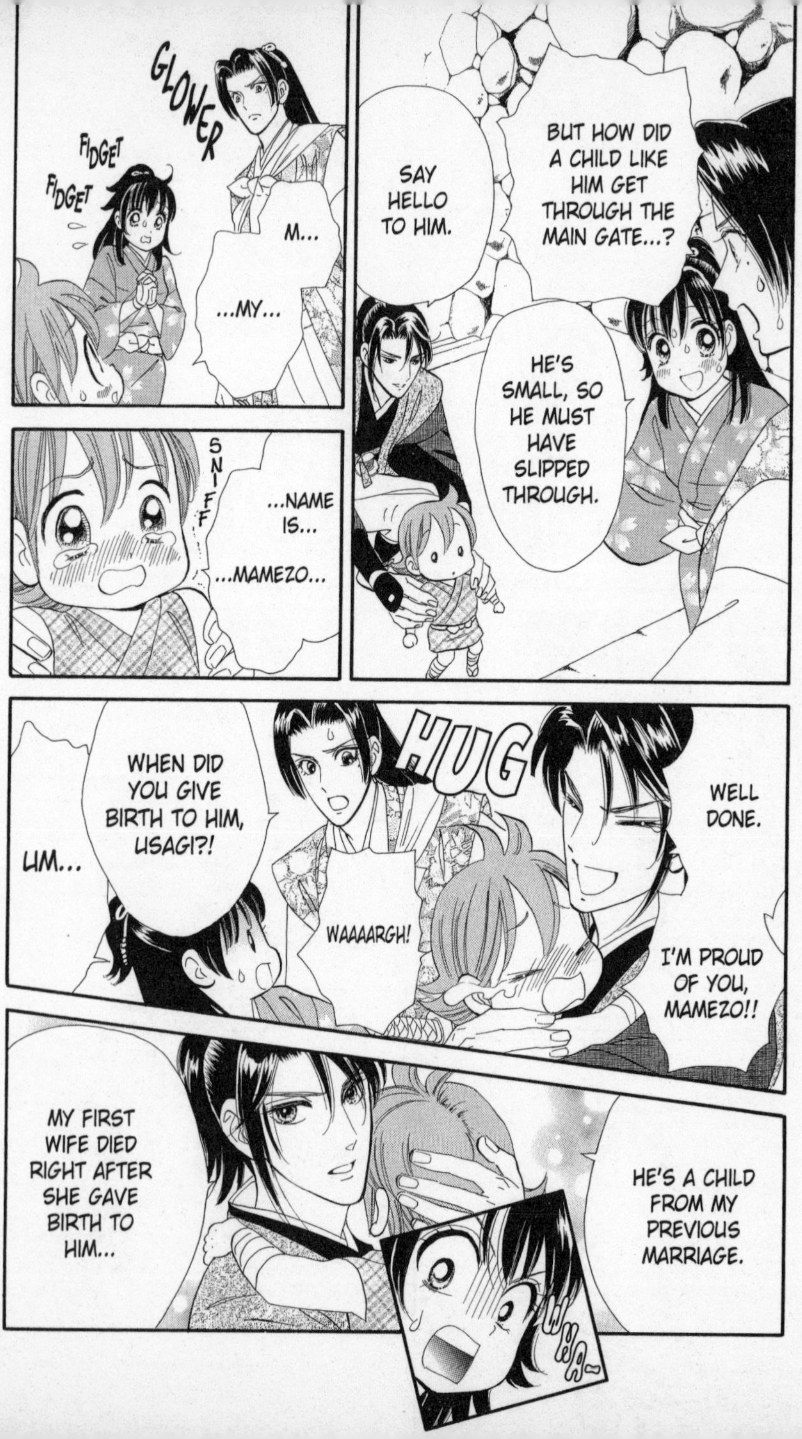

BUT HOW DID A CHILD LIKE HIM GET THROUGH THE MAIN GATE...?
HE'S SMALL, SO HE MUST HAVE SLIPPED THROUGH.
SAY HELLO TO HIM.
GLOWER
FIDGET FIDGET
M...
...MY...
SNIFF
...NAME IS...
...MAMEZO...
HUG
WELL DONE.
I'M PROUD OF YOU, MAMEZO!!
WAAAARGH!
WHEN DID YOU GIVE BIRTH TO HIM, USAGI?!
UM...
HE'S A CHILD FROM MY PREVIOUS MARRIAGE.
MY FIRST WIFE DIED RIGHT AFTER SHE GAVE BIRTH TO HIM...

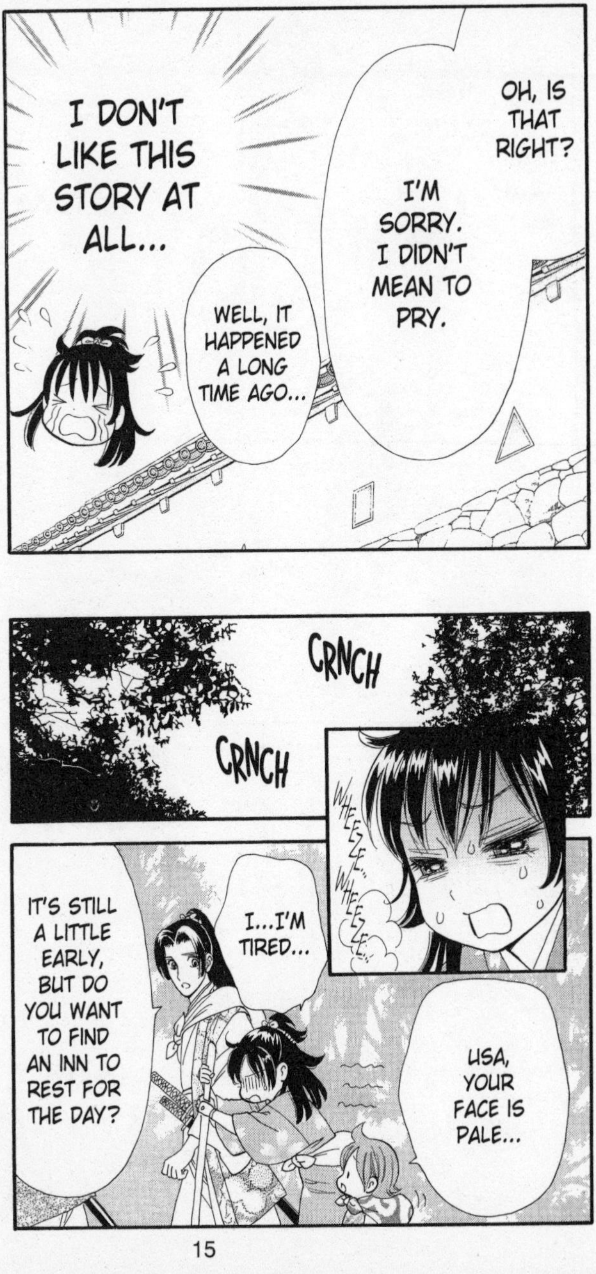
OH, IS THAT RIGHT?
I'M SORRY. I DIDN'T MEAN TO PRY.
WELL, IT HAPPENED A LONG TIME AGO...
I DON'T LIKE THIS STORY AT ALL...
CRNCH
CRNCH
WHEEZE... WHEEZE...
USA, YOUR FACE IS PALE...
I...I'M TIRED...
IT'S STILL A LITTLE EARLY, BUT DO YOU WANT TO FIND AN INN TO REST FOR THE DAY?

GREETINGS

Hello, it's Ue-Rin.

"Ue-Rin's Manga School" is gradually getting to the most interesting part...

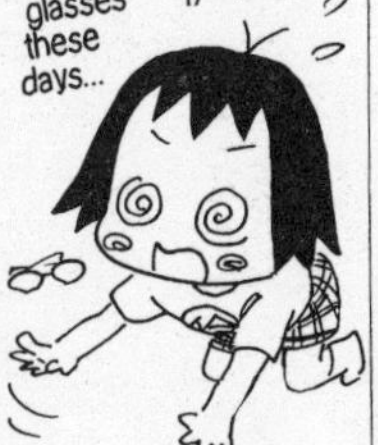
My glasses...
My glasses...
I keep misplacing my glasses these days...

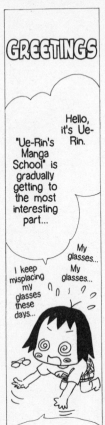

The story continues from the summer of my third year in middle school when I went down to Osaka to meet the editor with my two pieces of manga...

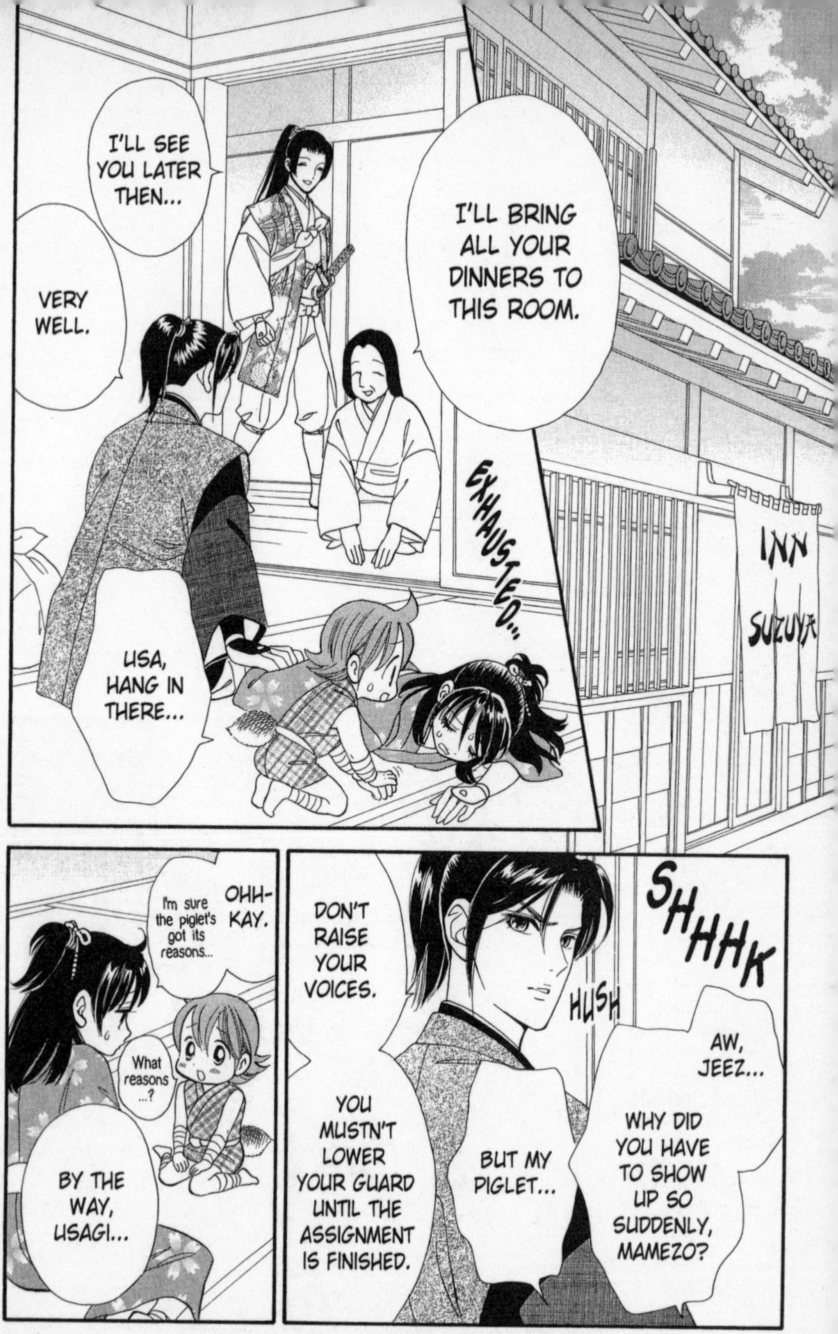
I'LL BRING ALL YOUR DINNERS TO THIS ROOM.
I'LL SEE YOU LATER THEN...
VERY WELL.
EXHAUSTED...
INN SUZUYA
USA, HANG IN THERE...
SHHHK
DON'T RAISE YOUR VOICES.
HUSH
AW, JEEZ...
WHY DID YOU HAVE TO SHOW UP SO SUDDENLY, MAMEZO?
BUT MY PIGLET...
YOU MUSTN'T LOWER YOUR GUARD UNTIL THE ASSIGNMENT IS FINISHED.
OHH-KAY.
I'm sure the piglet's got its reasons...
What reasons ...?
BY THE WAY, USAGI...

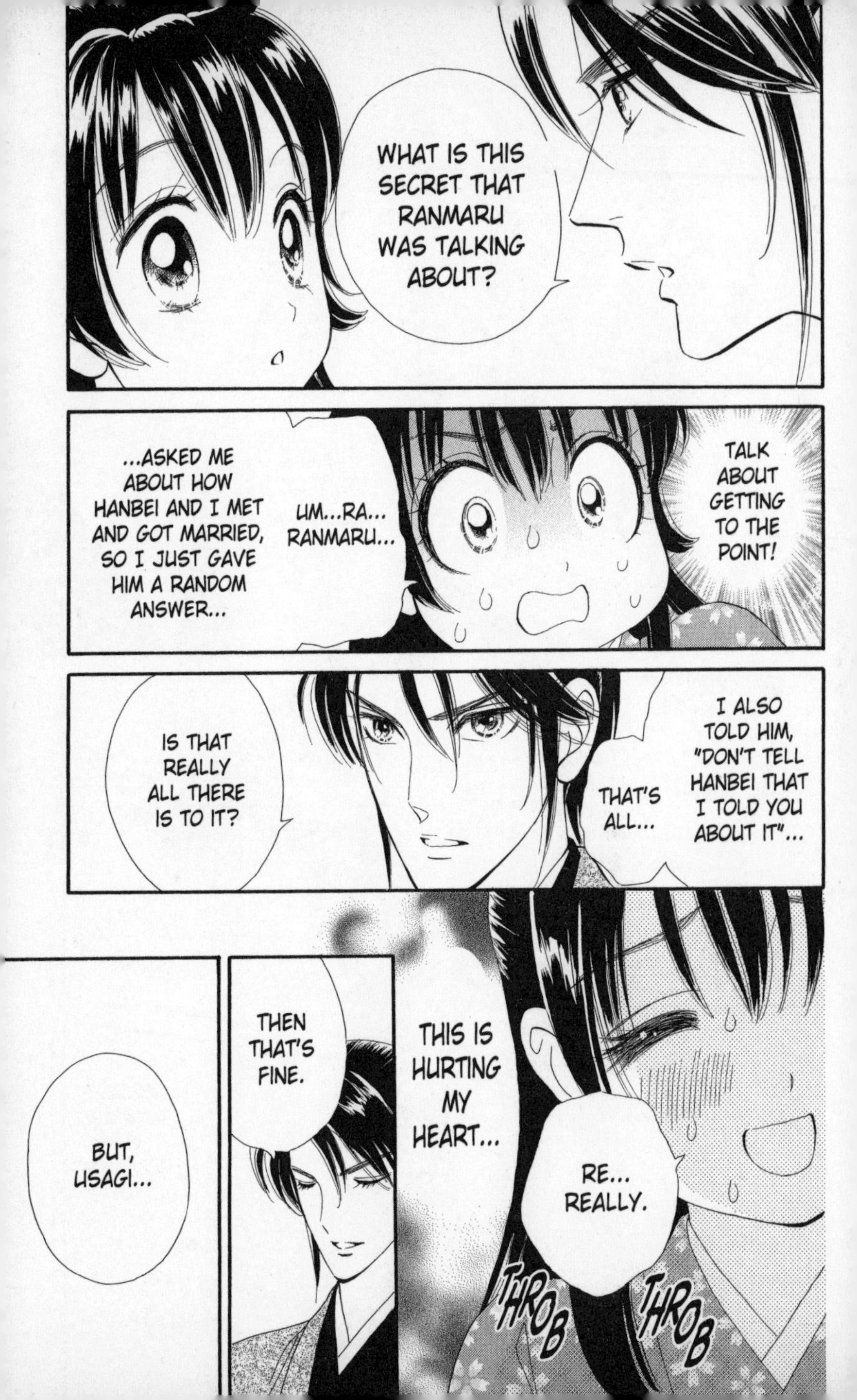
WHAT IS THIS SECRET THAT RANMARU WAS TALKING ABOUT?
TALK ABOUT GETTING TO THE POINT!
UM...RA... RANMARU...
...ASKED ME ABOUT HOW HANBEI AND I MET AND GOT MARRIED, SO I JUST GAVE HIM A RANDOM ANSWER...
I ALSO TOLD HIM, "DON'T TELL HANBEI THAT I TOLD YOU ABOUT IT"...
THAT'S ALL...
IS THAT REALLY ALL THERE IS TO IT?
THROB THROB
THIS IS HURTING MY HEART...
RE... REALLY.
THEN THAT'S FINE.
BUT, USAGI...

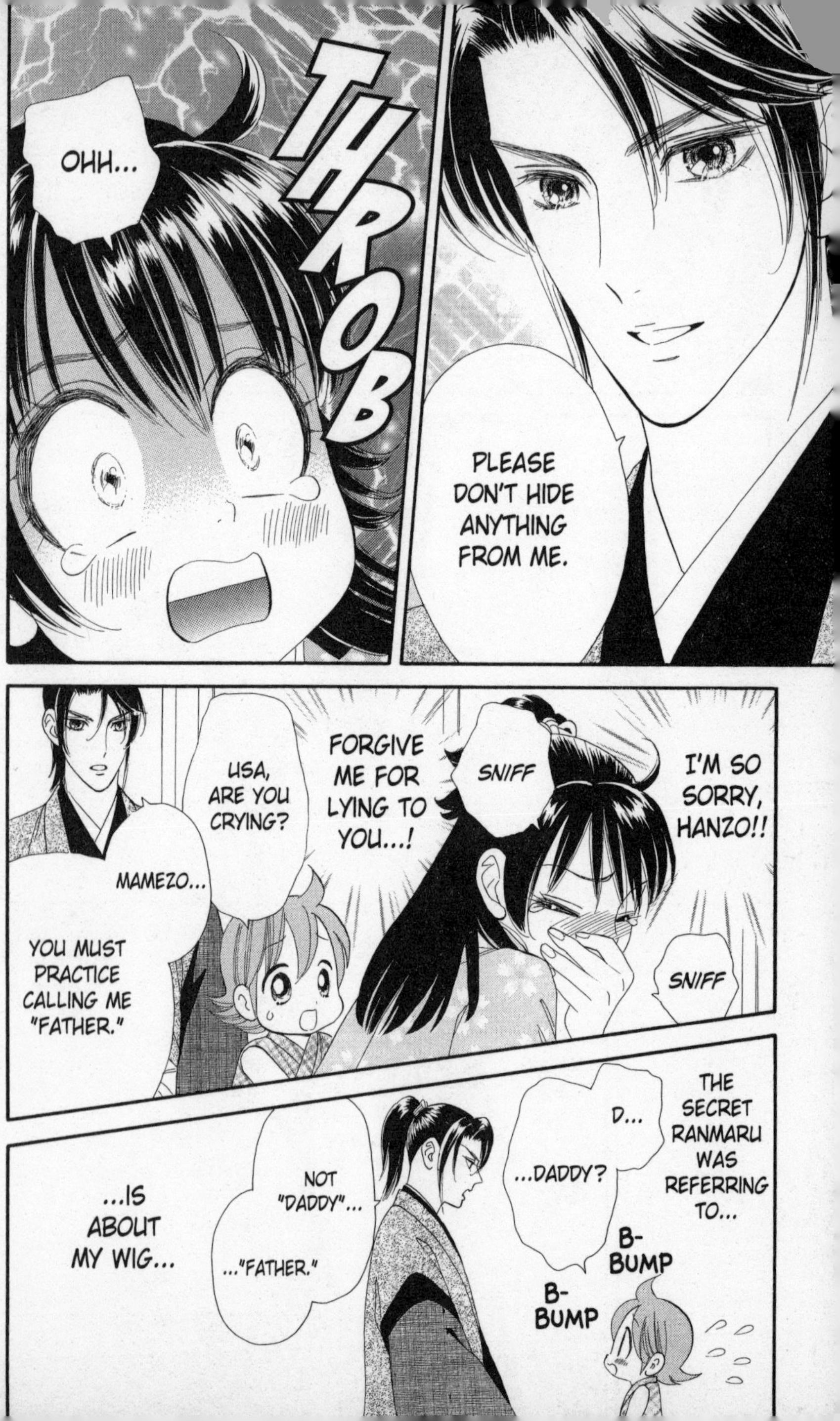
PLEASE DON'T HIDE ANYTHING FROM ME.
THROB
OHH...
I'M SO SORRY, HANZO!!
SNIFF
FORGIVE ME FOR LYING TO YOU...!
USA, ARE YOU CRYING?
SNIFF
MAMEZO...
YOU MUST PRACTICE CALLING ME "FATHER."
THE SECRET RANMARU WAS REFERRING TO...
D...
...DADDY?
B-BUMP
B-BUMP
NOT "DADDY"...
..."FATHER."
...IS ABOUT MY WIG...

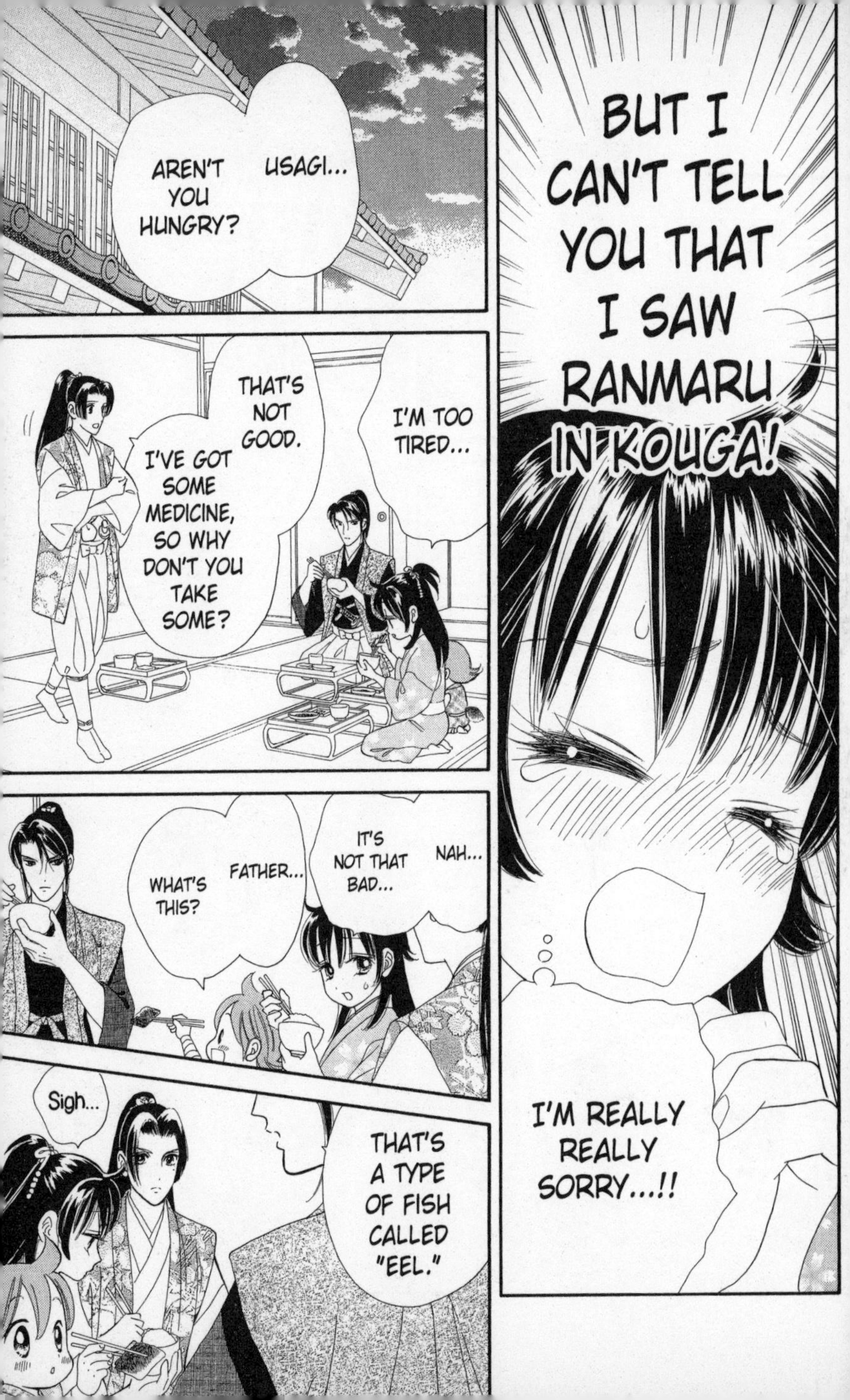
BUT I CAN'T TELL YOU THAT I SAW RANMARU IN KOUGA!
I'M REALLY REALLY SORRY...!!
USAGI...
AREN'T YOU HUNGRY?
I'M TOO TIRED...
THAT'S NOT GOOD.
I'VE GOT SOME MEDICINE, SO WHY DON'T YOU TAKE SOME?
NAH...
IT'S NOT THAT BAD...
FATHER...
WHAT'S THIS?
THAT'S A TYPE OF FISH CALLED "EEL."
Sigh...

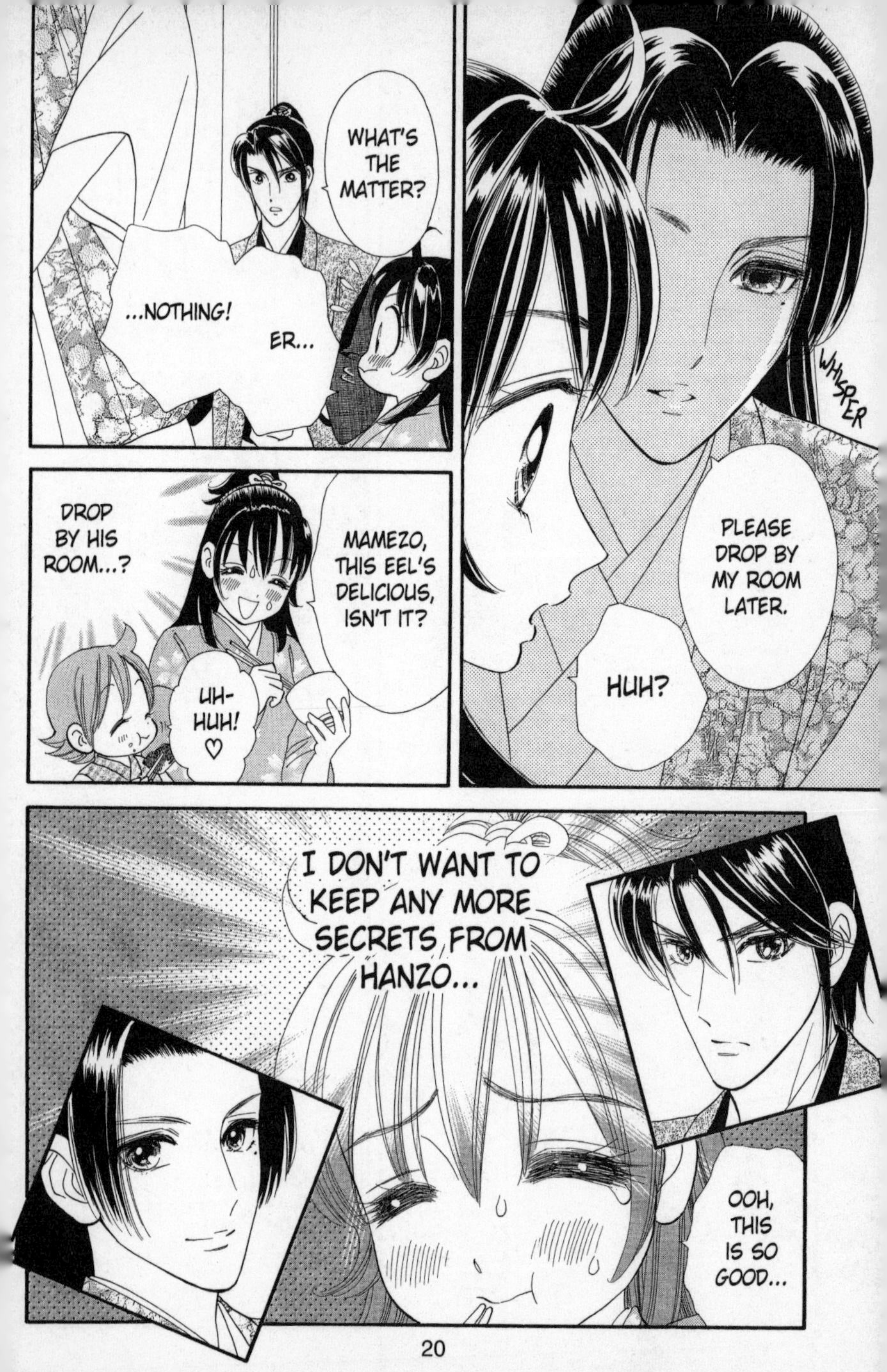
WHISPER
PLEASE DROP BY MY ROOM LATER.
HUH?
WHAT'S THE MATTER?
ER...
...NOTHING!
MAMEZO, THIS EEL'S DELICIOUS, ISN'T IT?
UH-HUH! ♡
DROP BY HIS ROOM...?
I DON'T WANT TO KEEP ANY MORE SECRETS FROM HANZO...
OOH, THIS IS SO GOOD...

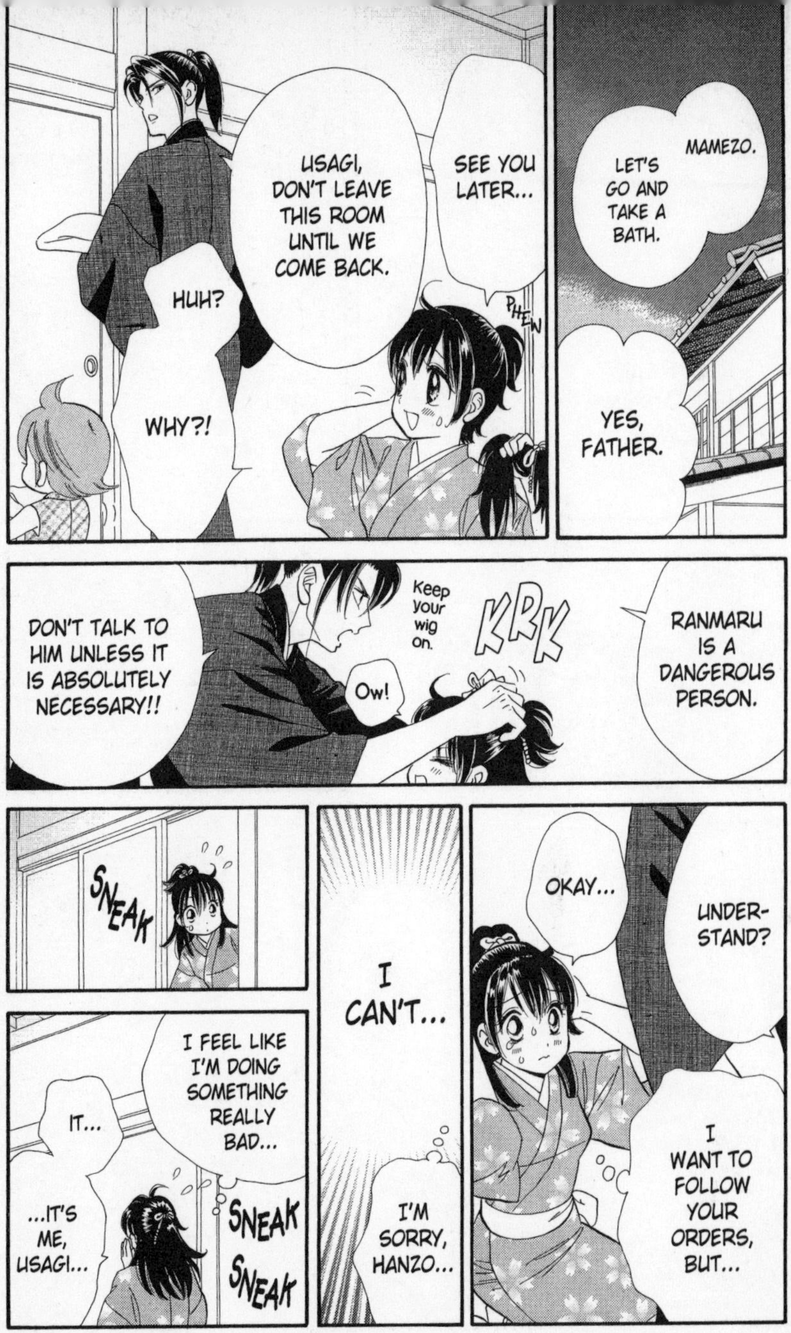
MAMEZO.
LET'S GO AND TAKE A BATH.
YES, FATHER.
SEE YOU LATER...
USAGI, DON'T LEAVE THIS ROOM UNTIL WE COME BACK.
PHEW
HUH?
WHY?!
RANMARU IS A DANGEROUS PERSON.
KRK
Keep your wig on.
Ow!
DON'T TALK TO HIM UNLESS IT IS ABSOLUTELY NECESSARY!!
UNDER-STAND?
OKAY...
I WANT TO FOLLOW YOUR ORDERS, BUT...
I CAN'T...
I'M SORRY, HANZO...
SNEAK
I FEEL LIKE I'M DOING SOMETHING REALLY BAD...
IT...
SNEAK
SNEAK
...IT'S ME, USAGI...

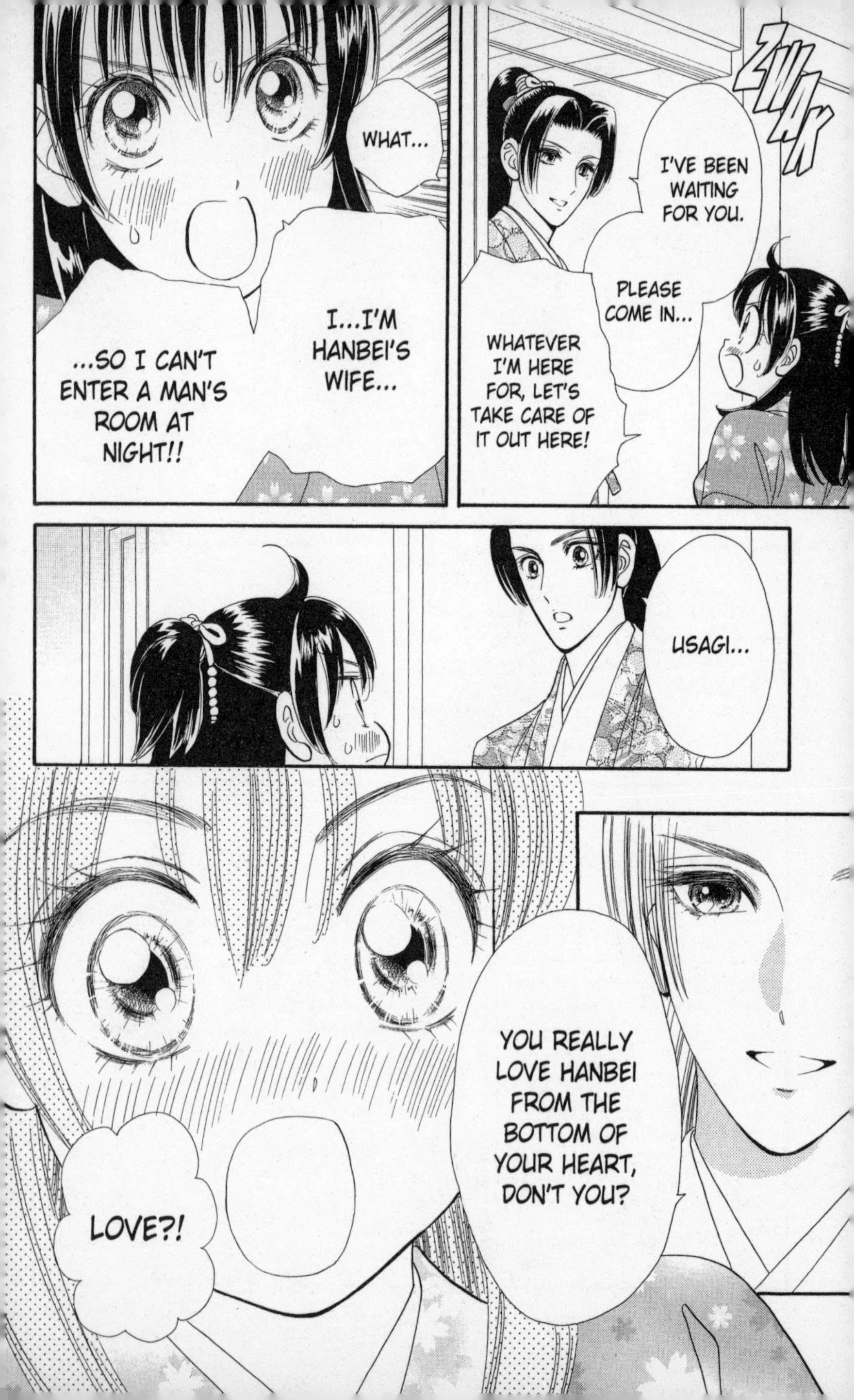
ZWAK
I'VE BEEN WAITING FOR YOU.
PLEASE COME IN...
WHATEVER I'M HERE FOR, LET'S TAKE CARE OF IT OUT HERE!
WHAT...
I...I'M HANBEI'S WIFE...
...SO I CAN'T ENTER A MAN'S ROOM AT NIGHT!!
USAGI...
YOU REALLY LOVE HANBEI FROM THE BOTTOM OF YOUR HEART, DON'T YOU?
LOVE?!

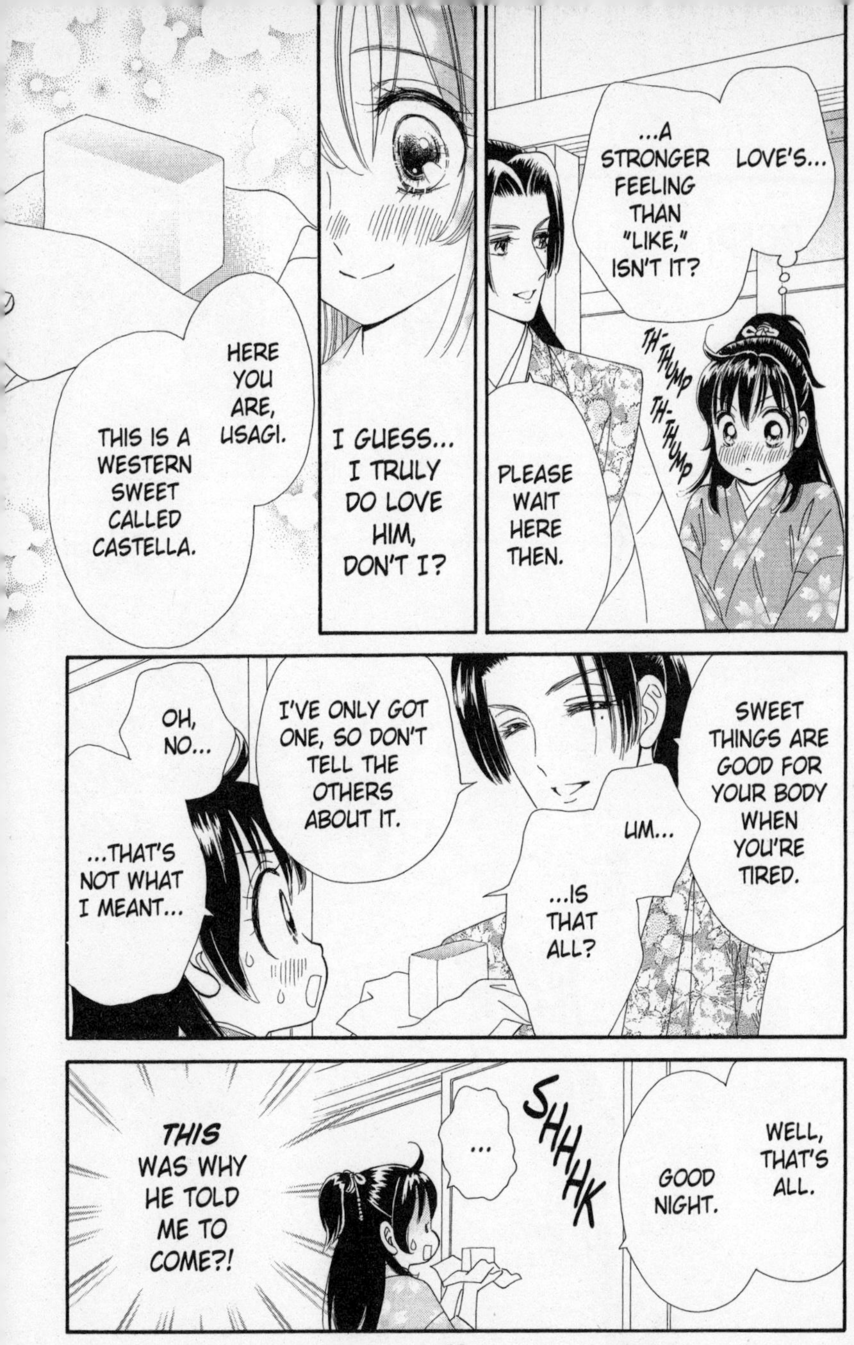
LOVE'S...
...A STRONGER FEELING THAN "LIKE," ISN'T IT?
TH-THUMP TH-THUMP
PLEASE WAIT HERE THEN.
I GUESS... I TRULY DO LOVE HIM, DON'T I?
HERE YOU ARE, USAGI.
THIS IS A WESTERN SWEET CALLED CASTELLA.
SWEET THINGS ARE GOOD FOR YOUR BODY WHEN YOU'RE TIRED.
UM...
...IS THAT ALL?
I'VE ONLY GOT ONE, SO DON'T TELL THE OTHERS ABOUT IT.
OH, NO...
...THAT'S NOT WHAT I MEANT...
WELL, THAT'S ALL.
GOOD NIGHT.
SHHHK
...
THIS WAS WHY HE TOLD ME TO COME?!

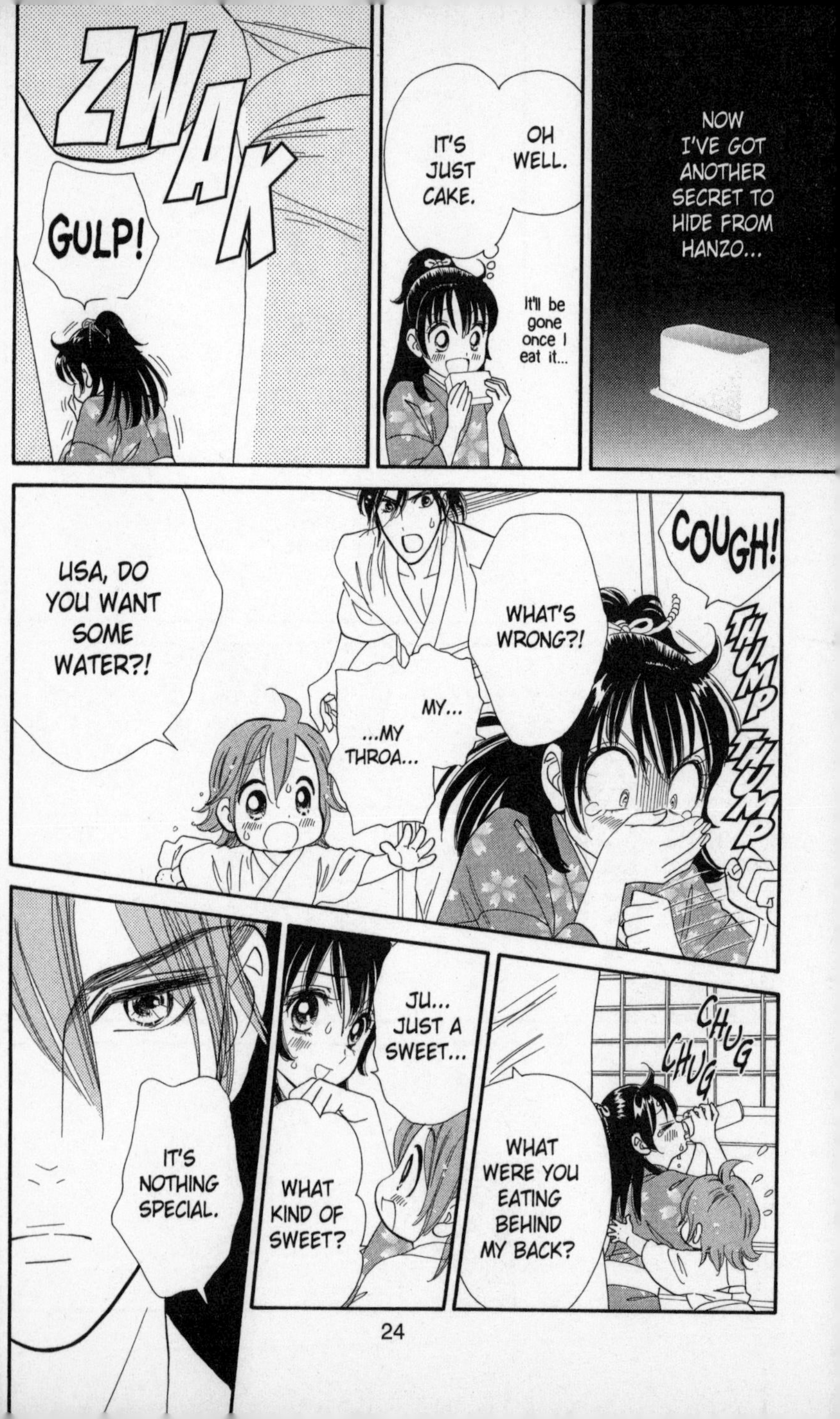
NOW I'VE GOT ANOTHER SECRET TO HIDE FROM HANZO...
OH WELL.
IT'S JUST CAKE.
It'll be gone once I eat it...
ZWAK
GULP!
COUGH!
THUMP THUMP
WHAT'S WRONG?!
MY...
...MY THROA...
USA, DO YOU WANT SOME WATER?!
CHUG CHUG
WHAT WERE YOU EATING BEHIND MY BACK?
JU... JUST A SWEET...
WHAT KIND OF SWEET?
IT'S NOTHING SPECIAL.

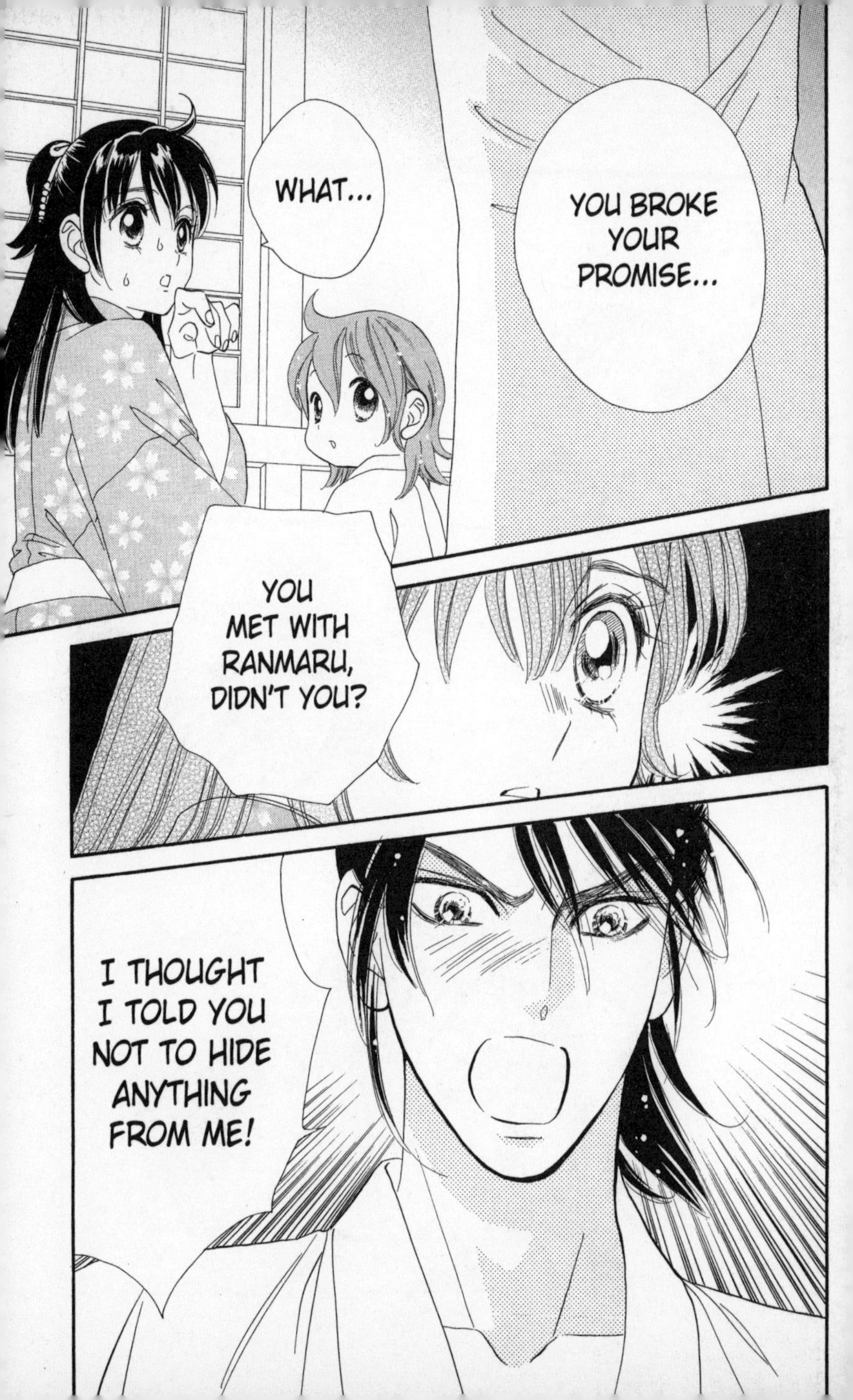
YOU BROKE YOUR PROMISE...
WHAT...
YOU MET WITH RANMARU, DIDN'T YOU?
I THOUGHT I TOLD YOU NOT TO HIDE ANYTHING FROM ME!

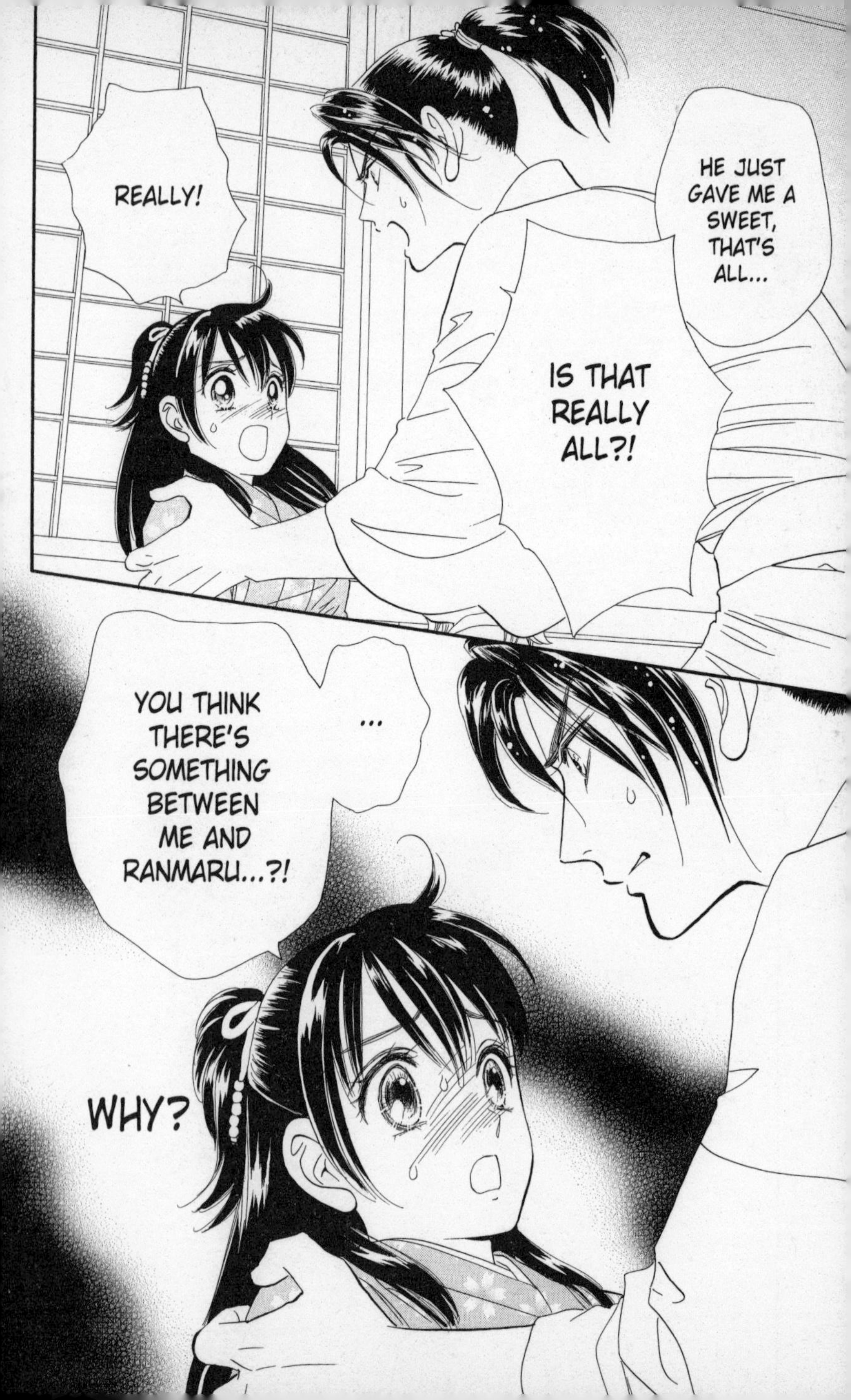
HE JUST GAVE ME A SWEET, THAT'S ALL...
IS THAT REALLY ALL?!
REALLY!
...
YOU THINK THERE'S SOMETHING BETWEEN ME AND RANMARU...?!
WHY?

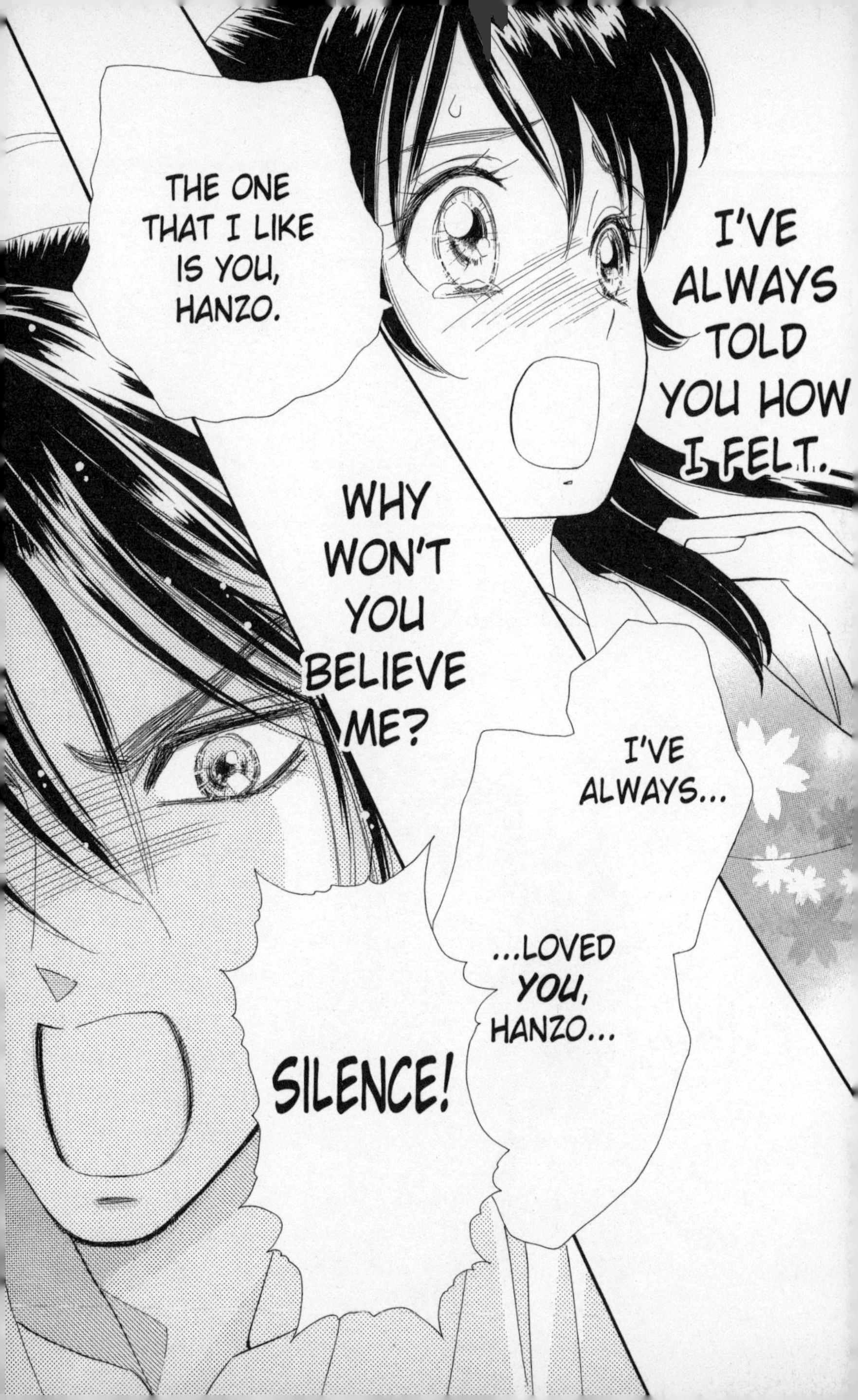
THE ONE THAT I LIKE IS YOU, HANZO.
I'VE ALWAYS TOLD YOU HOW I FELT..
WHY WON'T YOU BELIEVE ME?
I'VE ALWAYS...
...LOVED *YOU*, HANZO...
SILENCE!

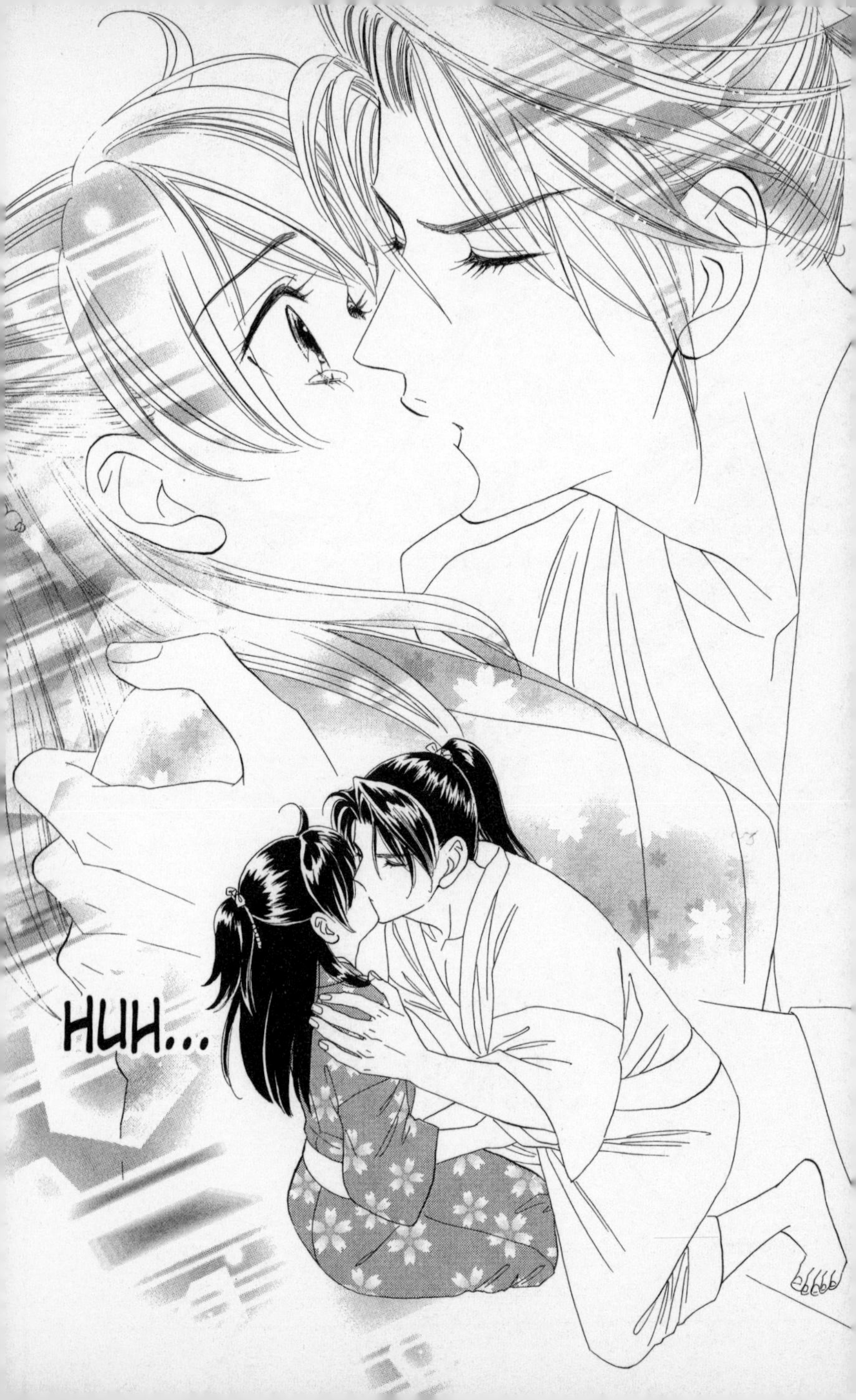
HUH...

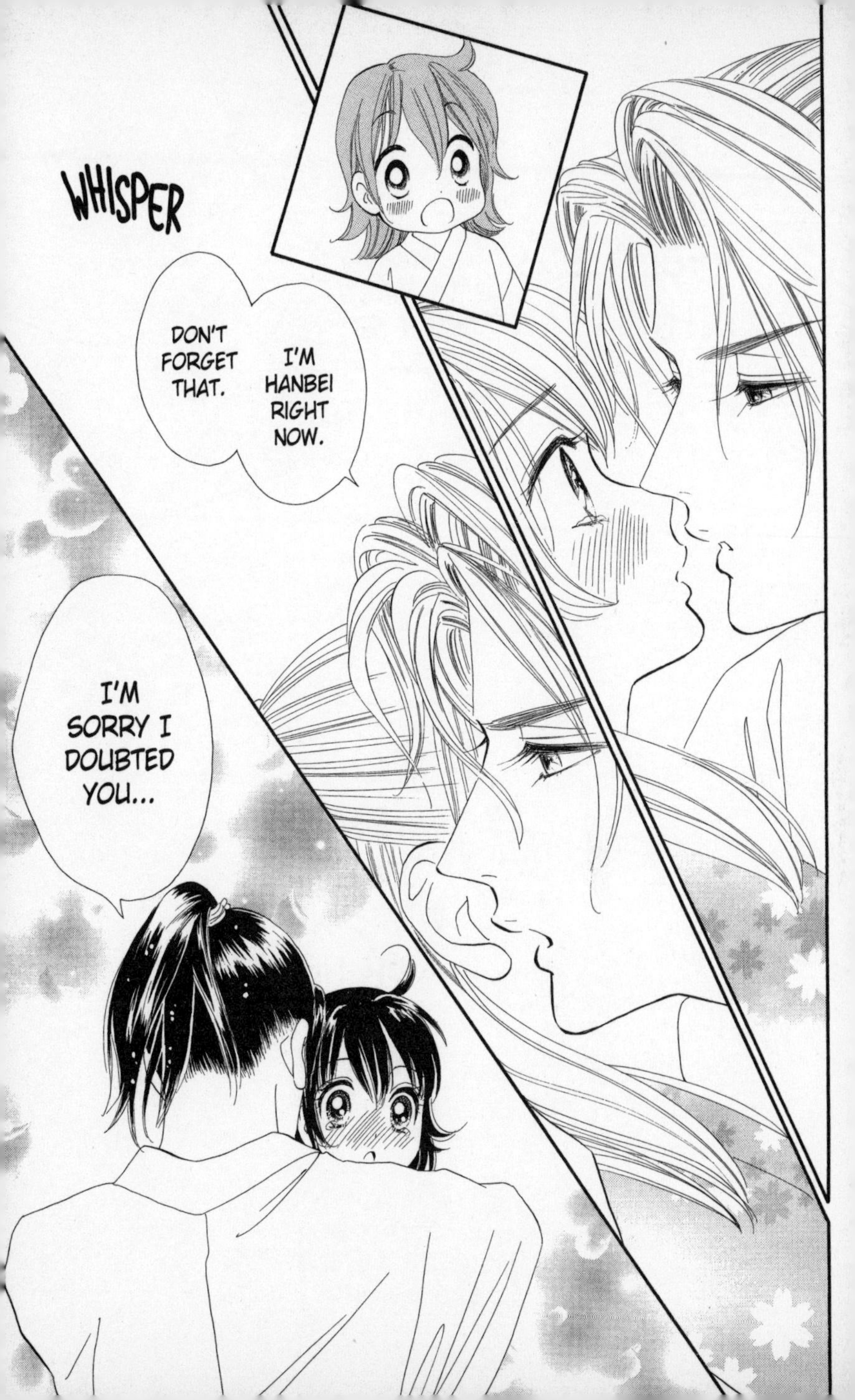
WHISPER
I'M HANBEI RIGHT NOW.
DON'T FORGET THAT.
I'M SORRY I DOUBTED YOU...

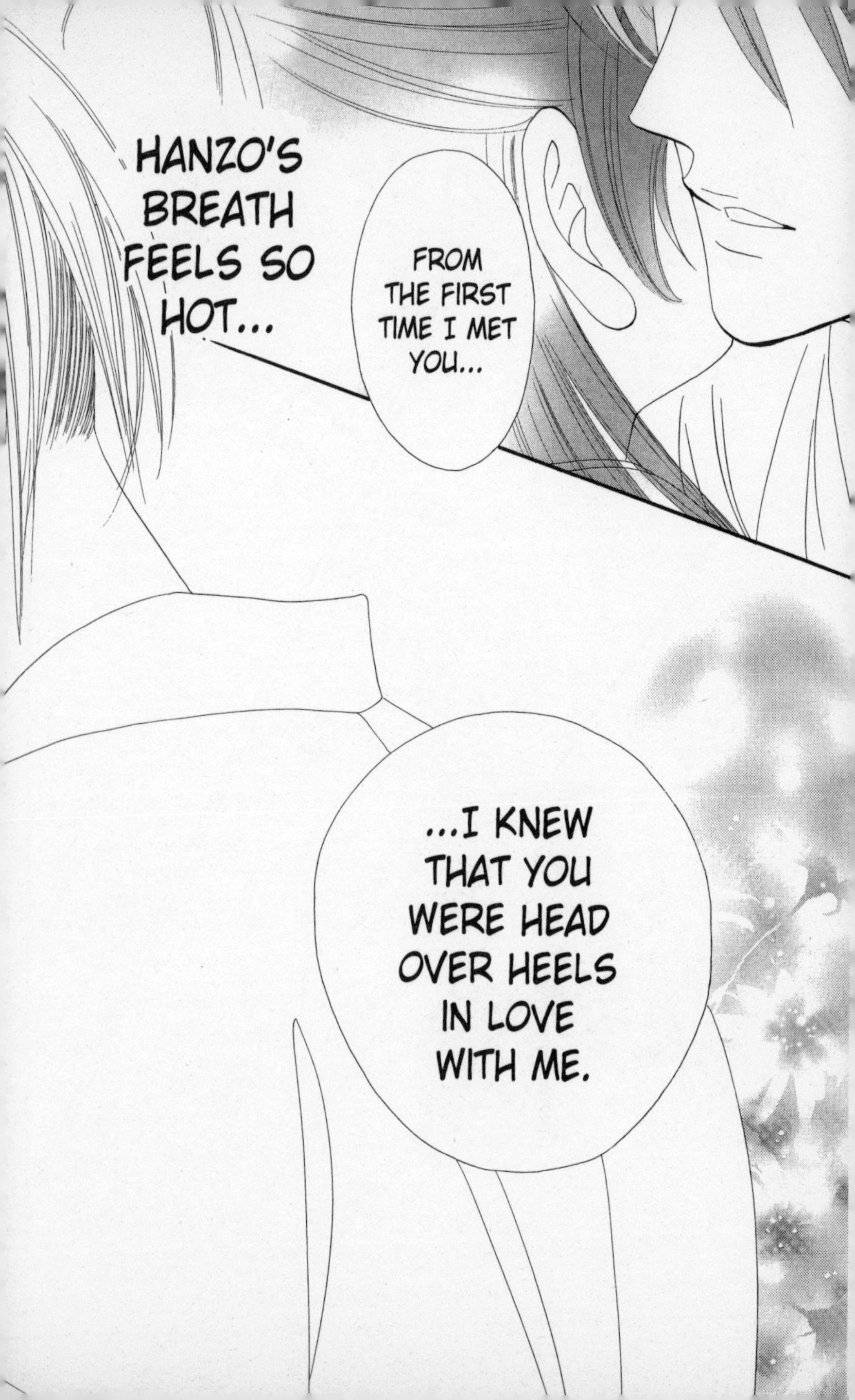
FROM THE FIRST TIME I MET YOU...
HANZO'S BREATH FEELS SO HOT...
...I KNEW THAT YOU WERE HEAD OVER HEELS IN LOVE WITH ME.

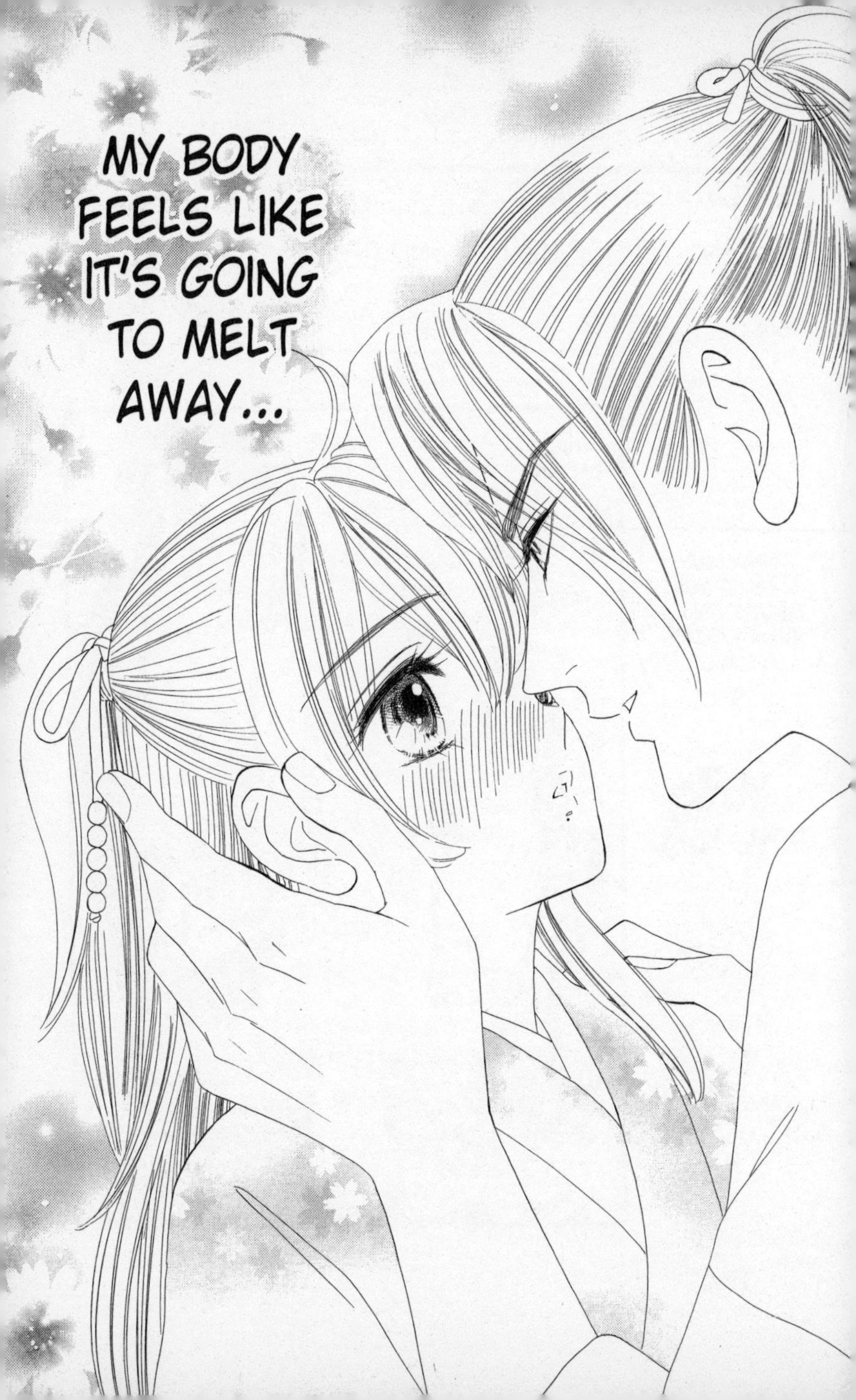
MY BODY FEELS LIKE IT'S GOING TO MELT AWAY...

TAIL OF THE MOON EXTRA: TODAY'S MISSION

"I WANT TO SEE HANZO AND BENKEI TOGETHER!"

-RYOKO, KYOTO

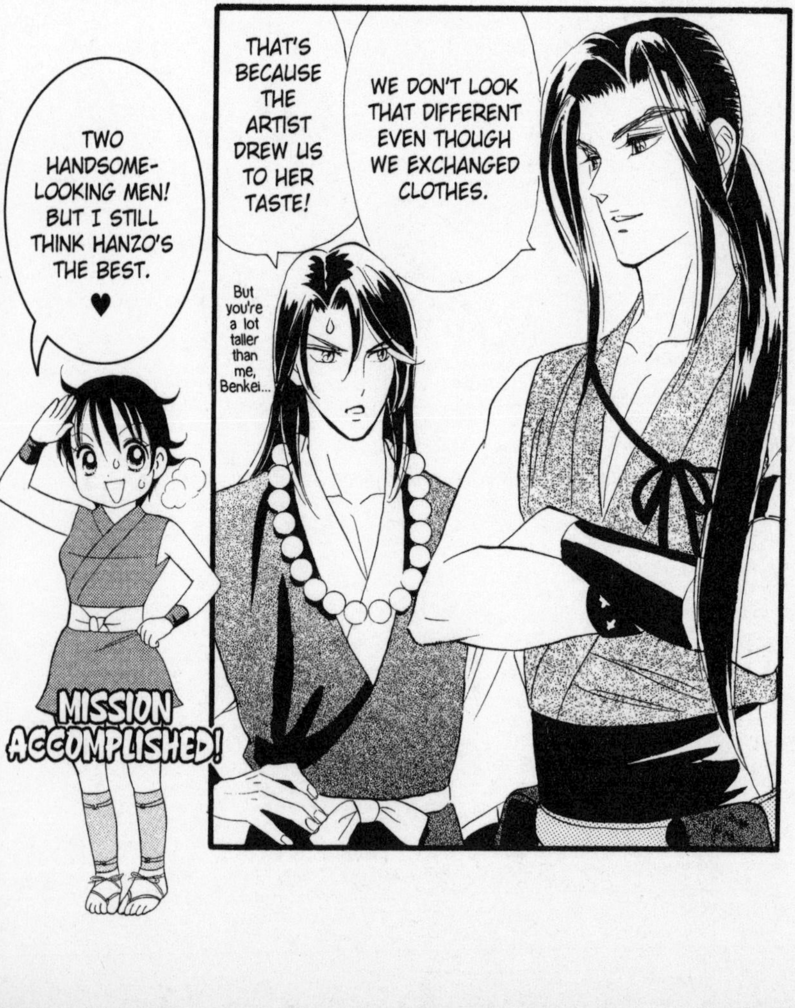
WE DON'T LOOK THAT DIFFERENT EVEN THOUGH WE EXCHANGED CLOTHES.
THAT'S BECAUSE THE ARTIST DREW US TO HER TASTE!
But you're a lot taller than me, Benkei...
TWO HANDSOME-LOOKING MEN! BUT I STILL THINK HANZO'S THE BEST. ♥
MISSION ACCOMPLISHED!

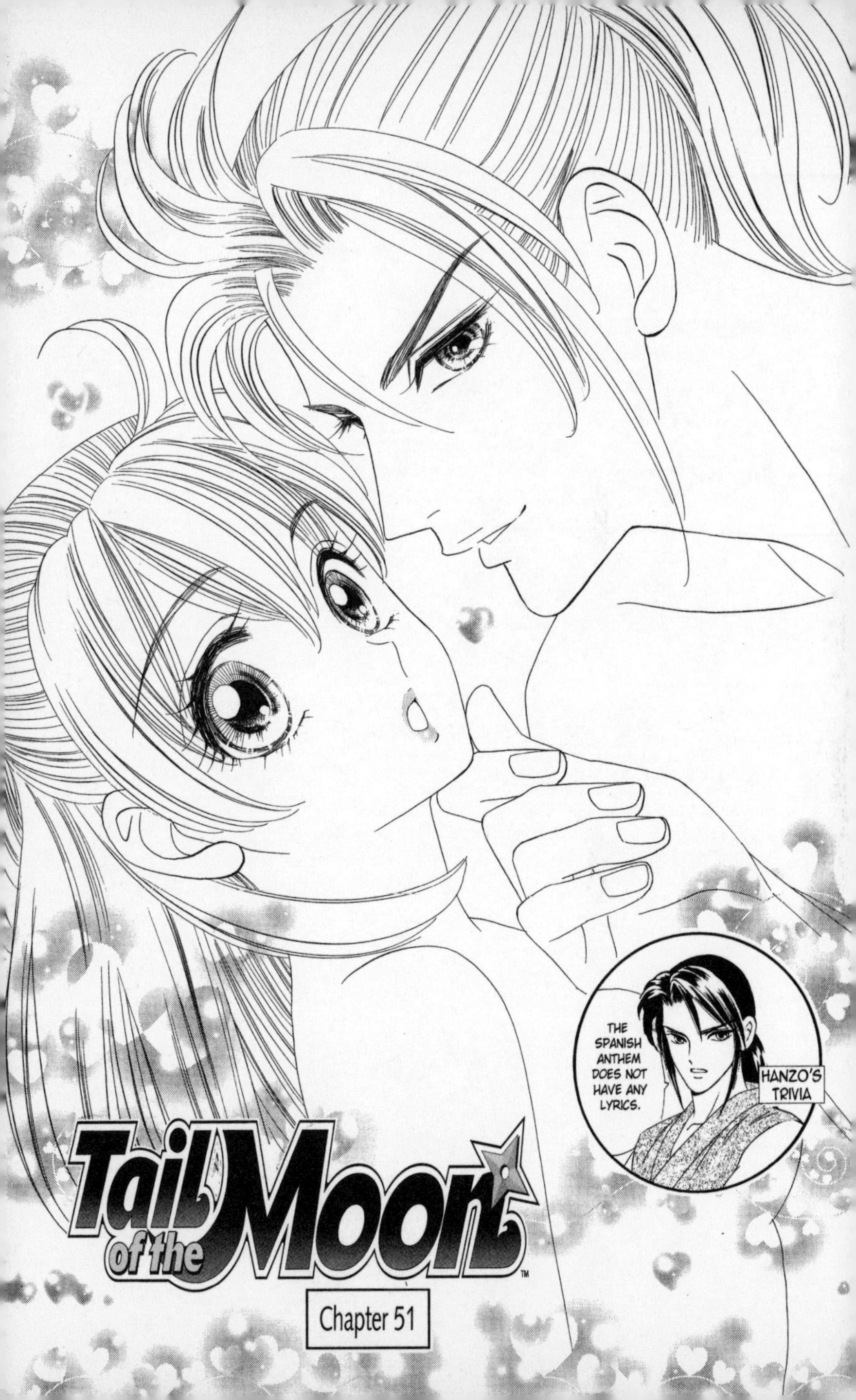
THE SPANISH ANTHEM DOES NOT HAVE ANY LYRICS.
HANZO'S TRIVIA
Tail of the Moon™
Chapter 51

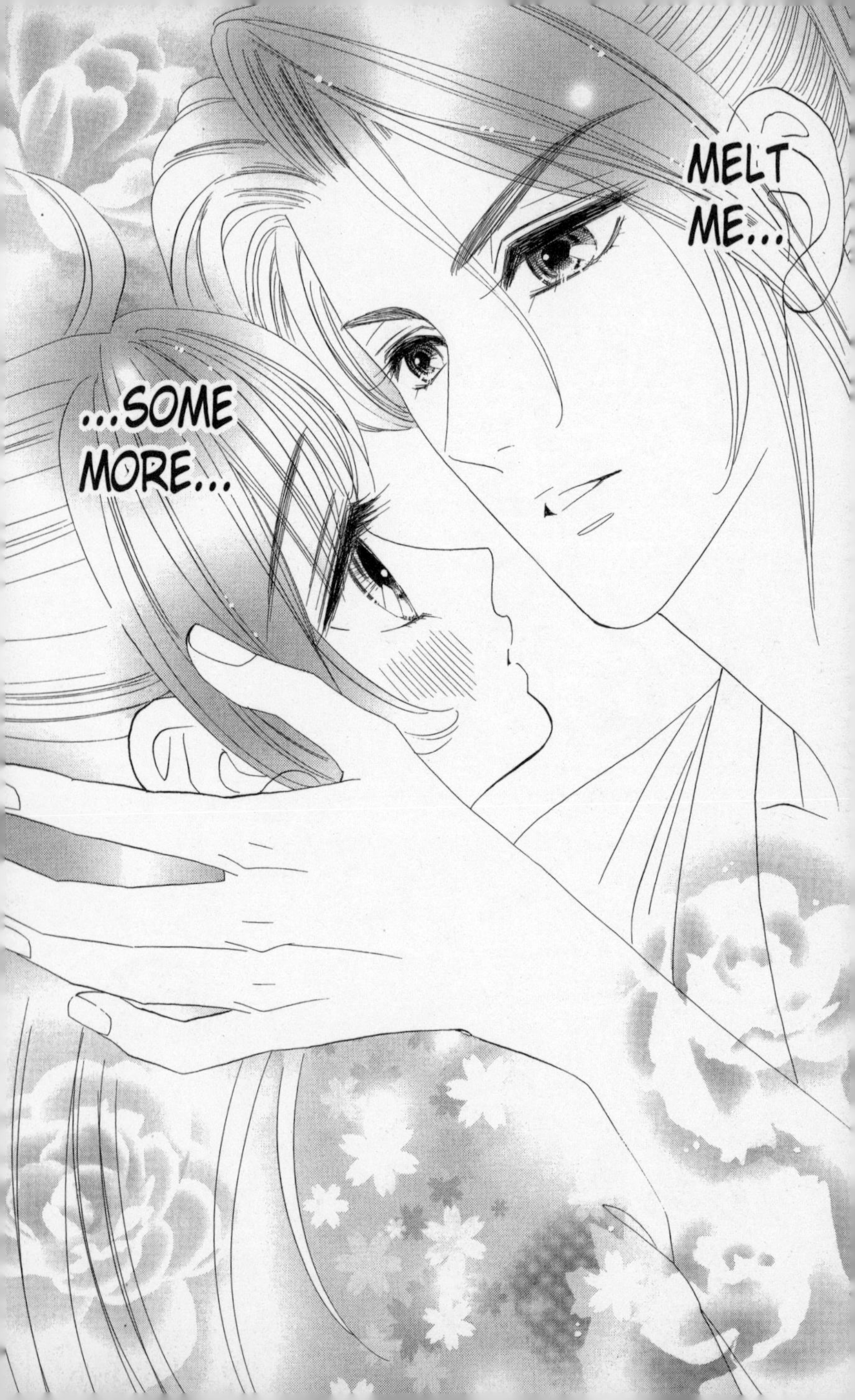
MELT ME...
...SOME MORE...

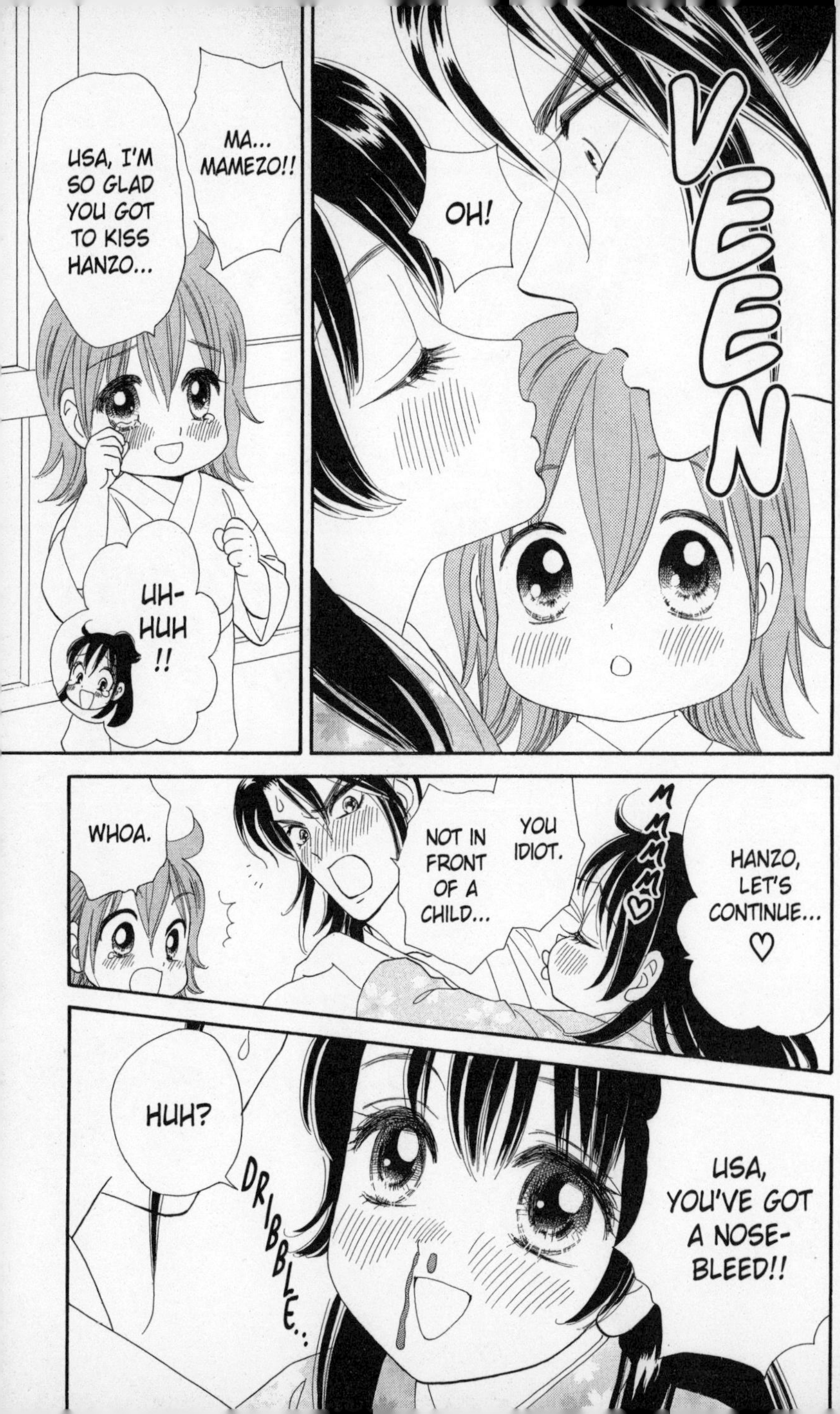
VEEN
OH!
MA... MAMEZO!!
USA, I'M SO GLAD YOU GOT TO KISS HANZO...
UH-HUH !!
HANZO, LET'S CONTINUE... ♡
MMMMM♡
YOU IDIOT.
NOT IN FRONT OF A CHILD...
WHOA.
USA, YOU'VE GOT A NOSE-BLEED!!
DRIBBLE...
HUH?

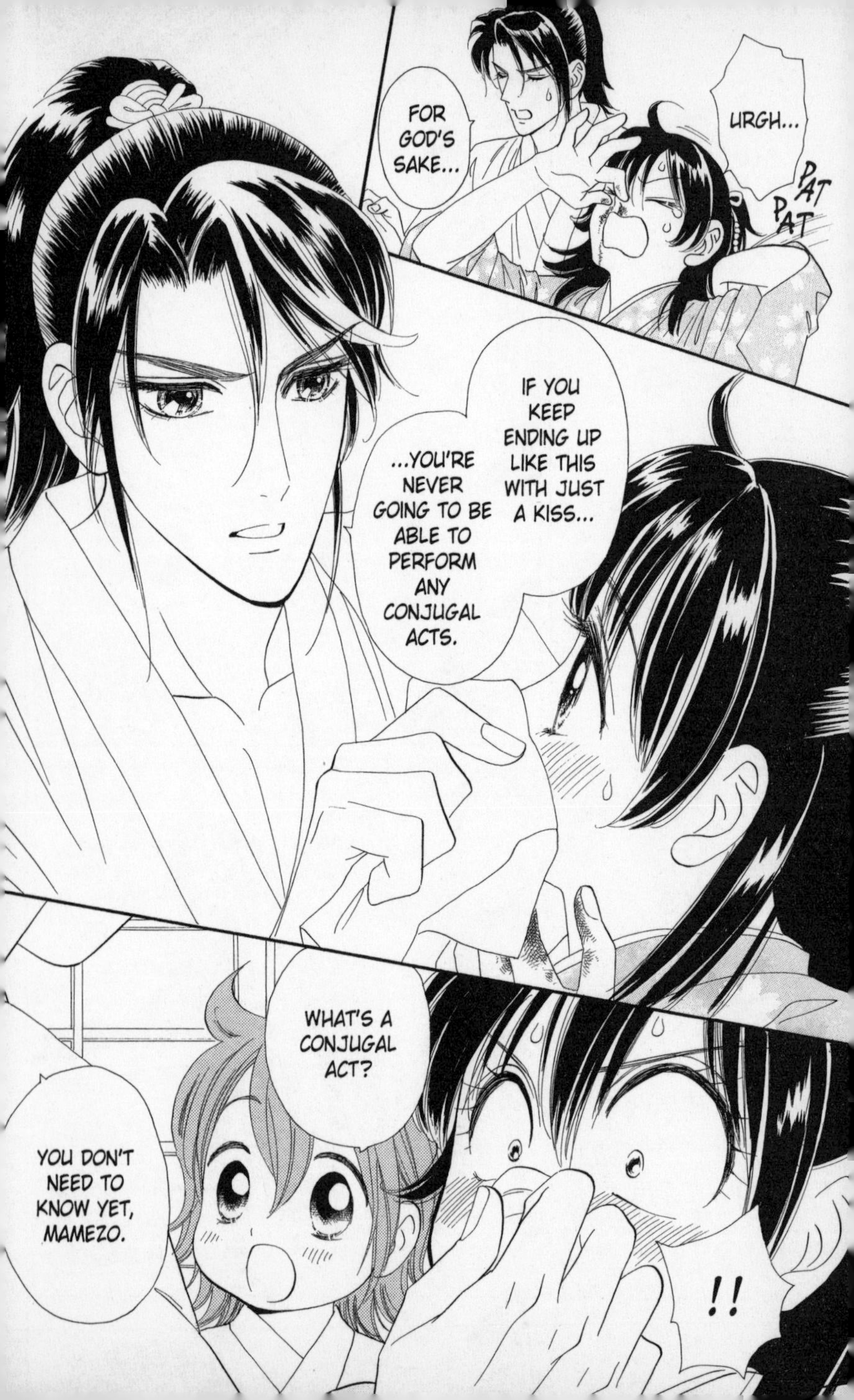
URGH...
PAT PAT
FOR GOD'S SAKE...
IF YOU KEEP ENDING UP LIKE THIS WITH JUST A KISS...
...YOU'RE NEVER GOING TO BE ABLE TO PERFORM ANY CONJUGAL ACTS.
WHAT'S A CONJUGAL ACT?
!!
YOU DON'T NEED TO KNOW YET, MAMEZO.

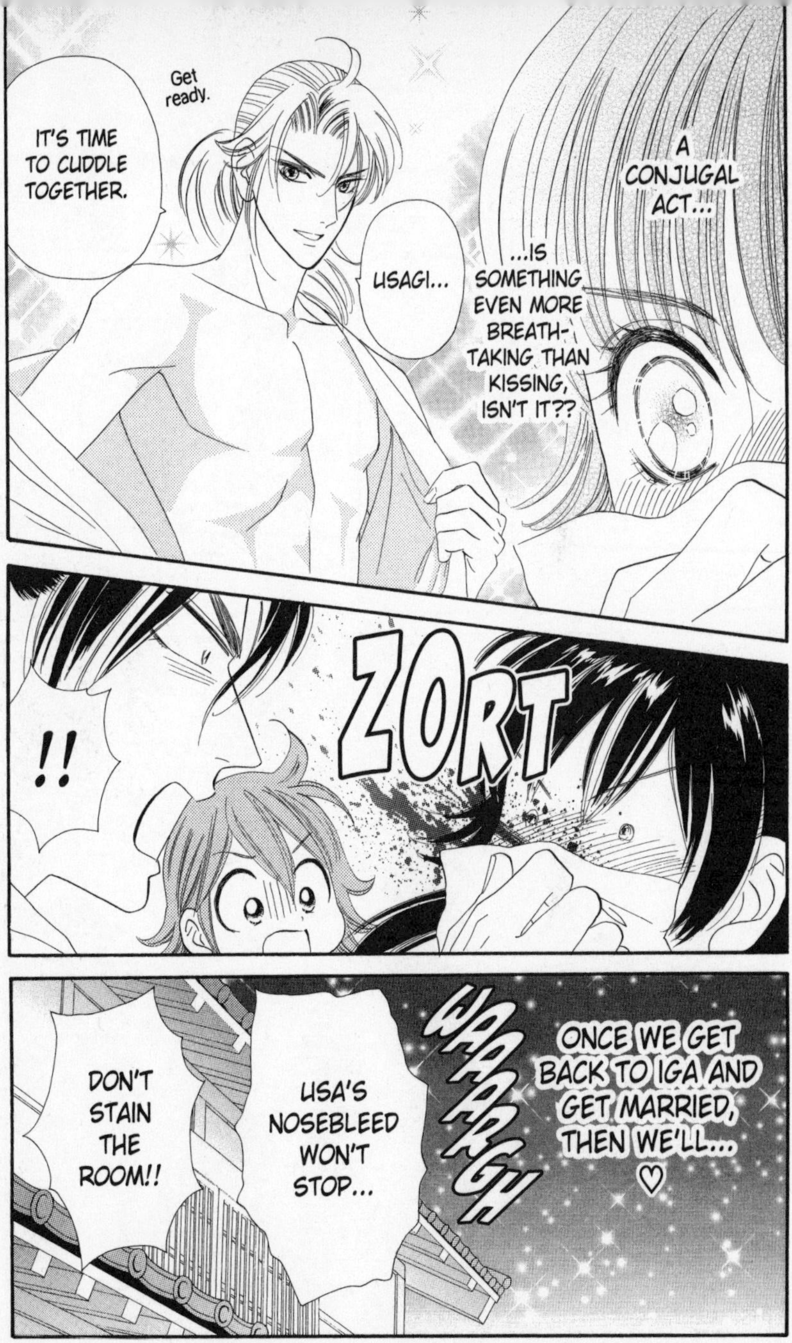
A CONJUGAL ACT...
...IS SOMETHING EVEN MORE BREATH-TAKING THAN KISSING, ISN'T IT??
USAGI...
Get ready.
IT'S TIME TO CUDDLE TOGETHER.
ZORT
!!
ONCE WE GET BACK TO IGA AND GET MARRIED, THEN WE'LL... ♡
WAAARGH
USA'S NOSEBLEED WON'T STOP...
DON'T STAIN THE ROOM!!

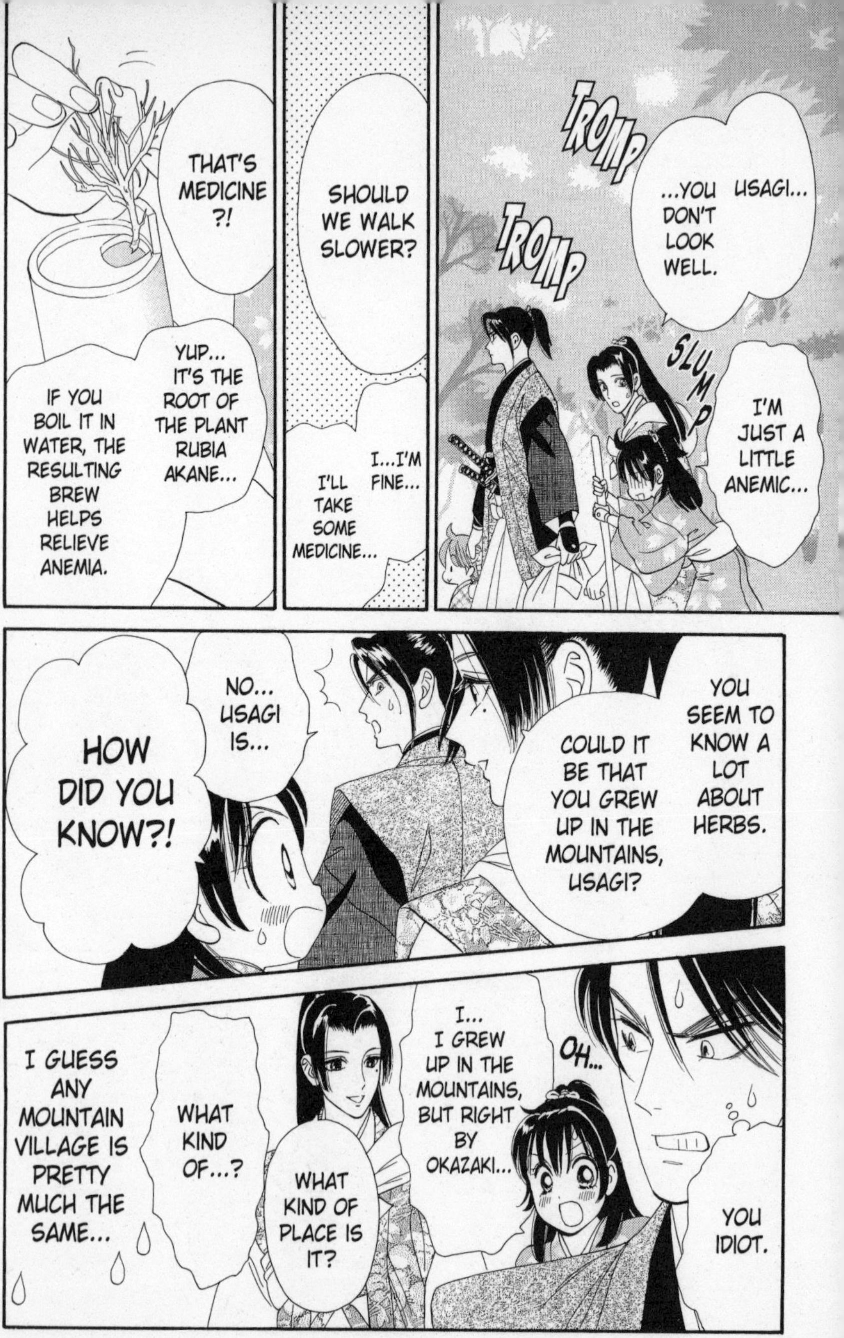
USAGI...
...YOU DON'T LOOK WELL.
TROMP
TROMP
I'M JUST A LITTLE ANEMIC...
SLUMP
SHOULD WE WALK SLOWER?
I...I'M FINE...
I'LL TAKE SOME MEDICINE...
THAT'S MEDICINE?!
YUP... IT'S THE ROOT OF THE PLANT RUBIA AKANE...
IF YOU BOIL IT IN WATER, THE RESULTING BREW HELPS RELIEVE ANEMIA.
YOU SEEM TO KNOW A LOT ABOUT HERBS.
COULD IT BE THAT YOU GREW UP IN THE MOUNTAINS, USAGI?
NO... USAGI IS...
HOW DID YOU KNOW?!
OH...
YOU IDIOT.
I... I GREW UP IN THE MOUNTAINS, BUT RIGHT BY OKAZAKI...
WHAT KIND OF PLACE IS IT?
WHAT KIND OF...?
I GUESS ANY MOUNTAIN VILLAGE IS PRETTY MUCH THE SAME...

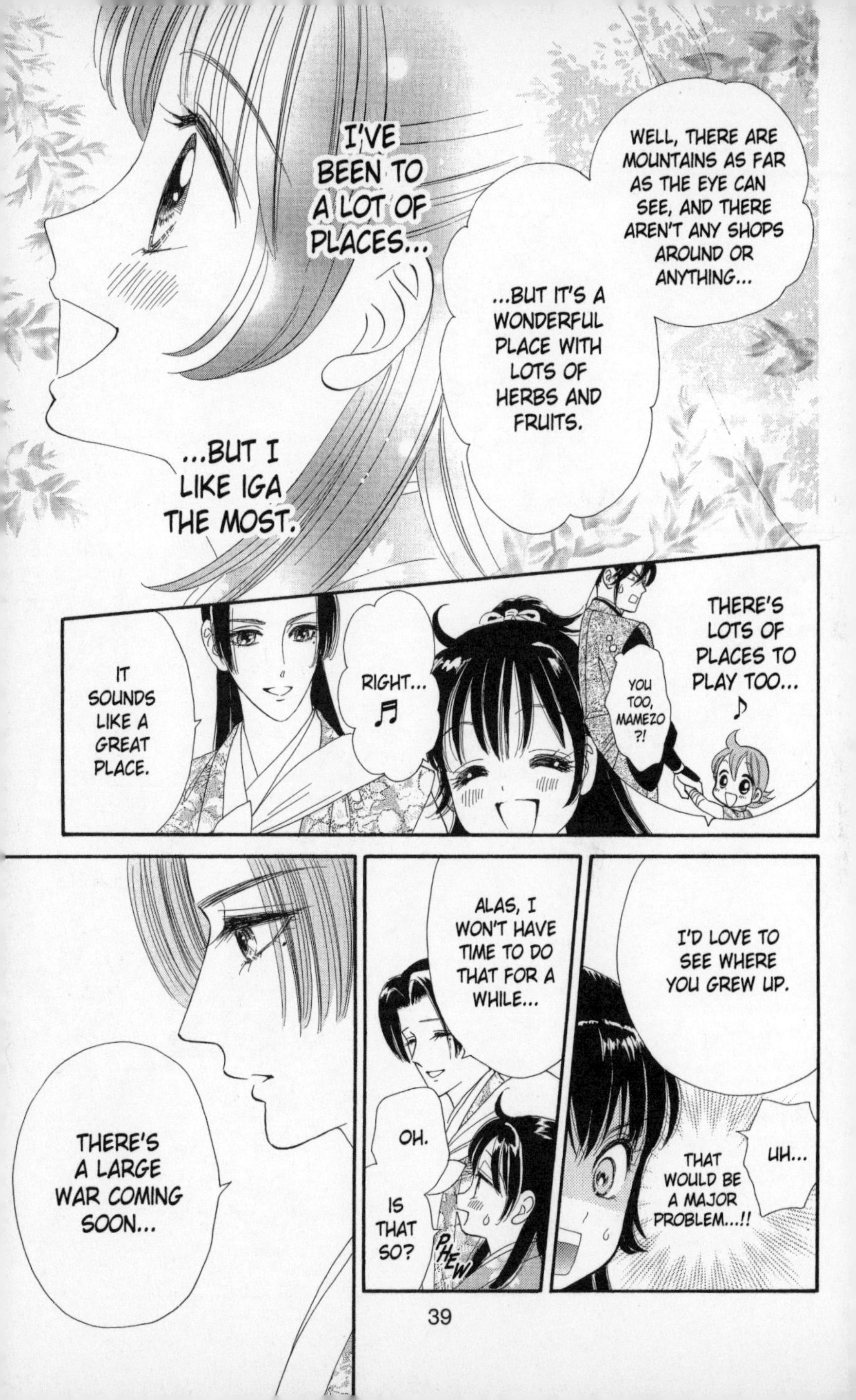
I'VE BEEN TO A LOT OF PLACES...
...BUT I LIKE IGA THE MOST.
WELL, THERE ARE MOUNTAINS AS FAR AS THE EYE CAN SEE, AND THERE AREN'T ANY SHOPS AROUND OR ANYTHING...
...BUT IT'S A WONDERFUL PLACE WITH LOTS OF HERBS AND FRUITS.
THERE'S LOTS OF PLACES TO PLAY TOO... ♪
YOU TOO, MAMEZO?!
RIGHT... ♬
IT SOUNDS LIKE A GREAT PLACE.
I'D LOVE TO SEE WHERE YOU GREW UP.
UH...
THAT WOULD BE A MAJOR PROBLEM...!!
ALAS, I WON'T HAVE TIME TO DO THAT FOR A WHILE...
OH.
IS THAT SO?
PHEW
THERE'S A LARGE WAR COMING SOON...

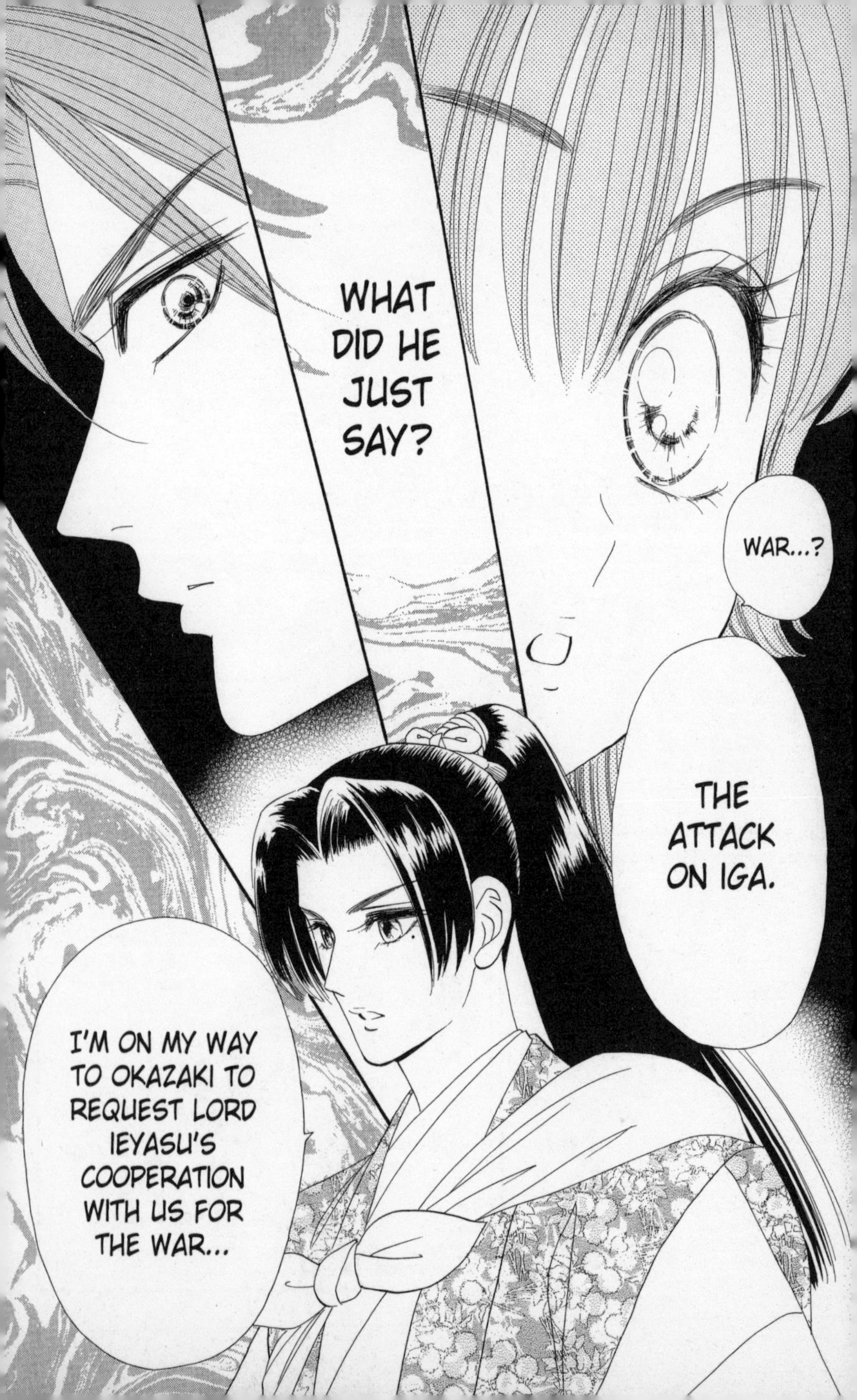
I'M ON MY WAY TO OKAZAKI TO REQUEST LORD IEYASU'S COOPERATION WITH US FOR THE WAR...
THE ATTACK ON IGA.
WAR...?
WHAT DID HE JUST SAY?

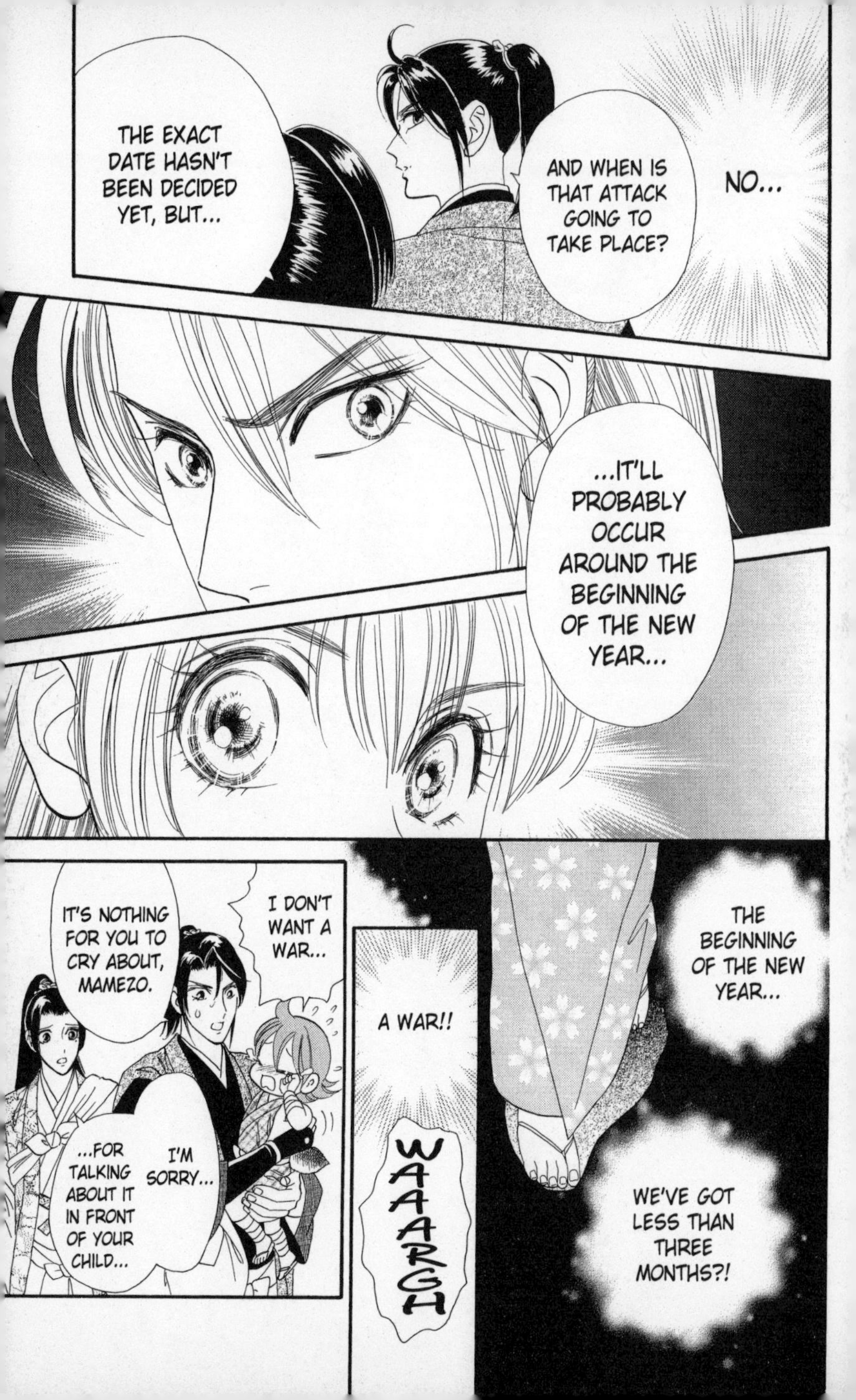
NO...
AND WHEN IS THAT ATTACK GOING TO TAKE PLACE?
THE EXACT DATE HASN'T BEEN DECIDED YET, BUT...
...IT'LL PROBABLY OCCUR AROUND THE BEGINNING OF THE NEW YEAR...
THE BEGINNING OF THE NEW YEAR...
WE'VE GOT LESS THAN THREE MONTHS?!
A WAR!!
WAAARGH
I DON'T WANT A WAR...
IT'S NOTHING FOR YOU TO CRY ABOUT, MAMEZO.
I'M SORRY...
...FOR TALKING ABOUT IT IN FRONT OF YOUR CHILD...

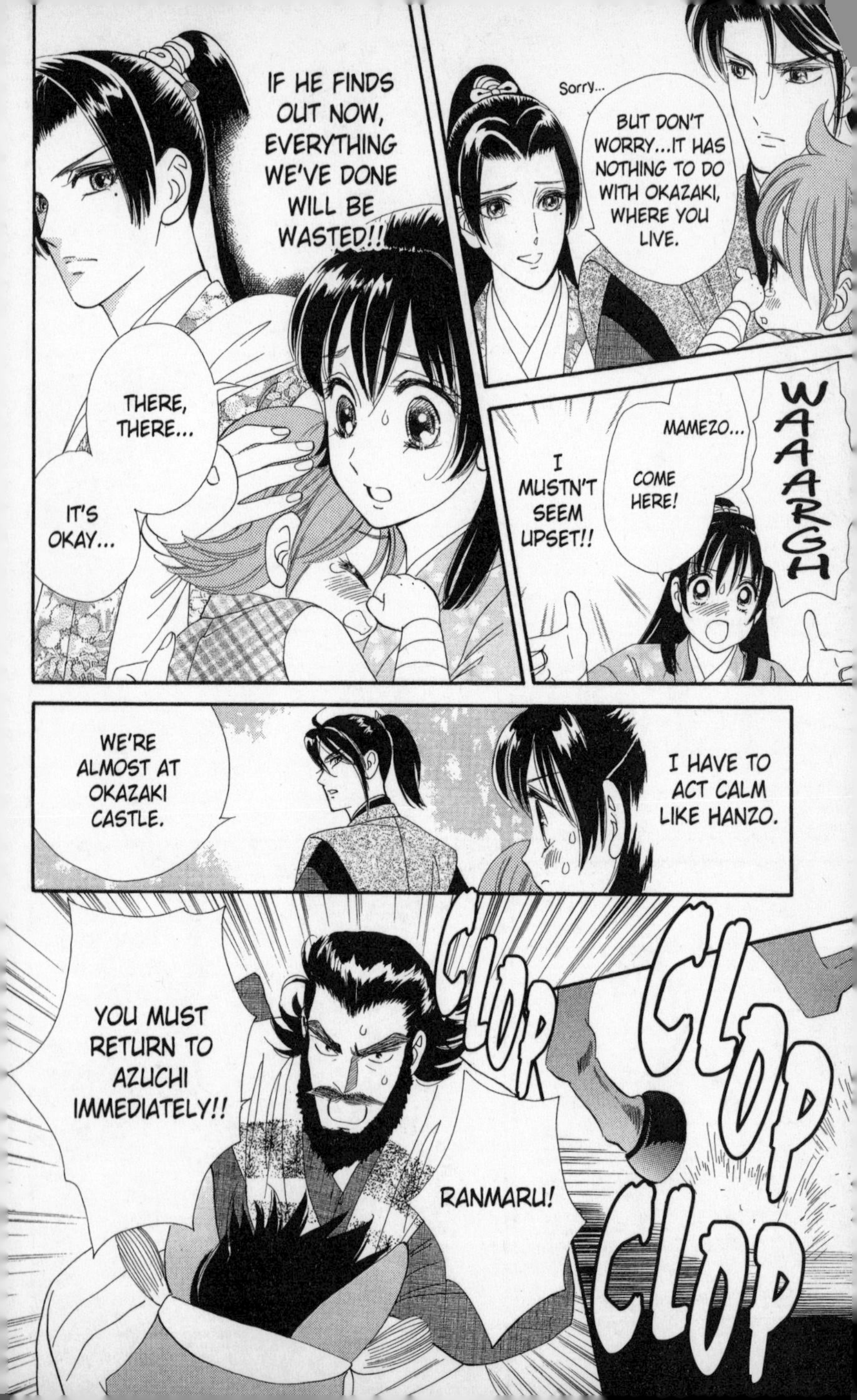
Sorry...
BUT DON'T WORRY...IT HAS NOTHING TO DO WITH OKAZAKI, WHERE YOU LIVE.
WAAARGH
MAMEZO...
COME HERE!
I MUSTN'T SEEM UPSET!!
IF HE FINDS OUT NOW, EVERYTHING WE'VE DONE WILL BE WASTED!!
THERE, THERE...
IT'S OKAY...
I HAVE TO ACT CALM LIKE HANZO.
WE'RE ALMOST AT OKAZAKI CASTLE.
CLOP
CLOP
CLOP
CLOP
RANMARU!
YOU MUST RETURN TO AZUCHI IMMEDIATELY!!

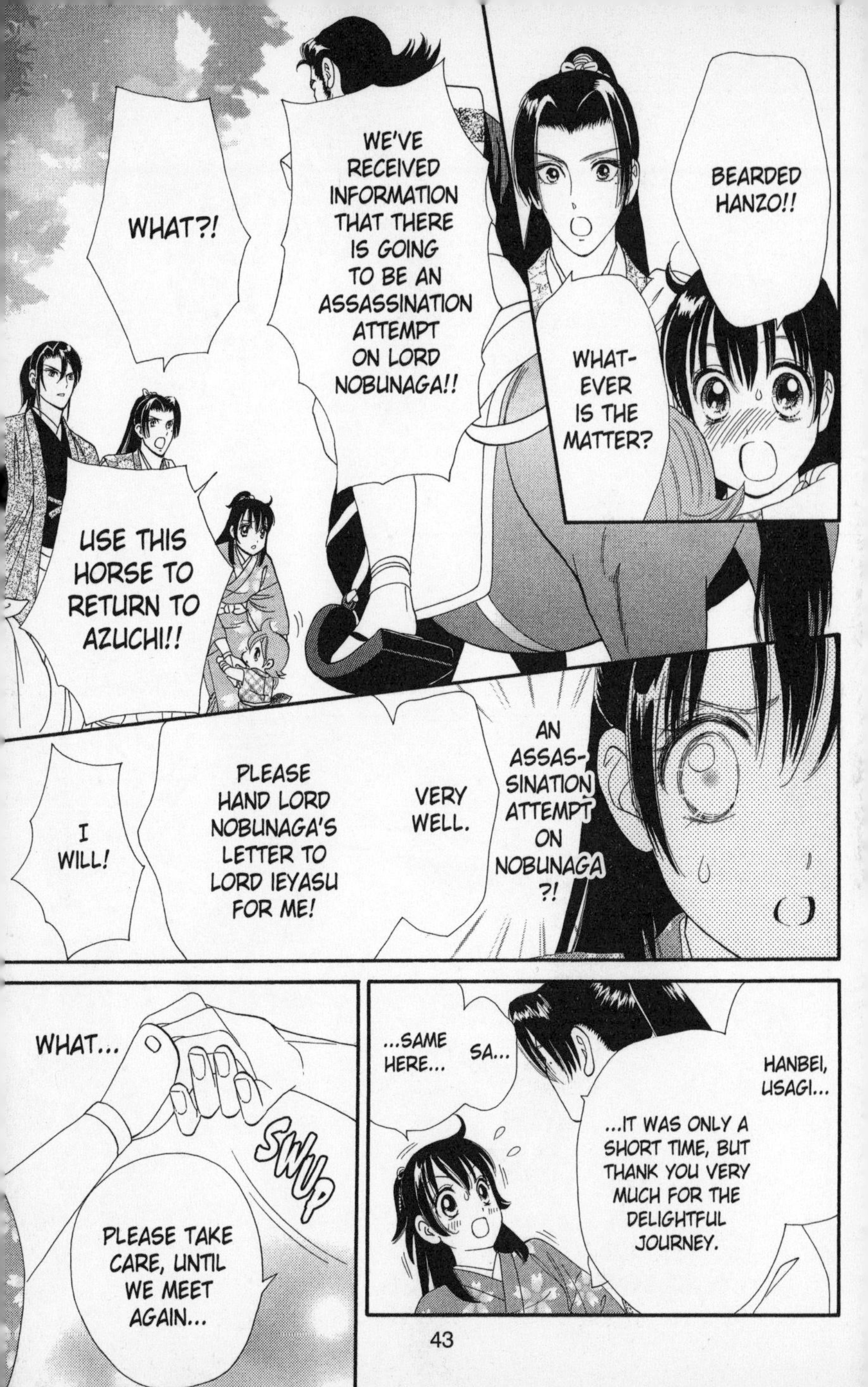
BEARDED HANZO!!
WHAT-EVER IS THE MATTER?
WE'VE RECEIVED INFORMATION THAT THERE IS GOING TO BE AN ASSASSINATION ATTEMPT ON LORD NOBUNAGA!!
WHAT?!
USE THIS HORSE TO RETURN TO AZUCHI!!
AN ASSAS-SINATION ATTEMPT ON NOBUNAGA?!
VERY WELL.
PLEASE HAND LORD NOBUNAGA'S LETTER TO LORD IEYASU FOR ME!
I WILL!
HANBEI, USAGI...
...IT WAS ONLY A SHORT TIME, BUT THANK YOU VERY MUCH FOR THE DELIGHTFUL JOURNEY.
SA...
...SAME HERE...
WHAT...
SWUP
PLEASE TAKE CARE, UNTIL WE MEET AGAIN...

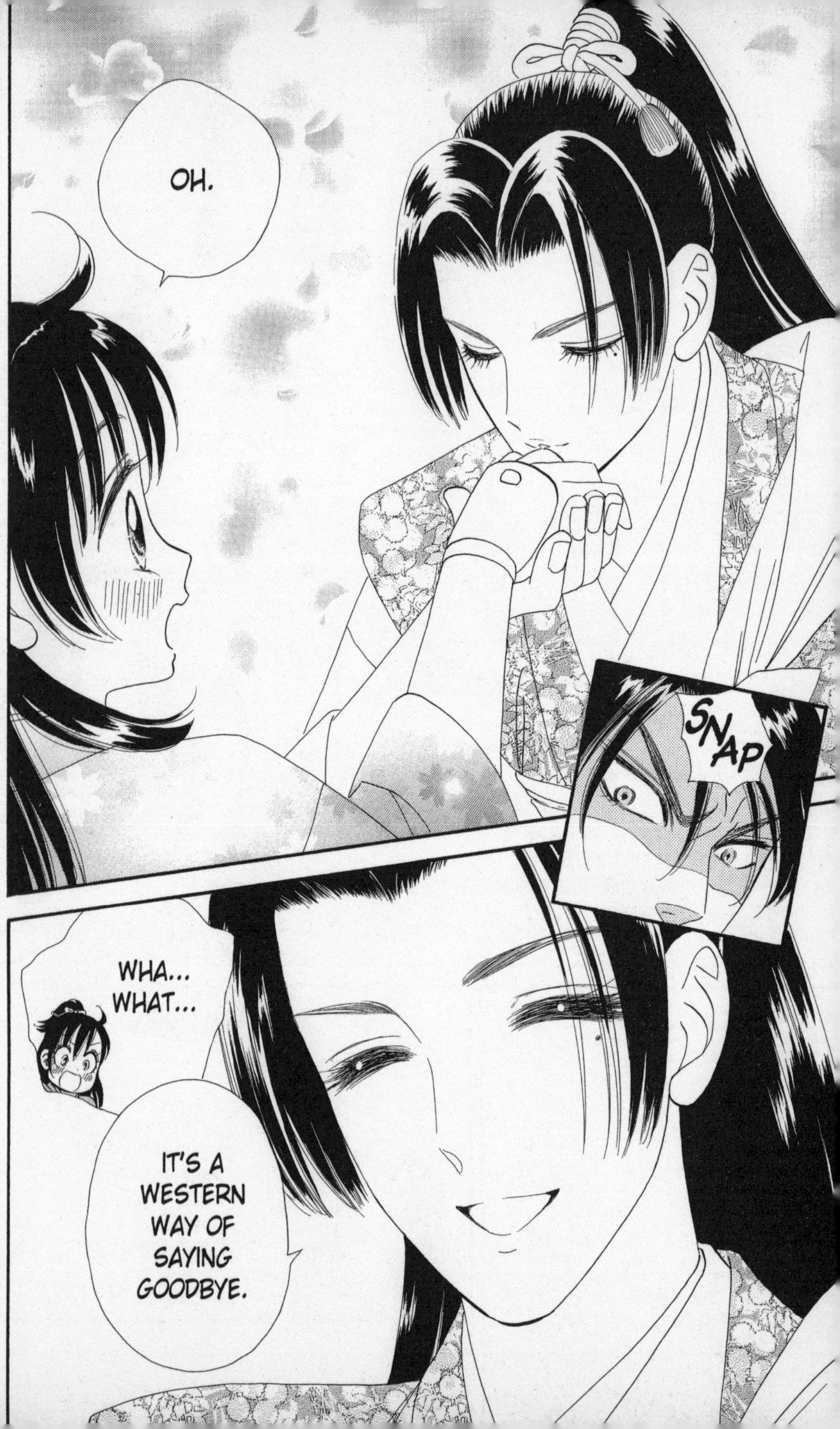
OH.
SNAP
WHA... WHAT...
IT'S A WESTERN WAY OF SAYING GOODBYE.

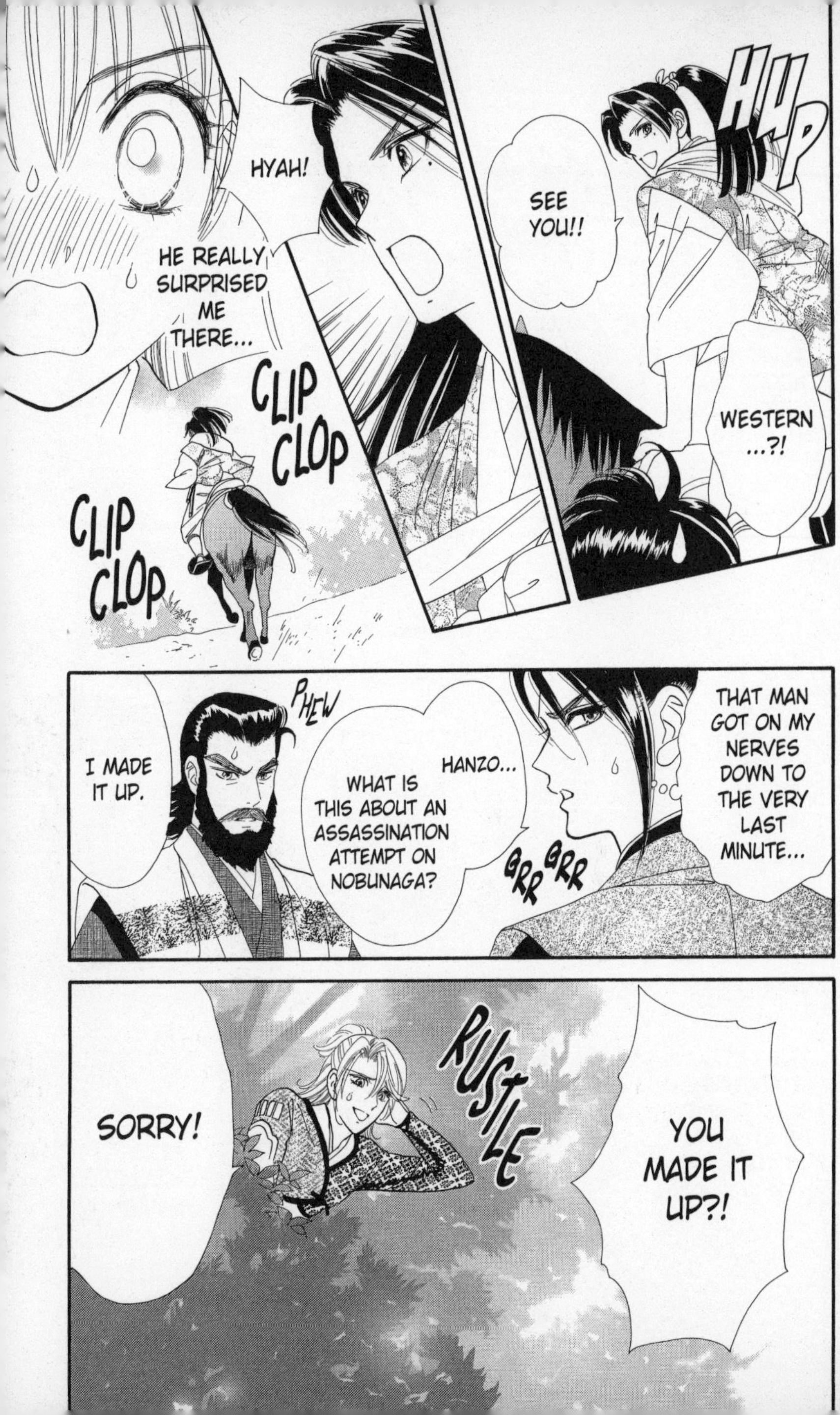
HUP
SEE YOU!!
WESTERN ...?!
HYAH!
HE REALLY SURPRISED ME THERE...
CLIP CLOP
CLIP CLOP
THAT MAN GOT ON MY NERVES DOWN TO THE VERY LAST MINUTE...
GRR GRR
HANZO...
WHAT IS THIS ABOUT AN ASSASSINATION ATTEMPT ON NOBUNAGA?
PHEW
I MADE IT UP.
YOU MADE IT UP?!
RUSTLE
SORRY!

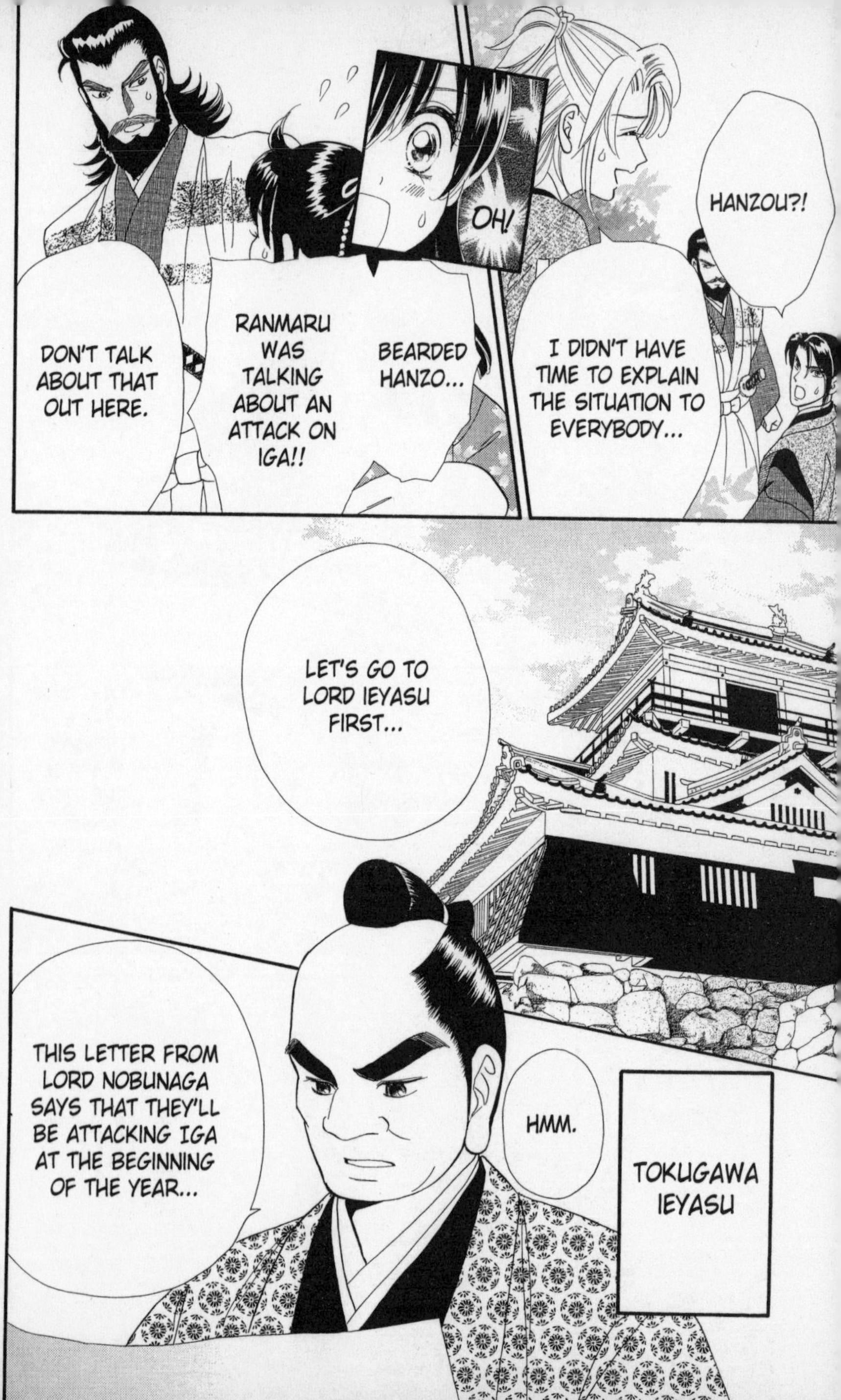
HANZOU?!
I DIDN'T HAVE TIME TO EXPLAIN THE SITUATION TO EVERYBODY...
OH!
BEARDED HANZO...
RANMARU WAS TALKING ABOUT AN ATTACK ON IGA!!
DON'T TALK ABOUT THAT OUT HERE.
LET'S GO TO LORD IEYASU FIRST...
TOKUGAWA IEYASU
HMM.
THIS LETTER FROM LORD NOBUNAGA SAYS THAT THEY'LL BE ATTACKING IGA AT THE BEGINNING OF THE YEAR...

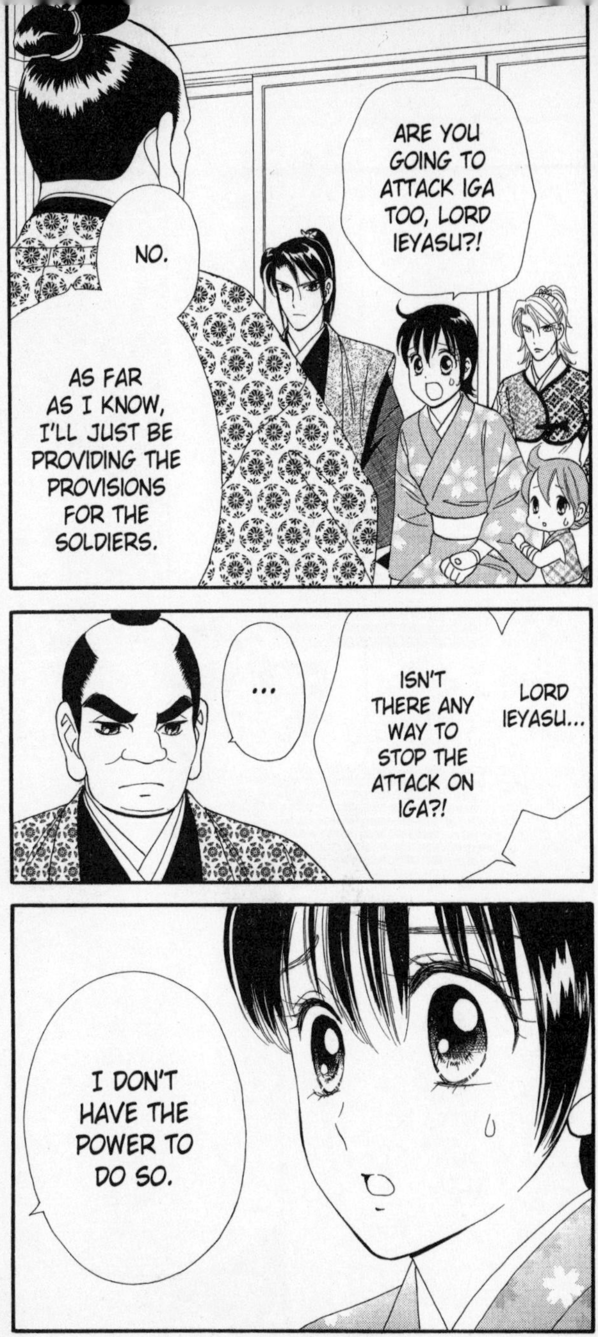
ARE YOU GOING TO ATTACK IGA TOO, LORD IEYASU?!
NO.
AS FAR AS I KNOW, I'LL JUST BE PROVIDING THE PROVISIONS FOR THE SOLDIERS.
LORD IEYASU...
ISN'T THERE ANY WAY TO STOP THE ATTACK ON IGA?!
...
I DON'T HAVE THE POWER TO DO SO.

UE-RIN'S WAY OF THE MANGA ⑫

I had this wily scheme of "It's going to be great if both of my works got accepted for the magazine!" But the words that came out of the editor that I met were...

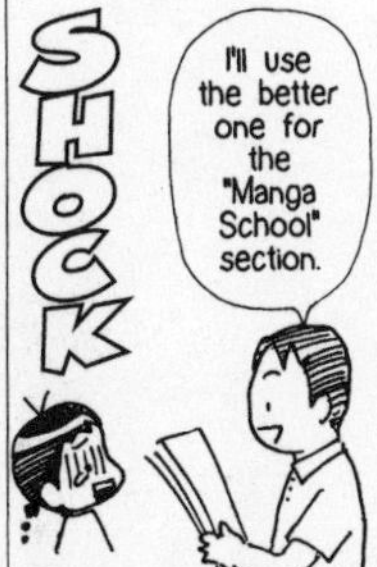
SHOCK
I'll use the better one for the "Manga School" section.

And so, the editor took the one he liked back with him to Tokyo.
Now that I think about it, he made the right decision. Plus, the other piece that didn't get taken was a good exercise for me, so the work wasn't wasted.

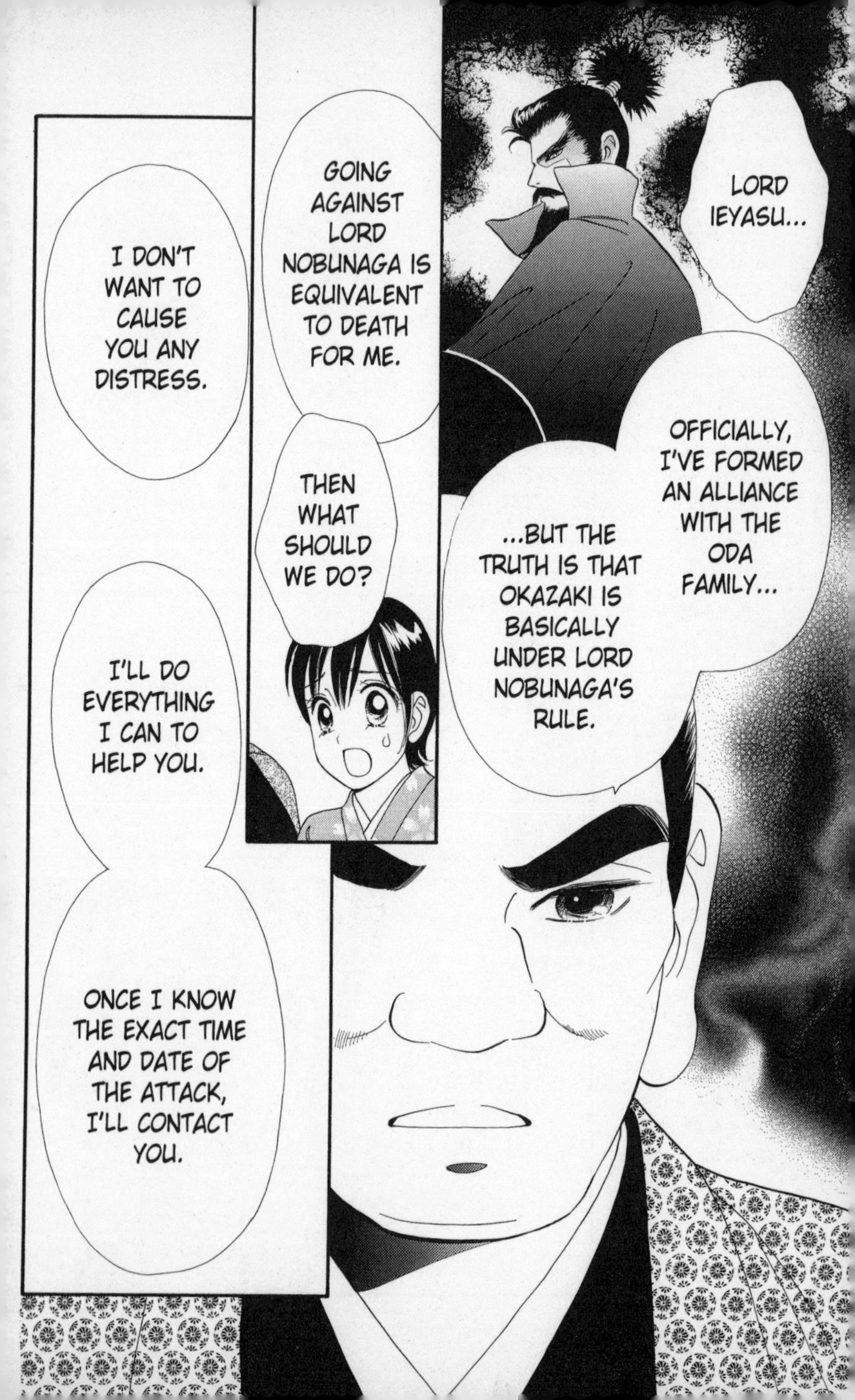
LORD IEYASU...
OFFICIALLY, I'VE FORMED AN ALLIANCE WITH THE ODA FAMILY...
...BUT THE TRUTH IS THAT OKAZAKI IS BASICALLY UNDER LORD NOBUNAGA'S RULE.
GOING AGAINST LORD NOBUNAGA IS EQUIVALENT TO DEATH FOR ME.
THEN WHAT SHOULD WE DO?
I DON'T WANT TO CAUSE YOU ANY DISTRESS.
I'LL DO EVERYTHING I CAN TO HELP YOU.
ONCE I KNOW THE EXACT TIME AND DATE OF THE ATTACK, I'LL CONTACT YOU.

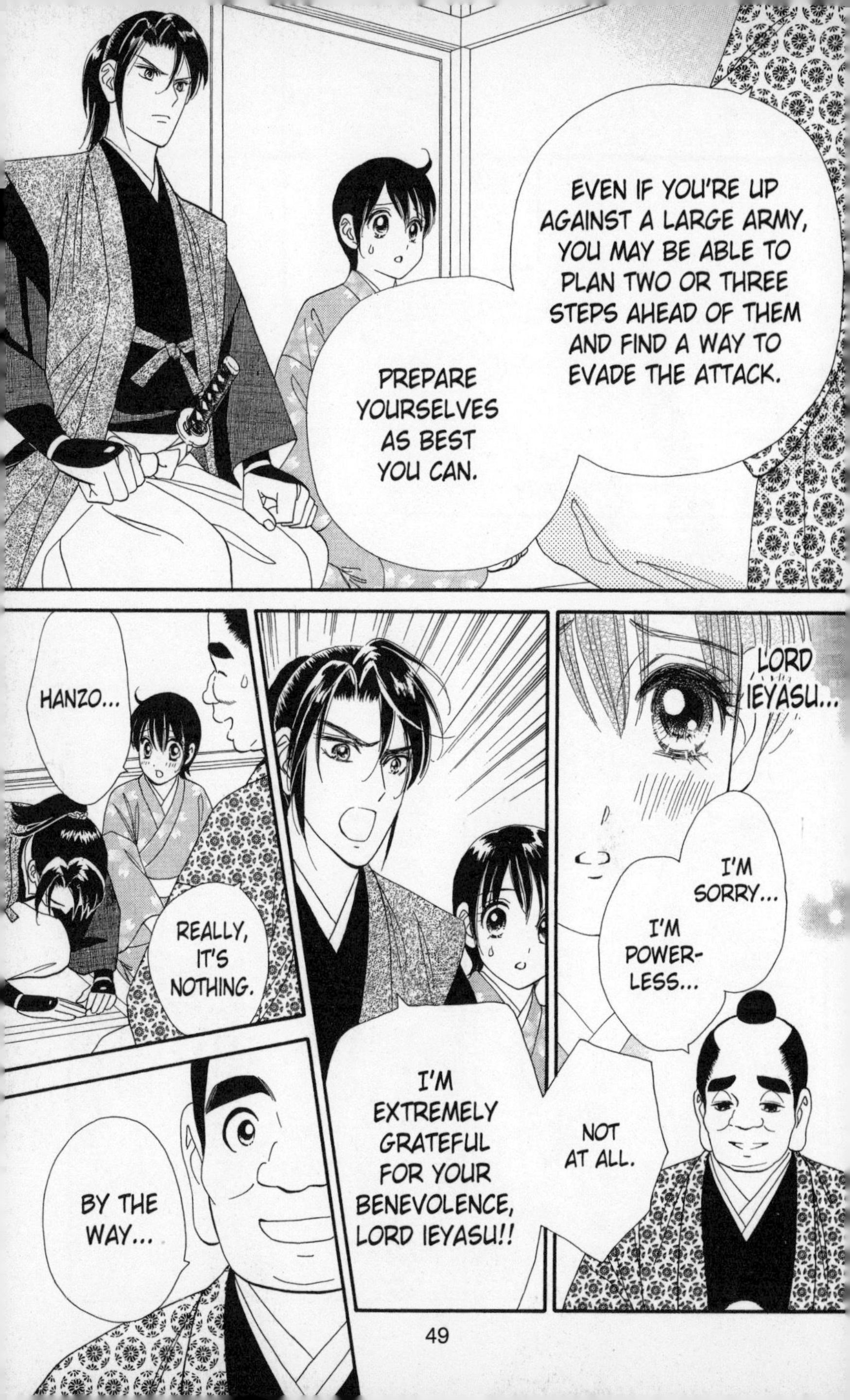
EVEN IF YOU'RE UP AGAINST A LARGE ARMY, YOU MAY BE ABLE TO PLAN TWO OR THREE STEPS AHEAD OF THEM AND FIND A WAY TO EVADE THE ATTACK.
PREPARE YOURSELVES AS BEST YOU CAN.
LORD IEYASU...
I'M SORRY...
I'M POWER-LESS...
I'M EXTREMELY GRATEFUL FOR YOUR BENEVOLENCE, LORD IEYASU!!
NOT AT ALL.
HANZO...
REALLY, IT'S NOTHING.
BY THE WAY...

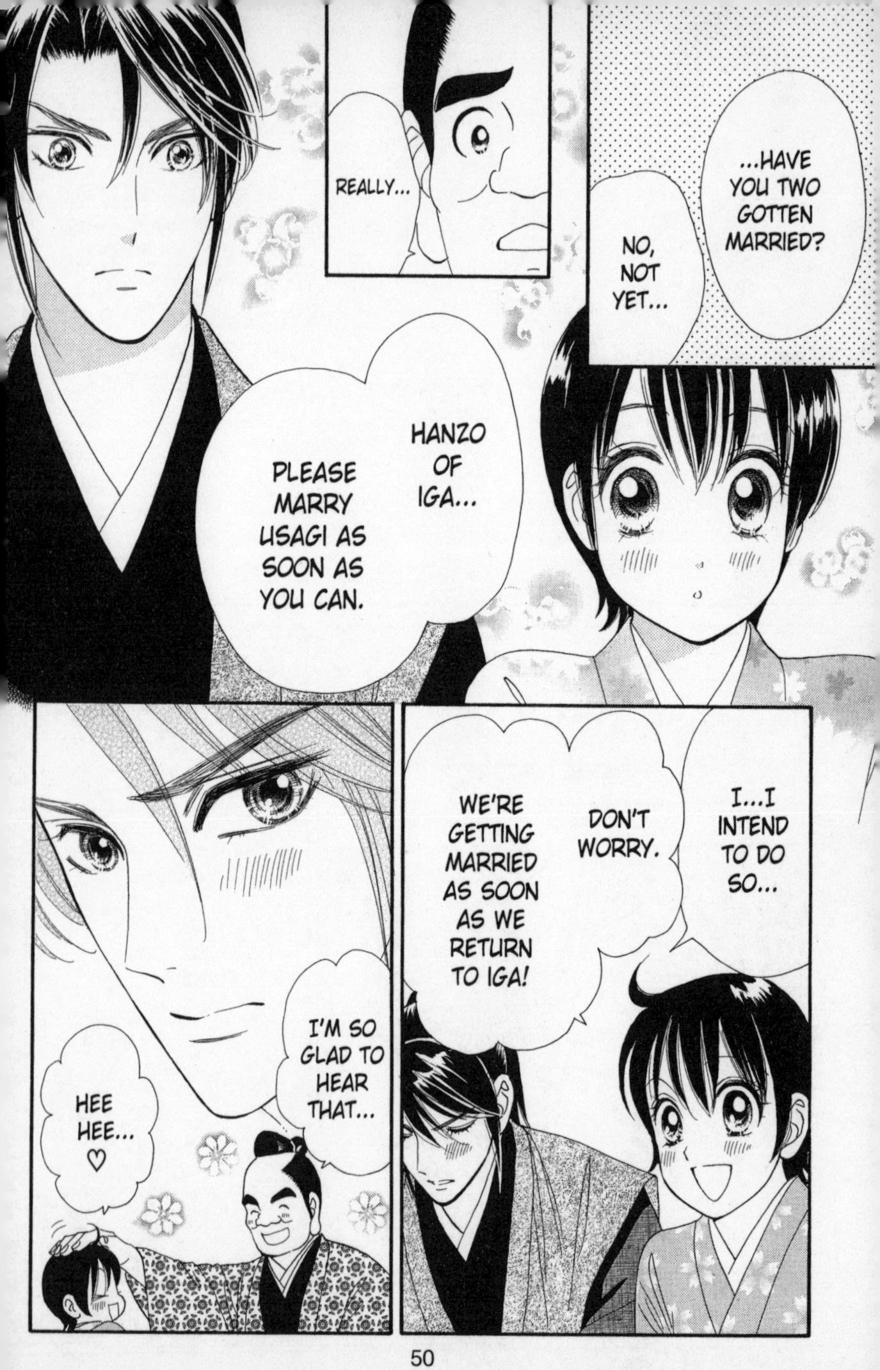
...HAVE YOU TWO GOTTEN MARRIED?
NO, NOT YET...
REALLY...
HANZO OF IGA...
PLEASE MARRY USAGI AS SOON AS YOU CAN.
I...I INTEND TO DO SO...
DON'T WORRY.
WE'RE GETTING MARRIED AS SOON AS WE RETURN TO IGA!
I'M SO GLAD TO HEAR THAT...
HEE HEE... ♡

LORD IEYASU, THANK YOU FOR EVERYTHING...

USAGI...

IF ANYTHING SHOULD HAPPEN, YOU CAN ALWAYS COME TO MY PLACE.

THANK YOU.

BUT NOTHING WILL HAPPEN!!

MY LORD...

I TRULY APOLOGIZE FOR LEAVING YOU AGAIN.

IT DOESN'T MATTER.

TAKE CARE OF YOURSELF, HANZOU.

I'M SORRY HE'S SUCH A FOOLISH SON...

THANK YOU VERY MUCH FOR YOUR KIND WORDS.

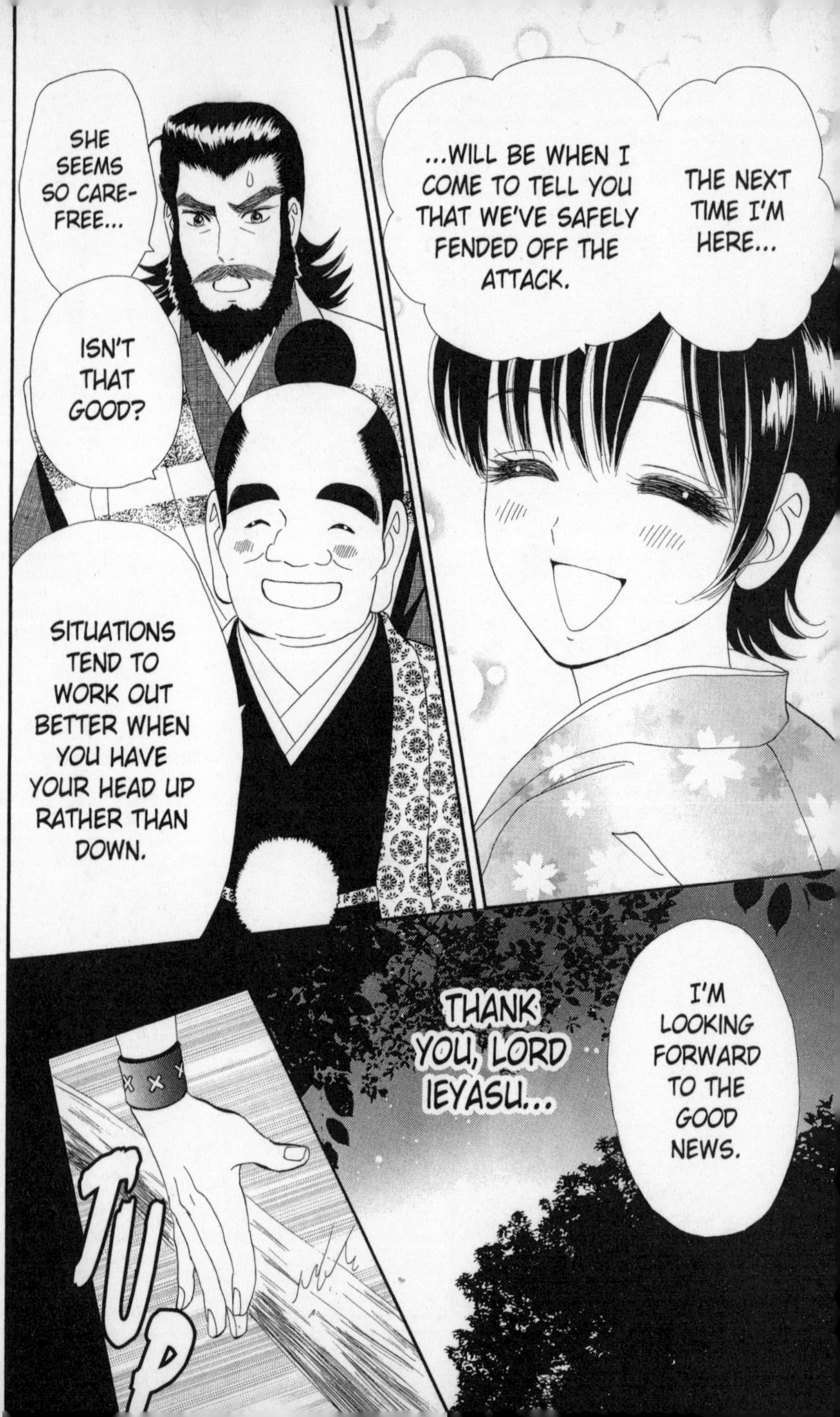
THE NEXT TIME I'M HERE...
...WILL BE WHEN I COME TO TELL YOU THAT WE'VE SAFELY FENDED OFF THE ATTACK.
SHE SEEMS SO CARE-FREE...
ISN'T THAT GOOD?
SITUATIONS TEND TO WORK OUT BETTER WHEN YOU HAVE YOUR HEAD UP RATHER THAN DOWN.
I'M LOOKING FORWARD TO THE GOOD NEWS.
THANK YOU, LORD IEYASU...
TUP

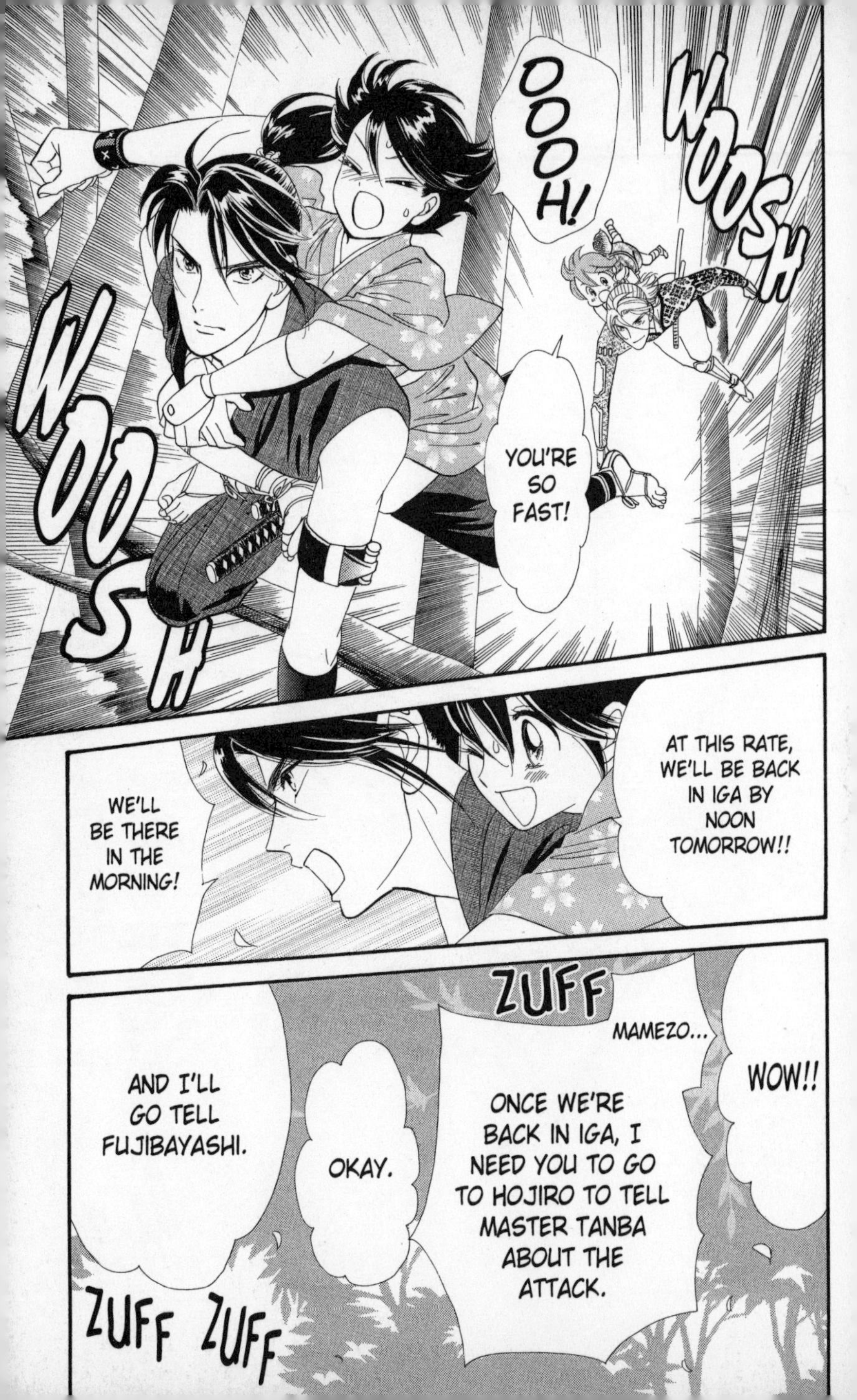
WOOSH
OOOOH!
YOU'RE SO FAST!
WOOSH
AT THIS RATE, WE'LL BE BACK IN IGA BY NOON TOMORROW!!
WE'LL BE THERE IN THE MORNING!
ZUFF
MAMEZO...
WOW!!
ONCE WE'RE BACK IN IGA, I NEED YOU TO GO TO HOJIRO TO TELL MASTER TANBA ABOUT THE ATTACK.
OKAY.
AND I'LL GO TELL FUJIBAYASHI.
ZUFF ZUFF

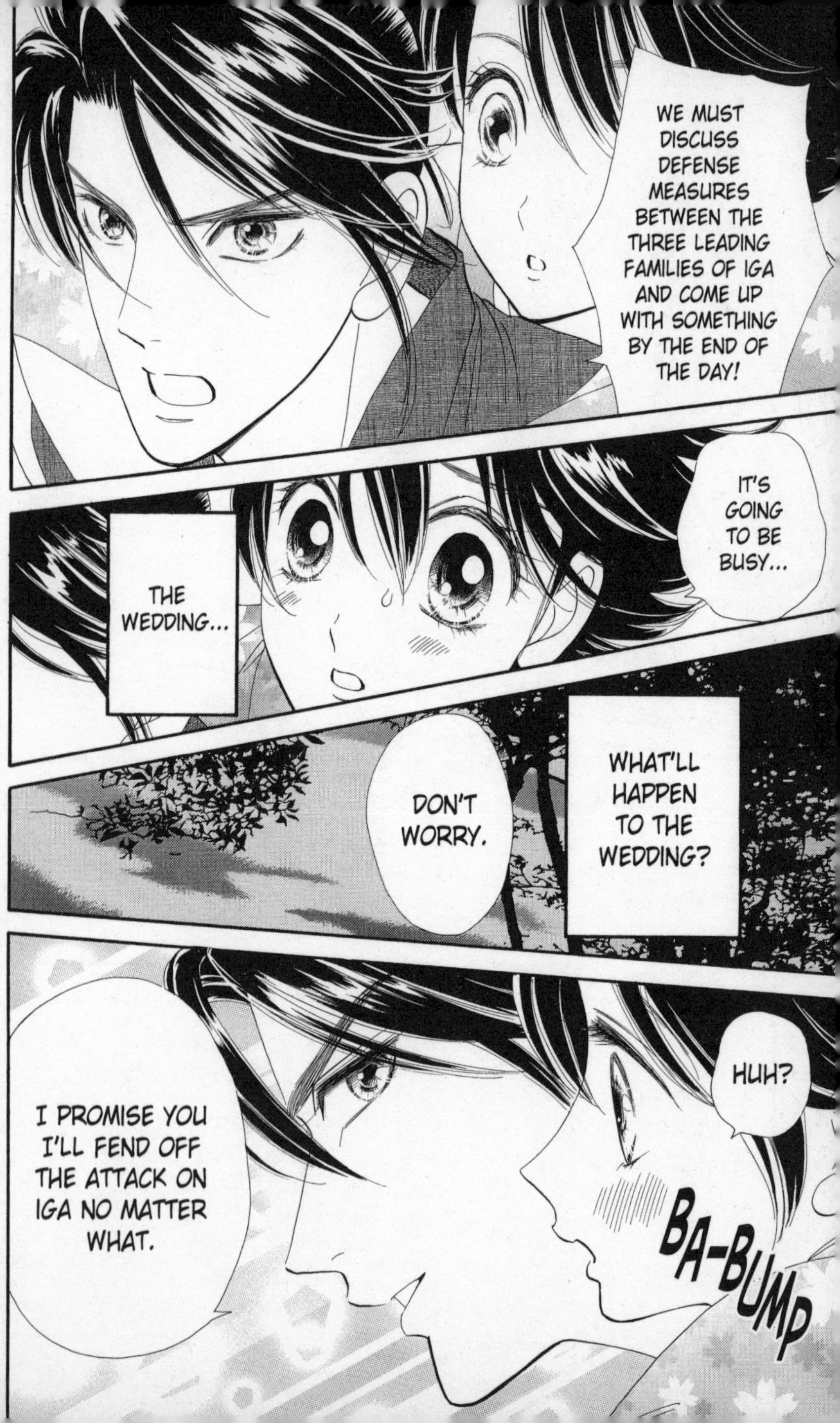
WE MUST DISCUSS DEFENSE MEASURES BETWEEN THE THREE LEADING FAMILIES OF IGA AND COME UP WITH SOMETHING BY THE END OF THE DAY!
IT'S GOING TO BE BUSY...
THE WEDDING...
WHAT'LL HAPPEN TO THE WEDDING?
DON'T WORRY.
HUH?
BA-BUMP
I PROMISE YOU I'LL FEND OFF THE ATTACK ON IGA NO MATTER WHAT.

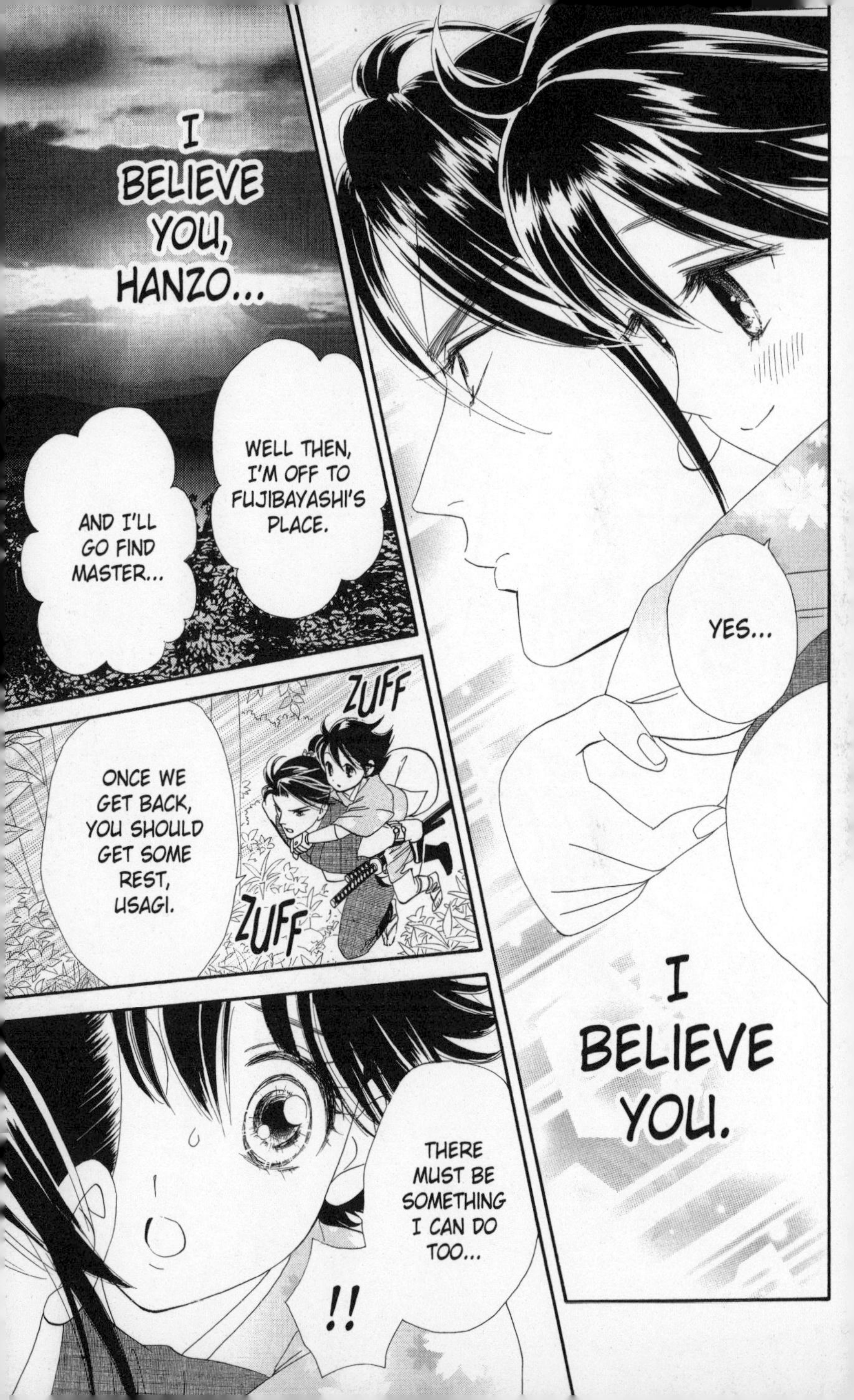
YES...
I BELIEVE YOU.
I BELIEVE YOU, HANZO...
WELL THEN, I'M OFF TO FUJIBAYASHI'S PLACE.
AND I'LL GO FIND MASTER...
ZUFF
ONCE WE GET BACK, YOU SHOULD GET SOME REST, USAGI.
ZUFF
THERE MUST BE SOMETHING I CAN DO TOO...
!!

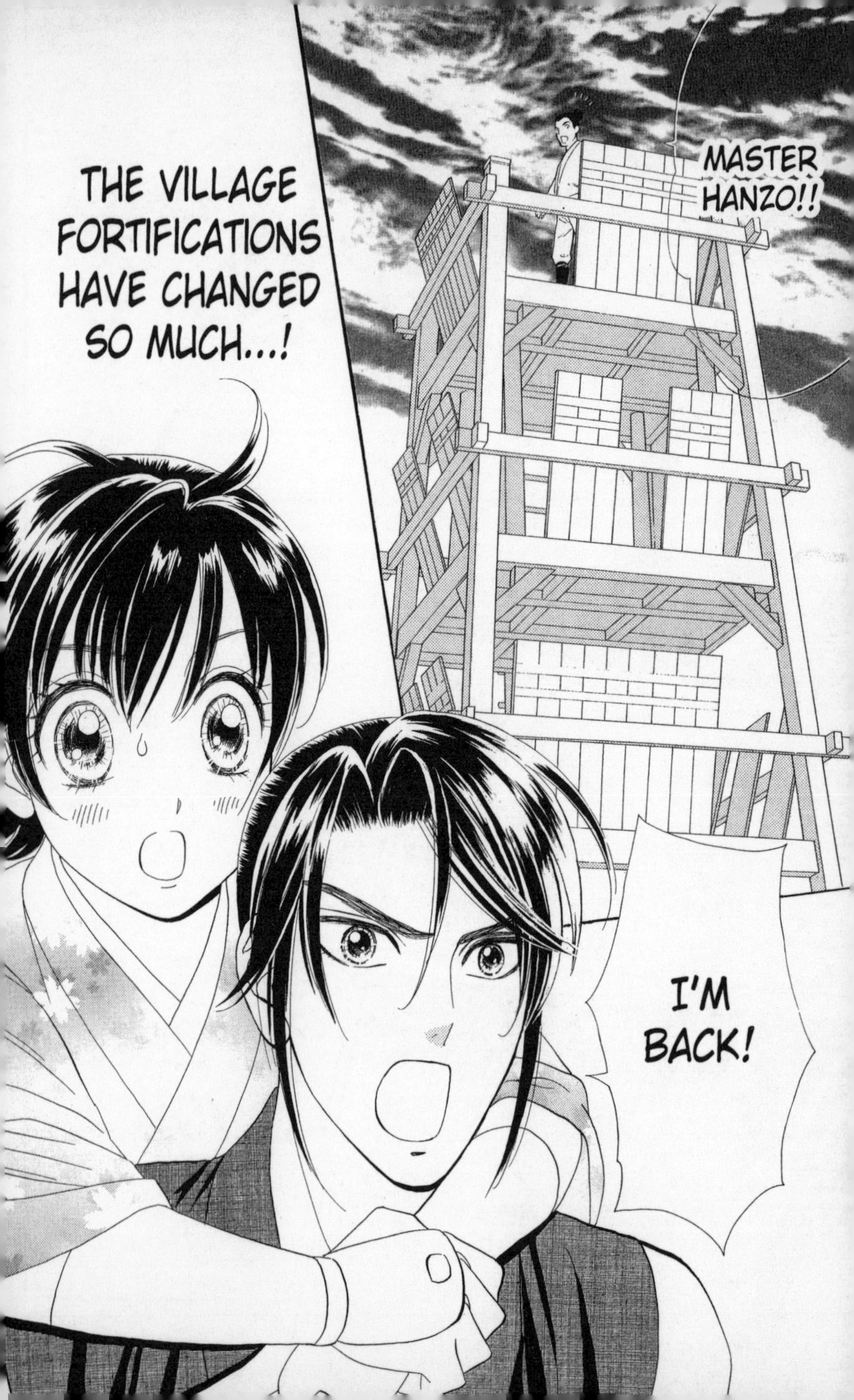
MASTER HANZO!!
THE VILLAGE FORTIFICATIONS HAVE CHANGED SO MUCH...!
I'M BACK!

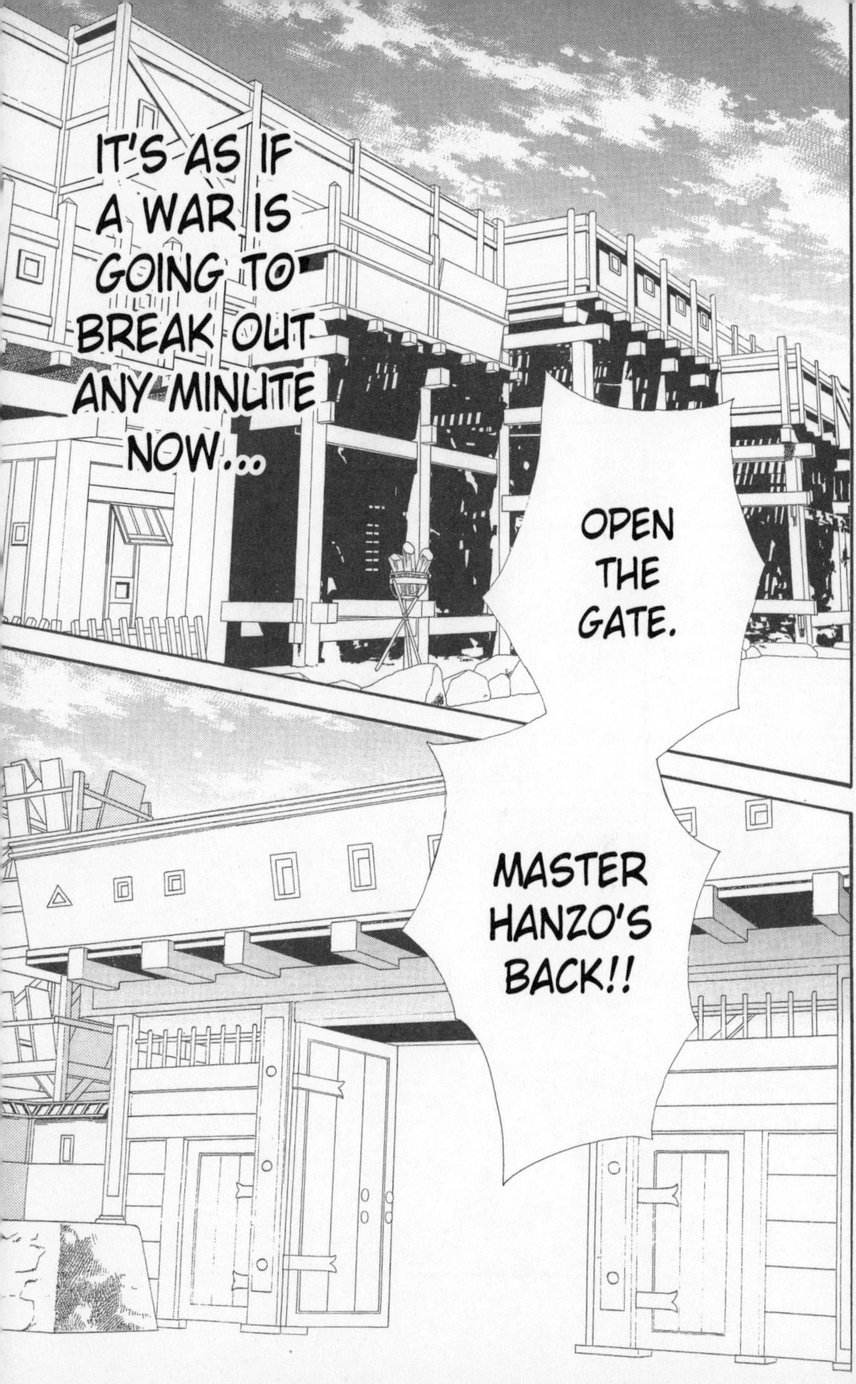
IT'S AS IF A WAR IS GOING TO BREAK OUT ANY MINUTE NOW...
OPEN THE GATE.
MASTER HANZO'S BACK!!

TAIL OF THE MOON EXTRA: **TODAY'S MISSION**

"I WANT TO SEE USAGI AND RYO TOGETHER!"

-AOI, KANAGAWA PREFECTURE

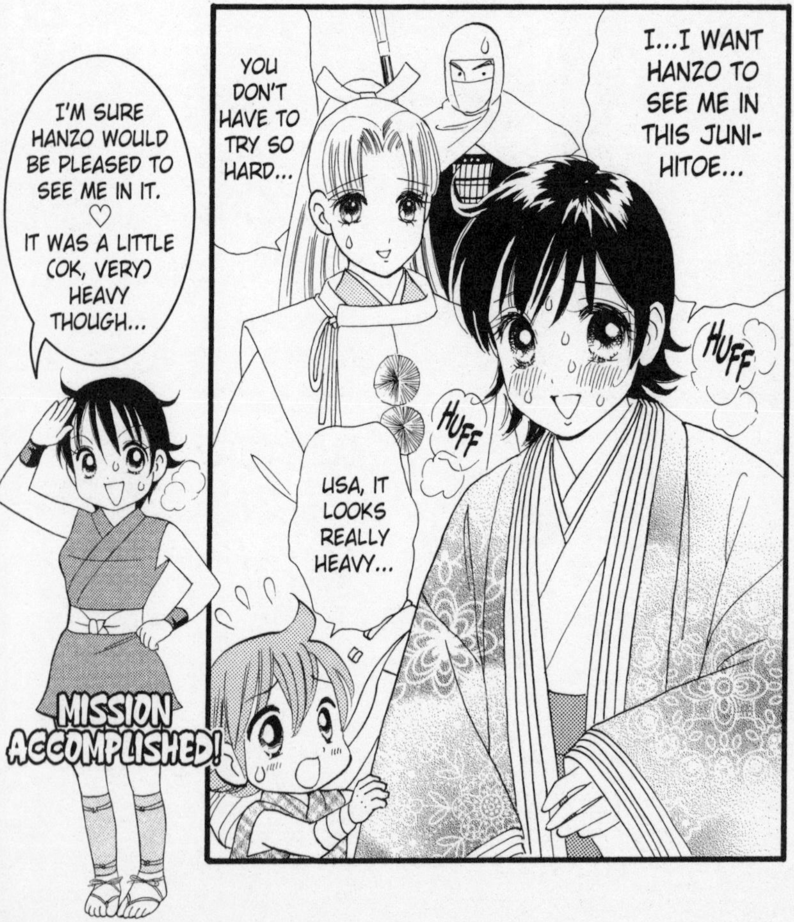
I...I WANT HANZO TO SEE ME IN THIS JUNI-HITOE...
YOU DON'T HAVE TO TRY SO HARD...
HUFF
HUFF
USA, IT LOOKS REALLY HEAVY...
I'M SURE HANZO WOULD BE PLEASED TO SEE ME IN IT. ♡ IT WAS A LITTLE (OK, VERY) HEAVY THOUGH...
MISSION ACCOMPLISHED!

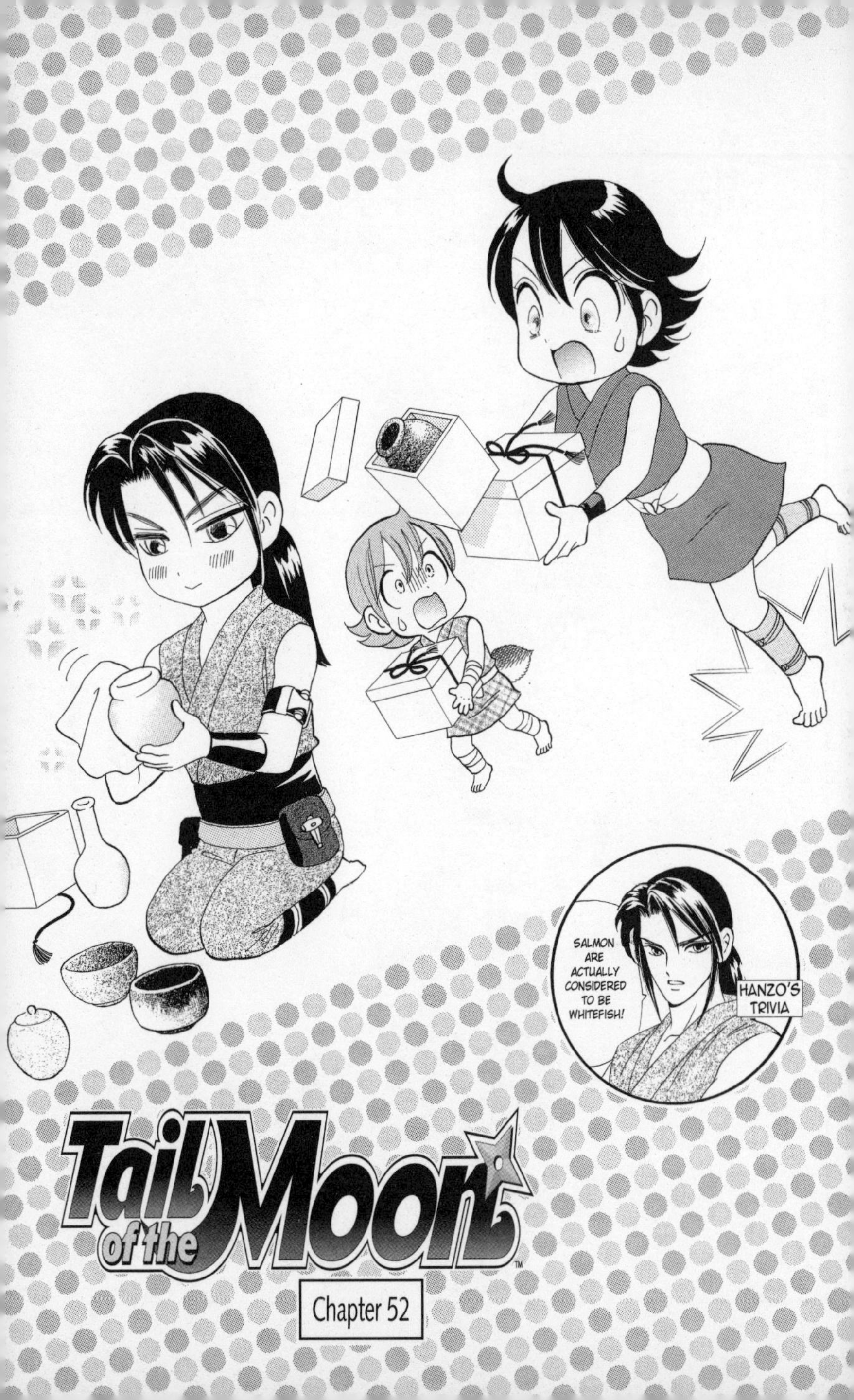
HANZO'S TRIVIA
SALMON ARE ACTUALLY CONSIDERED TO BE WHITEFISH!
Tail of the Moon™
Chapter 52

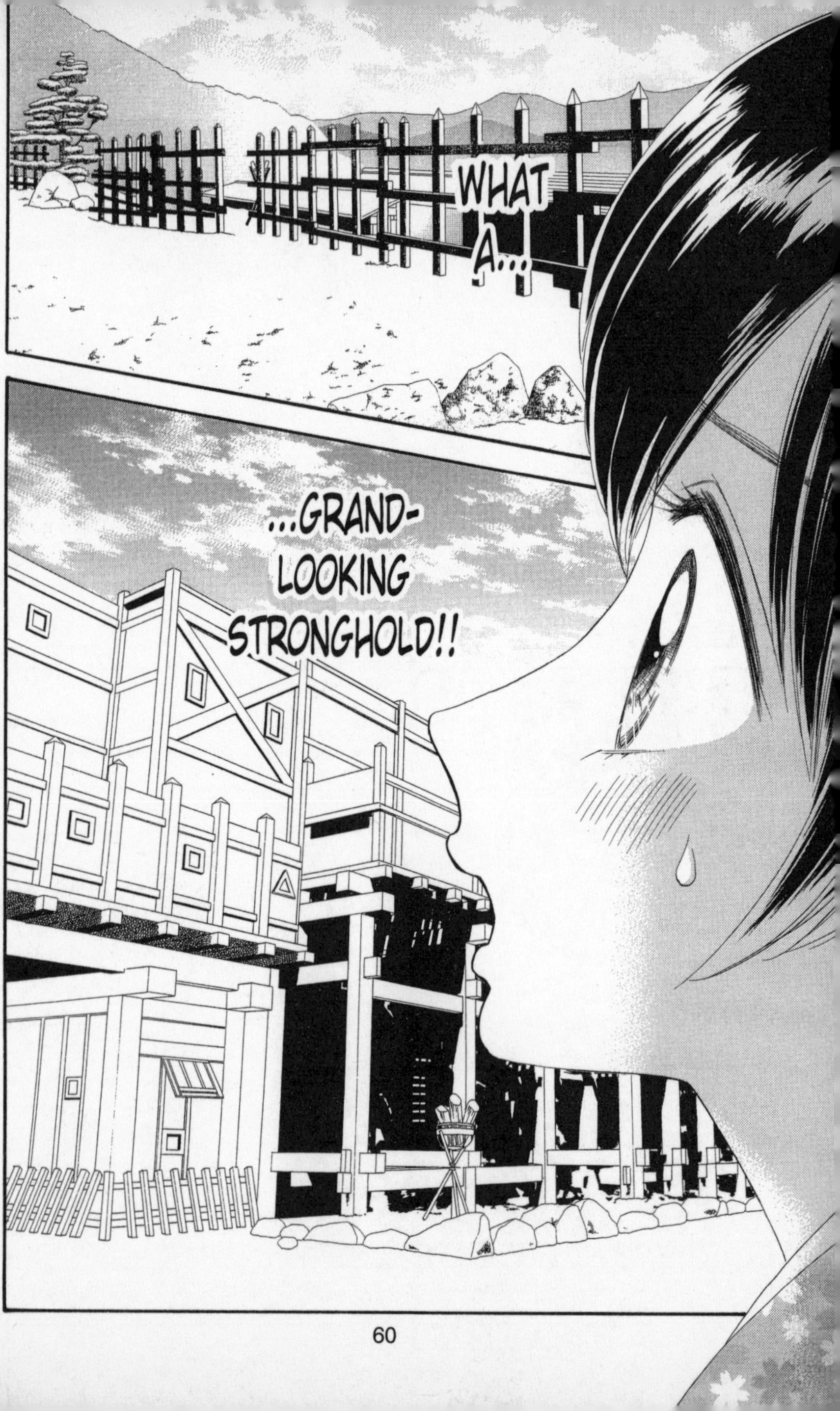
WHAT A...
...GRAND-LOOKING STRONGHOLD!!

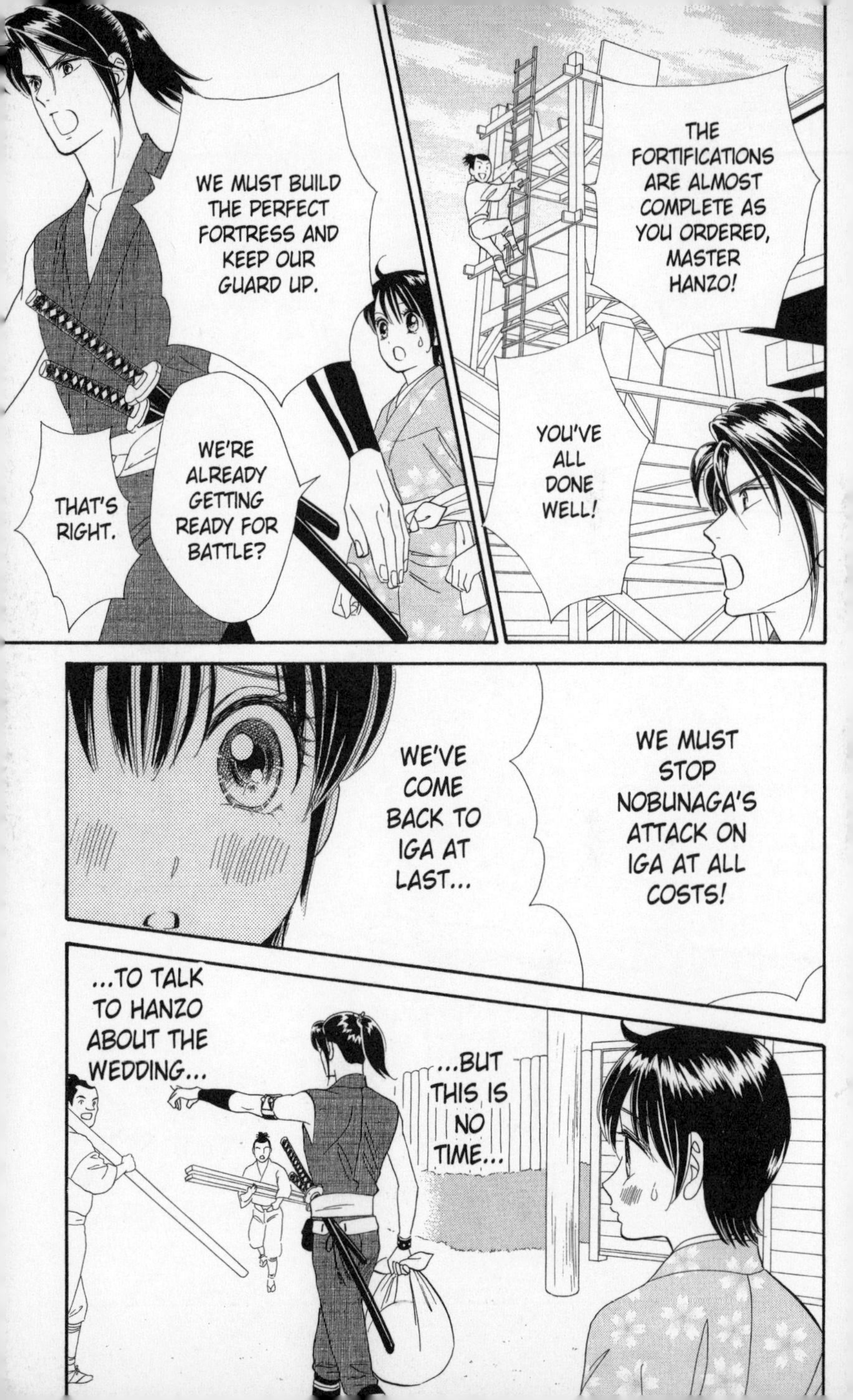
THE FORTIFICATIONS ARE ALMOST COMPLETE AS YOU ORDERED, MASTER HANZO!
YOU'VE ALL DONE WELL!
WE MUST BUILD THE PERFECT FORTRESS AND KEEP OUR GUARD UP.
WE'RE ALREADY GETTING READY FOR BATTLE?
THAT'S RIGHT.
WE MUST STOP NOBUNAGA'S ATTACK ON IGA AT ALL COSTS!
WE'VE COME BACK TO IGA AT LAST...
...TO TALK TO HANZO ABOUT THE WEDDING...
...BUT THIS IS NO TIME...

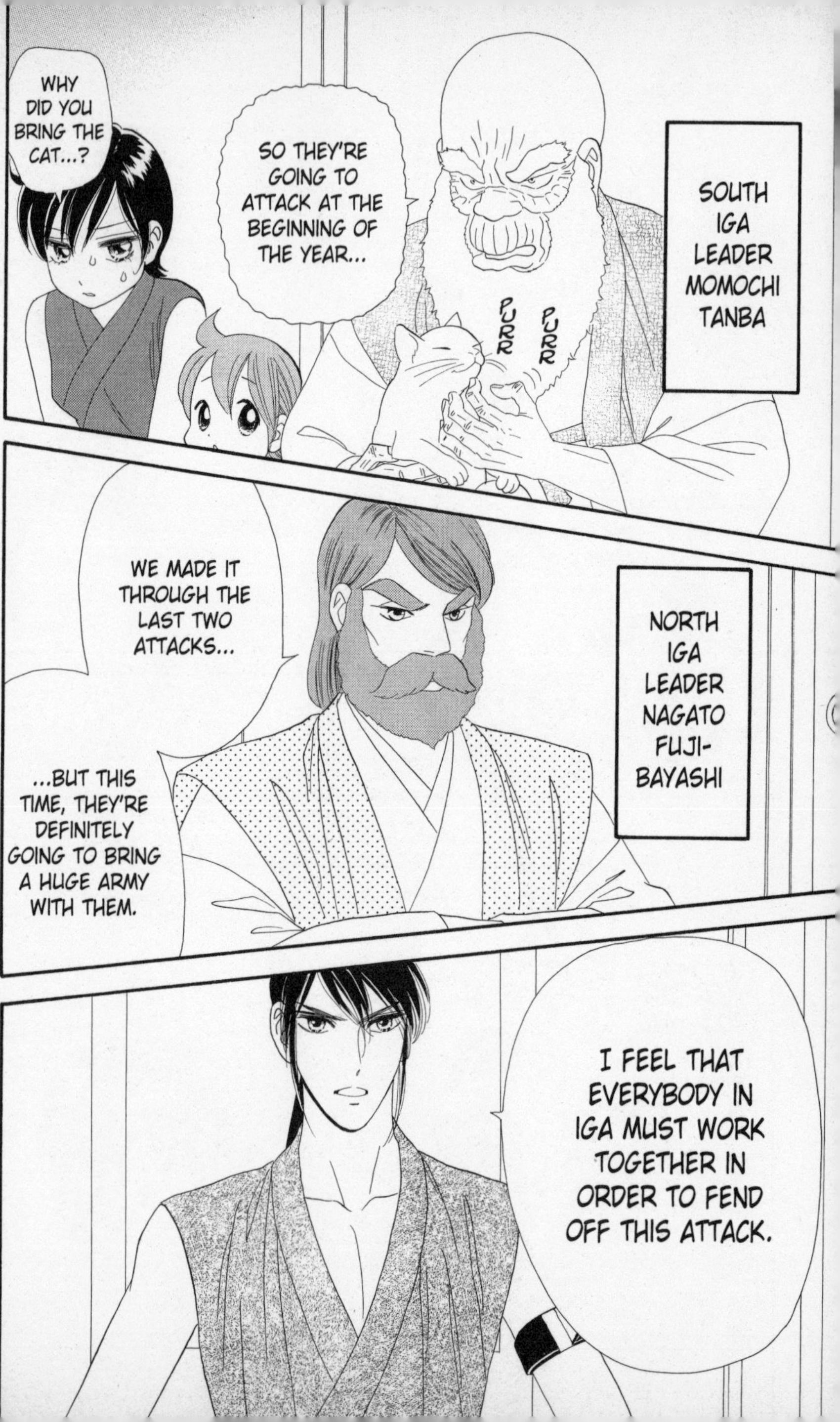
SOUTH IGA LEADER MOMOCHI TANBA
PURR PURR
SO THEY'RE GOING TO ATTACK AT THE BEGINNING OF THE YEAR...
WHY DID YOU BRING THE CAT...?
NORTH IGA LEADER NAGATO FUJI-BAYASHI
WE MADE IT THROUGH THE LAST TWO ATTACKS...
...BUT THIS TIME, THEY'RE DEFINITELY GOING TO BRING A HUGE ARMY WITH THEM.
I FEEL THAT EVERYBODY IN IGA MUST WORK TOGETHER IN ORDER TO FEND OFF THIS ATTACK.

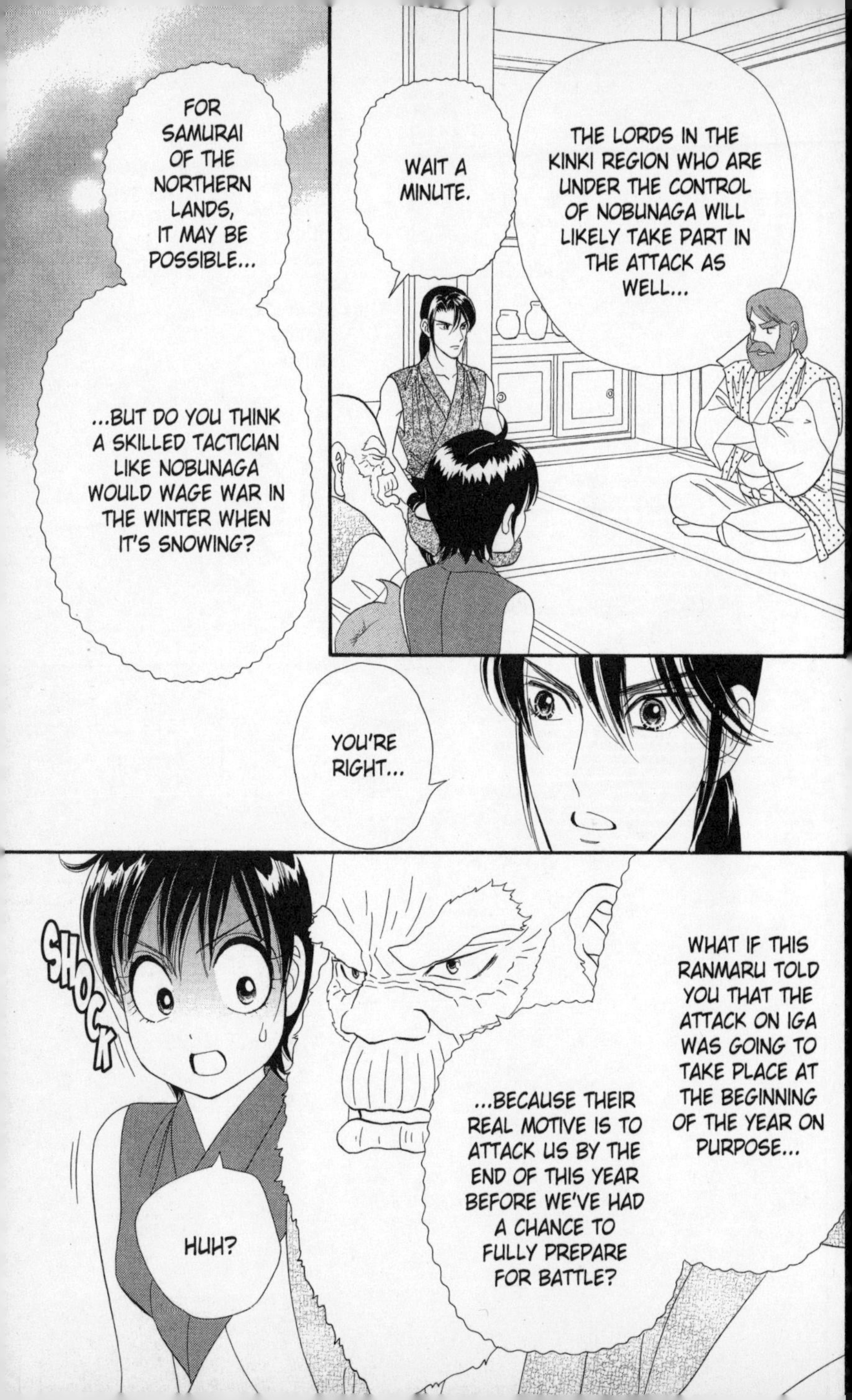
THE LORDS IN THE KINKI REGION WHO ARE UNDER THE CONTROL OF NOBUNAGA WILL LIKELY TAKE PART IN THE ATTACK AS WELL...
WAIT A MINUTE.
FOR SAMURAI OF THE NORTHERN LANDS, IT MAY BE POSSIBLE...
...BUT DO YOU THINK A SKILLED TACTICIAN LIKE NOBUNAGA WOULD WAGE WAR IN THE WINTER WHEN IT'S SNOWING?
YOU'RE RIGHT...
WHAT IF THIS RANMARU TOLD YOU THAT THE ATTACK ON IGA WAS GOING TO TAKE PLACE AT THE BEGINNING OF THE YEAR ON PURPOSE...
...BECAUSE THEIR REAL MOTIVE IS TO ATTACK US BY THE END OF THIS YEAR BEFORE WE'VE HAD A CHANCE TO FULLY PREPARE FOR BATTLE?
SHOCK
HUH?

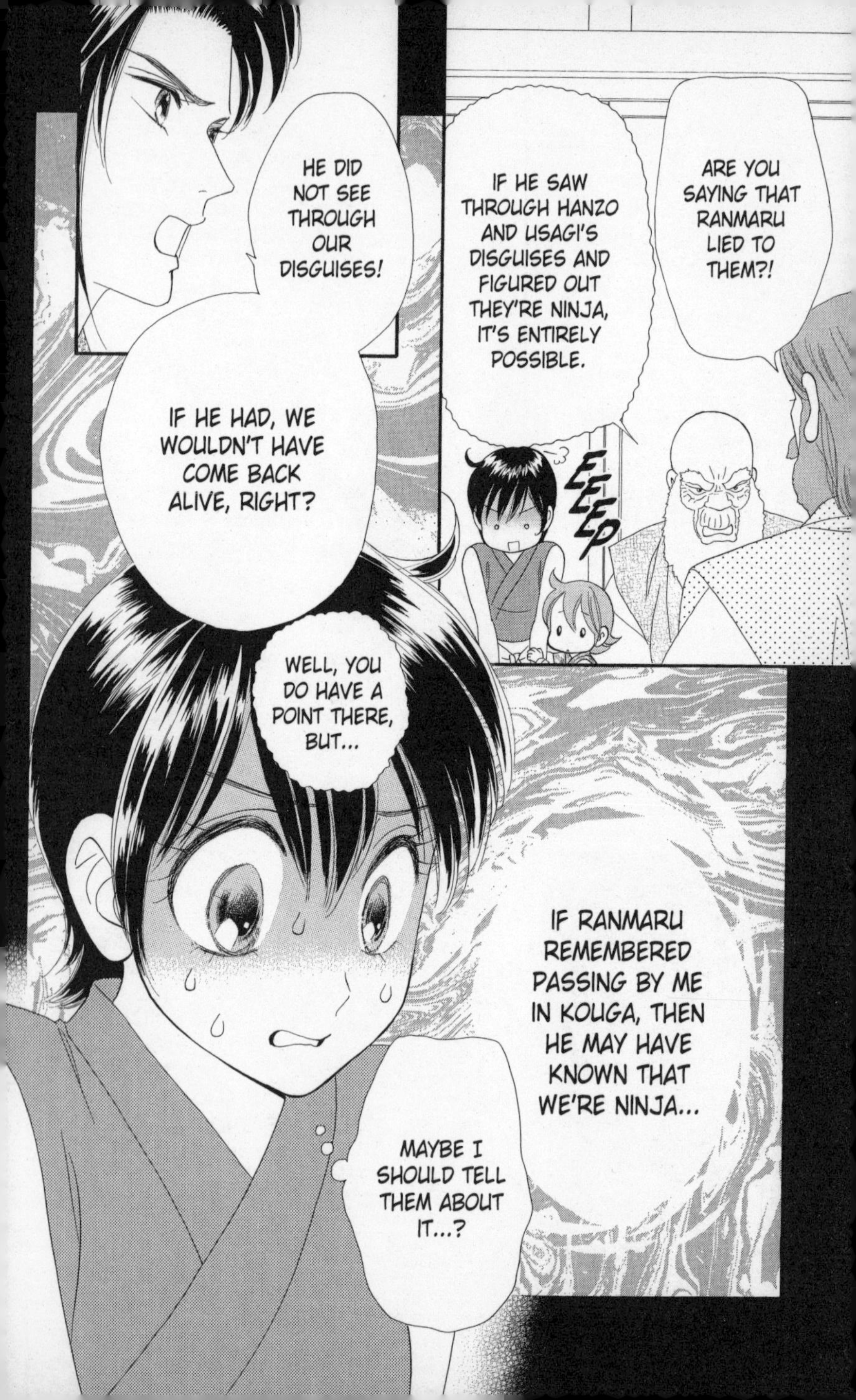
ARE YOU SAYING THAT RANMARU LIED TO THEM?!
IF HE SAW THROUGH HANZO AND USAGI'S DISGUISES AND FIGURED OUT THEY'RE NINJA, IT'S ENTIRELY POSSIBLE.
EEEP
HE DID NOT SEE THROUGH OUR DISGUISES!
IF HE HAD, WE WOULDN'T HAVE COME BACK ALIVE, RIGHT?
WELL, YOU DO HAVE A POINT THERE, BUT...
IF RANMARU REMEMBERED PASSING BY ME IN KOUGA, THEN HE MAY HAVE KNOWN THAT WE'RE NINJA...
MAYBE I SHOULD TELL THEM ABOUT IT...?

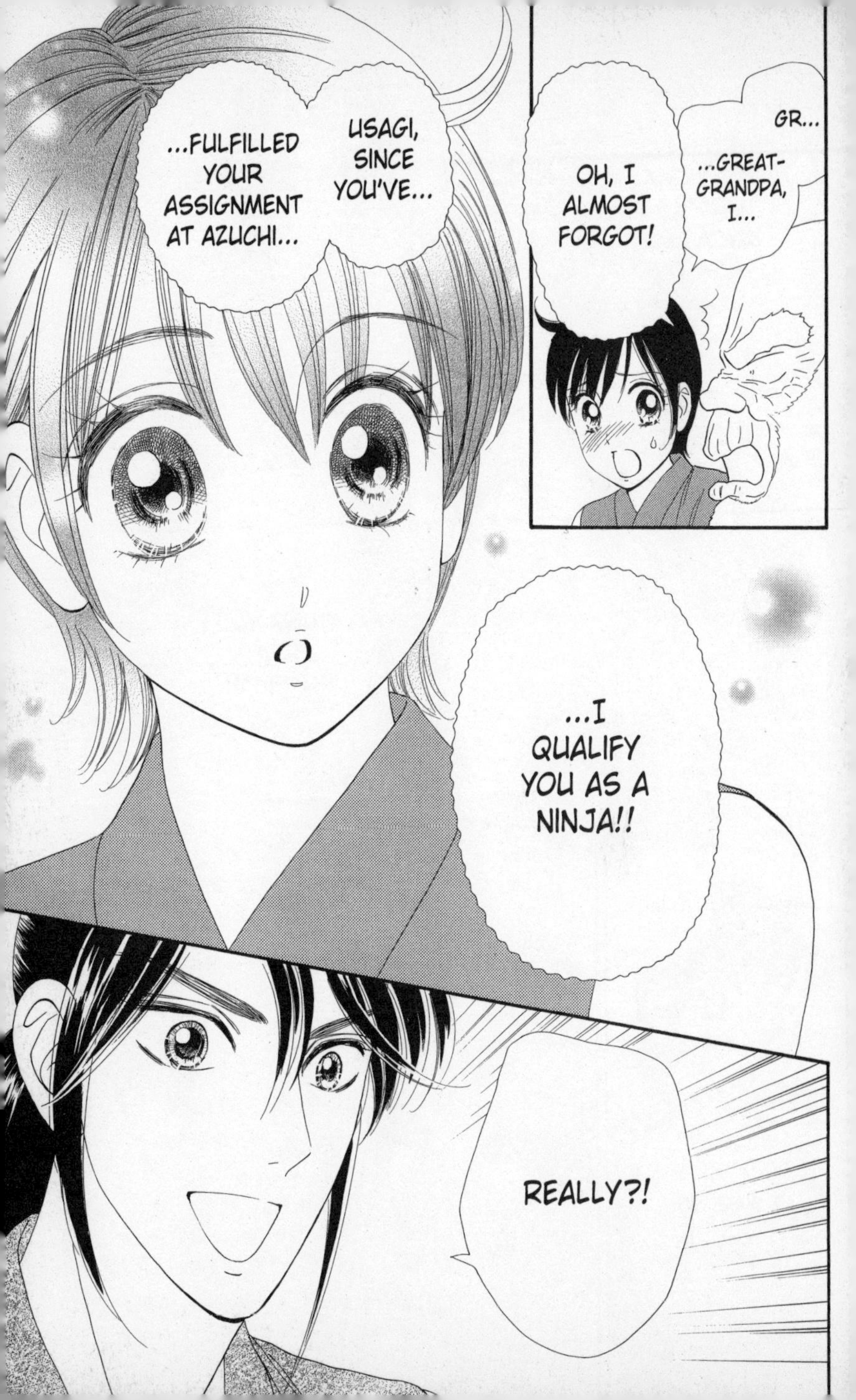
GR... ...GREAT-GRANDPA, I...
OH, I ALMOST FORGOT!
USAGI, SINCE YOU'VE...
...FULFILLED YOUR ASSIGNMENT AT AZUCHI...
...I QUALIFY YOU AS A NINJA!!
REALLY?!

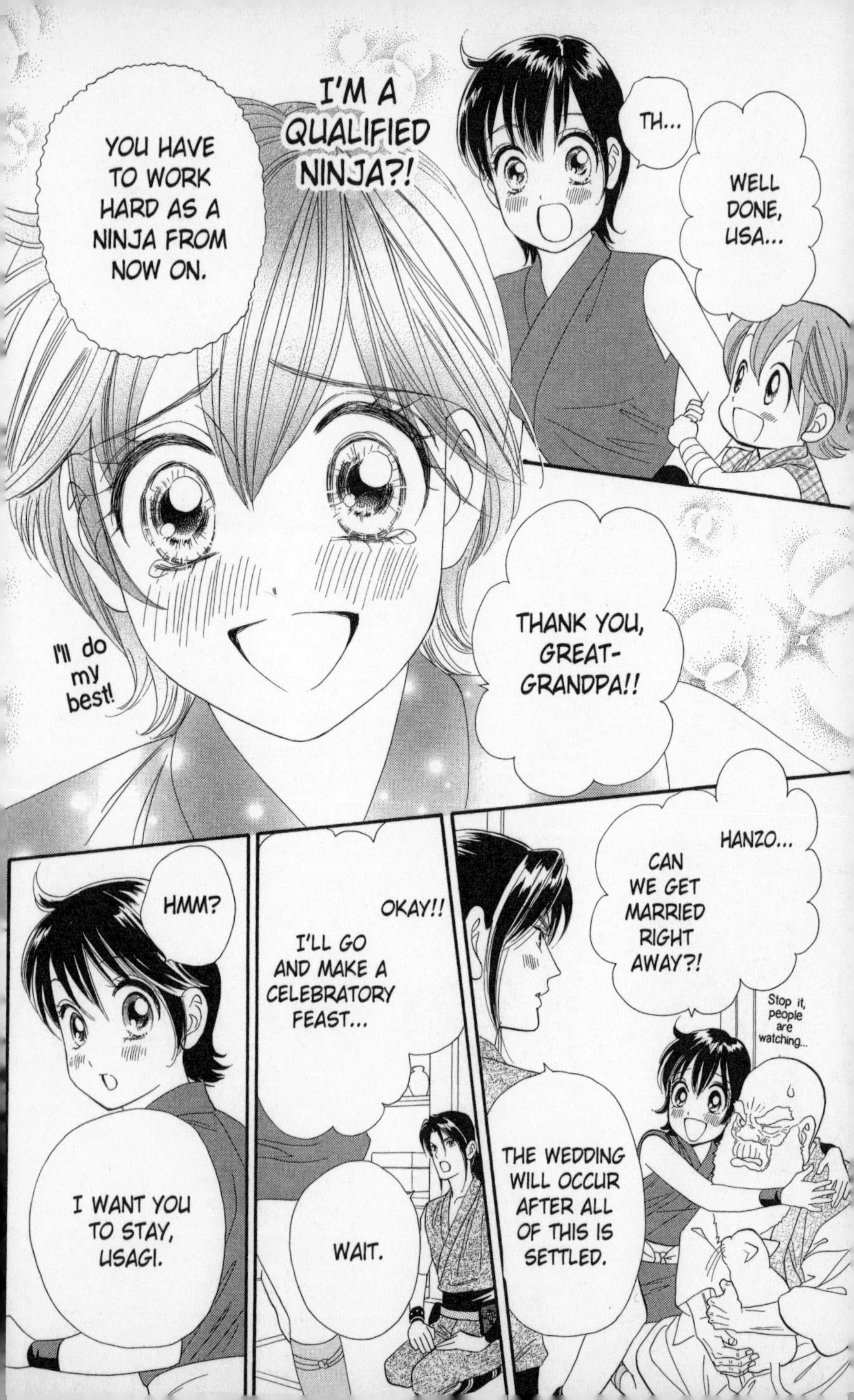
TH...
WELL DONE, USA...
YOU HAVE TO WORK HARD AS A NINJA FROM NOW ON.
I'M A QUALIFIED NINJA?!
THANK YOU, GREAT-GRANDPA!!
I'll do my best!
HANZO... CAN WE GET MARRIED RIGHT AWAY?!
Stop it, people are watching...
THE WEDDING WILL OCCUR AFTER ALL OF THIS IS SETTLED.
OKAY!!
I'LL GO AND MAKE A CELEBRATORY FEAST...
WAIT.
HMM?
I WANT YOU TO STAY, USAGI.

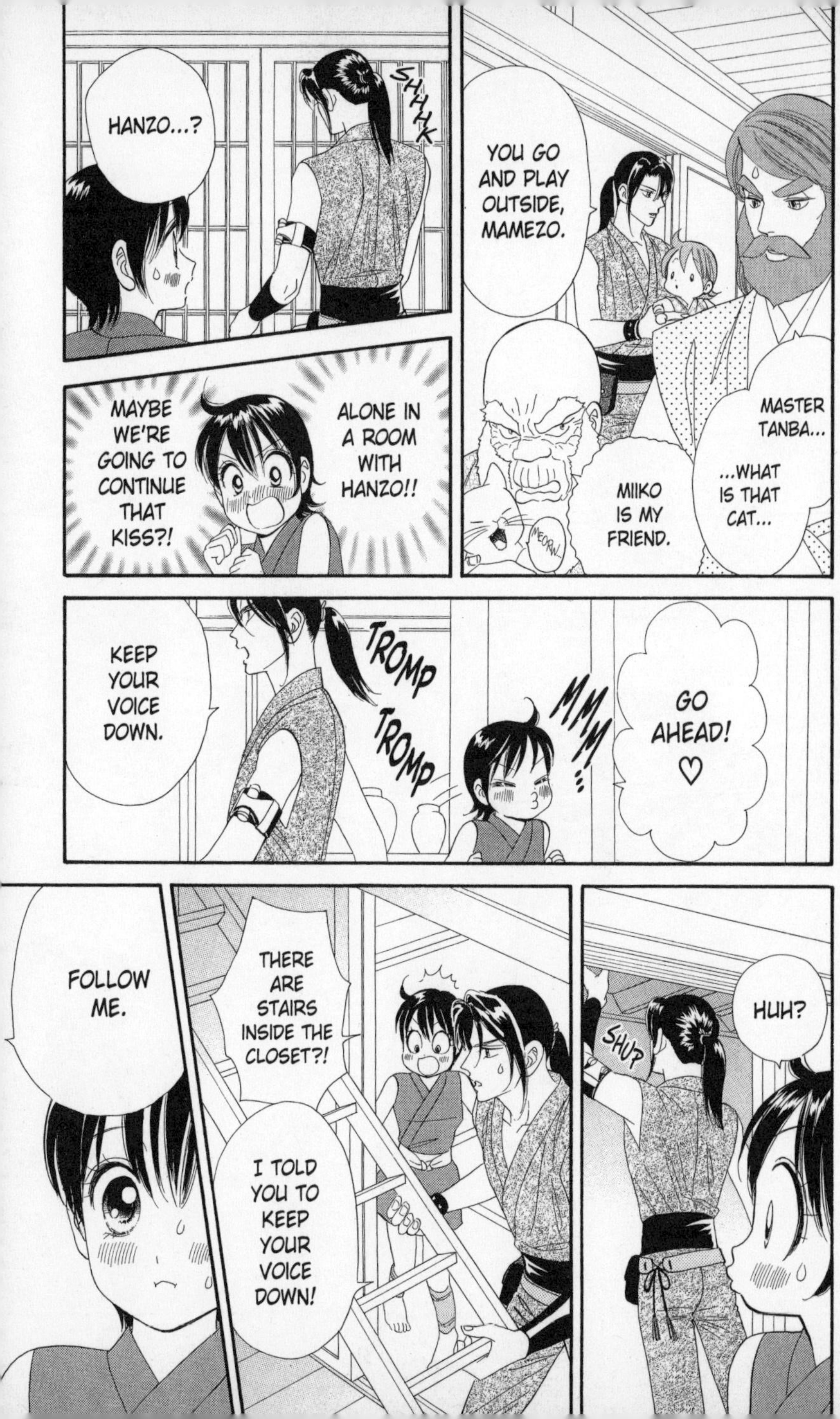
YOU GO AND PLAY OUTSIDE, MAMEZO.
MASTER TANBA...
...WHAT IS THAT CAT...
MIIKO IS MY FRIEND.
MEORW...
SHHHK
HANZO...?
ALONE IN A ROOM WITH HANZO!!
MAYBE WE'RE GOING TO CONTINUE THAT KISS?!
GO AHEAD! ♡
MMM...
TROMP
TROMP
KEEP YOUR VOICE DOWN.
HUH?
SHUP
THERE ARE STAIRS INSIDE THE CLOSET?!
I TOLD YOU TO KEEP YOUR VOICE DOWN!
FOLLOW ME.

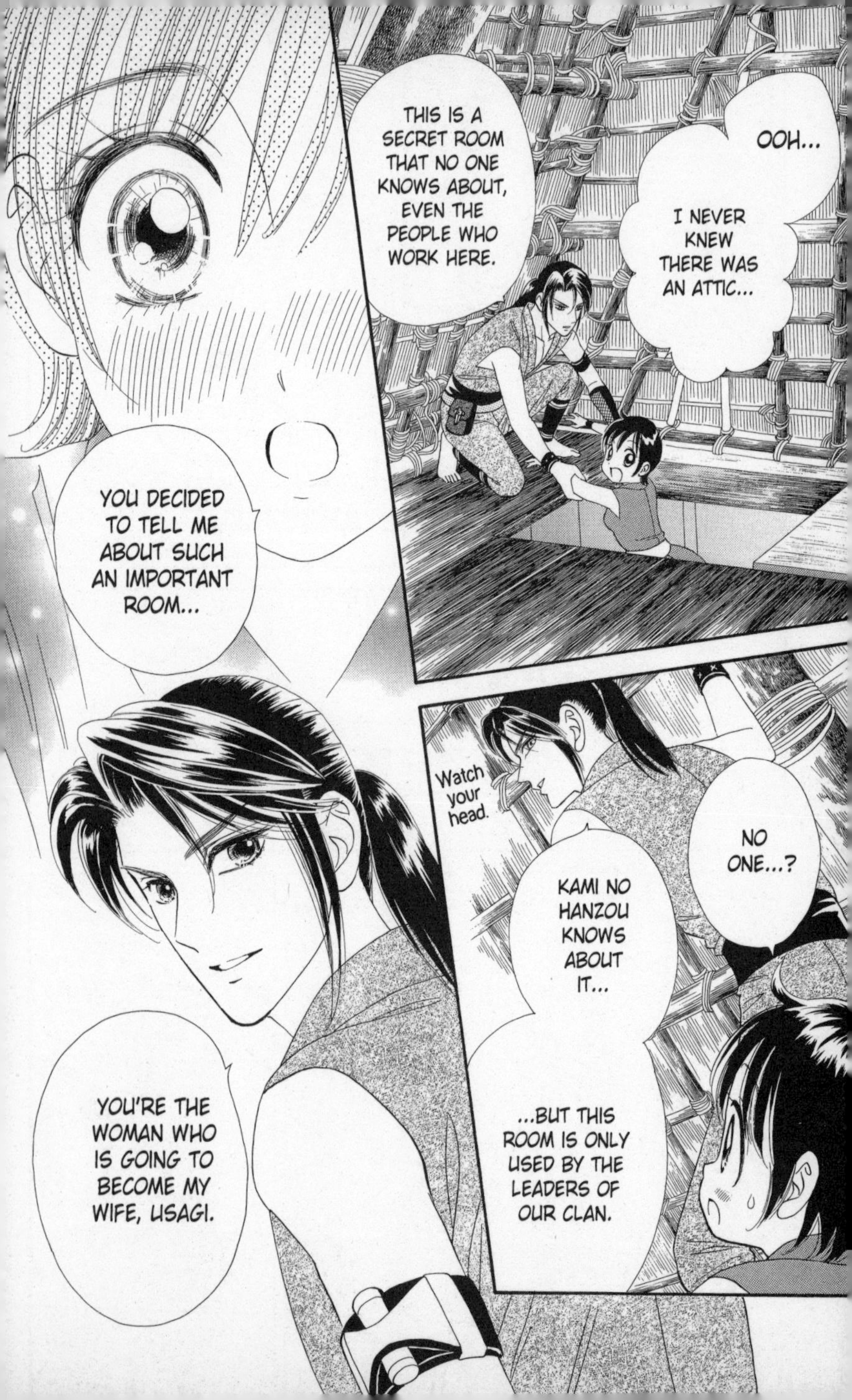
OOH...
I NEVER KNEW THERE WAS AN ATTIC...
THIS IS A SECRET ROOM THAT NO ONE KNOWS ABOUT, EVEN THE PEOPLE WHO WORK HERE.
NO ONE...?
Watch your head.
KAMI NO HANZOU KNOWS ABOUT IT...
...BUT THIS ROOM IS ONLY USED BY THE LEADERS OF OUR CLAN.
YOU DECIDED TO TELL ME ABOUT SUCH AN IMPORTANT ROOM...
YOU'RE THE WOMAN WHO IS GOING TO BECOME MY WIFE, USAGI.

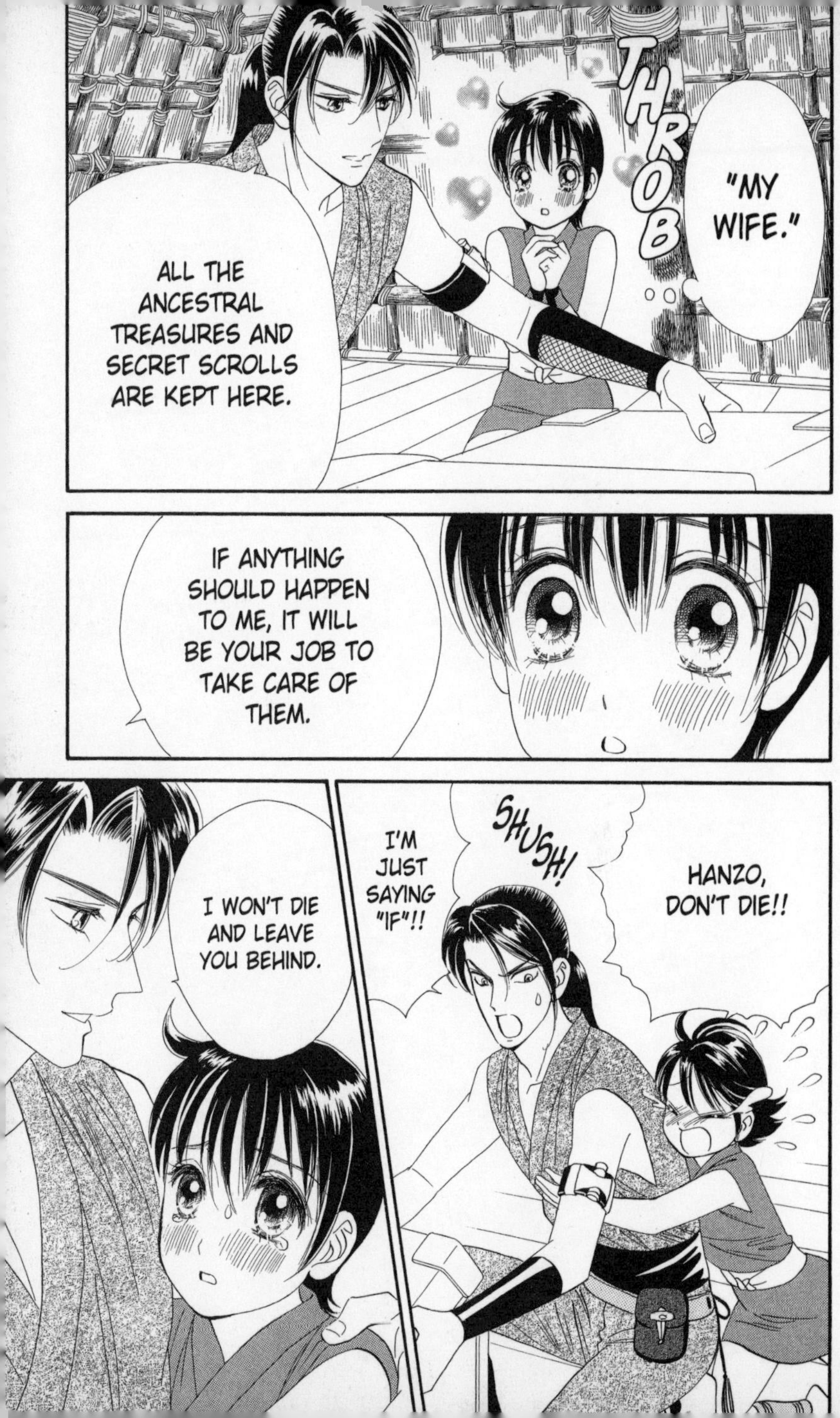
"MY WIFE."
THROB
ALL THE ANCESTRAL TREASURES AND SECRET SCROLLS ARE KEPT HERE.
IF ANYTHING SHOULD HAPPEN TO ME, IT WILL BE YOUR JOB TO TAKE CARE OF THEM.
HANZO, DON'T DIE!!
SHUSH!
I'M JUST SAYING "IF"!!
I WON'T DIE AND LEAVE YOU BEHIND.

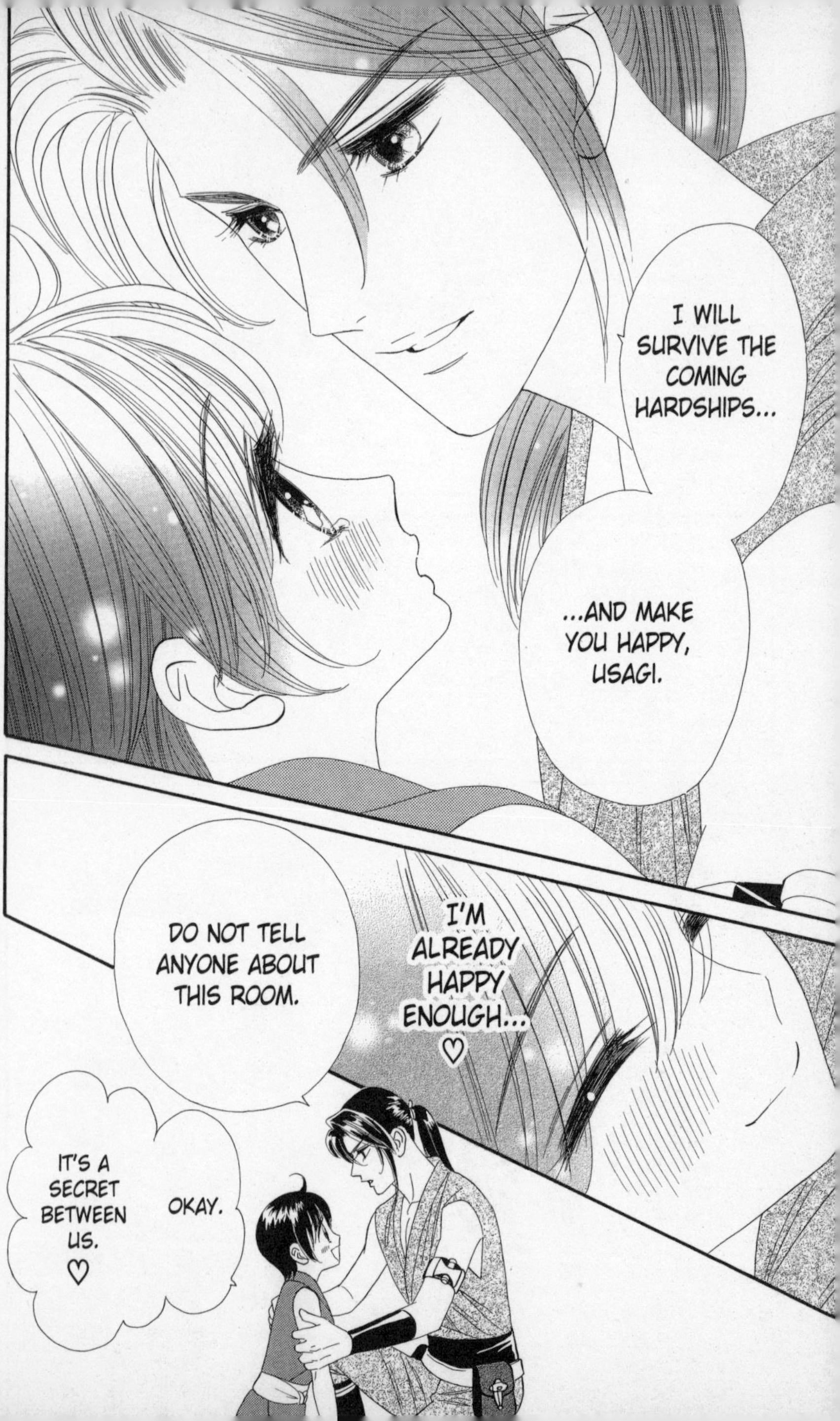
I WILL SURVIVE THE COMING HARDSHIPS...
...AND MAKE YOU HAPPY, USAGI.
I'M ALREADY HAPPY ENOUGH... ♡
DO NOT TELL ANYONE ABOUT THIS ROOM.
OKAY.
IT'S A SECRET BETWEEN US. ♡

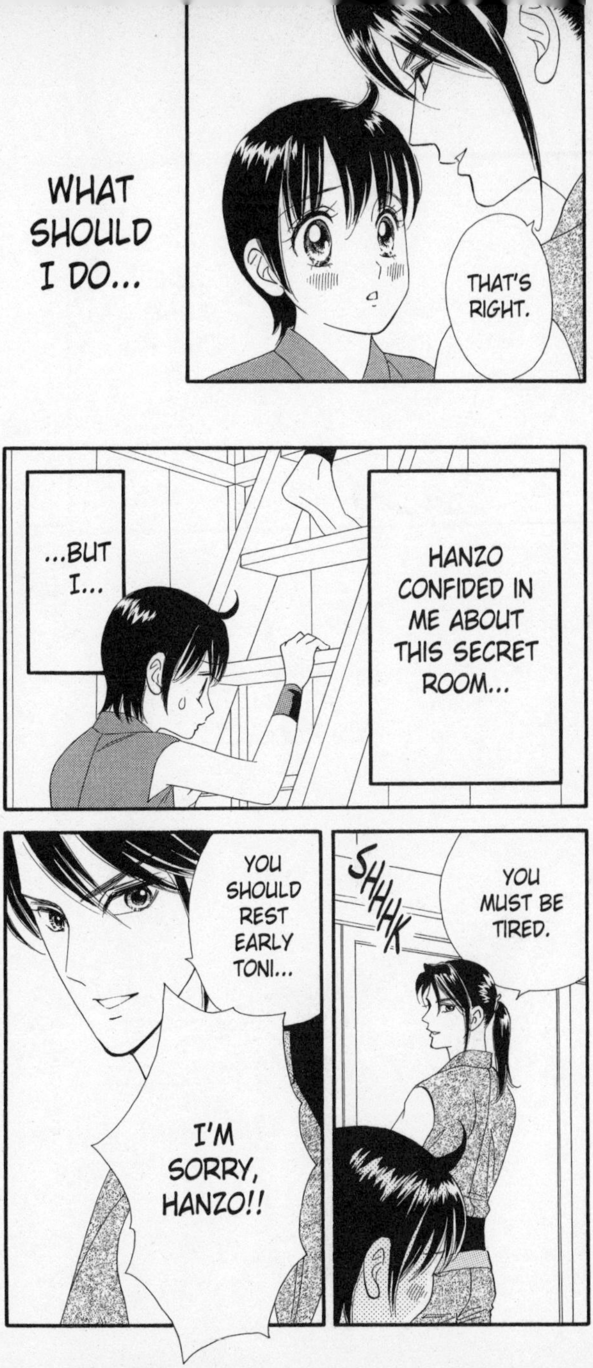
THAT'S RIGHT.
WHAT SHOULD I DO...
HANZO CONFIDED IN ME ABOUT THIS SECRET ROOM...
...BUT I...
SHHHK
YOU MUST BE TIRED.
YOU SHOULD REST EARLY TONI...
I'M SORRY, HANZO!!

UE-RIN'S WAY OF THE MANGA ⑬

During the meeting in Osaka, I got to learn about different tools and techniques from other girls who were there, so it was a really enlightening experience for me.

Since I didn't tell my own friends about drawing manga, meeting people who also drew manga was a great inspiration for me. And so, I continued to draw and send manga and hardly studied for my exams after that. The reason I was still able to attend school without missing classes was because my house was kitty-corner to my school, so I was able to make it in time even if I left my house after the school bell rang.

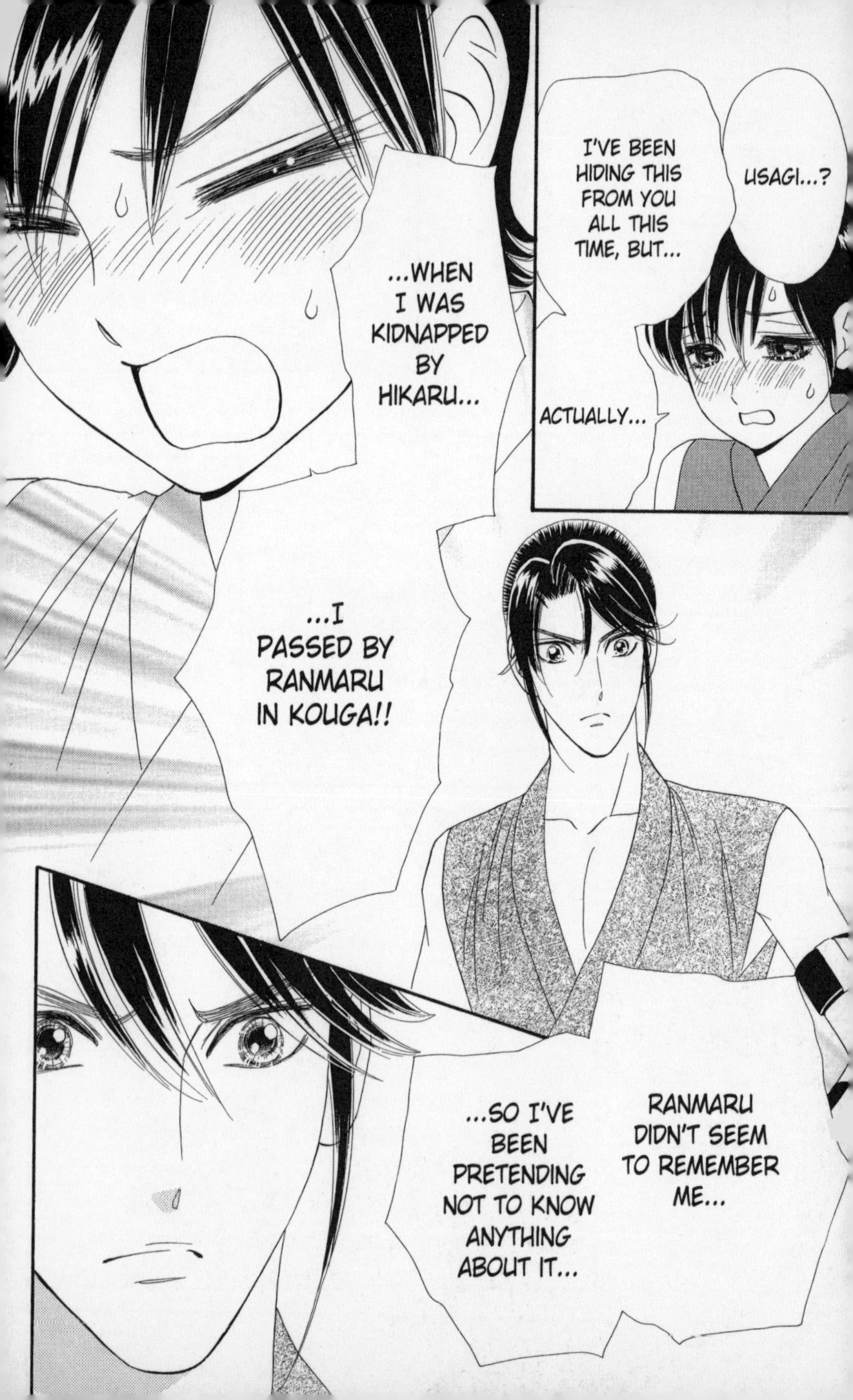
USAGI...?
I'VE BEEN HIDING THIS FROM YOU ALL THIS TIME, BUT...
ACTUALLY...
...WHEN I WAS KIDNAPPED BY HIKARU...
...I PASSED BY RANMARU IN KOUGA!!
RANMARU DIDN'T SEEM TO REMEMBER ME...
...SO I'VE BEEN PRETENDING NOT TO KNOW ANYTHING ABOUT IT...

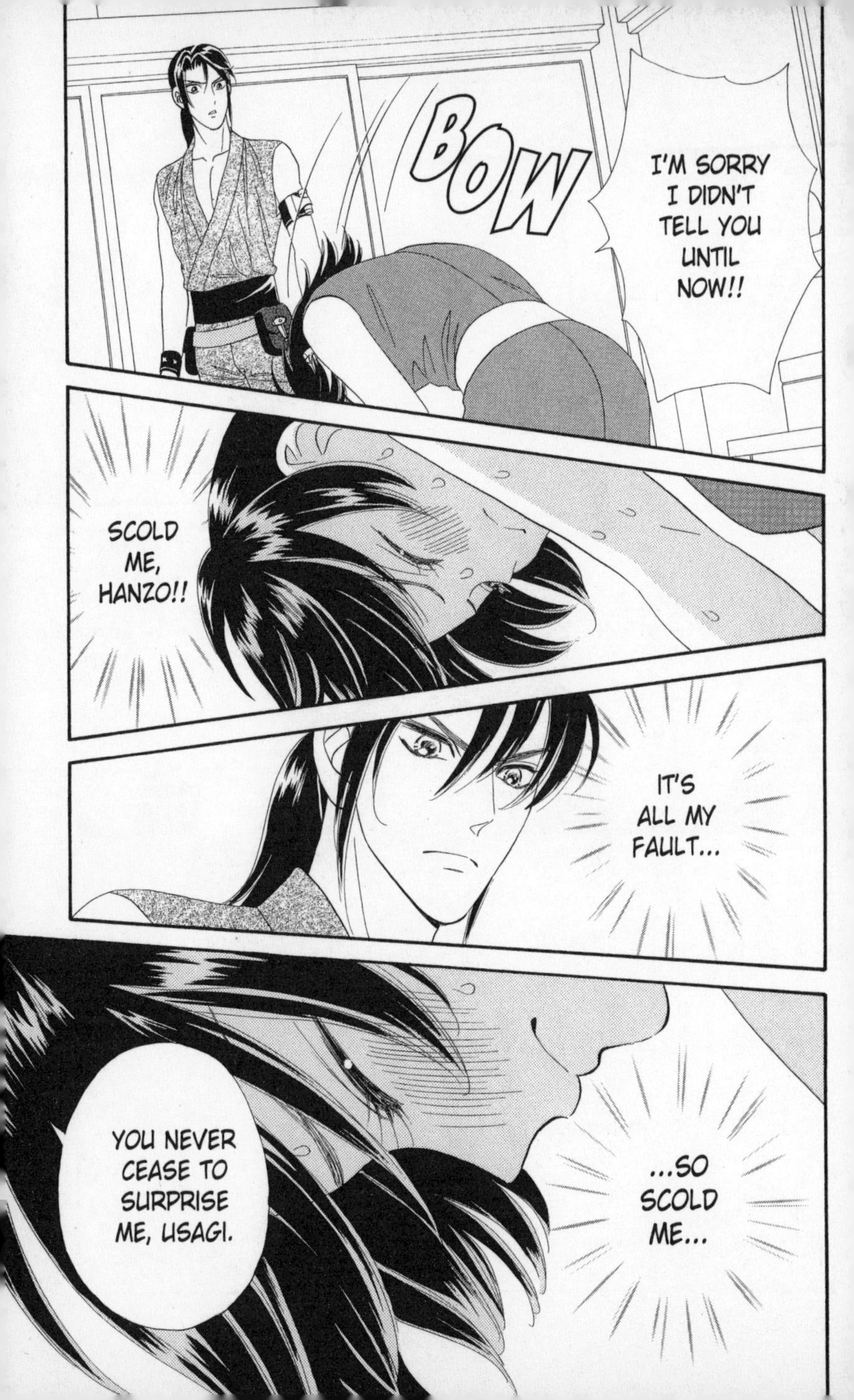
I'M SORRY I DIDN'T TELL YOU UNTIL NOW!!
BOW
SCOLD ME, HANZO!!
IT'S ALL MY FAULT...
...SO SCOLD ME...
YOU NEVER CEASE TO SURPRISE ME, USAGI.

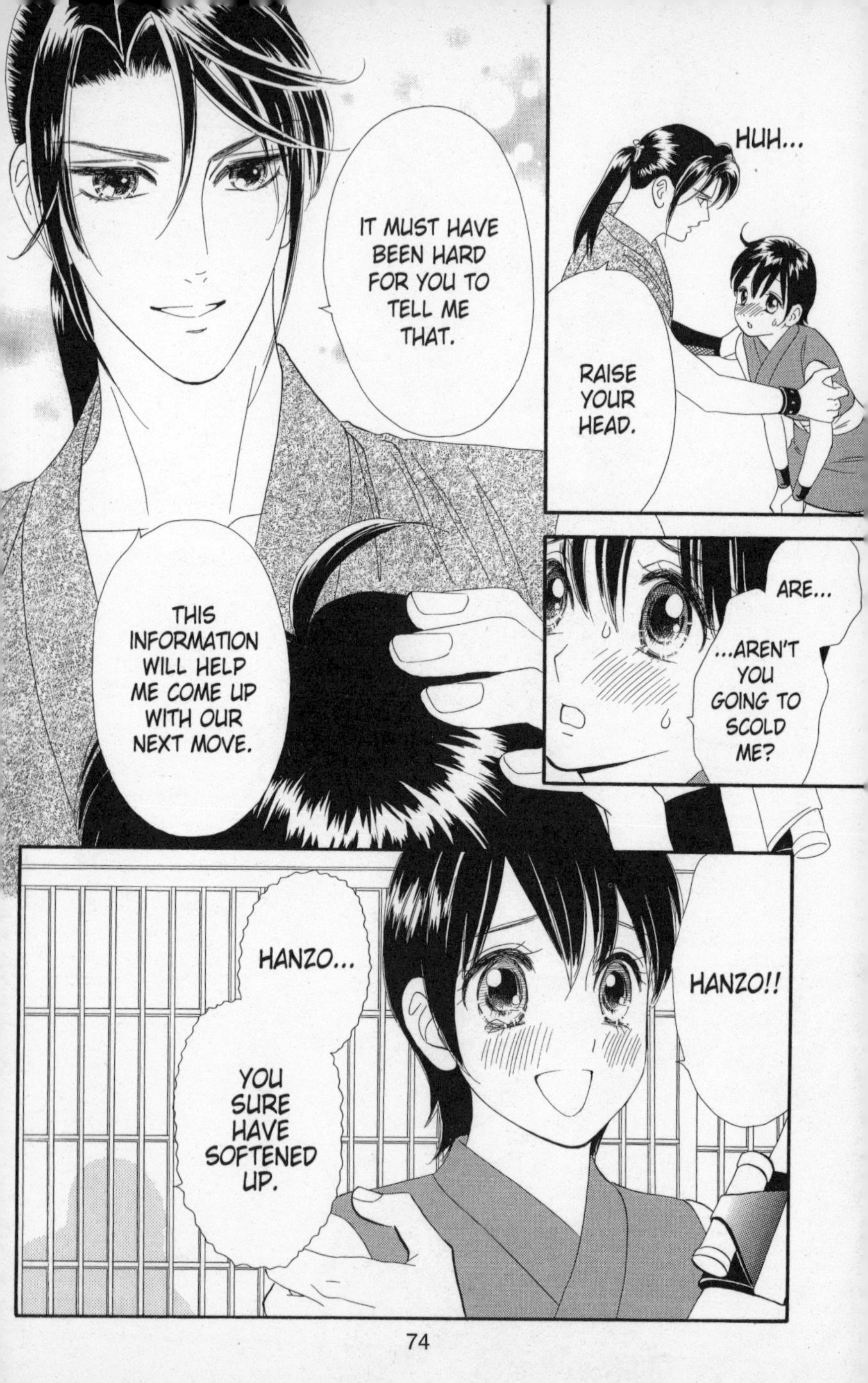
HUH...
RAISE YOUR HEAD.
ARE...
...AREN'T YOU GOING TO SCOLD ME?
IT MUST HAVE BEEN HARD FOR YOU TO TELL ME THAT.
THIS INFORMATION WILL HELP ME COME UP WITH OUR NEXT MOVE.
HANZO!!
HANZO...
YOU SURE HAVE SOFTENED UP.

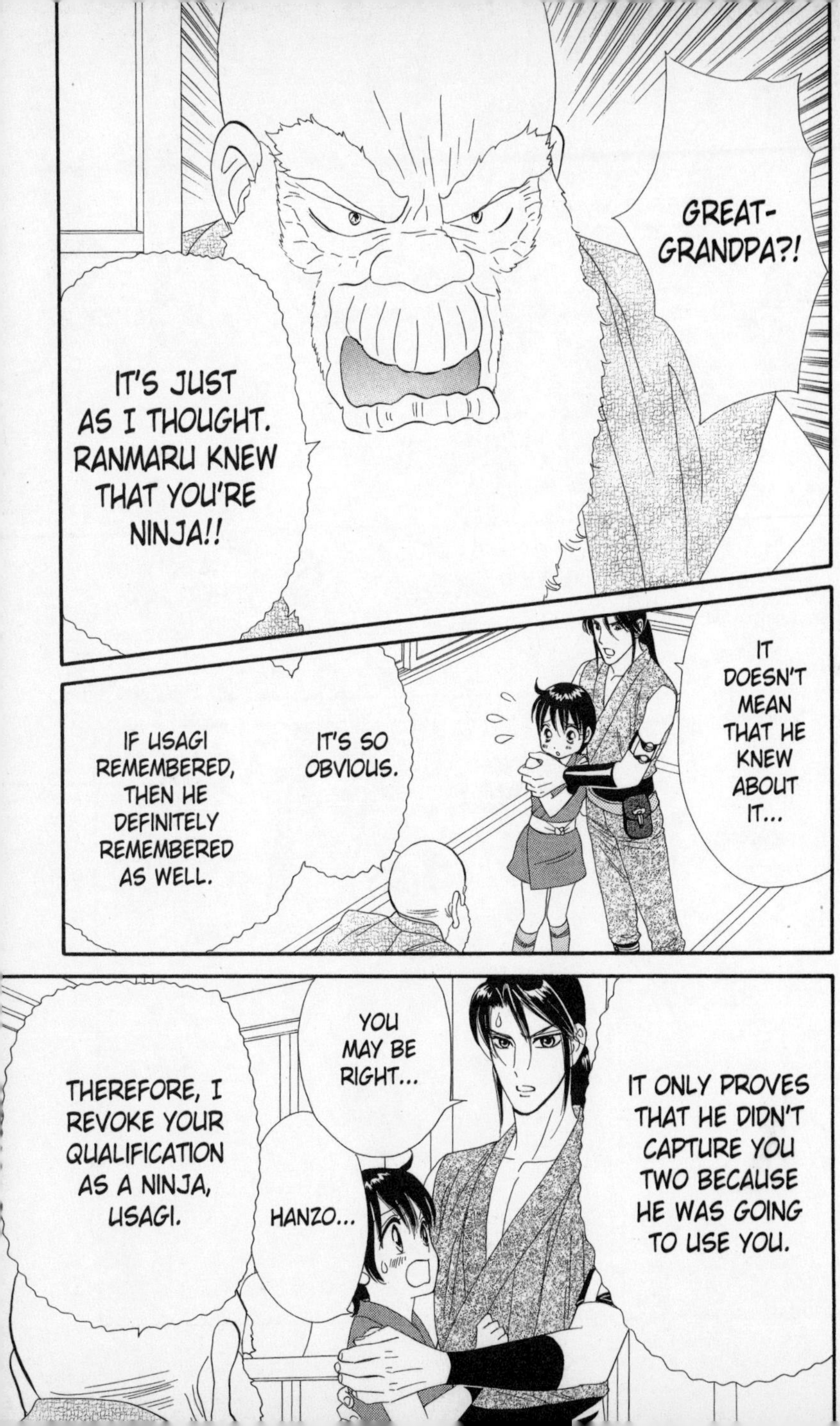
GREAT-GRANDPA?!
IT'S JUST AS I THOUGHT. RANMARU KNEW THAT YOU'RE NINJA!!
IT DOESN'T MEAN THAT HE KNEW ABOUT IT...
IT'S SO OBVIOUS.
IF USAGI REMEMBERED, THEN HE DEFINITELY REMEMBERED AS WELL.
IT ONLY PROVES THAT HE DIDN'T CAPTURE YOU TWO BECAUSE HE WAS GOING TO USE YOU.
YOU MAY BE RIGHT...
HANZO...
THEREFORE, I REVOKE YOUR QUALIFICATION AS A NINJA, USAGI.

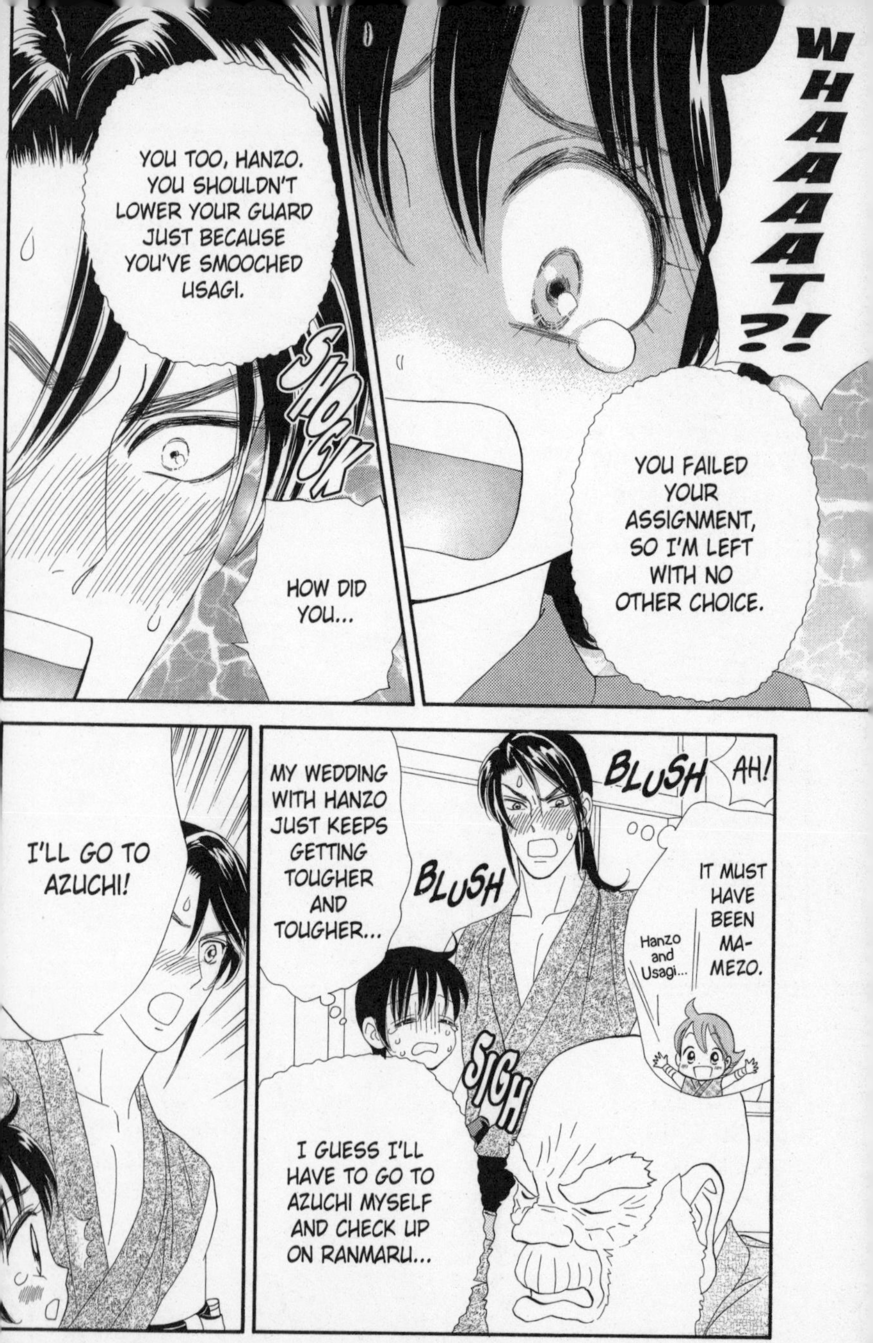
WHAAAAT?!
YOU FAILED YOUR ASSIGNMENT, SO I'M LEFT WITH NO OTHER CHOICE.
YOU TOO, HANZO. YOU SHOULDN'T LOWER YOUR GUARD JUST BECAUSE YOU'VE SMOOCHED USAGI.
SHOCK
HOW DID YOU...
AH!
BLUSH
IT MUST HAVE BEEN MA-MEZO.
Hanzo and Usagi...
MY WEDDING WITH HANZO JUST KEEPS GETTING TOUGHER AND TOUGHER...
BLUSH
SIGH
I GUESS I'LL HAVE TO GO TO AZUCHI MYSELF AND CHECK UP ON RANMARU...
I'LL GO TO AZUCHI!

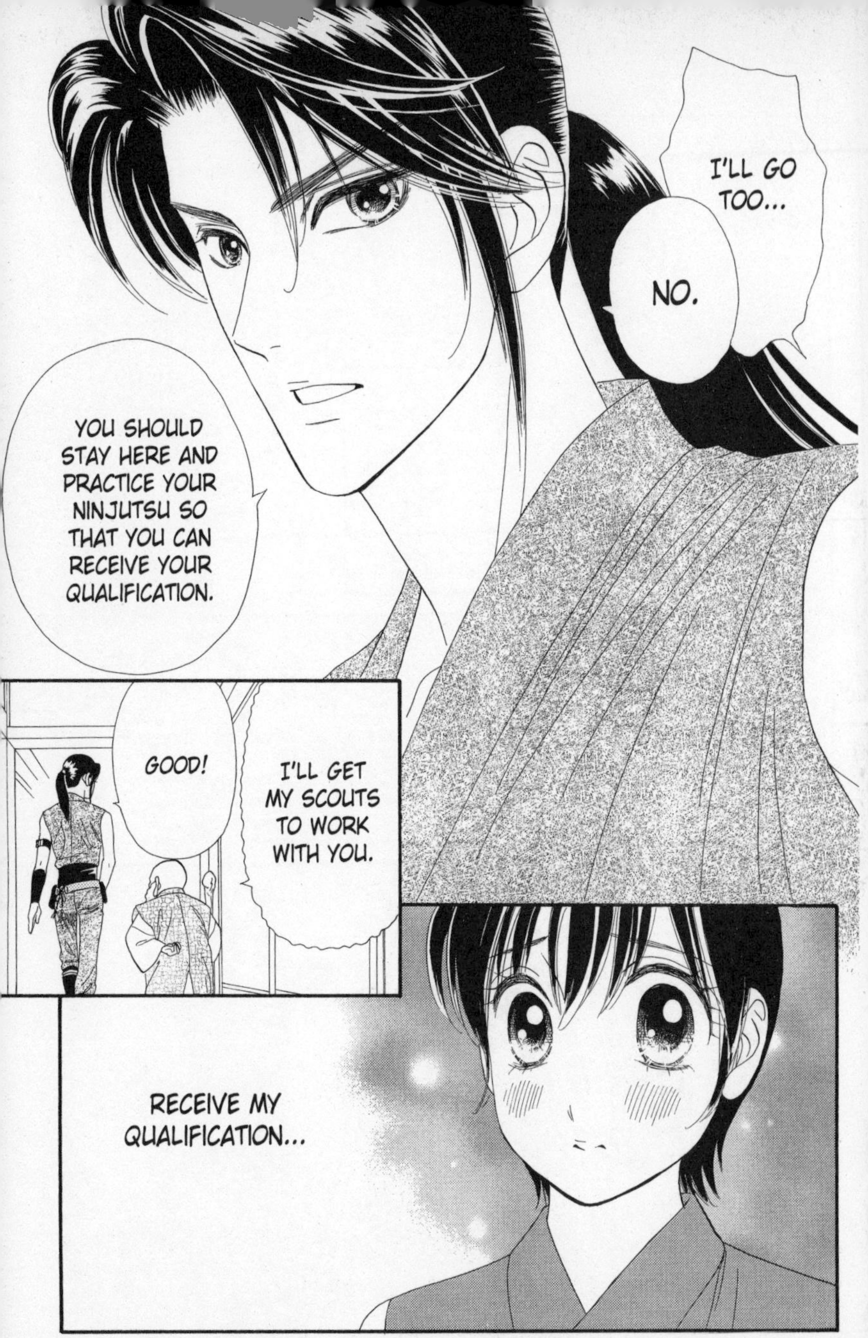
I'LL GO TOO...
NO.
YOU SHOULD STAY HERE AND PRACTICE YOUR NINJUTSU SO THAT YOU CAN RECEIVE YOUR QUALIFICATION.
I'LL GET MY SCOUTS TO WORK WITH YOU.
GOOD!
RECEIVE MY QUALIFICATION...

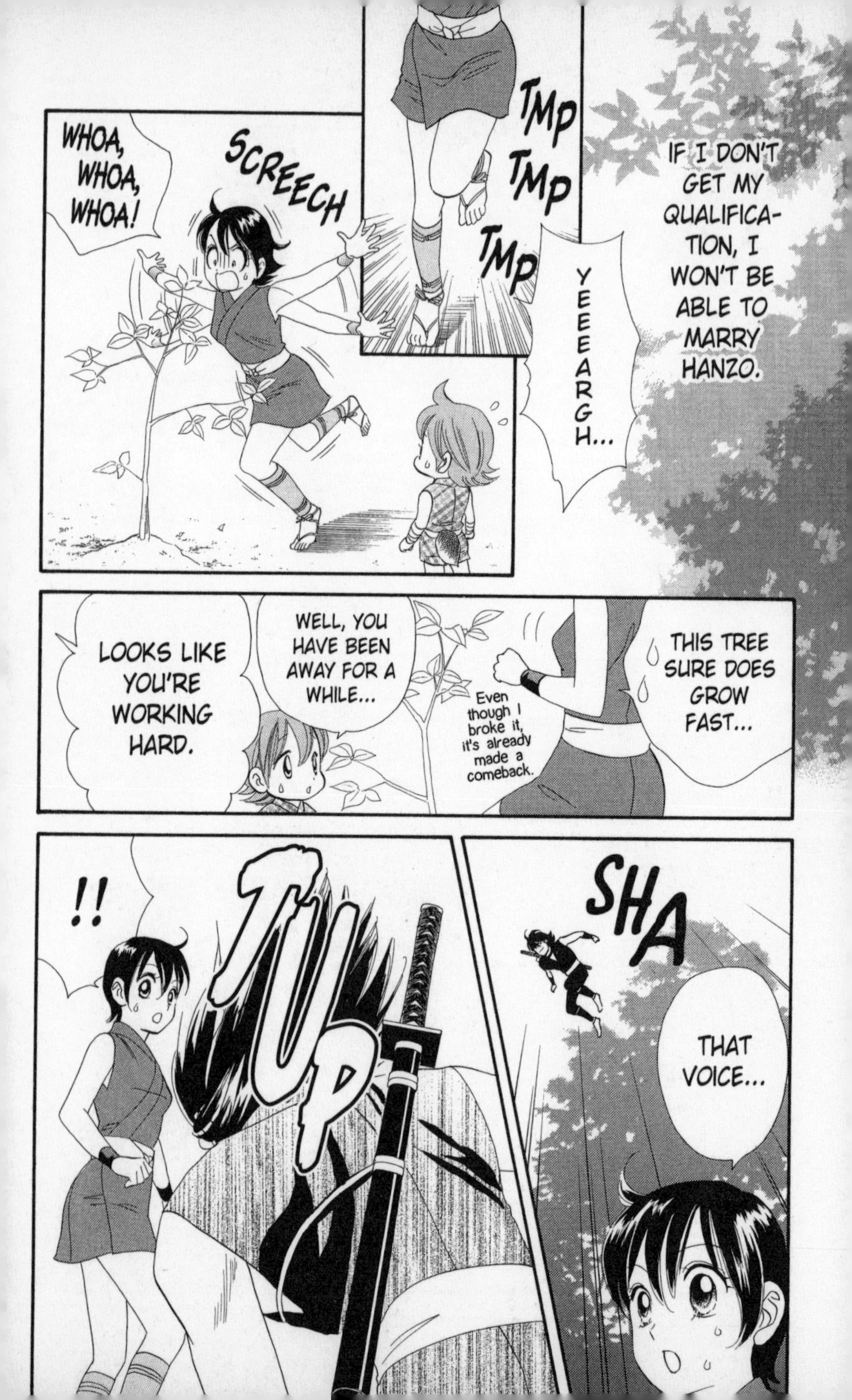
IF I DON'T GET MY QUALIFICATION, I WON'T BE ABLE TO MARRY HANZO.
TMP TMP TMP
YEEEEARGH...
SCREECH
WHOA, WHOA, WHOA!
THIS TREE SURE DOES GROW FAST...
Even though I broke it, it's already made a comeback.
WELL, YOU HAVE BEEN AWAY FOR A WHILE...
LOOKS LIKE YOU'RE WORKING HARD.
SHA
THAT VOICE...
TUP
!!

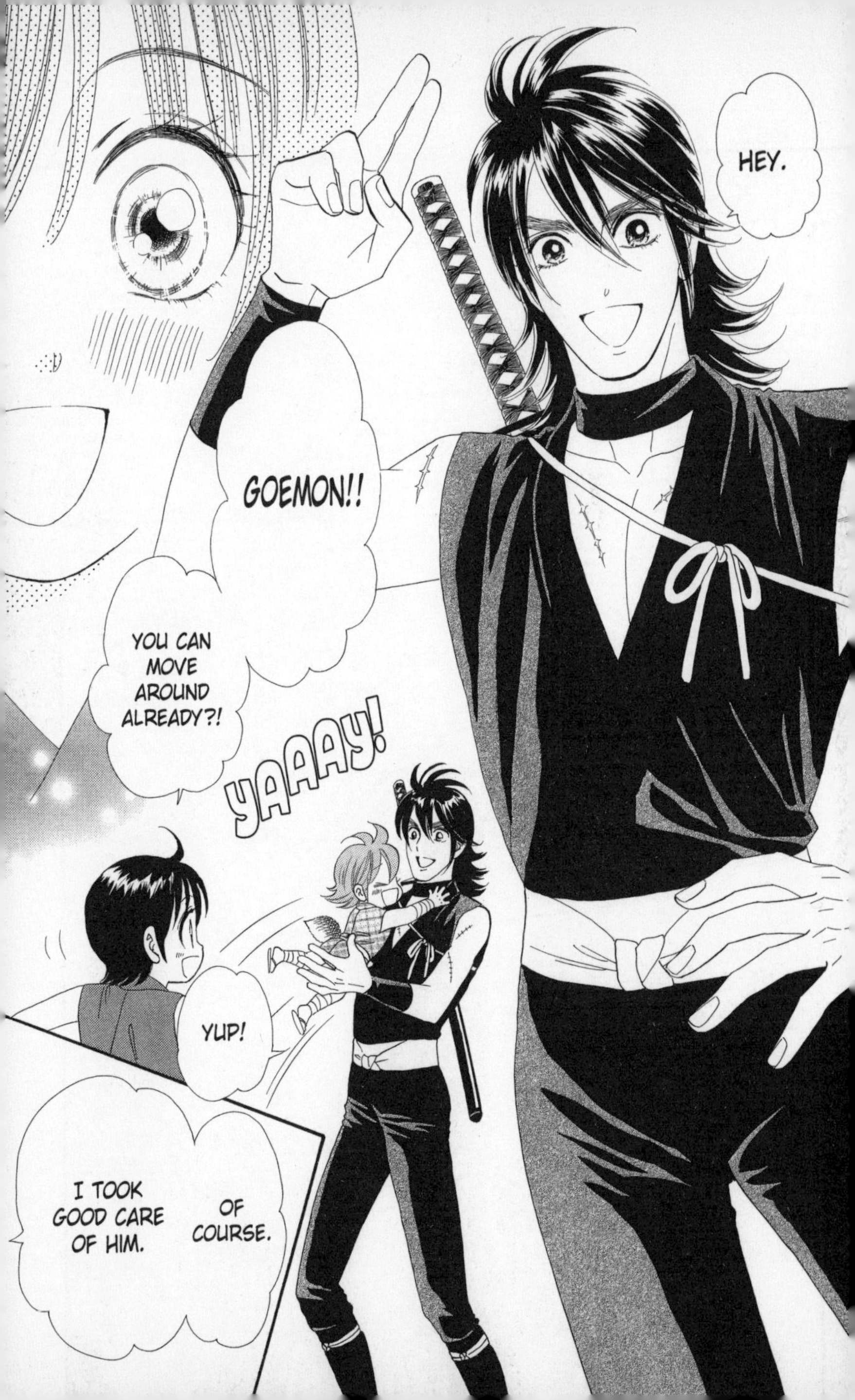
HEY.
GOEMON!!
YOU CAN MOVE AROUND ALREADY?!
YAAAY!
YUP!
OF COURSE.
I TOOK GOOD CARE OF HIM.

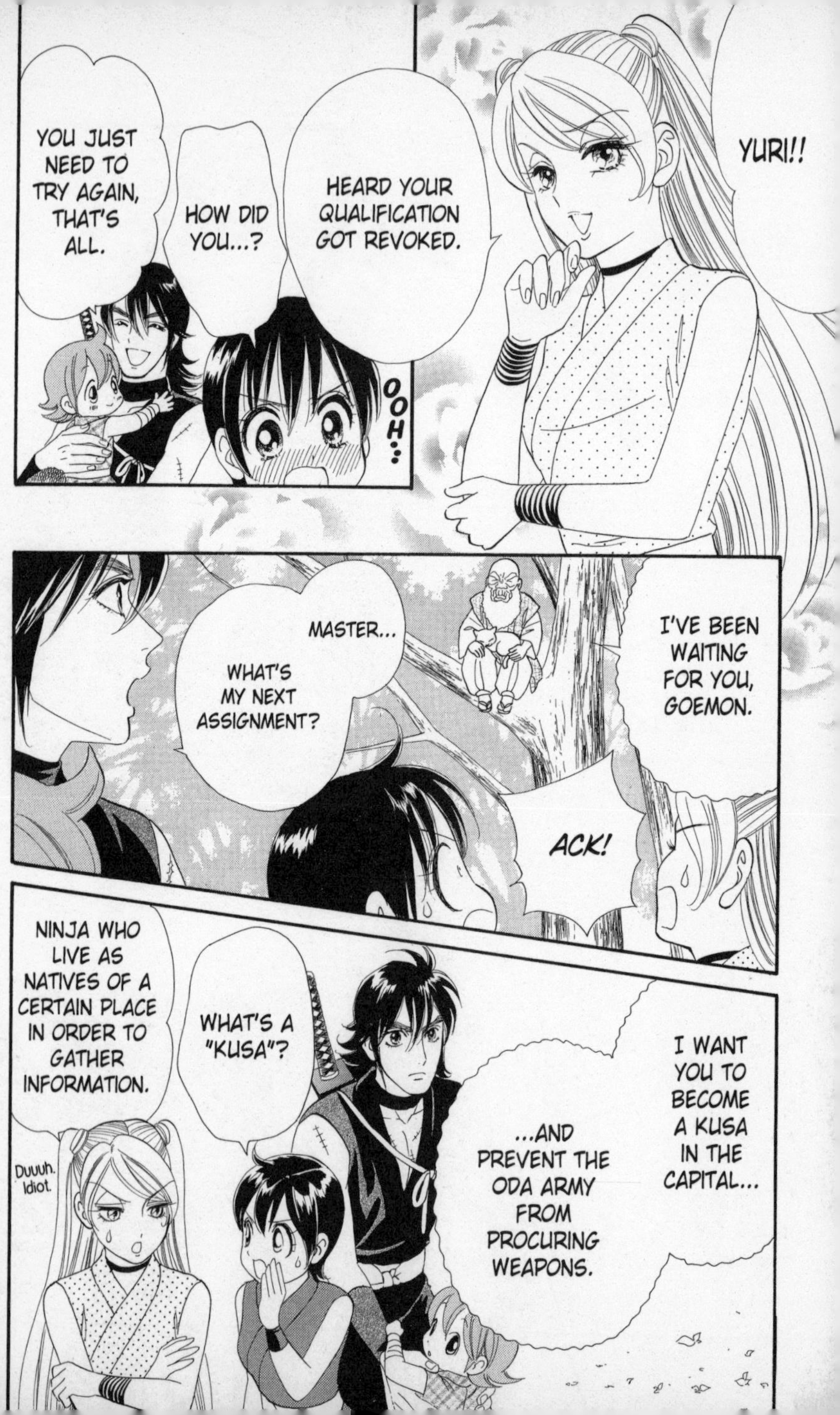
YURI!!
HEARD YOUR QUALIFICATION GOT REVOKED.
OOH...
HOW DID YOU...?
YOU JUST NEED TO TRY AGAIN, THAT'S ALL.
I'VE BEEN WAITING FOR YOU, GOEMON.
ACK!
MASTER...
WHAT'S MY NEXT ASSIGNMENT?
I WANT YOU TO BECOME A KUSA IN THE CAPITAL...
...AND PREVENT THE ODA ARMY FROM PROCURING WEAPONS.
WHAT'S A "KUSA"?
NINJA WHO LIVE AS NATIVES OF A CERTAIN PLACE IN ORDER TO GATHER INFORMATION.
Duuuh. Idiot.

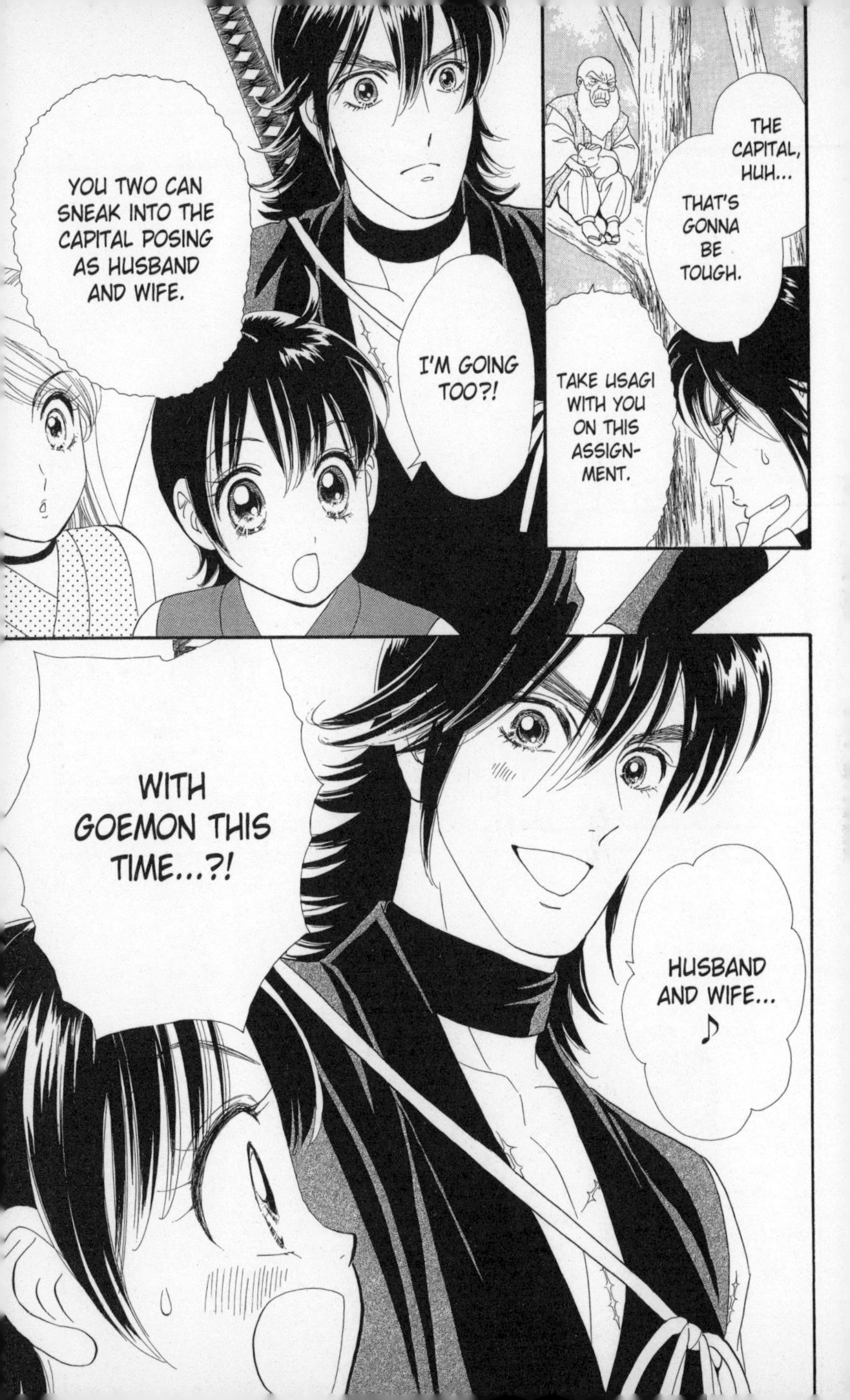
THE CAPITAL, HUH...
THAT'S GONNA BE TOUGH.
TAKE USAGI WITH YOU ON THIS ASSIGNMENT.
YOU TWO CAN SNEAK INTO THE CAPITAL POSING AS HUSBAND AND WIFE.
I'M GOING TOO?!
HUSBAND AND WIFE... ♪
WITH GOEMON THIS TIME...?!

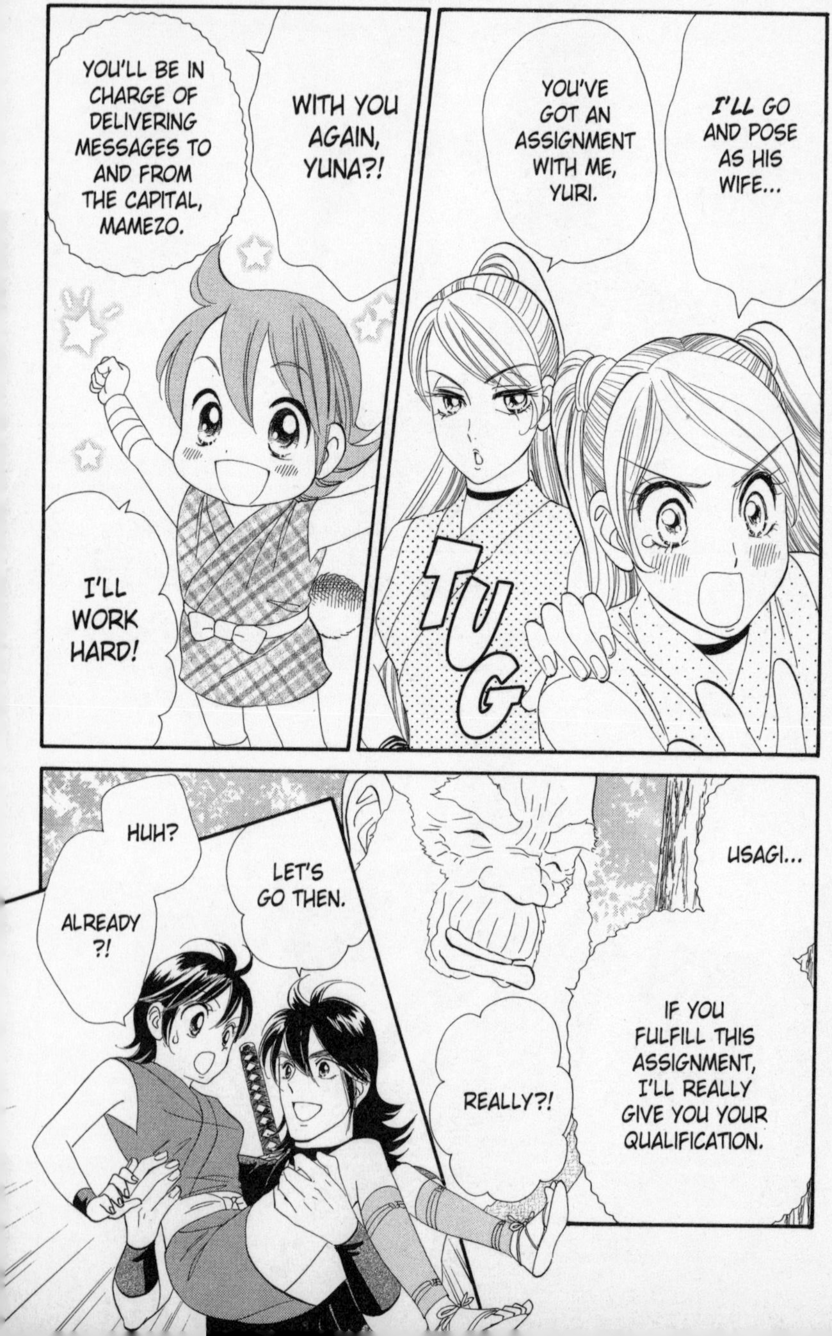
I'LL GO AND POSE AS HIS WIFE...
YOU'VE GOT AN ASSIGNMENT WITH ME, YURI.
TUG
WITH YOU AGAIN, YUNA?!
YOU'LL BE IN CHARGE OF DELIVERING MESSAGES TO AND FROM THE CAPITAL, MAMEZO.
I'LL WORK HARD!
USAGI...
IF YOU FULFILL THIS ASSIGNMENT, I'LL REALLY GIVE YOU YOUR QUALIFICATION.
REALLY?!
LET'S GO THEN.
HUH?
ALREADY?!

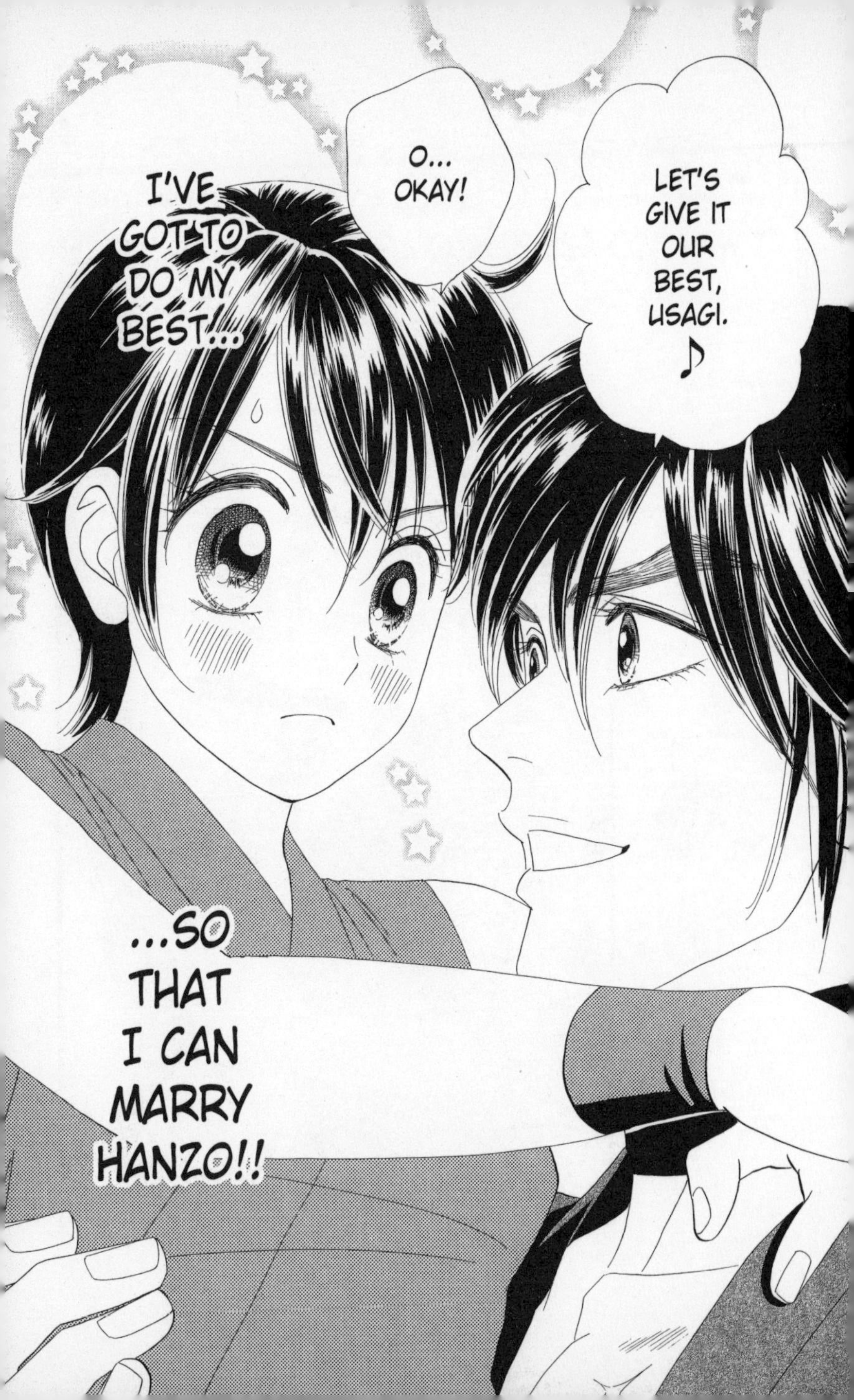
LET'S GIVE IT OUR BEST, USAGI. ♪
O... OKAY!
I'VE GOT TO DO MY BEST...
...SO THAT I CAN MARRY HANZO!!

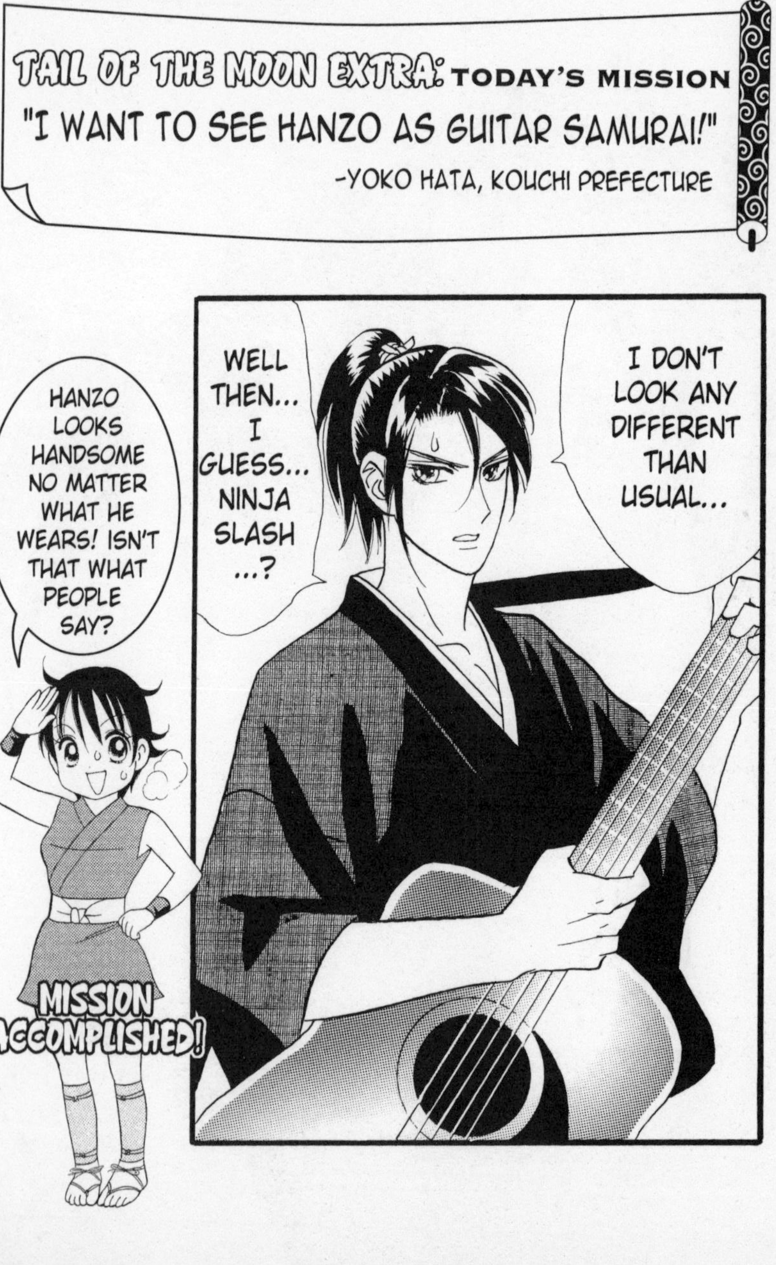
TAIL OF THE MOON EXTRA: TODAY'S MISSION
"I WANT TO SEE HANZO AS GUITAR SAMURAI!"
-YOKO HATA, KOUCHI PREFECTURE
I DON'T LOOK ANY DIFFERENT THAN USUAL...
WELL THEN... I GUESS... NINJA SLASH ...?
HANZO LOOKS HANDSOME NO MATTER WHAT HE WEARS! ISN'T THAT WHAT PEOPLE SAY?
MISSION ACCOMPLISHED!

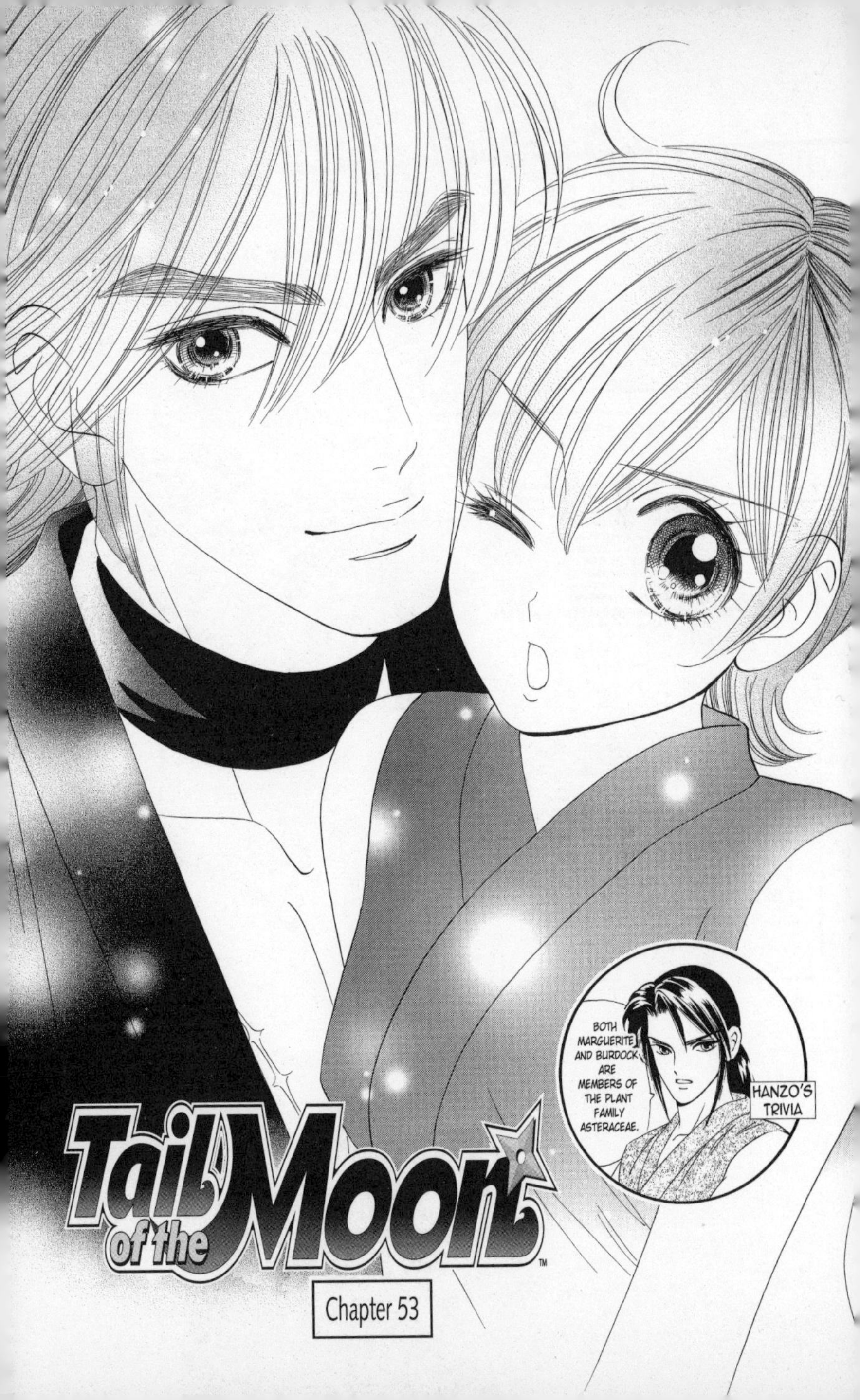
Tail of the Moon™
Chapter 53
HANZO'S TRIVIA
BOTH MARGUERITE AND BURDOCK ARE MEMBERS OF THE PLANT FAMILY ASTERACEAE.

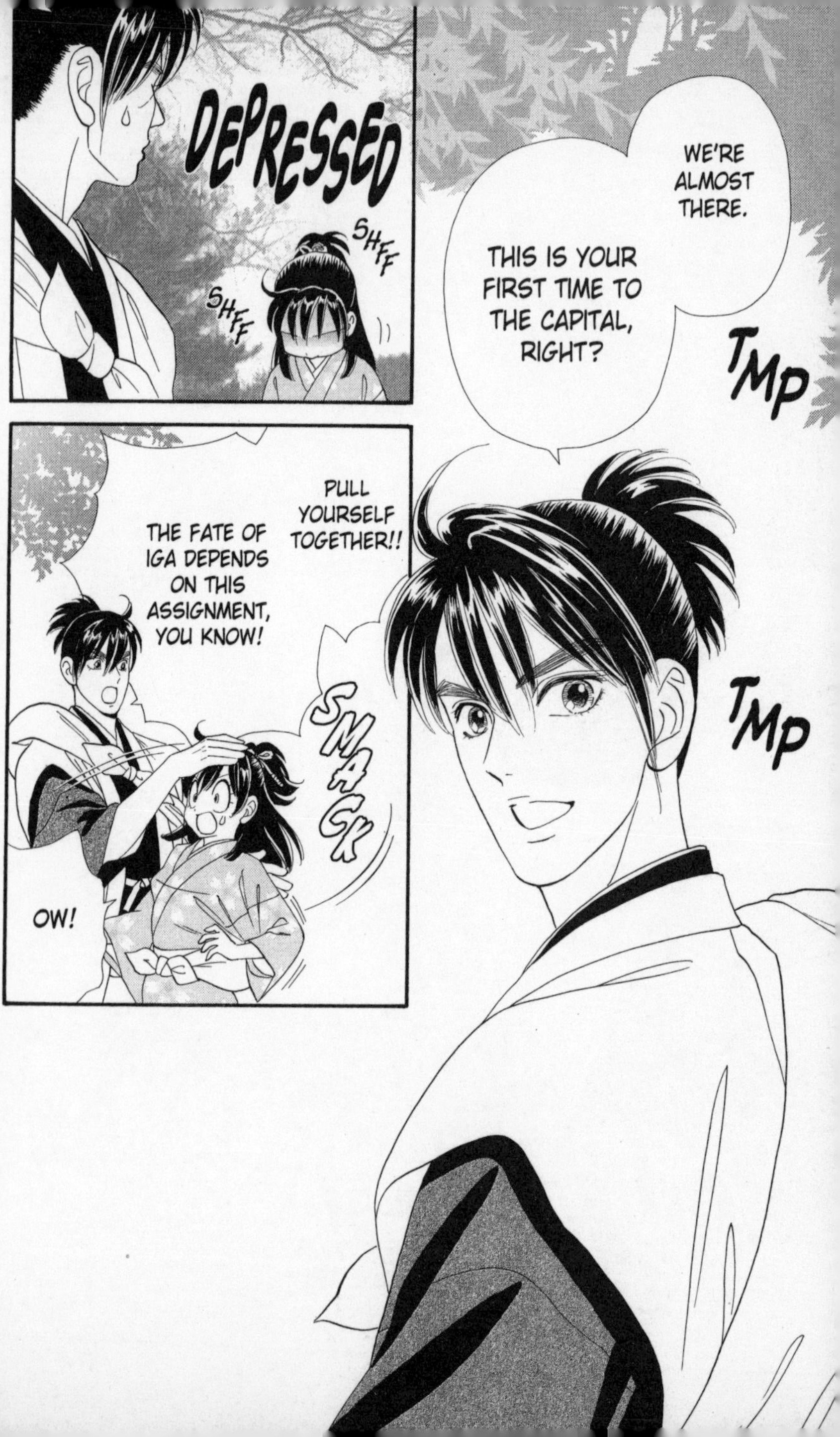
WE'RE ALMOST THERE.
THIS IS YOUR FIRST TIME TO THE CAPITAL, RIGHT?
TMP
TMP
DEPRESSED
SHFF
SHFF
PULL YOURSELF TOGETHER!!
THE FATE OF IGA DEPENDS ON THIS ASSIGNMENT, YOU KNOW!
SMACK
OW!

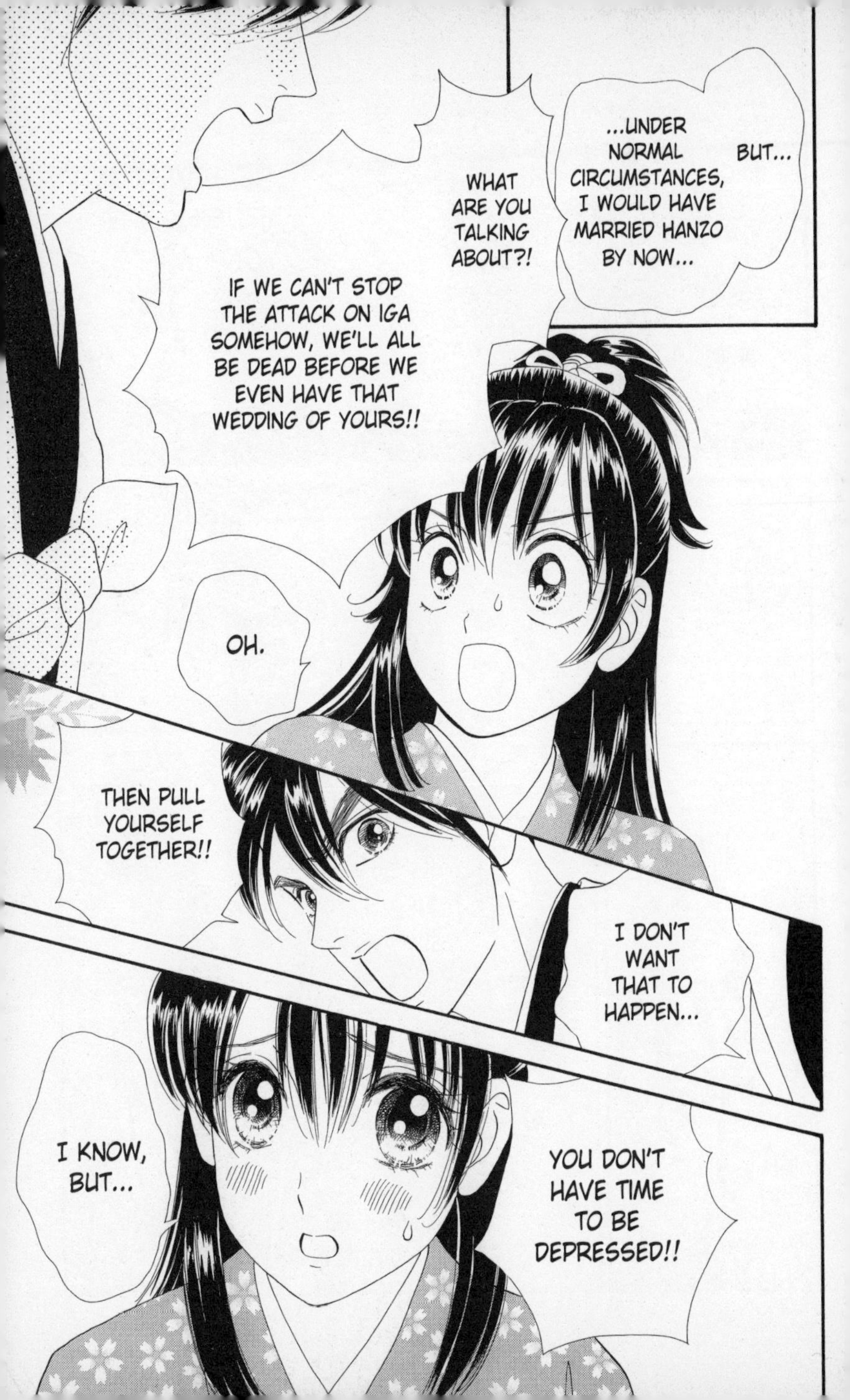

...UNDER NORMAL CIRCUMSTANCES, I WOULD HAVE MARRIED HANZO BY NOW...
BUT...
WHAT ARE YOU TALKING ABOUT?!
IF WE CAN'T STOP THE ATTACK ON IGA SOMEHOW, WE'LL ALL BE DEAD BEFORE WE EVEN HAVE THAT WEDDING OF YOURS!!
OH.
I DON'T WANT THAT TO HAPPEN...
THEN PULL YOURSELF TOGETHER!!
YOU DON'T HAVE TIME TO BE DEPRESSED!!
I KNOW, BUT...

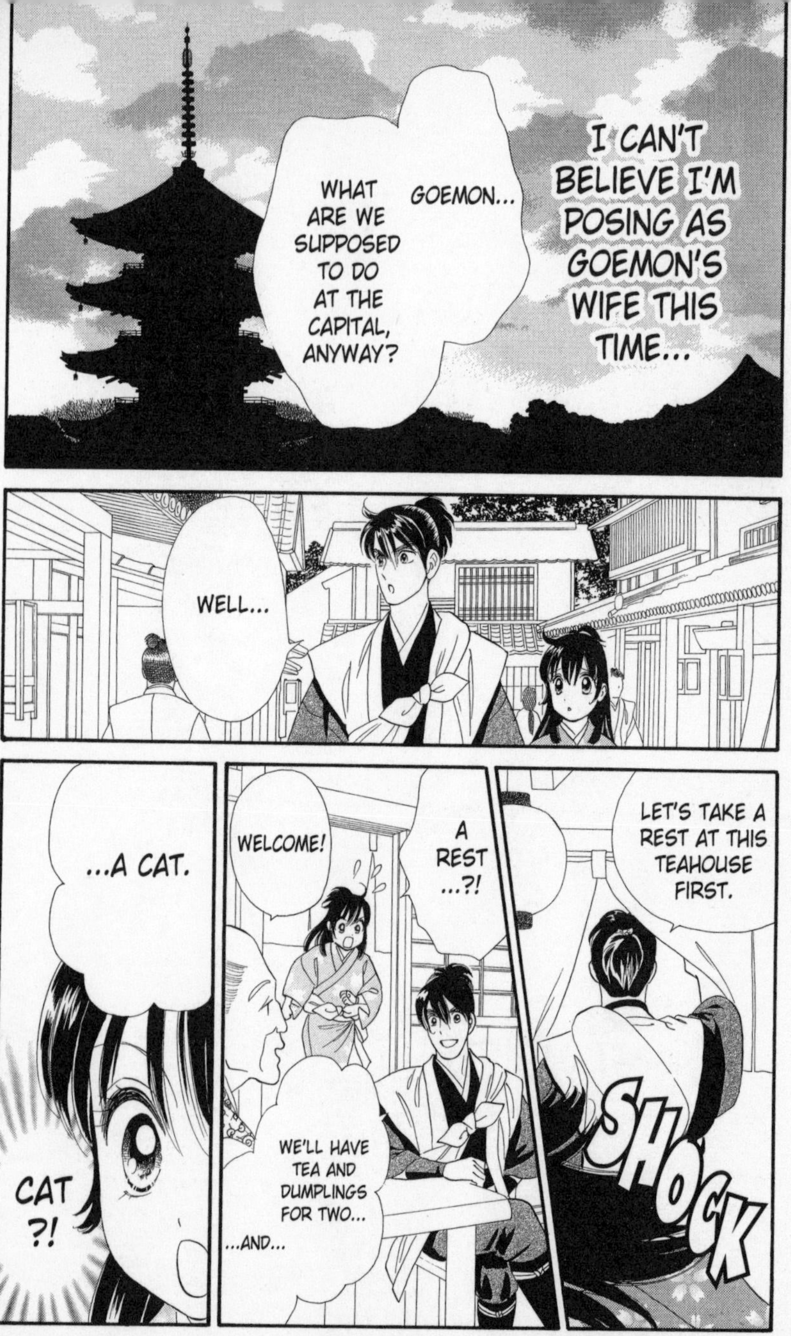
I CAN'T BELIEVE I'M POSING AS GOEMON'S WIFE THIS TIME...
GOEMON...
WHAT ARE WE SUPPOSED TO DO AT THE CAPITAL, ANYWAY?
WELL...
LET'S TAKE A REST AT THIS TEAHOUSE FIRST.
SHOCK
A REST ...?!
WELCOME!
WE'LL HAVE TEA AND DUMPLINGS FOR TWO...
...AND...
...A CAT.
CAT ?!

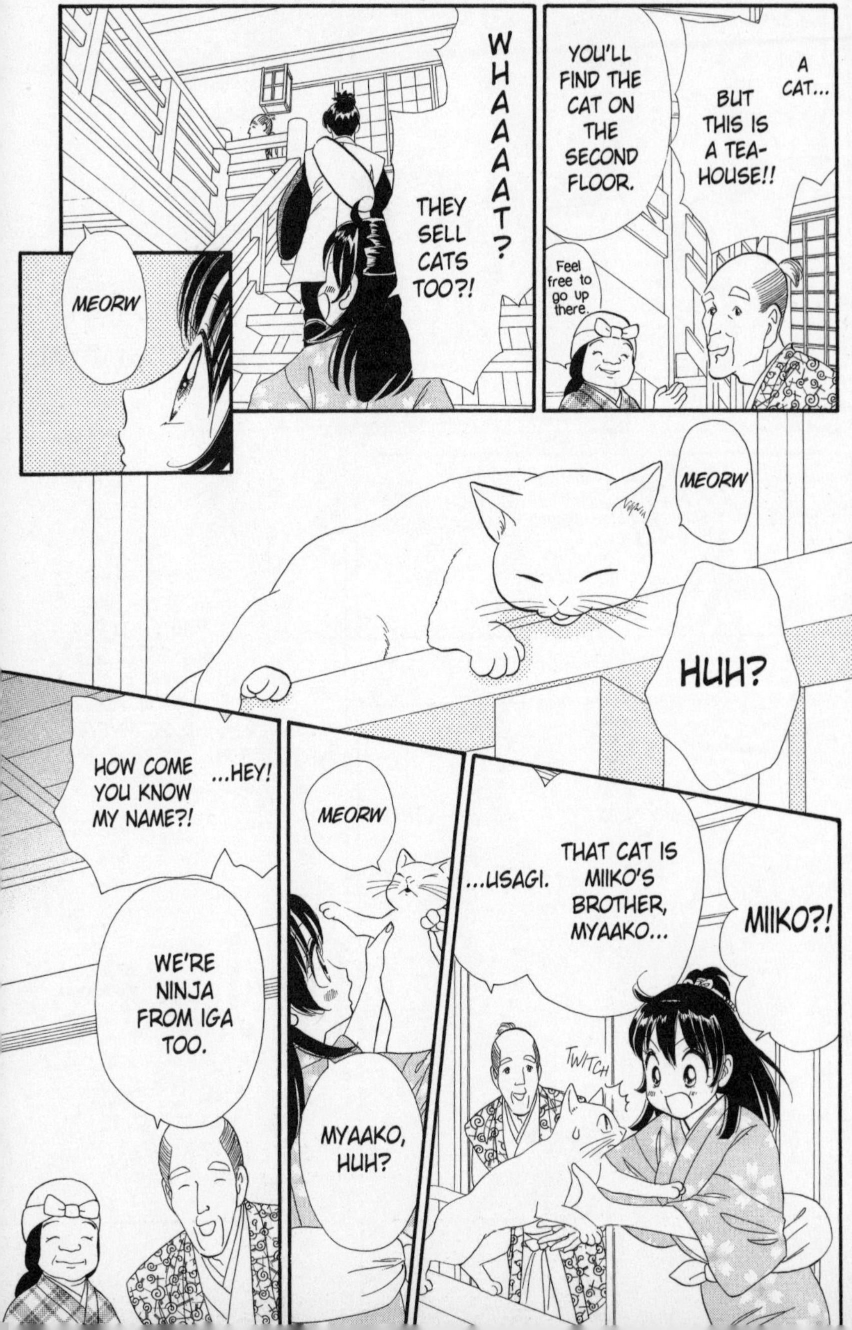

A CAT...
BUT THIS IS A TEA-HOUSE!!
YOU'LL FIND THE CAT ON THE SECOND FLOOR.
Feel free to go up there.
WHAAAAAT?
THEY SELL CATS TOO?!
MEORW
MEORW
HUH?
MIIKO?!
THAT CAT IS MIIKO'S BROTHER, MYAAKO...
...USAGI.
TWITCH
MEORW
MYAAKO, HUH?
...HEY!
HOW COME YOU KNOW MY NAME?!
WE'RE NINJA FROM IGA TOO.

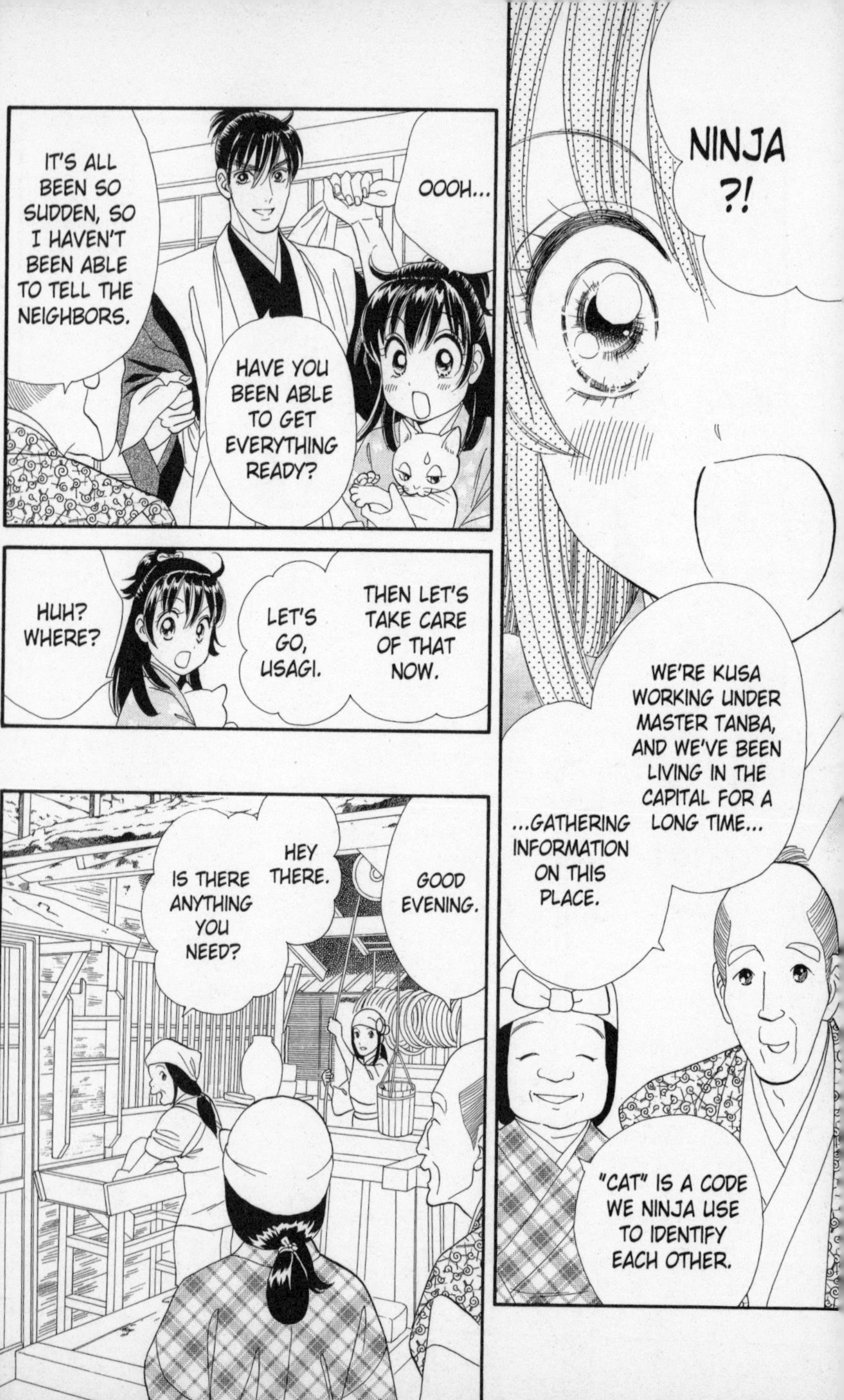
NINJA ?!
WE'RE KUSA WORKING UNDER MASTER TANBA, AND WE'VE BEEN LIVING IN THE CAPITAL FOR A LONG TIME...
...GATHERING INFORMATION ON THIS PLACE.
"CAT" IS A CODE WE NINJA USE TO IDENTIFY EACH OTHER.
OOOH...
IT'S ALL BEEN SO SUDDEN, SO I HAVEN'T BEEN ABLE TO TELL THE NEIGHBORS.
HAVE YOU BEEN ABLE TO GET EVERYTHING READY?
THEN LET'S TAKE CARE OF THAT NOW.
LET'S GO, USAGI.
HUH? WHERE?
GOOD EVENING.
HEY THERE.
IS THERE ANYTHING YOU NEED?

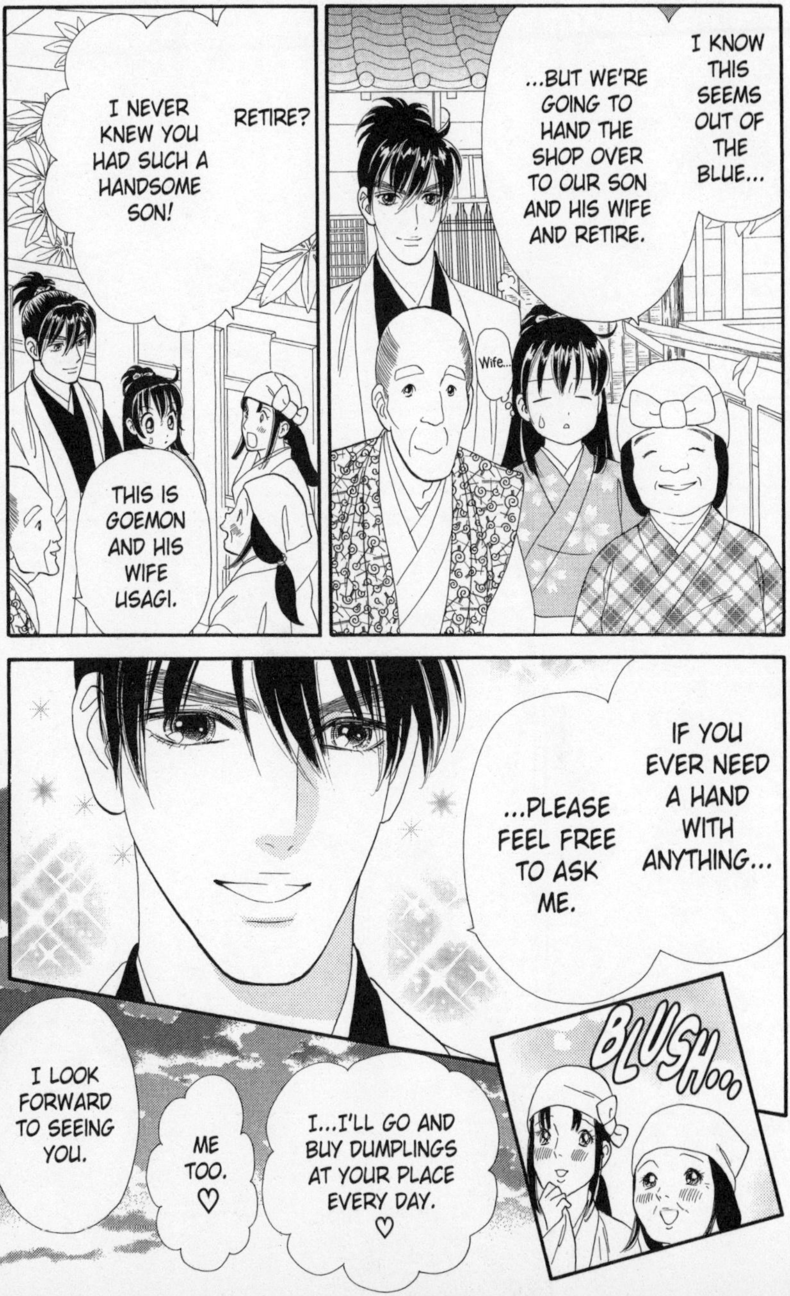
I KNOW THIS SEEMS OUT OF THE BLUE...
...BUT WE'RE GOING TO HAND THE SHOP OVER TO OUR SON AND HIS WIFE AND RETIRE.
Wife...
RETIRE?
I NEVER KNEW YOU HAD SUCH A HANDSOME SON!
THIS IS GOEMON AND HIS WIFE USAGI.
IF YOU EVER NEED A HAND WITH ANYTHING...
...PLEASE FEEL FREE TO ASK ME.
BLUSHOOO
I...I'LL GO AND BUY DUMPLINGS AT YOUR PLACE EVERY DAY. ♡
ME TOO. ♡
I LOOK FORWARD TO SEEING YOU.

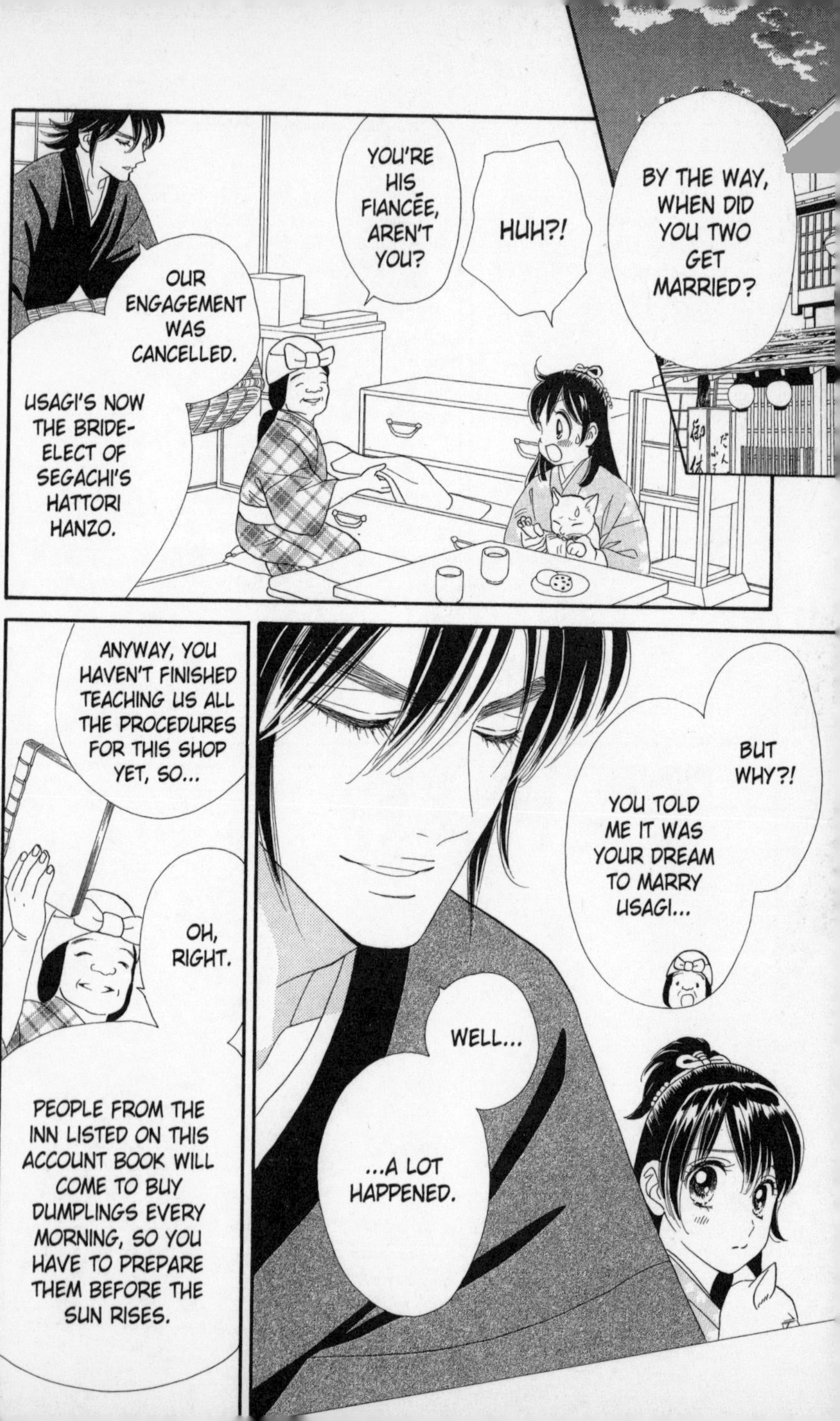
BY THE WAY, WHEN DID YOU TWO GET MARRIED?
HUH?!
YOU'RE HIS FIANCÉE, AREN'T YOU?
OUR ENGAGEMENT WAS CANCELLED.
USAGI'S NOW THE BRIDE-ELECT OF SEGACHI'S HATTORI HANZO.
BUT WHY?!
YOU TOLD ME IT WAS YOUR DREAM TO MARRY USAGI...
WELL...
...A LOT HAPPENED.
ANYWAY, YOU HAVEN'T FINISHED TEACHING US ALL THE PROCEDURES FOR THIS SHOP YET, SO...
OH, RIGHT.
PEOPLE FROM THE INN LISTED ON THIS ACCOUNT BOOK WILL COME TO BUY DUMPLINGS EVERY MORNING, SO YOU HAVE TO PREPARE THEM BEFORE THE SUN RISES.

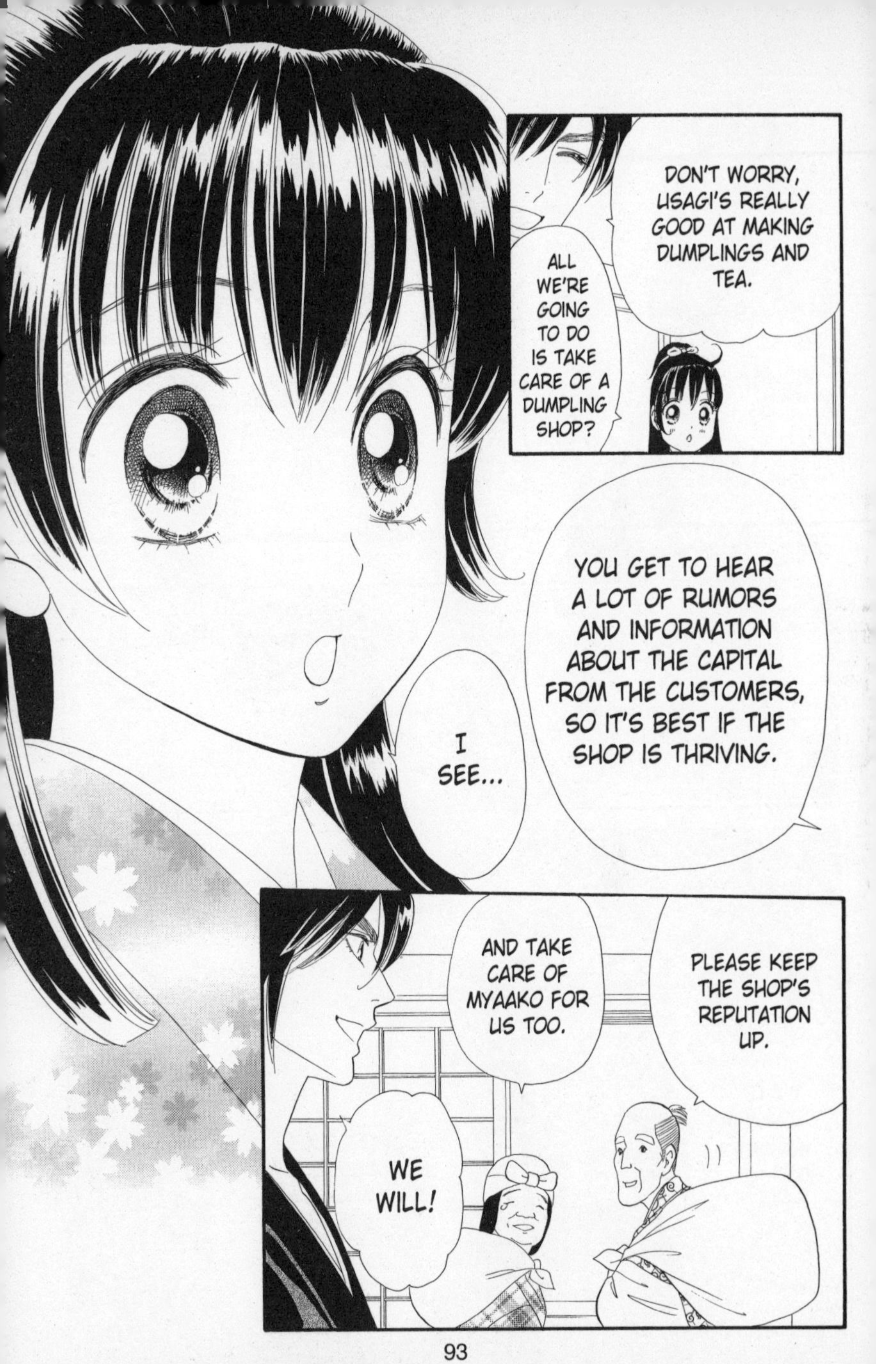
DON'T WORRY, USAGI'S REALLY GOOD AT MAKING DUMPLINGS AND TEA.
ALL WE'RE GOING TO DO IS TAKE CARE OF A DUMPLING SHOP?
YOU GET TO HEAR A LOT OF RUMORS AND INFORMATION ABOUT THE CAPITAL FROM THE CUSTOMERS, SO IT'S BEST IF THE SHOP IS THRIVING.
I SEE...
PLEASE KEEP THE SHOP'S REPUTATION UP.
AND TAKE CARE OF MYAAKO FOR US TOO.
WE WILL!

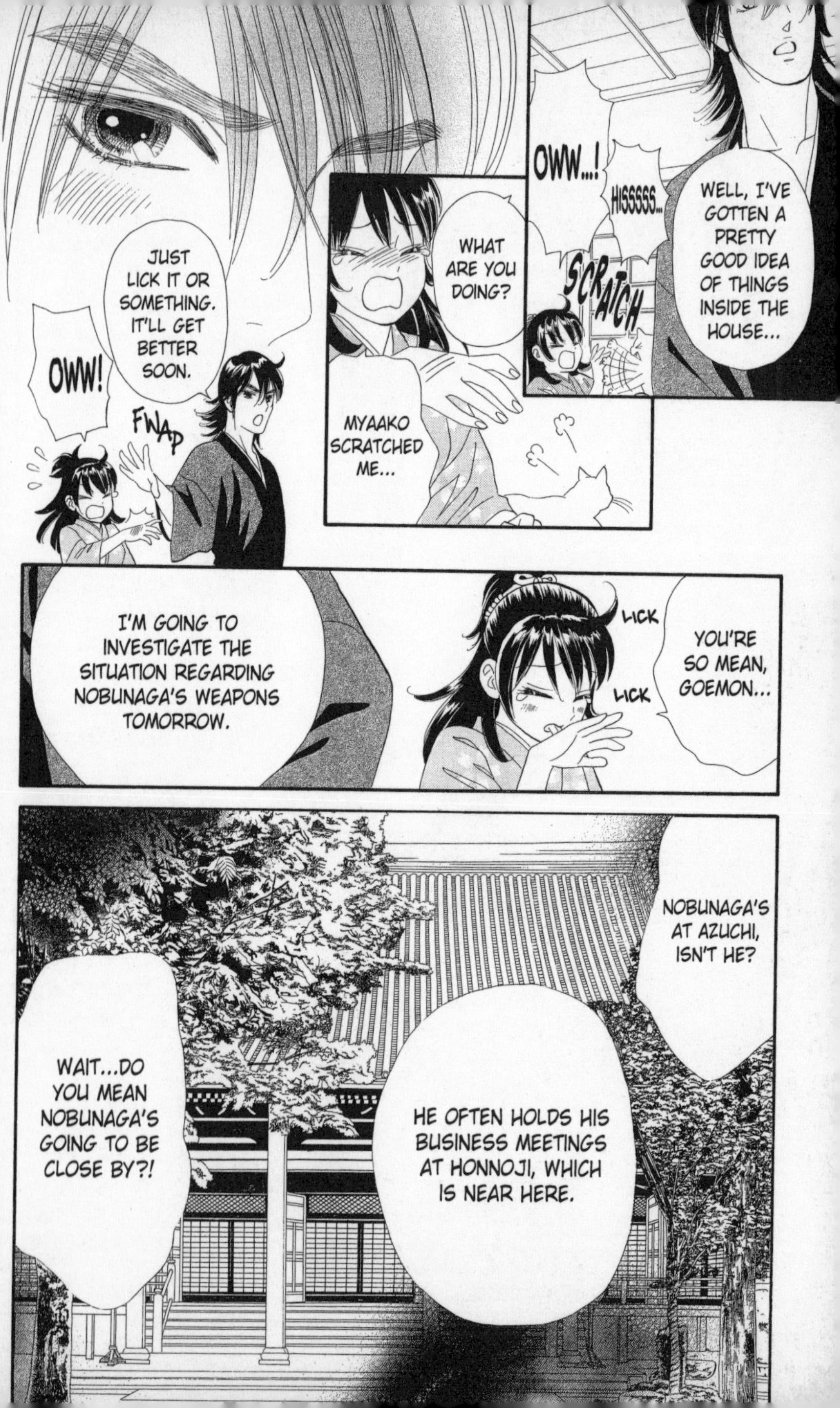
WELL, I'VE GOTTEN A PRETTY GOOD IDEA OF THINGS INSIDE THE HOUSE...
OWW...!
HISSSSS...
SCRATCH
WHAT ARE YOU DOING?
MYAAKO SCRATCHED ME...
JUST LICK IT OR SOMETHING. IT'LL GET BETTER SOON.
OWW!
FWAP
YOU'RE SO MEAN, GOEMON...
LICK
LICK
I'M GOING TO INVESTIGATE THE SITUATION REGARDING NOBUNAGA'S WEAPONS TOMORROW.
NOBUNAGA'S AT AZUCHI, ISN'T HE?
HE OFTEN HOLDS HIS BUSINESS MEETINGS AT HONNOJI, WHICH IS NEAR HERE.
WAIT...DO YOU MEAN NOBUNAGA'S GOING TO BE CLOSE BY?!

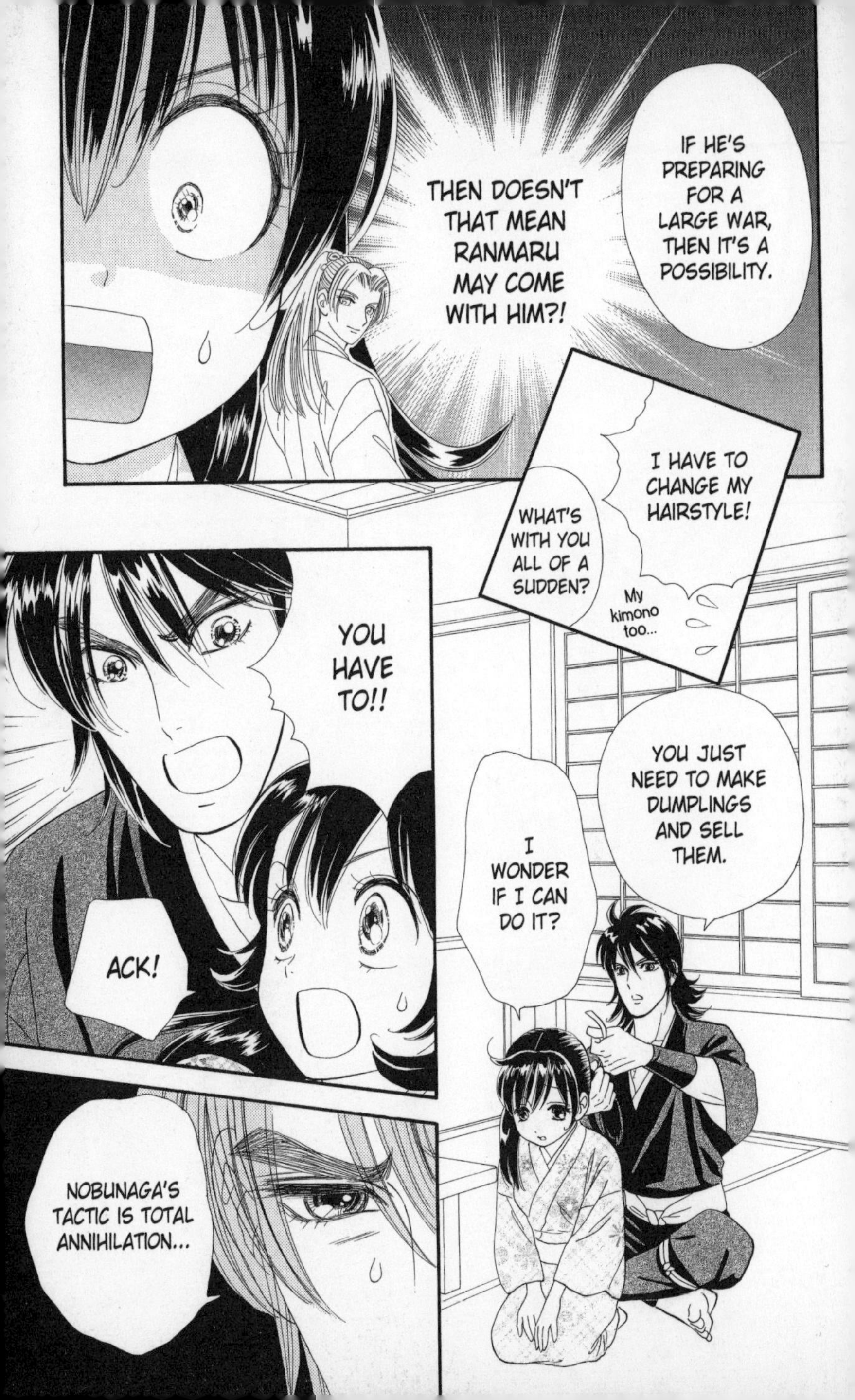
IF HE'S PREPARING FOR A LARGE WAR, THEN IT'S A POSSIBILITY.
THEN DOESN'T THAT MEAN RANMARU MAY COME WITH HIM?!
I HAVE TO CHANGE MY HAIRSTYLE!
My kimono too...
WHAT'S WITH YOU ALL OF A SUDDEN?
YOU JUST NEED TO MAKE DUMPLINGS AND SELL THEM.
I WONDER IF I CAN DO IT?
YOU HAVE TO!!
ACK!
NOBUNAGA'S TACTIC IS TOTAL ANNIHILATION...

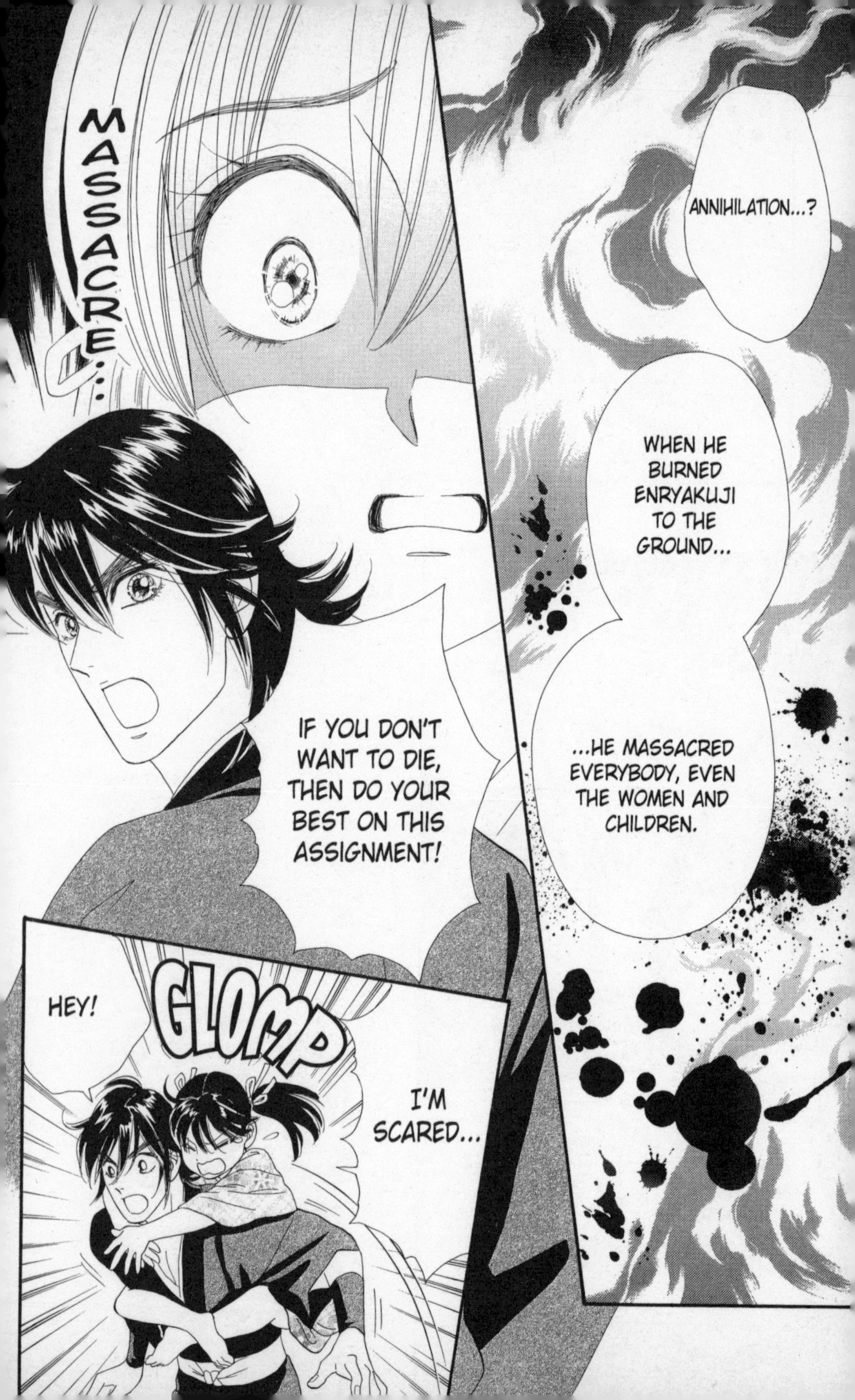
ANNIHILATION...?
WHEN HE BURNED ENRYAKUJI TO THE GROUND...
...HE MASSACRED EVERYBODY, EVEN THE WOMEN AND CHILDREN.
MASSACRE...
IF YOU DON'T WANT TO DIE, THEN DO YOUR BEST ON THIS ASSIGNMENT!
GLOMP
I'M SCARED...
HEY!

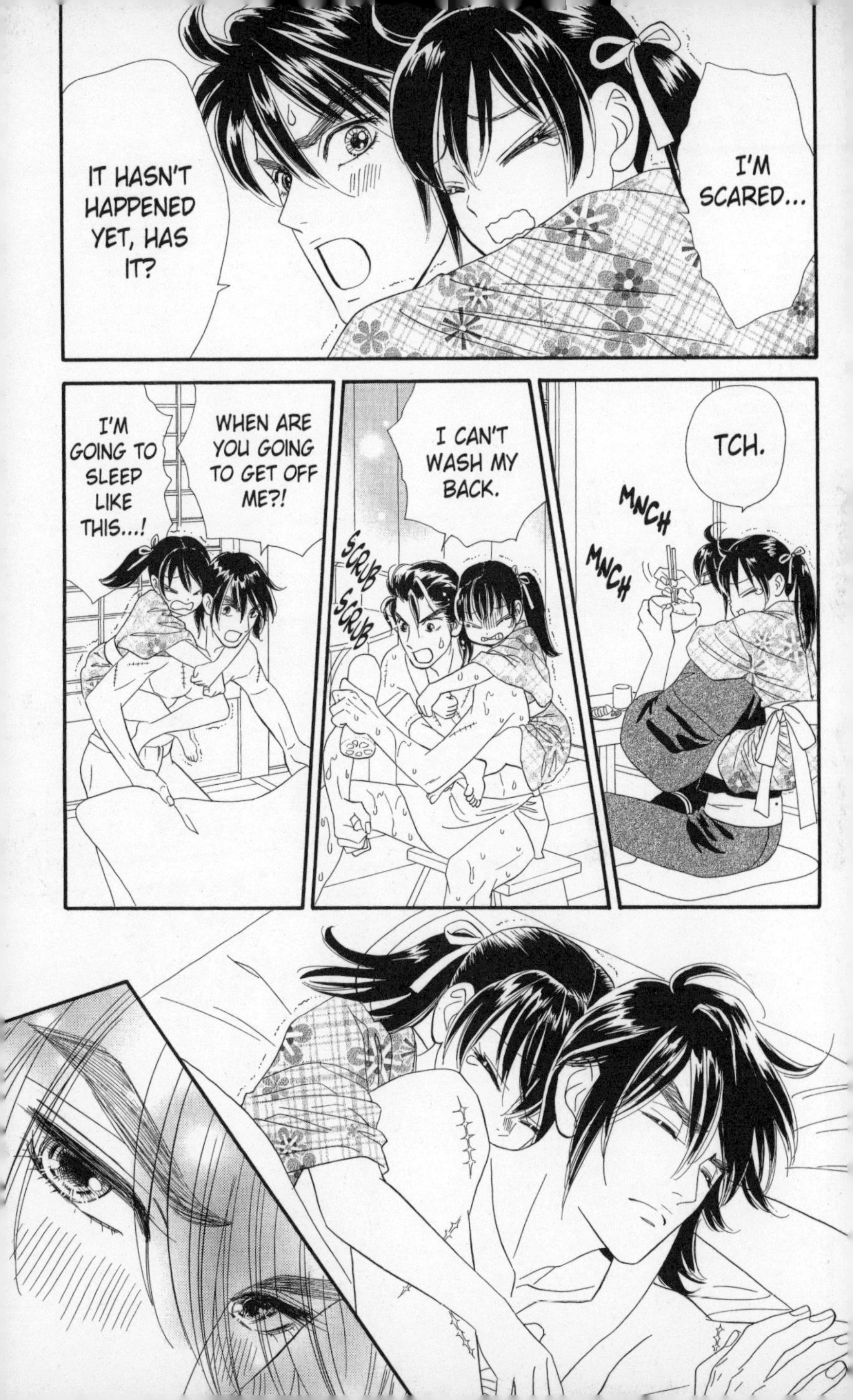
I'M SCARED...
IT HASN'T HAPPENED YET, HAS IT?
TCH.
MNCH
MNCH
I CAN'T WASH MY BACK.
SCRUB
SCRUB
WHEN ARE YOU GOING TO GET OFF ME?!
I'M GOING TO SLEEP LIKE THIS...!

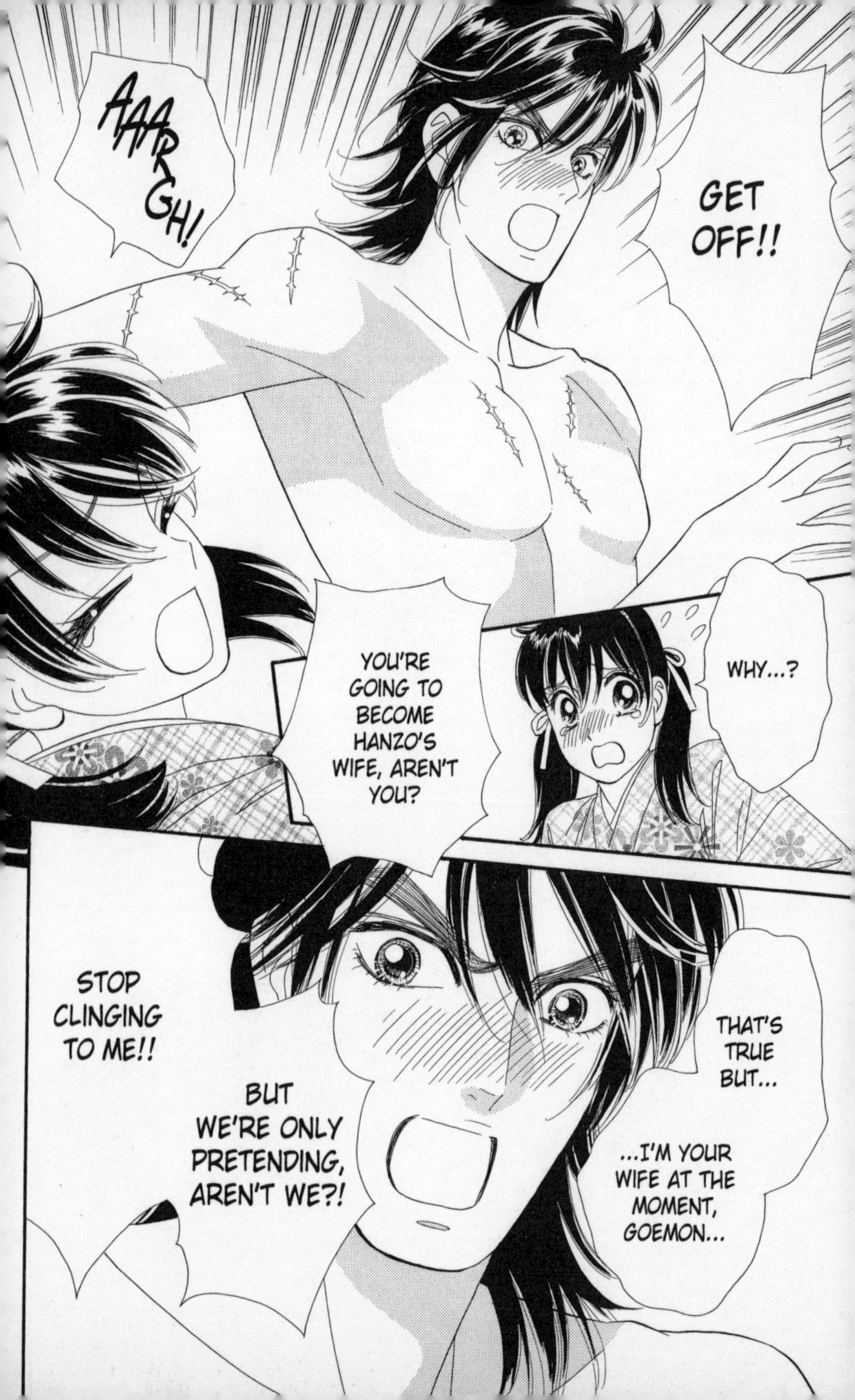
GET OFF!!
AAARGH!
WHY...?
YOU'RE GOING TO BECOME HANZO'S WIFE, AREN'T YOU?
THAT'S TRUE BUT...
...I'M YOUR WIFE AT THE MOMENT, GOEMON...
BUT WE'RE ONLY PRETENDING, AREN'T WE?!
STOP CLINGING TO ME!!

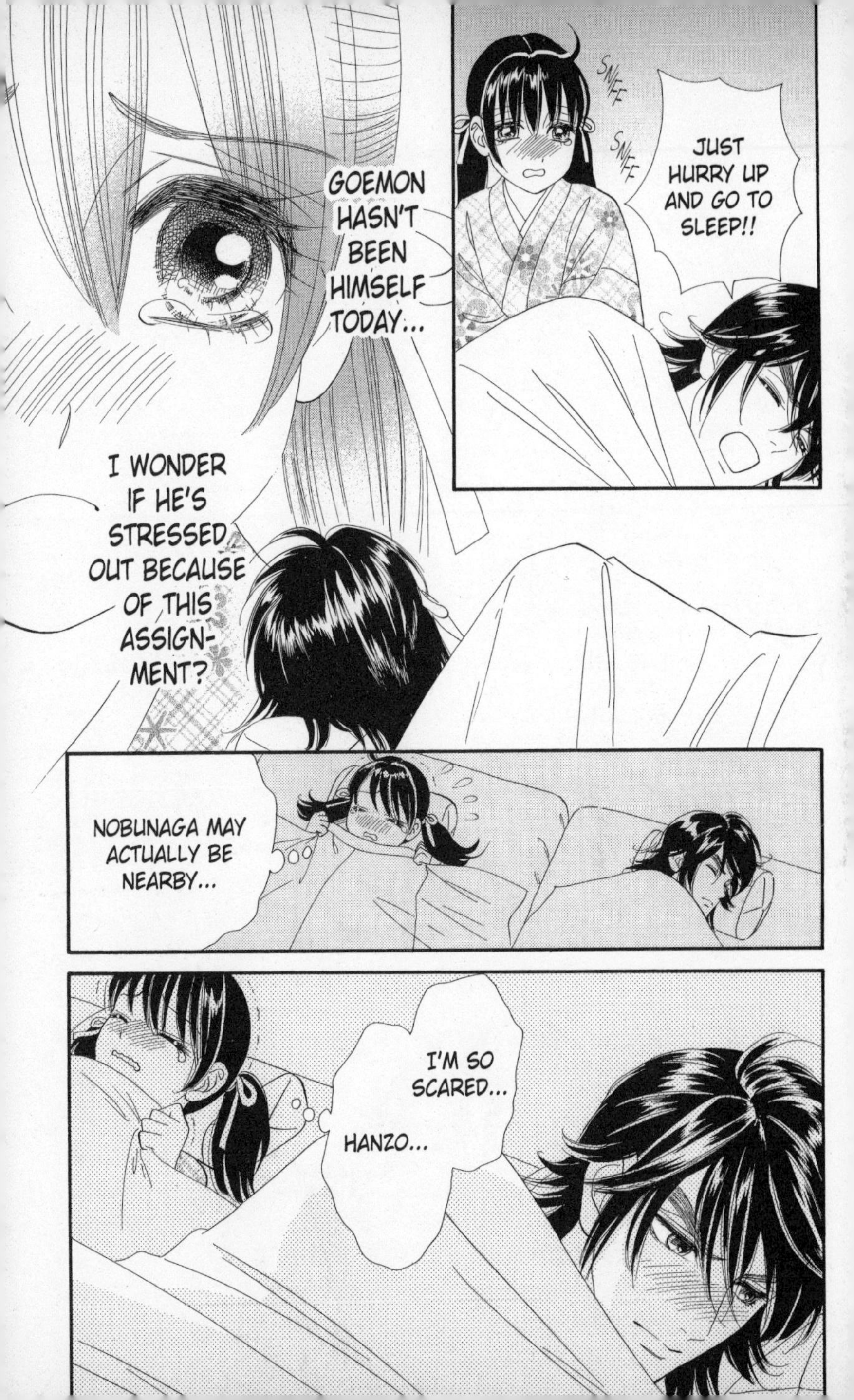
SNIFF
SNIFF
JUST HURRY UP AND GO TO SLEEP!!
GOEMON HASN'T BEEN HIMSELF TODAY...
I WONDER IF HE'S STRESSED OUT BECAUSE OF THIS ASSIGN-MENT?
NOBUNAGA MAY ACTUALLY BE NEARBY...
I'M SO SCARED...
HANZO...

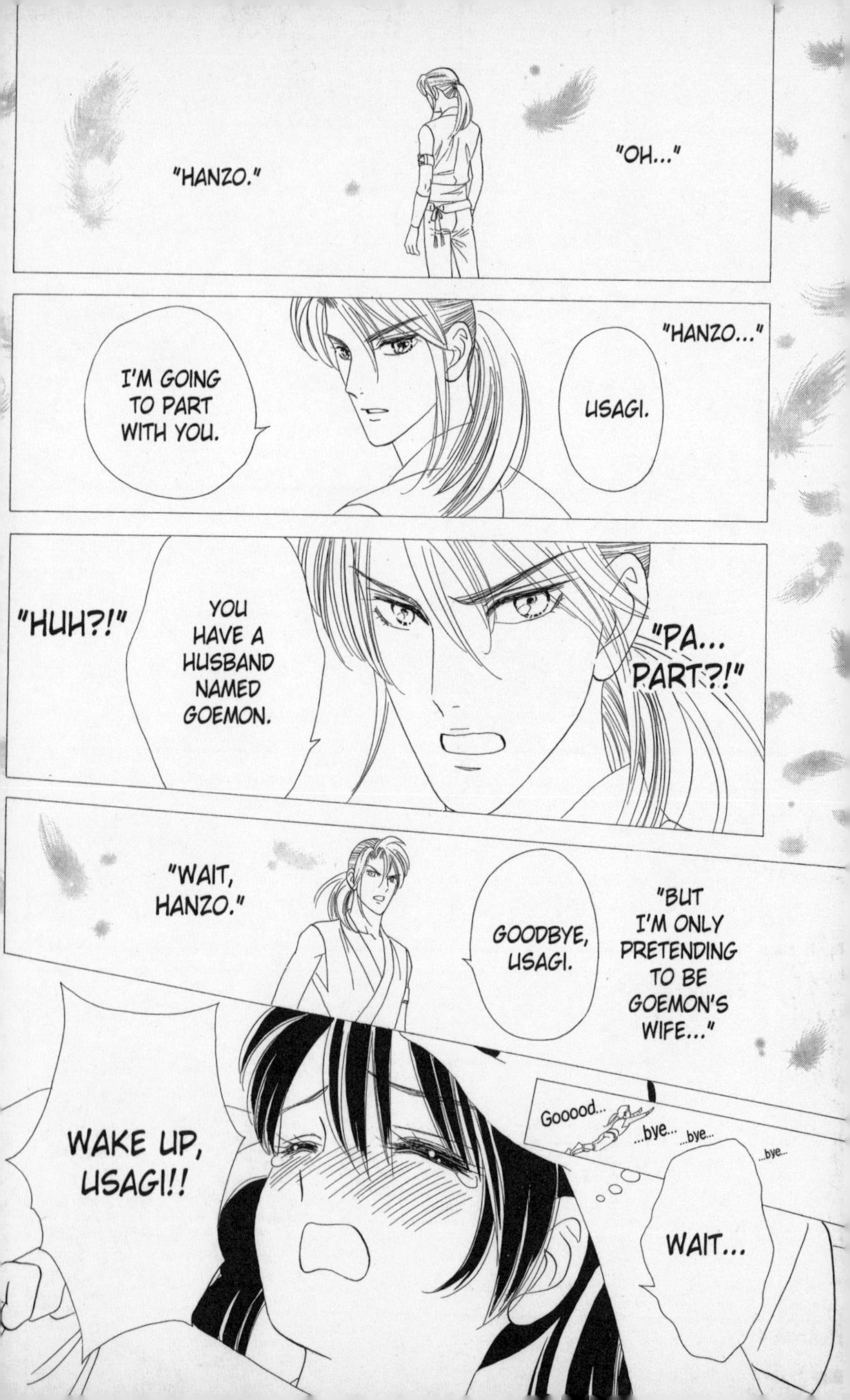
"OH..."
"HANZO."
"HANZO..."
USAGI.
I'M GOING TO PART WITH YOU.
"PA... PART?!"
YOU HAVE A HUSBAND NAMED GOEMON.
"HUH?!"
"BUT I'M ONLY PRETENDING TO BE GOEMON'S WIFE..."
GOODBYE, USAGI.
"WAIT, HANZO."
Gooood... ...bye... ...bye... ...bye...
WAIT...
WAKE UP, USAGI!!

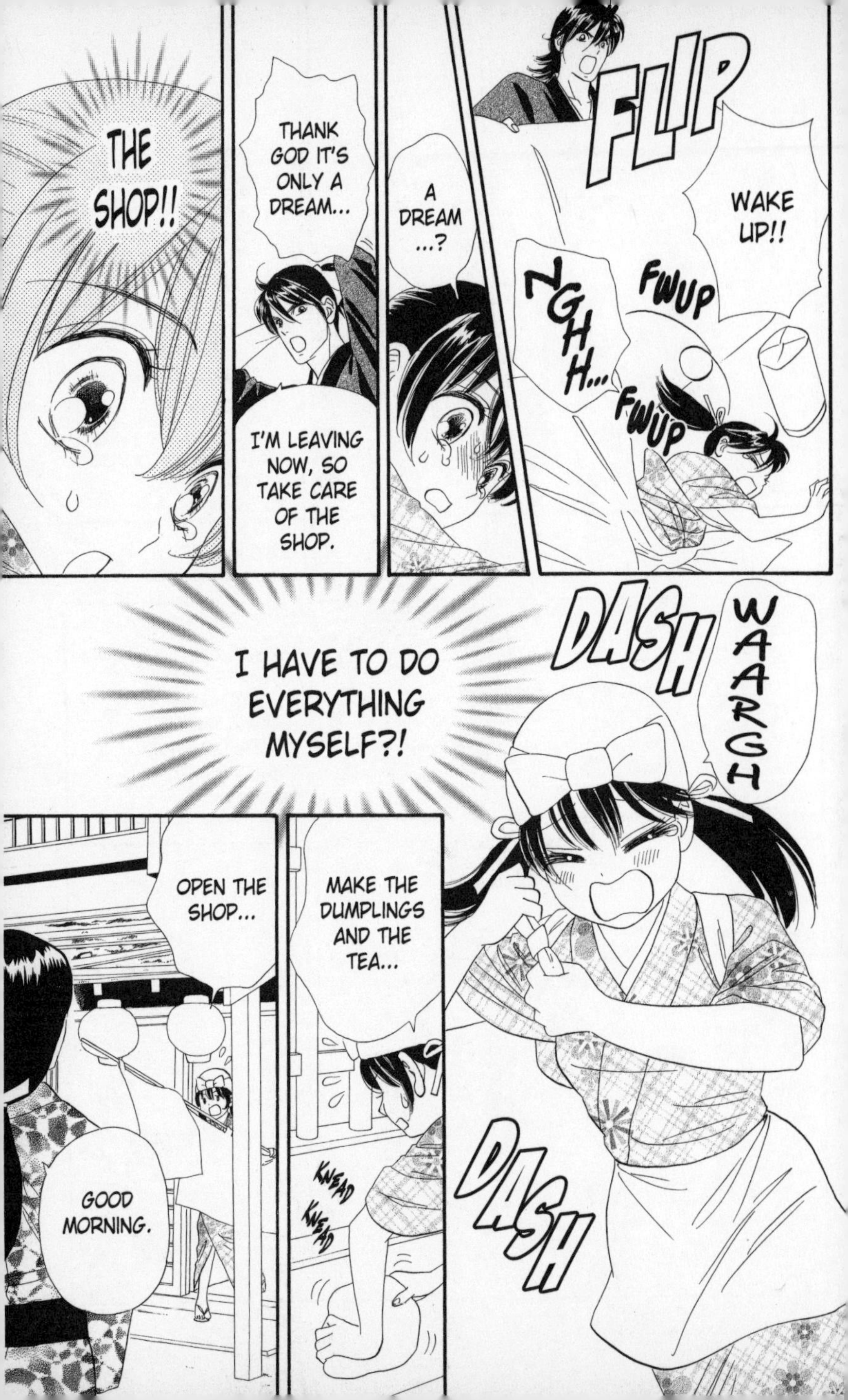
FLIP
WAKE UP!!
FWUP
NGHH...
FWUP
A DREAM ...?
THANK GOD IT'S ONLY A DREAM...
I'M LEAVING NOW, SO TAKE CARE OF THE SHOP.
THE SHOP!!
DASH
WAARGH
I HAVE TO DO EVERYTHING MYSELF?!
DASH
MAKE THE DUMPLINGS AND THE TEA...
KNEAD
KNEAD
OPEN THE SHOP...
GOOD MORNING.

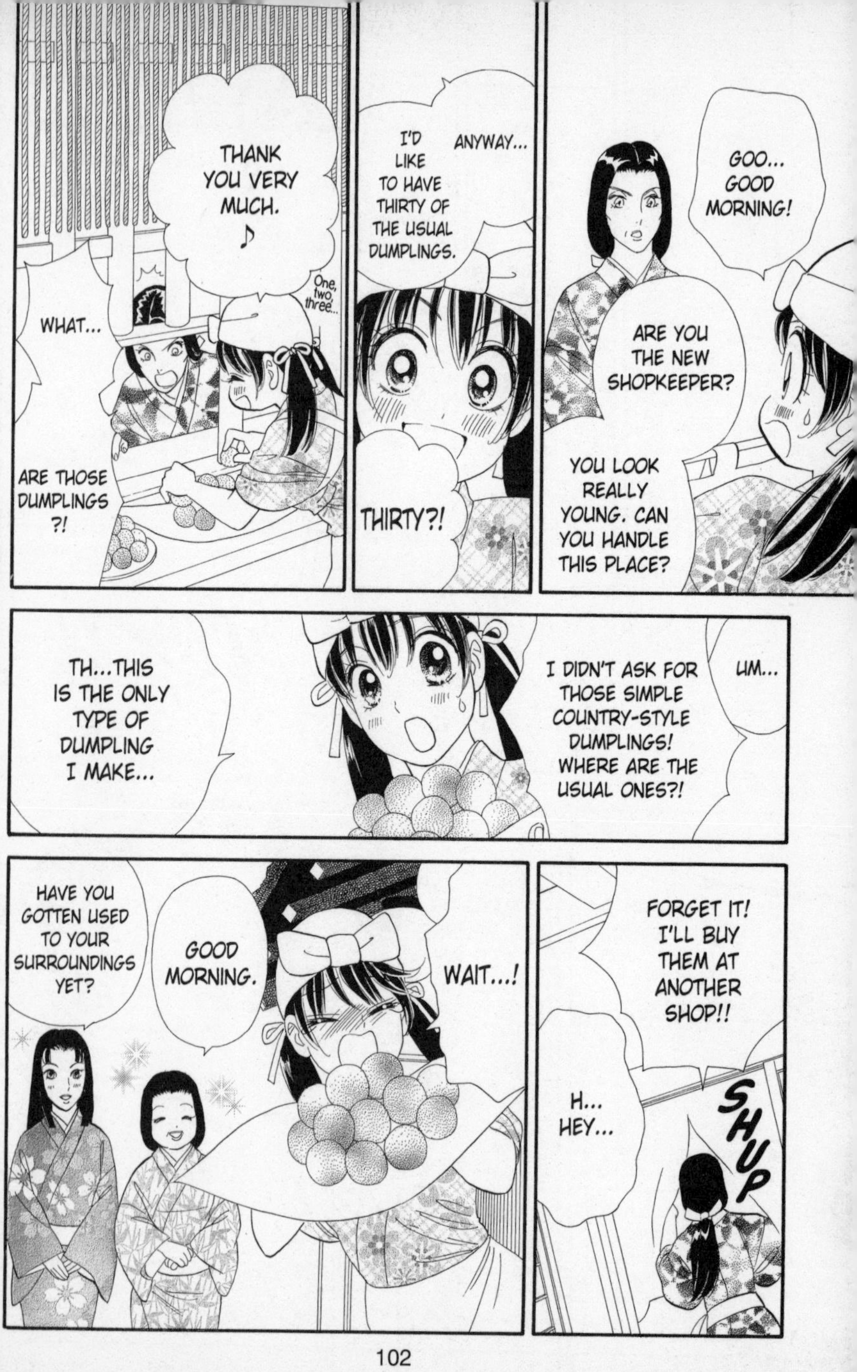
GOO... GOOD MORNING!
ARE YOU THE NEW SHOPKEEPER?
YOU LOOK REALLY YOUNG. CAN YOU HANDLE THIS PLACE?
ANYWAY...
I'D LIKE TO HAVE THIRTY OF THE USUAL DUMPLINGS.
THIRTY?!
THANK YOU VERY MUCH. ♪
One, two, three...
WHAT...
ARE THOSE DUMPLINGS ?!
UM...
I DIDN'T ASK FOR THOSE SIMPLE COUNTRY-STYLE DUMPLINGS! WHERE ARE THE USUAL ONES?!
TH...THIS IS THE ONLY TYPE OF DUMPLING I MAKE...
FORGET IT! I'LL BUY THEM AT ANOTHER SHOP!!
SHUP
H... HEY...
WAIT...!
GOOD MORNING.
HAVE YOU GOTTEN USED TO YOUR SURROUNDINGS YET?

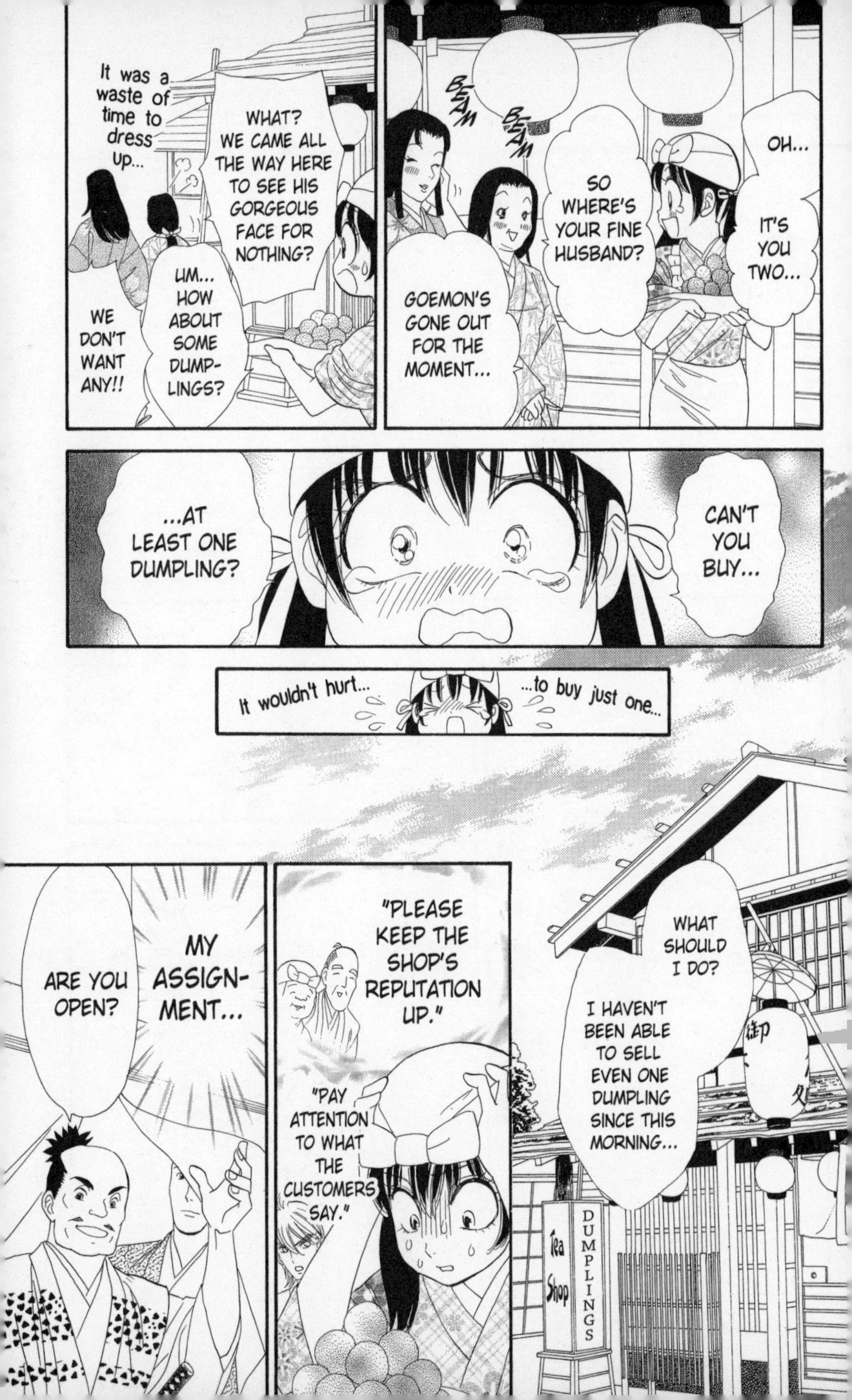
OH...
IT'S YOU TWO...
BEAM
BEAM
SO WHERE'S YOUR FINE HUSBAND?
GOEMON'S GONE OUT FOR THE MOMENT...
WHAT? WE CAME ALL THE WAY HERE TO SEE HIS GORGEOUS FACE FOR NOTHING?
It was a waste of time to dress up...
UM... HOW ABOUT SOME DUMP-LINGS?
WE DON'T WANT ANY!!
CAN'T YOU BUY...
...AT LEAST ONE DUMPLING?
It wouldn't hurt...
...to buy just one...
WHAT SHOULD I DO?
I HAVEN'T BEEN ABLE TO SELL EVEN ONE DUMPLING SINCE THIS MORNING...
Tea Shop
DUMPLINGS
"PLEASE KEEP THE SHOP'S REPUTATION UP."
"PAY ATTENTION TO WHAT THE CUSTOMERS SAY."
MY ASSIGN-MENT...
ARE YOU OPEN?

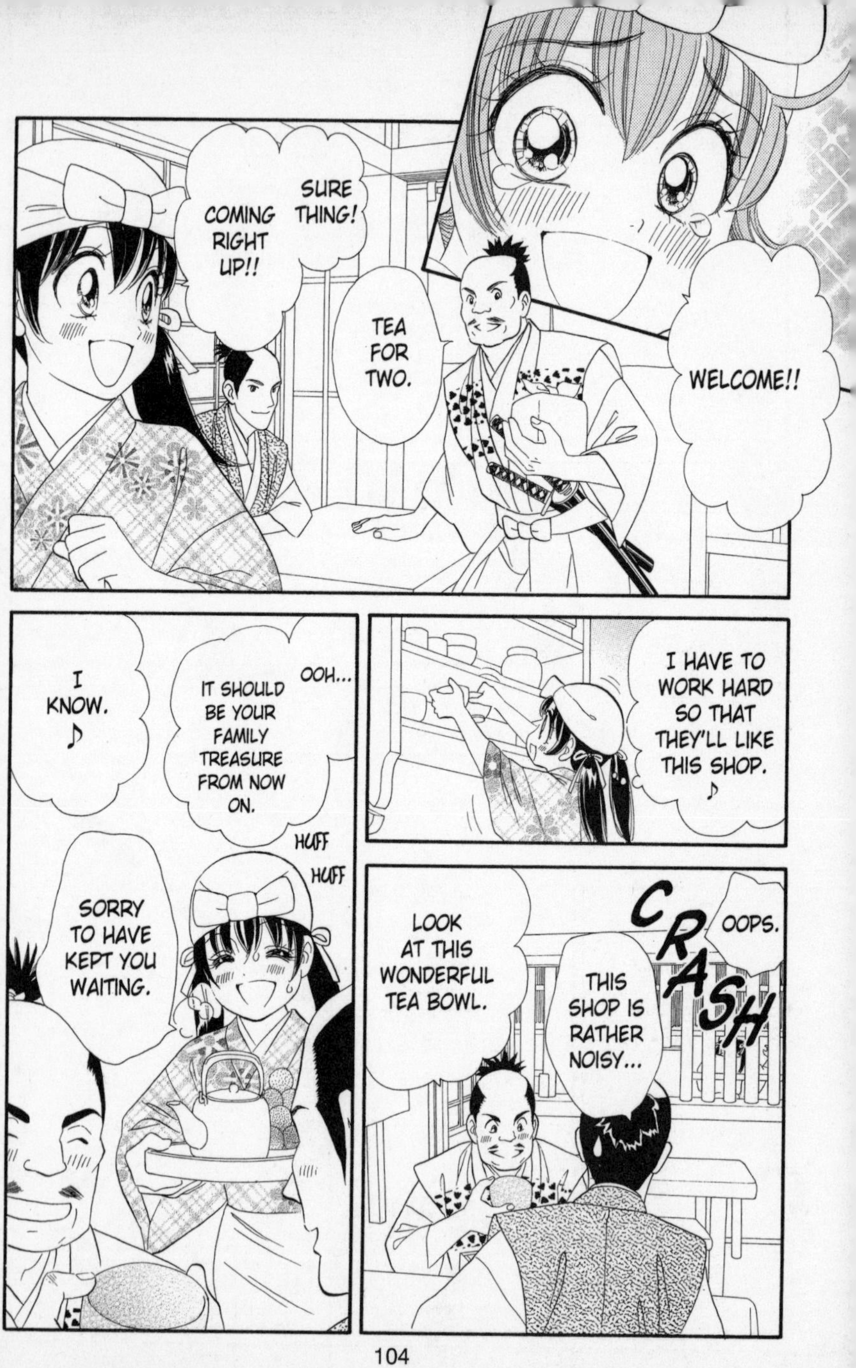
WELCOME!!
TEA FOR TWO.
SURE THING!
COMING RIGHT UP!!
I HAVE TO WORK HARD SO THAT THEY'LL LIKE THIS SHOP. ♪
OOPS.
CRASH
THIS SHOP IS RATHER NOISY...
LOOK AT THIS WONDERFUL TEA BOWL.
OOH...
IT SHOULD BE YOUR FAMILY TREASURE FROM NOW ON.
I KNOW. ♪
HUFF HUFF
SORRY TO HAVE KEPT YOU WAITING.

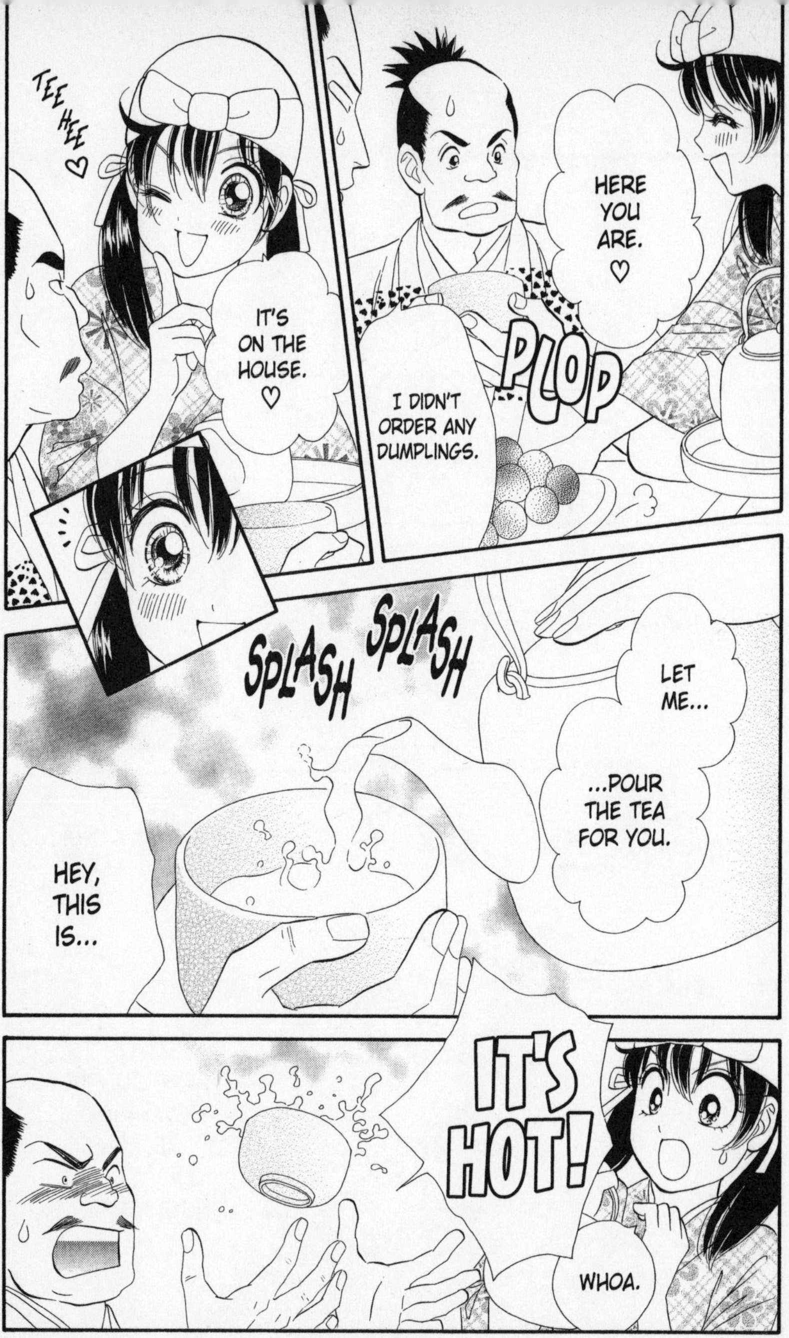
HERE YOU ARE. ♡
PLOP
I DIDN'T ORDER ANY DUMPLINGS.
TEE HEE ♡
IT'S ON THE HOUSE. ♡
LET ME...
...POUR THE TEA FOR YOU.
SPLASH
SPLASH
HEY, THIS IS...
IT'S HOT!
WHOA.

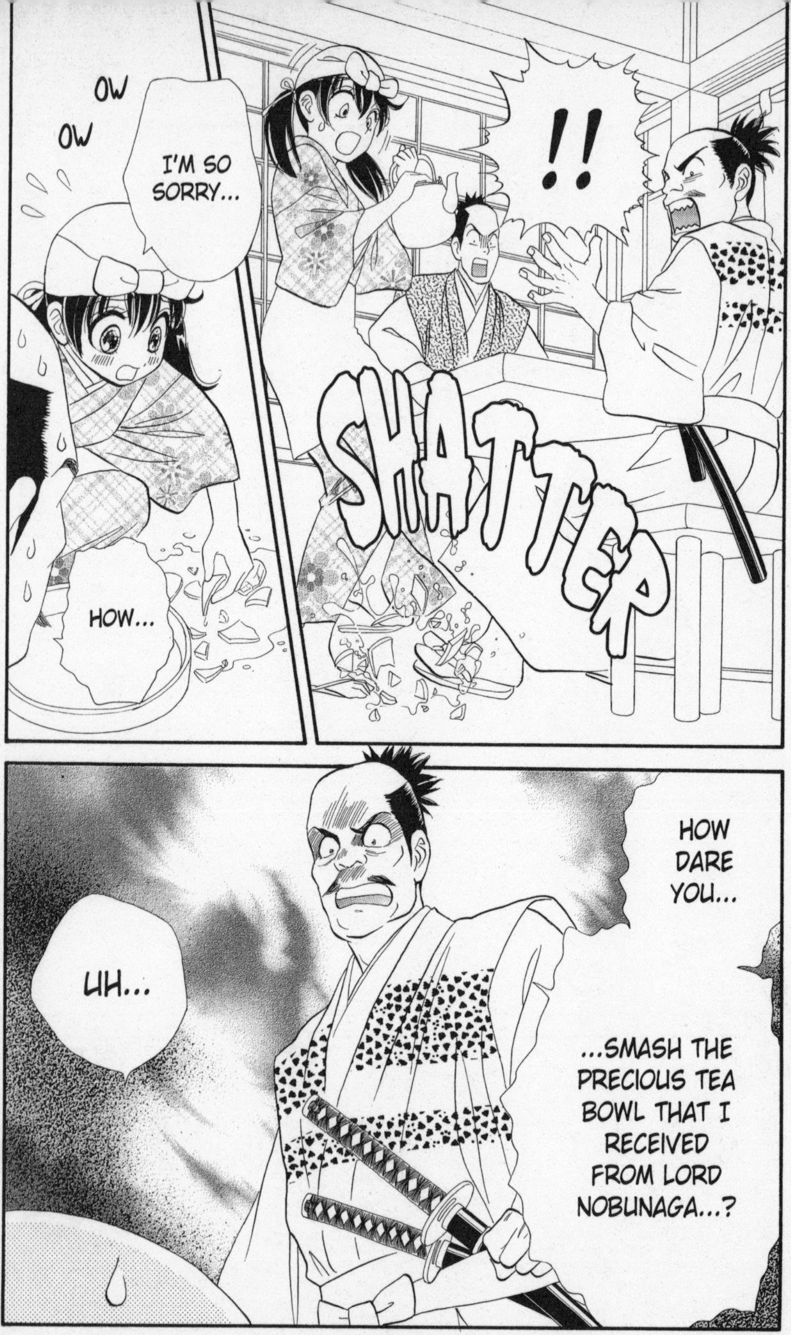
!!
SHATTER
I'M SO SORRY...
OW
OW
HOW...
HOW DARE YOU...
...SMASH THE PRECIOUS TEA BOWL THAT I RECEIVED FROM LORD NOBUNAGA...?
UH...

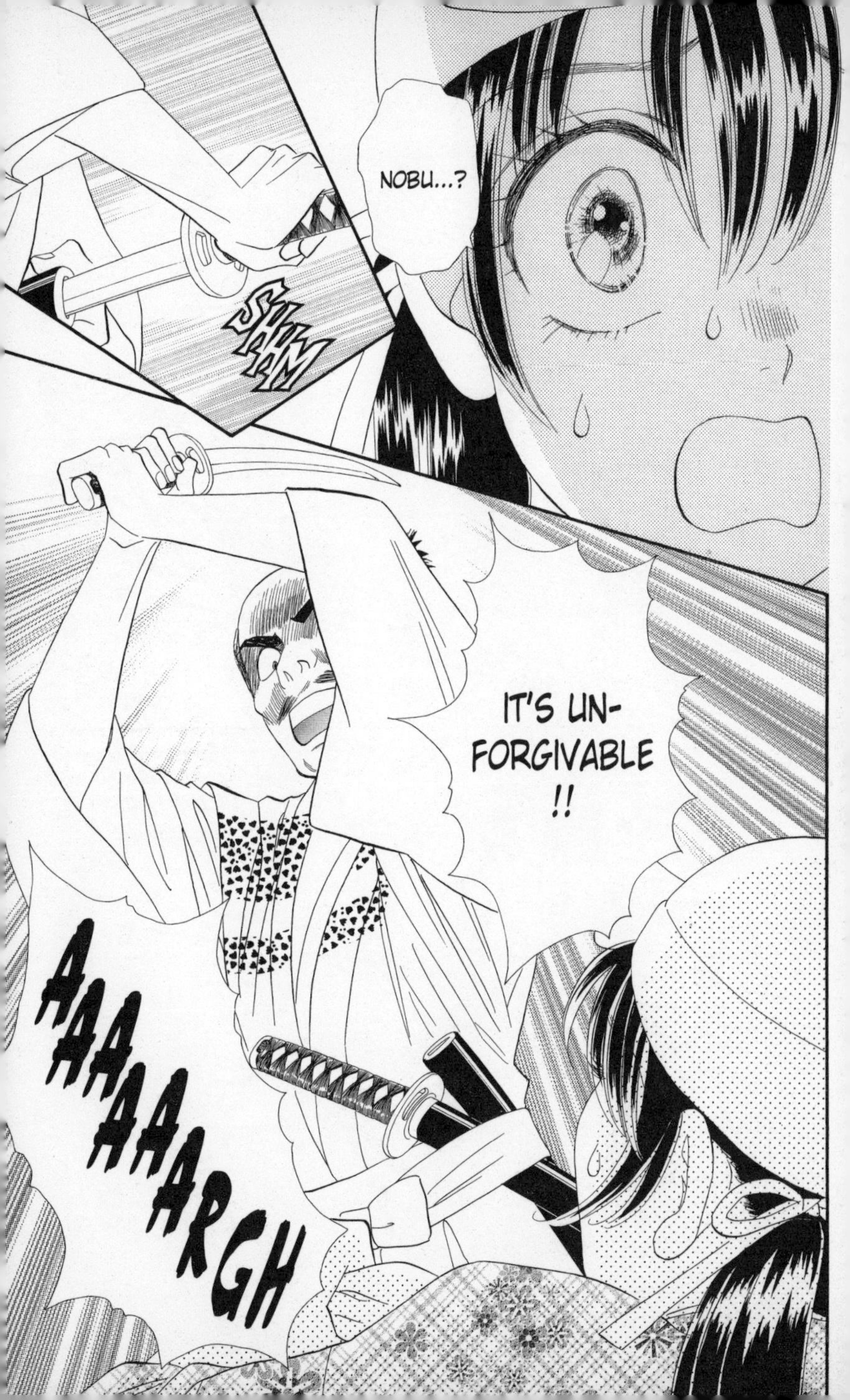
NOBU...?
SHWM
IT'S UN-
FORGIVABLE
!!
AAAAAARGH

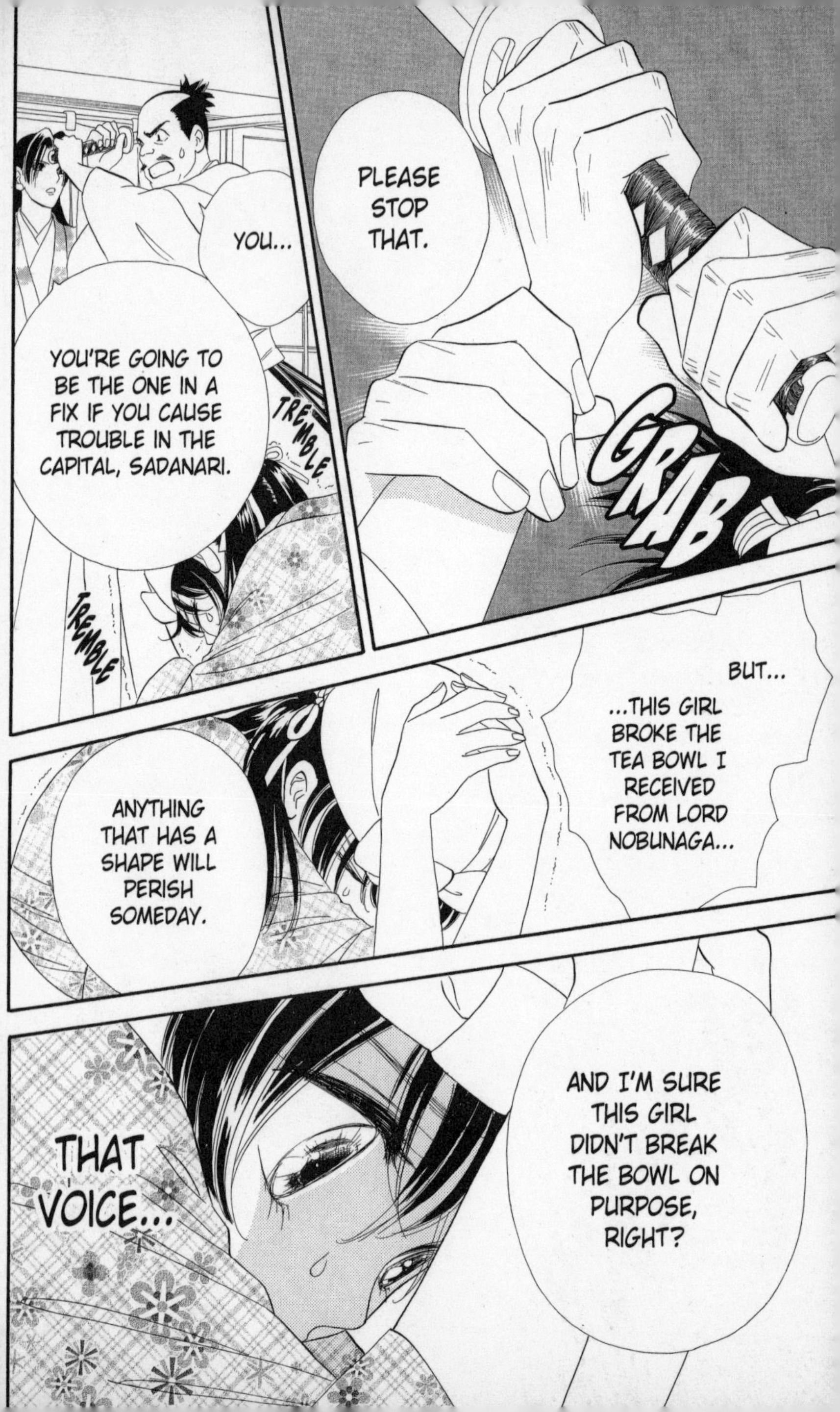
PLEASE STOP THAT.
GRAB
YOU...
YOU'RE GOING TO BE THE ONE IN A FIX IF YOU CAUSE TROUBLE IN THE CAPITAL, SADANARI.
TREMBLE
TREMBLE
BUT...
...THIS GIRL BROKE THE TEA BOWL I RECEIVED FROM LORD NOBUNAGA...
ANYTHING THAT HAS A SHAPE WILL PERISH SOMEDAY.
AND I'M SURE THIS GIRL DIDN'T BREAK THE BOWL ON PURPOSE, RIGHT?
THAT VOICE...

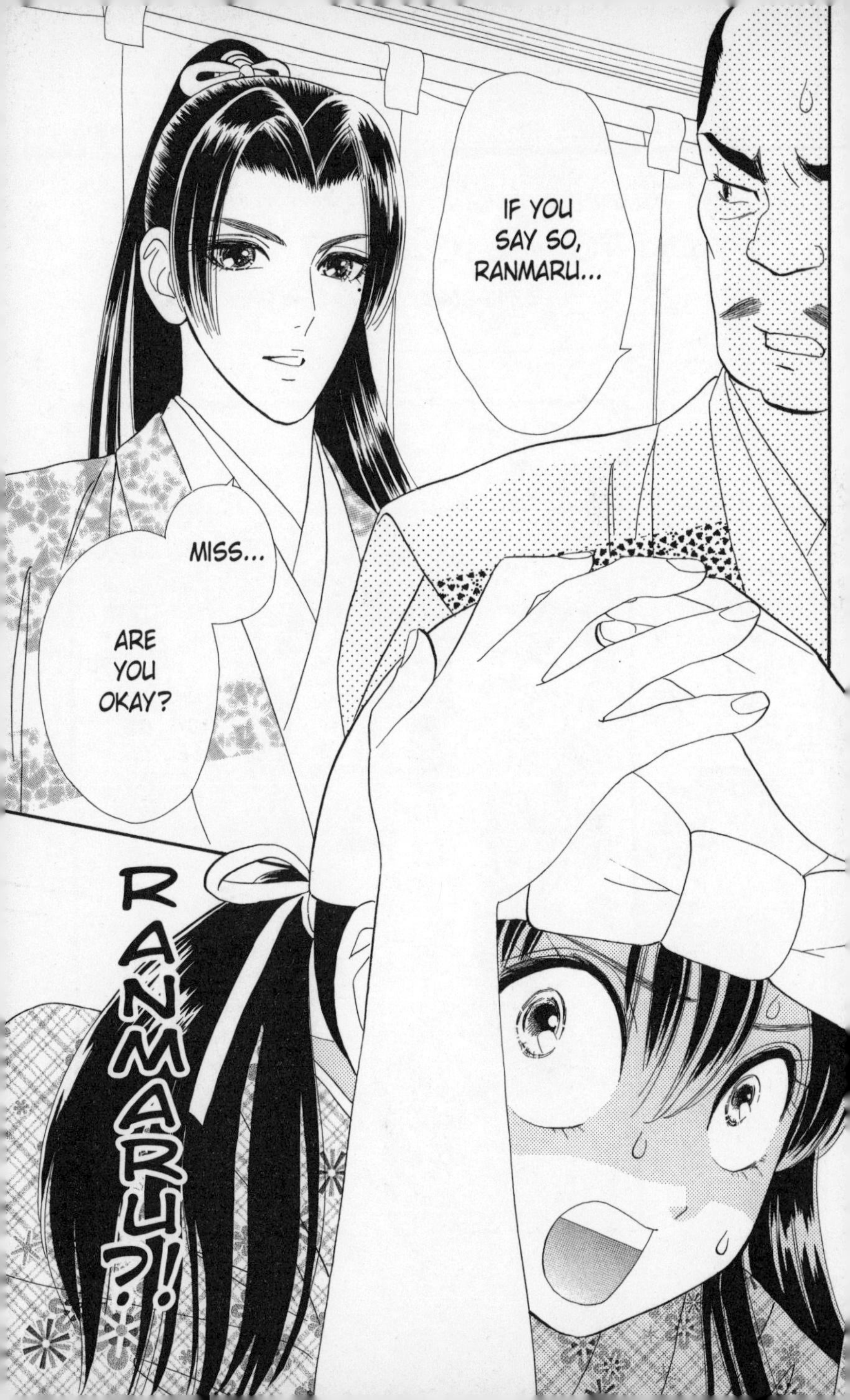
IF YOU SAY SO, RANMARU...
MISS...
ARE YOU OKAY?
RANMARU?!

TAIL OF THE MOON EXTRA: TODAY'S MISSION

"I WANT TO SEE USAGI AS A MAID!"

-AKIHABARA, YAMANASHI PREFECTURE

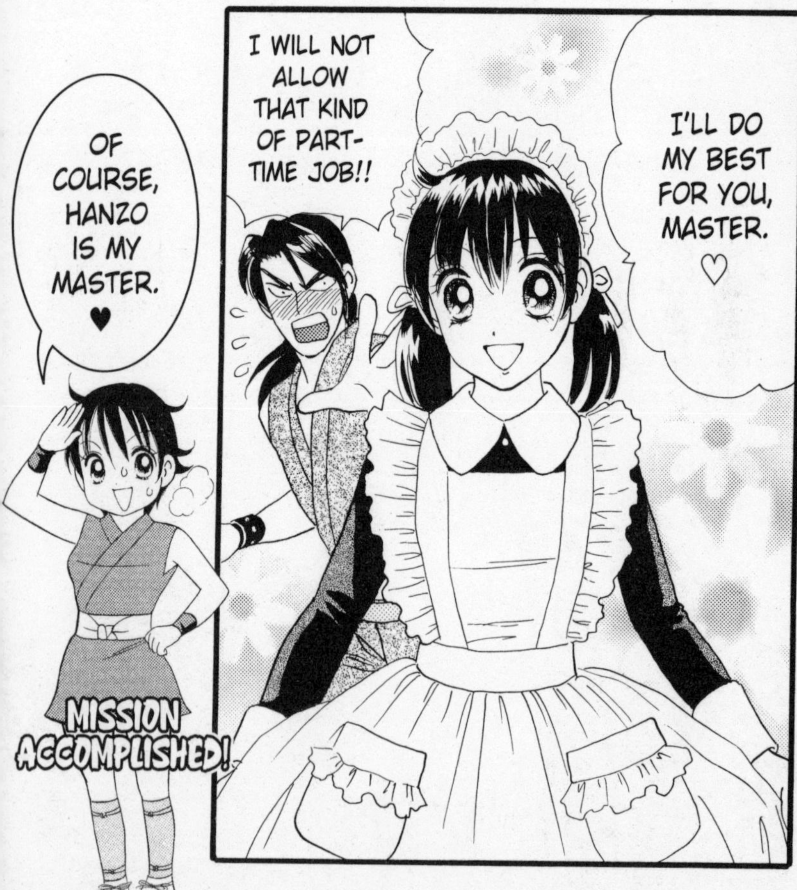
I'LL DO MY BEST FOR YOU, MASTER. ♡
I WILL NOT ALLOW THAT KIND OF PART-TIME JOB!!
OF COURSE, HANZO IS MY MASTER. ♥
MISSION ACCOMPLISHED!

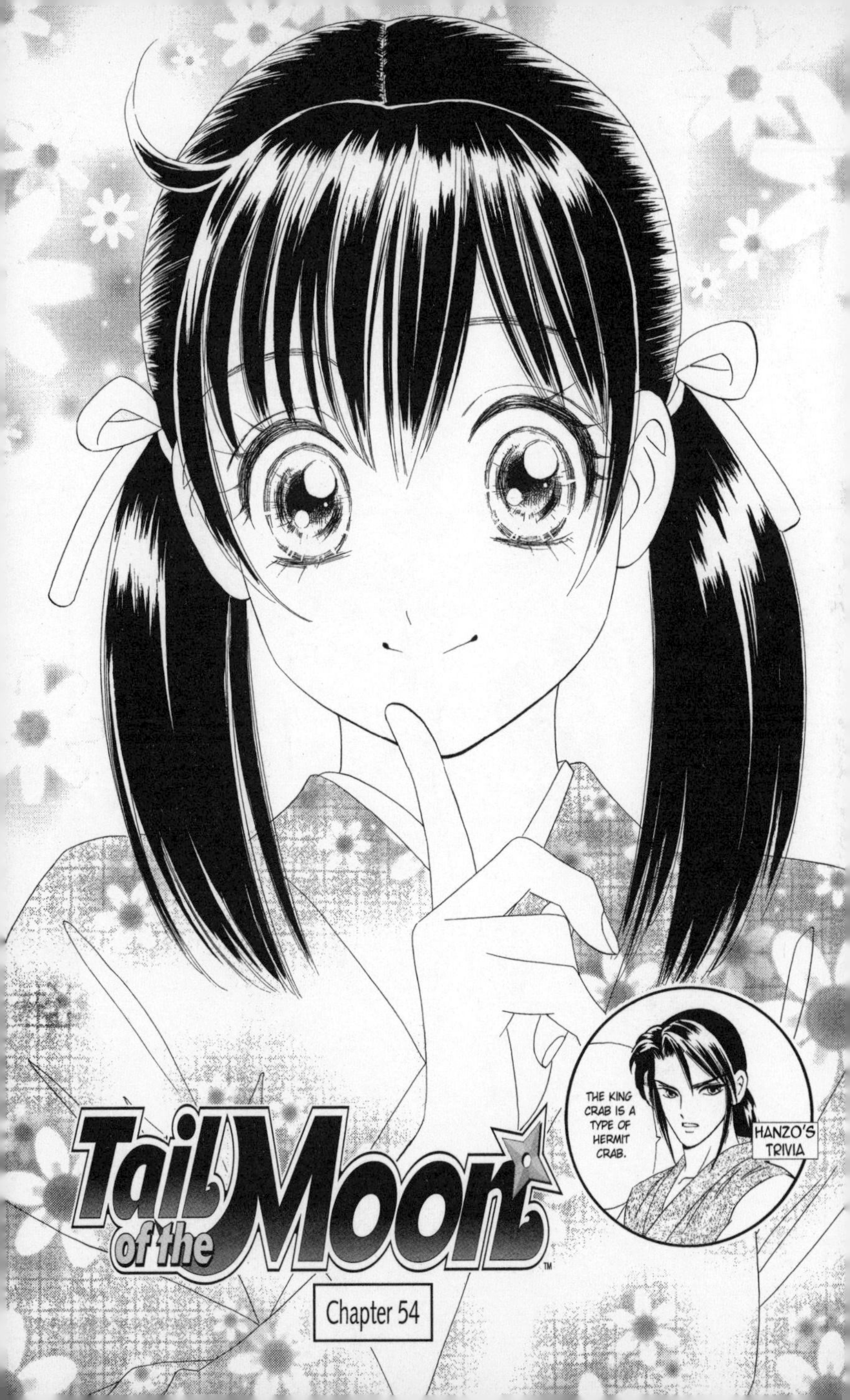
Tail of the Moon™
Chapter 54
THE KING CRAB IS A TYPE OF HERMIT CRAB.
HANZO'S TRIVIA

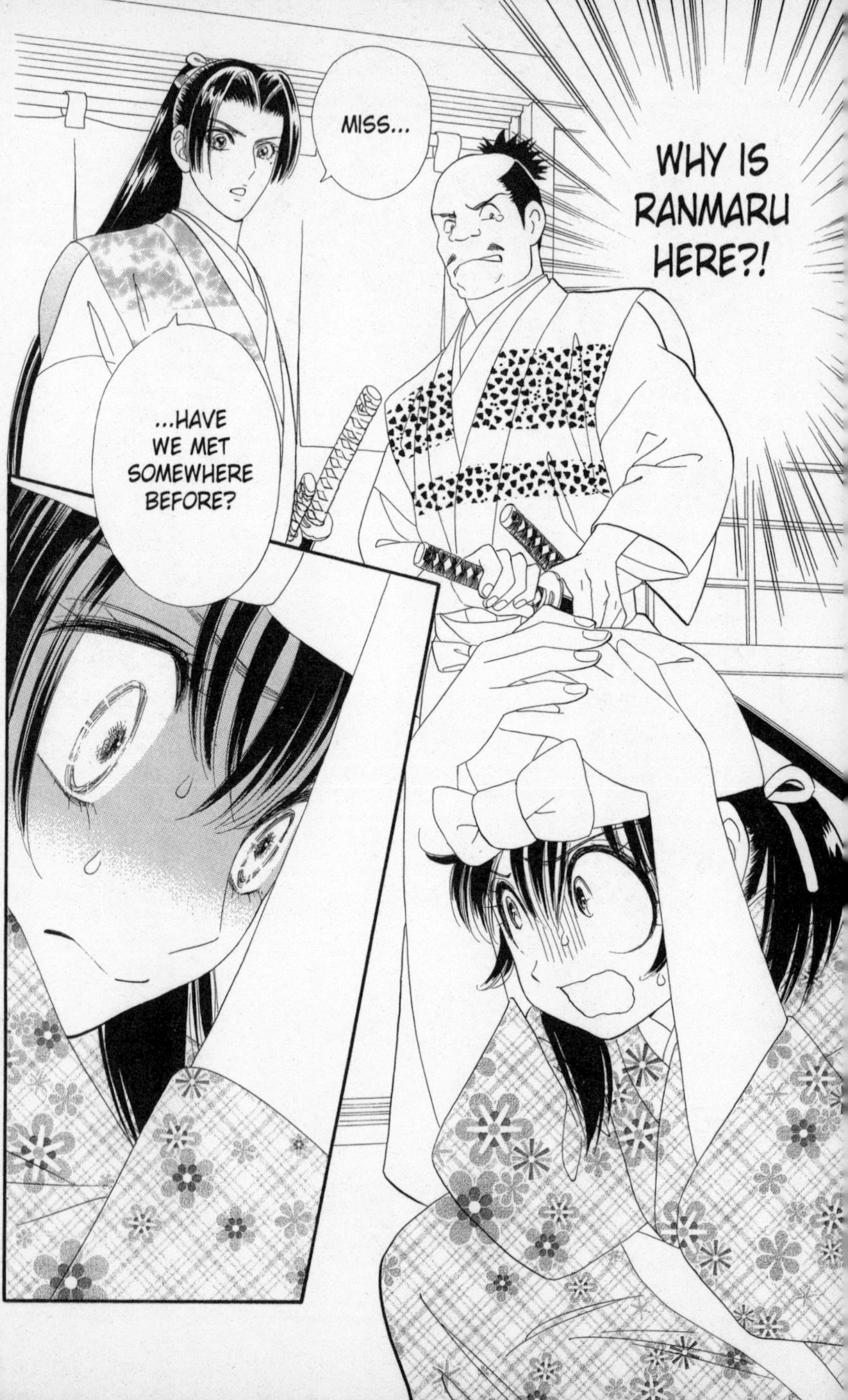
WHY IS RANMARU HERE?!
MISS...
...HAVE WE MET SOMEWHERE BEFORE?

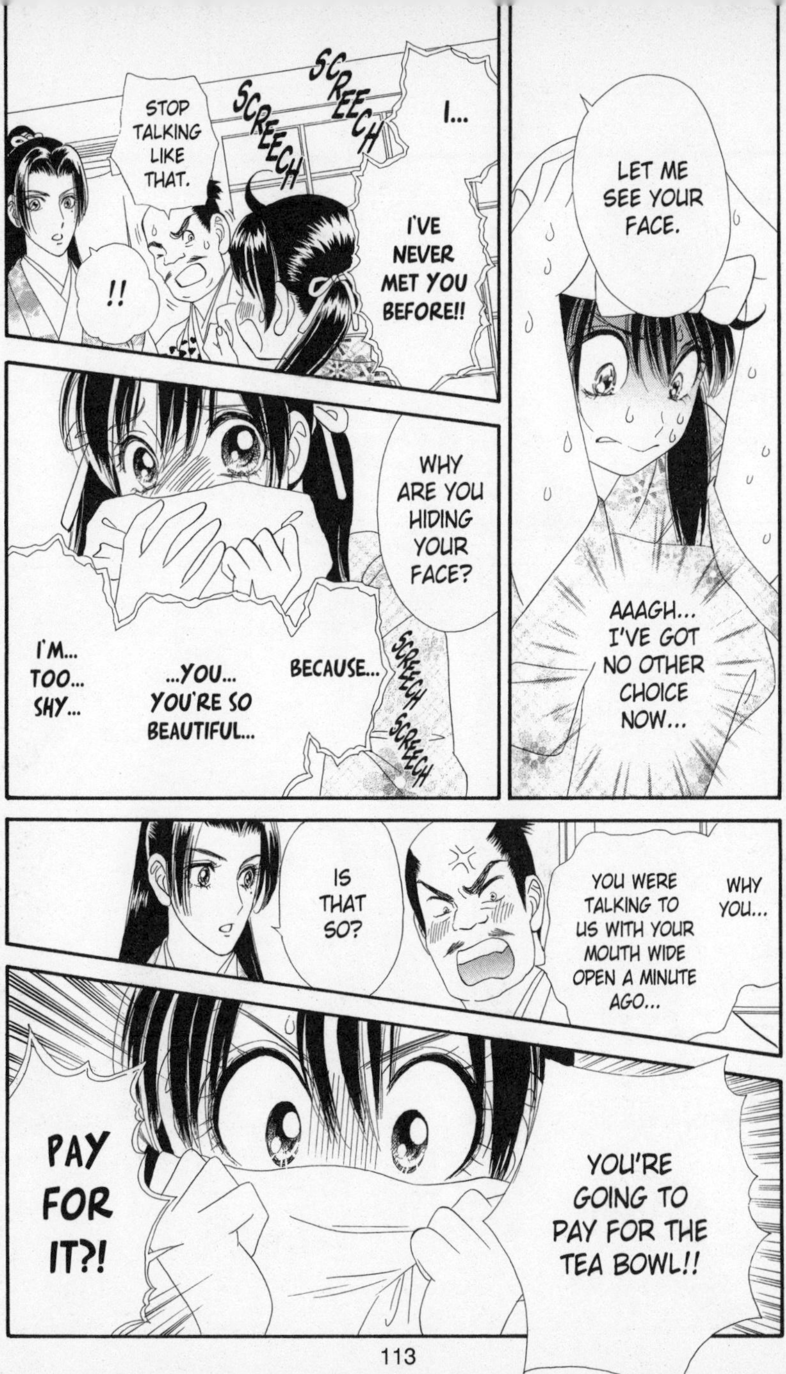
LET ME SEE YOUR FACE.
AAAGH... I'VE GOT NO OTHER CHOICE NOW...
I...
SCREECH
SCREECH
I'VE NEVER MET YOU BEFORE!!
STOP TALKING LIKE THAT.
!!
WHY ARE YOU HIDING YOUR FACE?
BECAUSE...
SCREECH
SCREECH
...YOU... YOU'RE SO BEAUTIFUL...
I'M... TOO... SHY...
WHY YOU...
YOU WERE TALKING TO US WITH YOUR MOUTH WIDE OPEN A MINUTE AGO...
IS THAT SO?
YOU'RE GOING TO PAY FOR THE TEA BOWL!!
PAY FOR IT?!

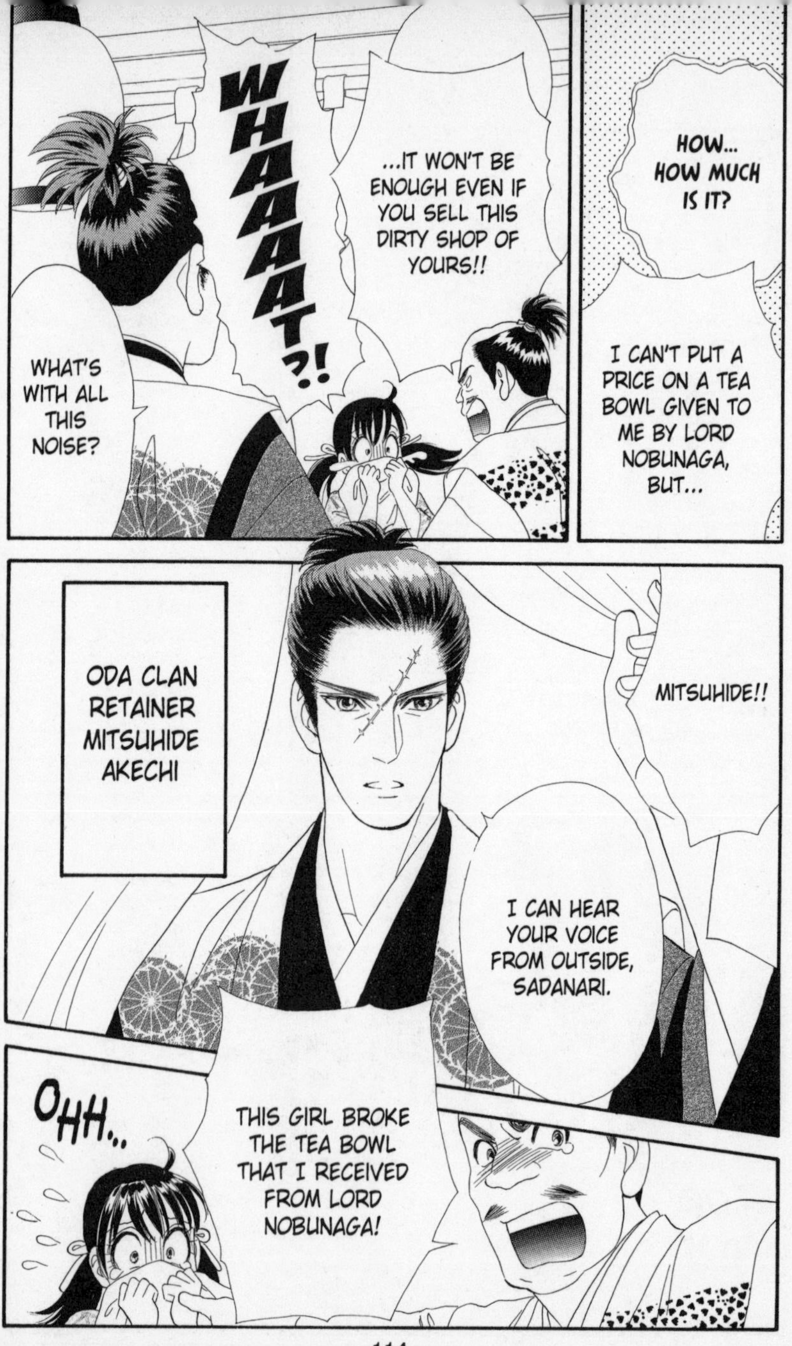
HOW... HOW MUCH IS IT?
I CAN'T PUT A PRICE ON A TEA BOWL GIVEN TO ME BY LORD NOBUNAGA, BUT...
...IT WON'T BE ENOUGH EVEN IF YOU SELL THIS DIRTY SHOP OF YOURS!!
WHAAAAT?!
WHAT'S WITH ALL THIS NOISE?
MITSUHIDE!!
ODA CLAN RETAINER MITSUHIDE AKECHI
I CAN HEAR YOUR VOICE FROM OUTSIDE, SADANARI.
THIS GIRL BROKE THE TEA BOWL THAT I RECEIVED FROM LORD NOBUNAGA!
OHH...

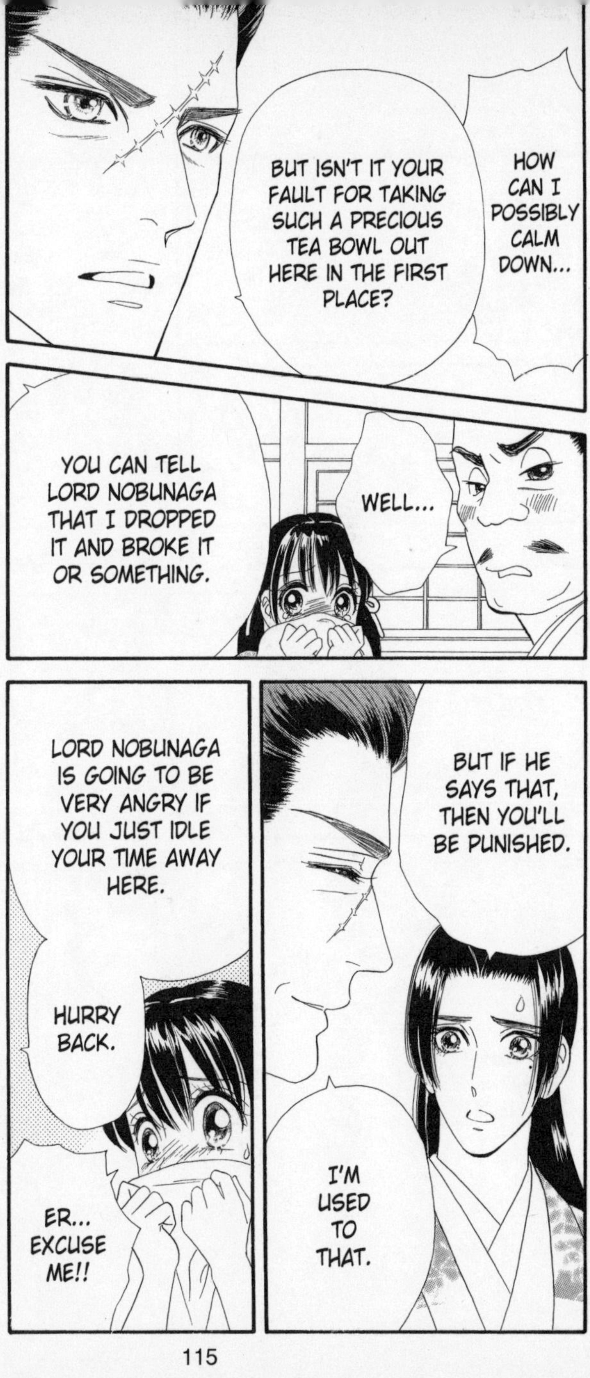
HOW CAN I POSSIBLY CALM DOWN...
BUT ISN'T IT YOUR FAULT FOR TAKING SUCH A PRECIOUS TEA BOWL OUT HERE IN THE FIRST PLACE?
WELL...
YOU CAN TELL LORD NOBUNAGA THAT I DROPPED IT AND BROKE IT OR SOMETHING.
BUT IF HE SAYS THAT, THEN YOU'LL BE PUNISHED.
I'M USED TO THAT.
LORD NOBUNAGA IS GOING TO BE VERY ANGRY IF YOU JUST IDLE YOUR TIME AWAY HERE.
HURRY BACK.
ER... EXCUSE ME!!

UE-RIN'S WAY OF THE MANGA ⑭

Back then, I had extracurricular activities, so I would swim three kilometers after school every day. I also attended cram school twice a week and was even learning calligraphy and piano during the weekends. I had to cut my sleeping time in order to draw my manga. Basically, the time I had to draw manga was very precious to me.

I hadn't made my debut yet, but I had an editor who would take a look at my manga and fix certain areas before it was submitted to a magazine. This happened to be a very stressful thing for me.

And the reason for that was...

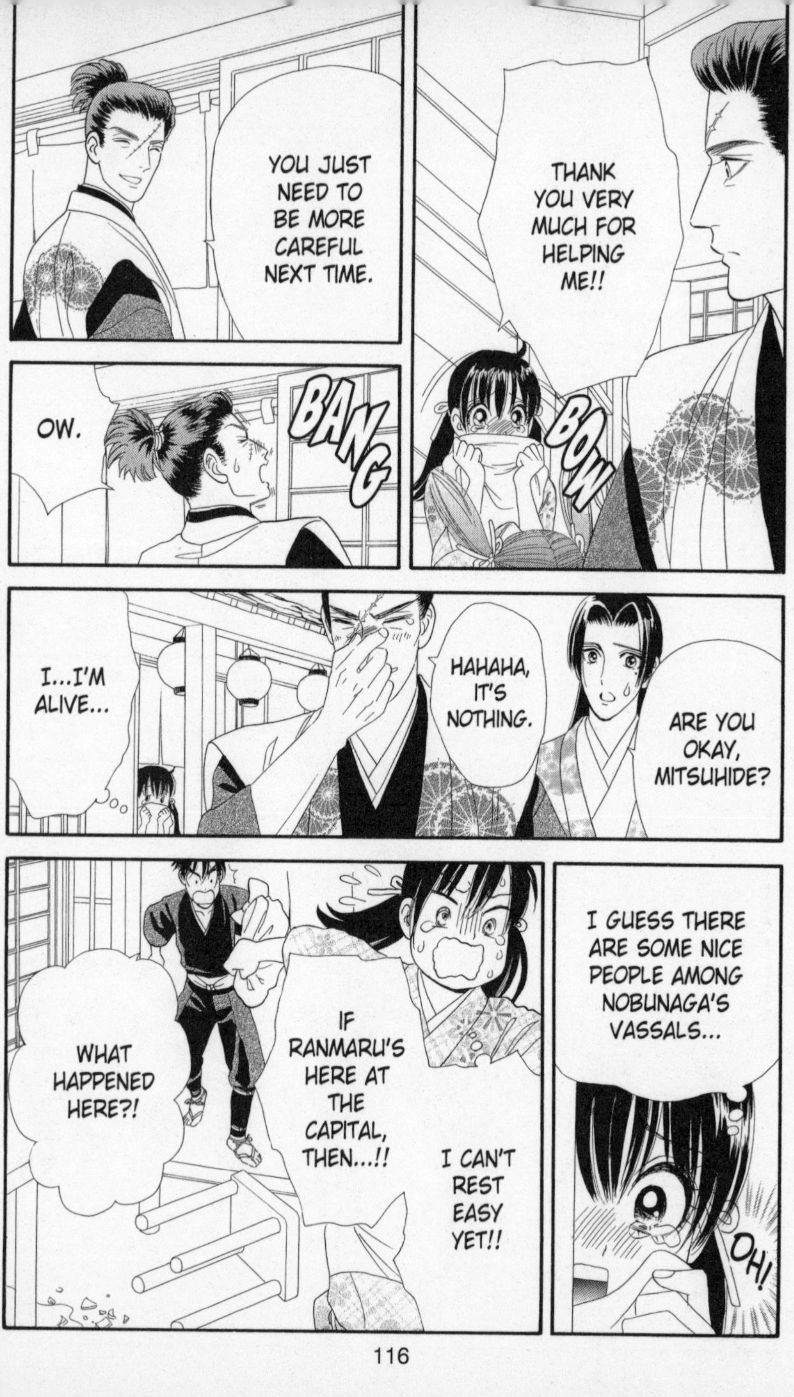
THANK YOU VERY MUCH FOR HELPING ME!!
BOW
YOU JUST NEED TO BE MORE CAREFUL NEXT TIME.
BANG
OW.
ARE YOU OKAY, MITSUHIDE?
HAHAHA, IT'S NOTHING.
I...I'M ALIVE...
I GUESS THERE ARE SOME NICE PEOPLE AMONG NOBUNAGA'S VASSALS...
OH!
I CAN'T REST EASY YET!!
IF RANMARU'S HERE AT THE CAPITAL, THEN...!!
WHAT HAPPENED HERE?!

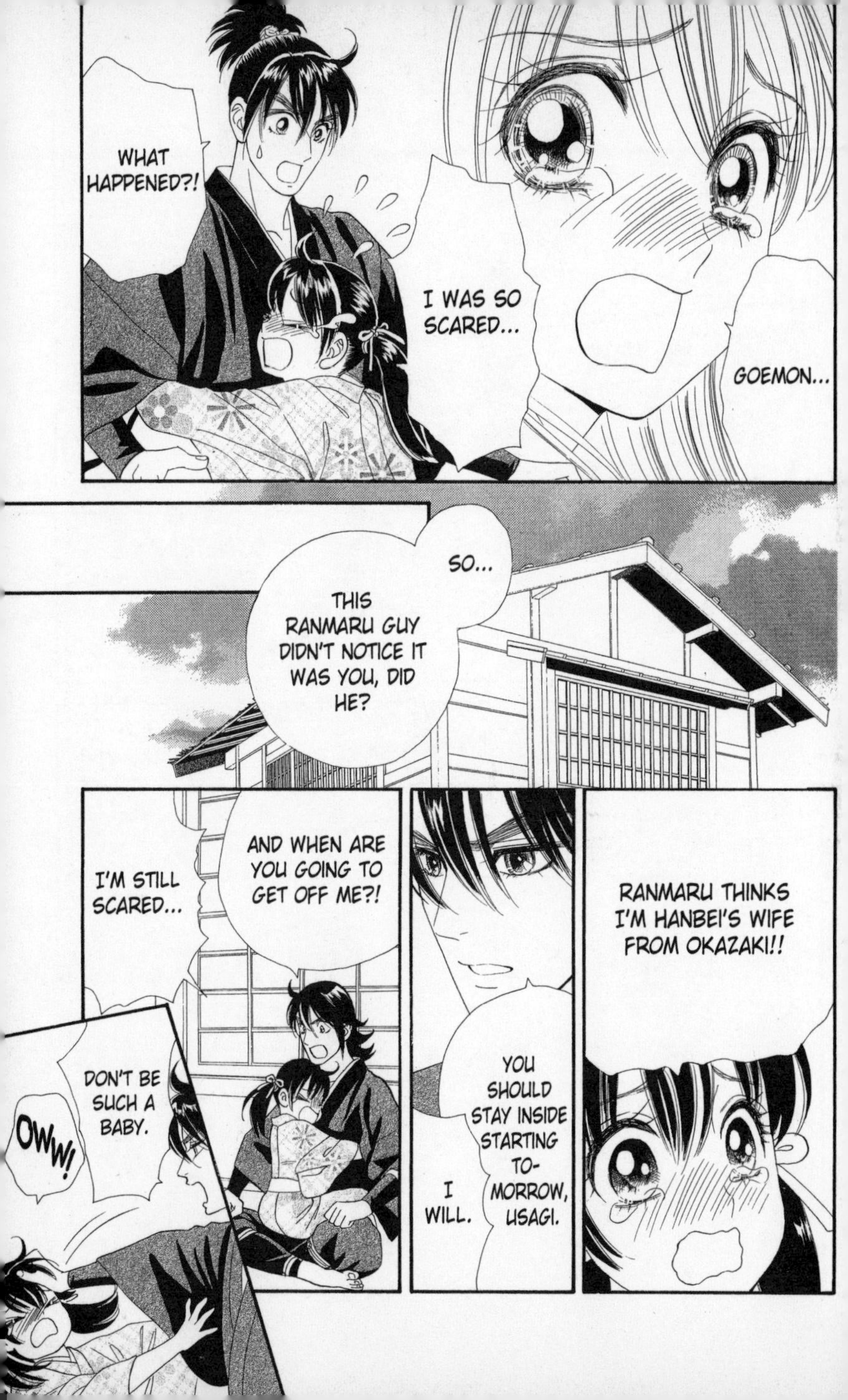
GOEMON...
I WAS SO SCARED...
WHAT HAPPENED?!
SO...
THIS RANMARU GUY DIDN'T NOTICE IT WAS YOU, DID HE?
RANMARU THINKS I'M HANBEI'S WIFE FROM OKAZAKI!!
YOU SHOULD STAY INSIDE STARTING TO-MORROW, USAGI.
I WILL.
AND WHEN ARE YOU GOING TO GET OFF ME?!
I'M STILL SCARED...
DON'T BE SUCH A BABY.
OWW!

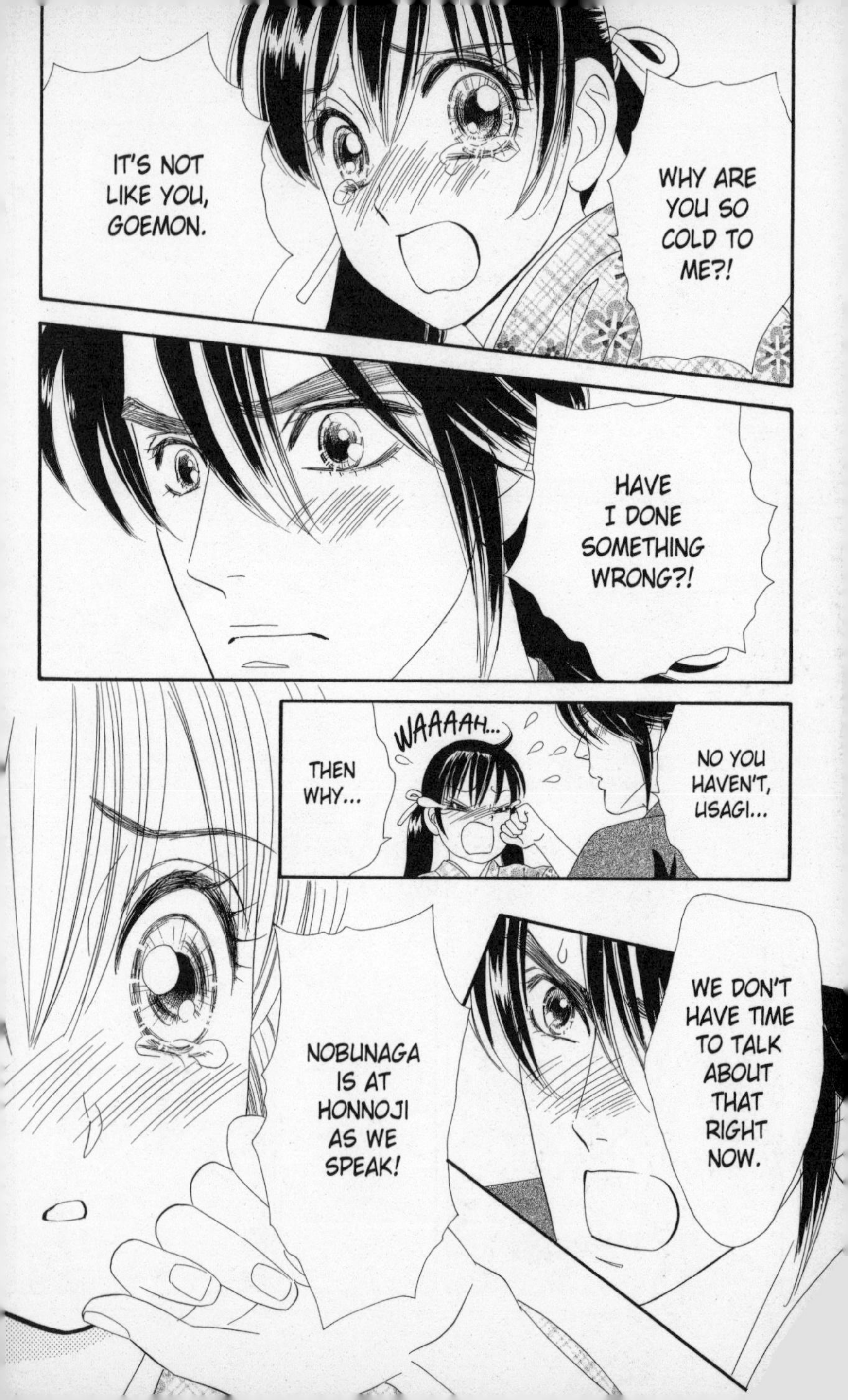
WHY ARE YOU SO COLD TO ME?!
IT'S NOT LIKE YOU, GOEMON.
HAVE I DONE SOMETHING WRONG?!
NO YOU HAVEN'T, USAGI...
WAAAAH...
THEN WHY...
WE DON'T HAVE TIME TO TALK ABOUT THAT RIGHT NOW.
NOBUNAGA IS AT HONNOJI AS WE SPEAK!

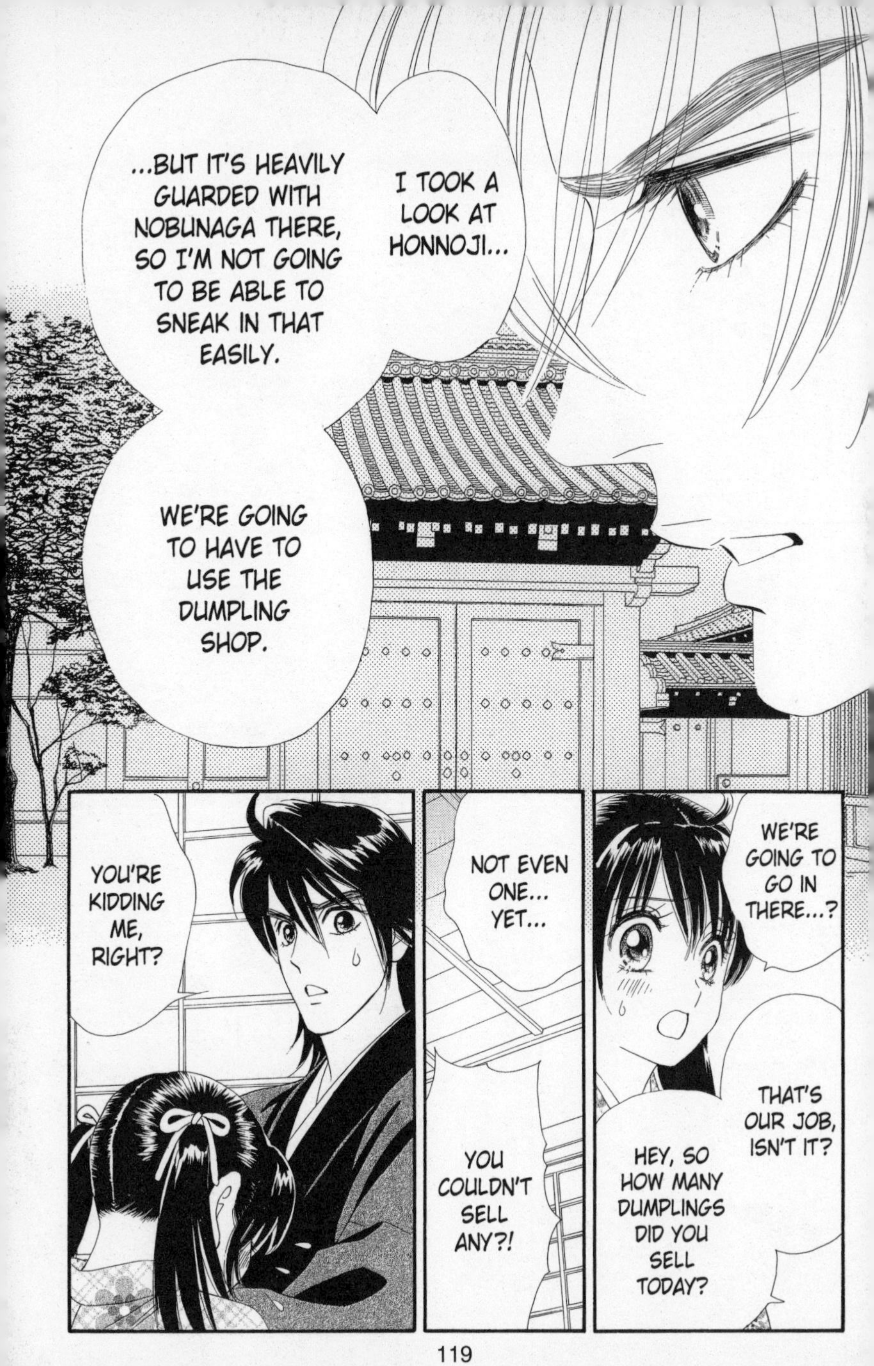
I TOOK A LOOK AT HONNOJI...
...BUT IT'S HEAVILY GUARDED WITH NOBUNAGA THERE, SO I'M NOT GOING TO BE ABLE TO SNEAK IN THAT EASILY.
WE'RE GOING TO HAVE TO USE THE DUMPLING SHOP.
WE'RE GOING TO GO IN THERE...?
THAT'S OUR JOB, ISN'T IT?
HEY, SO HOW MANY DUMPLINGS DID YOU SELL TODAY?
NOT EVEN ONE... YET...
YOU COULDN'T SELL ANY?!
YOU'RE KIDDING ME, RIGHT?

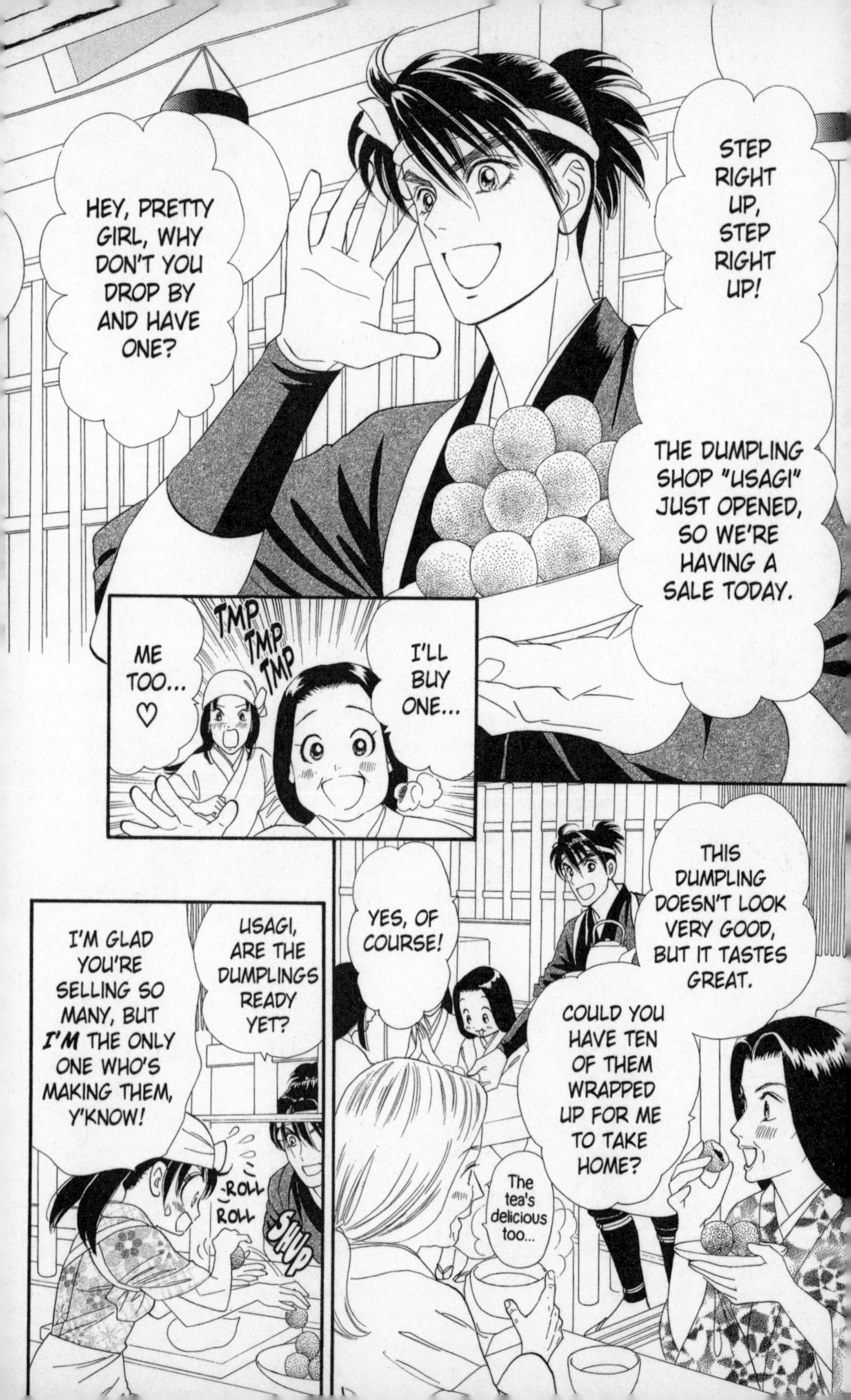
STEP RIGHT UP, STEP RIGHT UP!
HEY, PRETTY GIRL, WHY DON'T YOU DROP BY AND HAVE ONE?
THE DUMPLING SHOP "USAGI" JUST OPENED, SO WE'RE HAVING A SALE TODAY.
I'LL BUY ONE...
TMP TMP TMP
ME TOO... ♡
THIS DUMPLING DOESN'T LOOK VERY GOOD, BUT IT TASTES GREAT.
YES, OF COURSE!
COULD YOU HAVE TEN OF THEM WRAPPED UP FOR ME TO TAKE HOME?
The tea's delicious too...
USAGI, ARE THE DUMPLINGS READY YET?
I'M GLAD YOU'RE SELLING SO MANY, BUT *I'M* THE ONLY ONE WHO'S MAKING THEM, Y'KNOW!
ROLL ROLL
SHUP

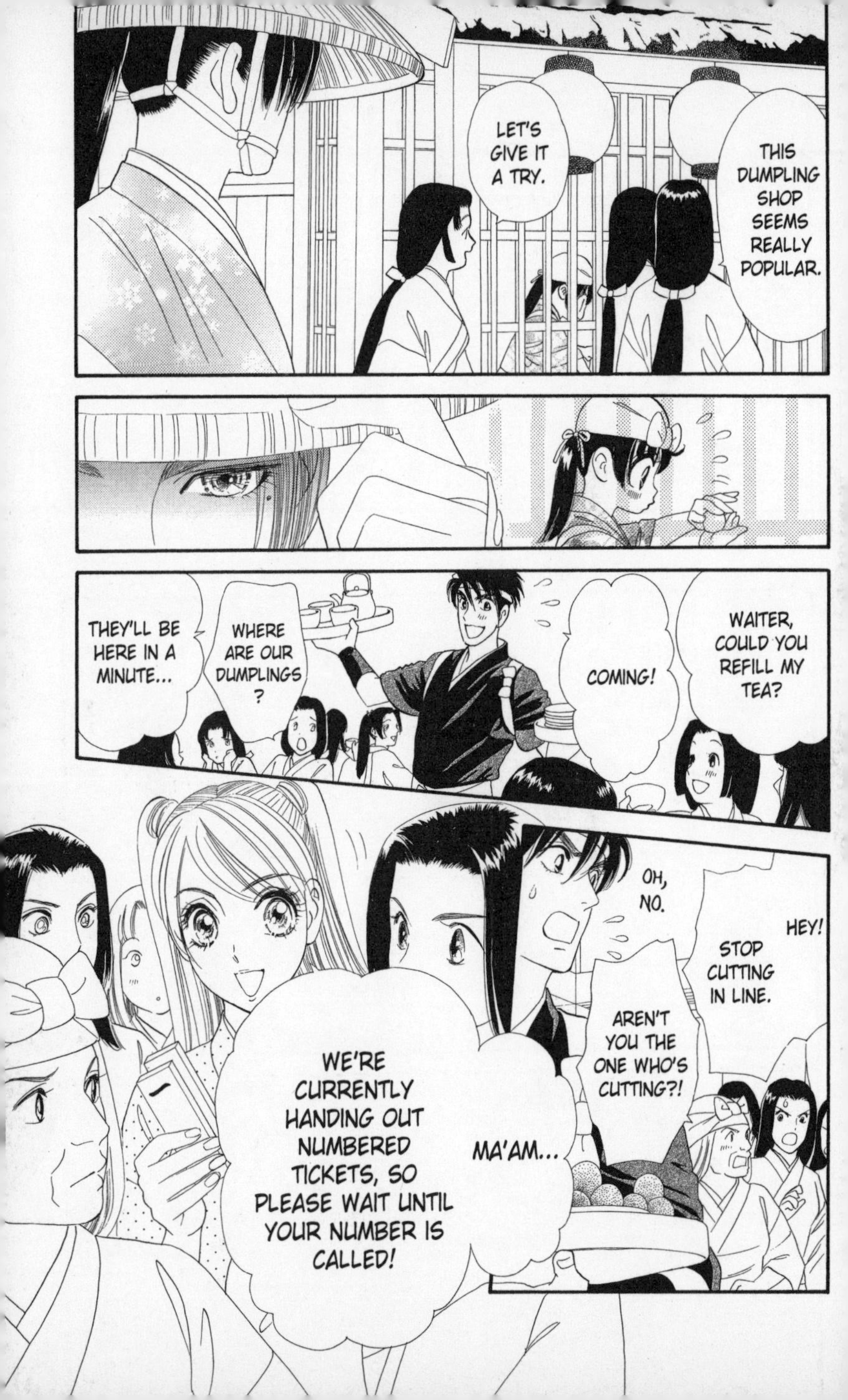
THIS DUMPLING SHOP SEEMS REALLY POPULAR.
LET'S GIVE IT A TRY.
WAITER, COULD YOU REFILL MY TEA?
COMING!
WHERE ARE OUR DUMPLINGS?
THEY'LL BE HERE IN A MINUTE...
HEY!
STOP CUTTING IN LINE.
OH, NO.
AREN'T YOU THE ONE WHO'S CUTTING?!
MA'AM...
WE'RE CURRENTLY HANDING OUT NUMBERED TICKETS, SO PLEASE WAIT UNTIL YOUR NUMBER IS CALLED!

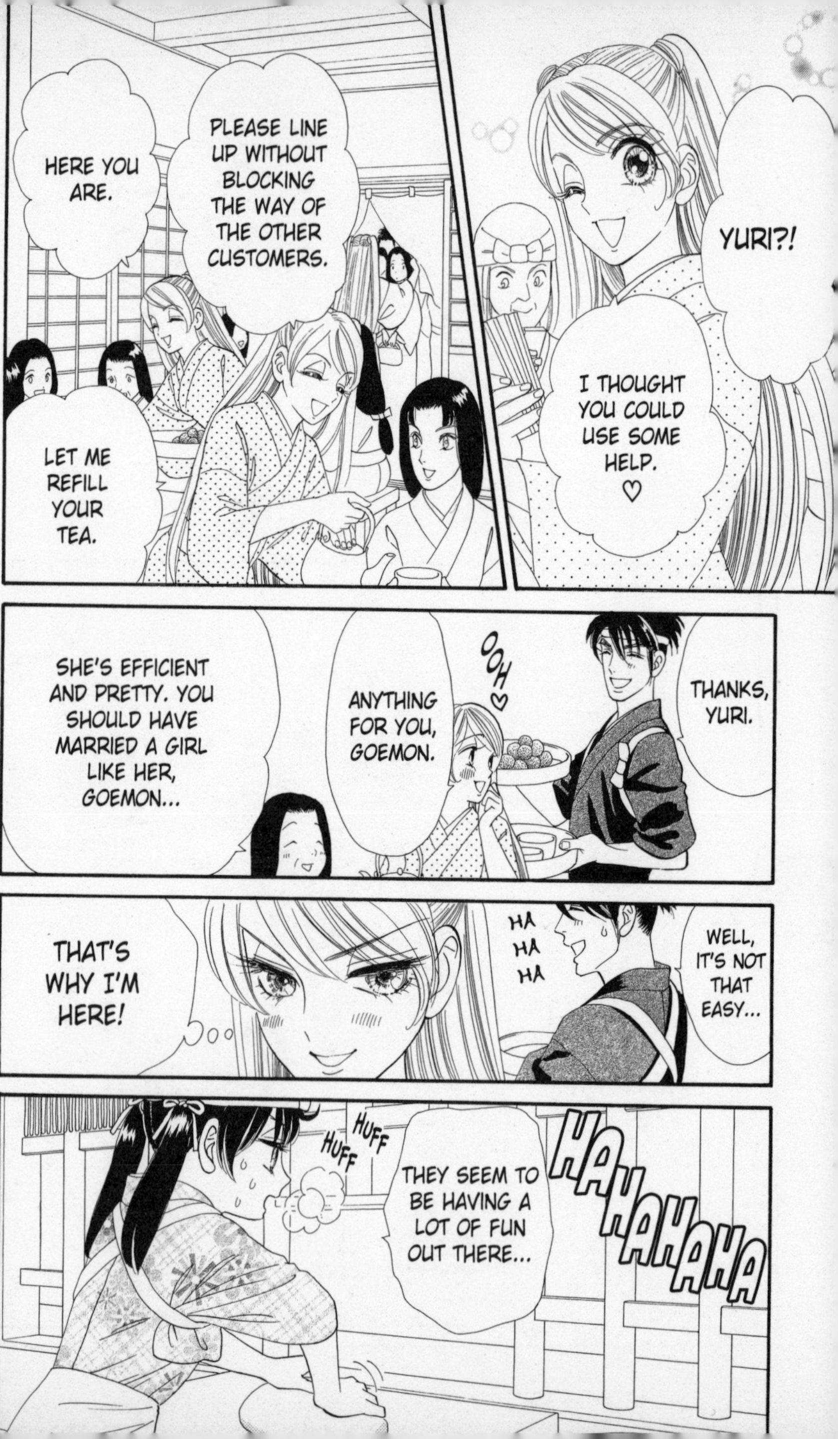
YURI?!
I THOUGHT YOU COULD USE SOME HELP. ♡
PLEASE LINE UP WITHOUT BLOCKING THE WAY OF THE OTHER CUSTOMERS.
HERE YOU ARE.
LET ME REFILL YOUR TEA.
THANKS, YURI.
OOH ♡
ANYTHING FOR YOU, GOEMON.
SHE'S EFFICIENT AND PRETTY. YOU SHOULD HAVE MARRIED A GIRL LIKE HER, GOEMON...
WELL, IT'S NOT THAT EASY...
HA HA HA
THAT'S WHY I'M HERE!
HAHAHAHA
THEY SEEM TO BE HAVING A LOT OF FUN OUT THERE...
HUFF HUFF

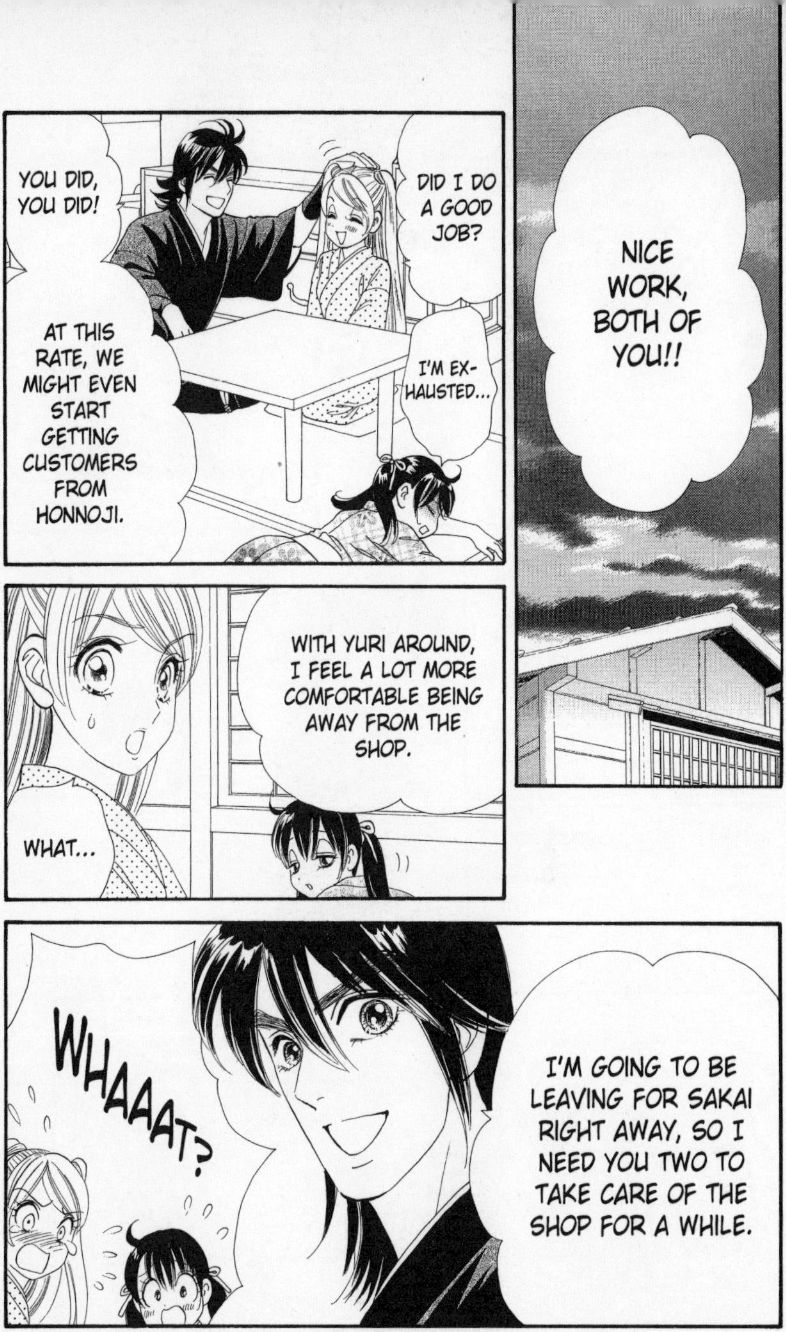
NICE WORK, BOTH OF YOU!!
DID I DO A GOOD JOB?
YOU DID, YOU DID!
I'M EX-HAUSTED...
AT THIS RATE, WE MIGHT EVEN START GETTING CUSTOMERS FROM HONNOJI.
WITH YURI AROUND, I FEEL A LOT MORE COMFORTABLE BEING AWAY FROM THE SHOP.
WHAT...
I'M GOING TO BE LEAVING FOR SAKAI RIGHT AWAY, SO I NEED YOU TWO TO TAKE CARE OF THE SHOP FOR A WHILE.
WHAAAAT?

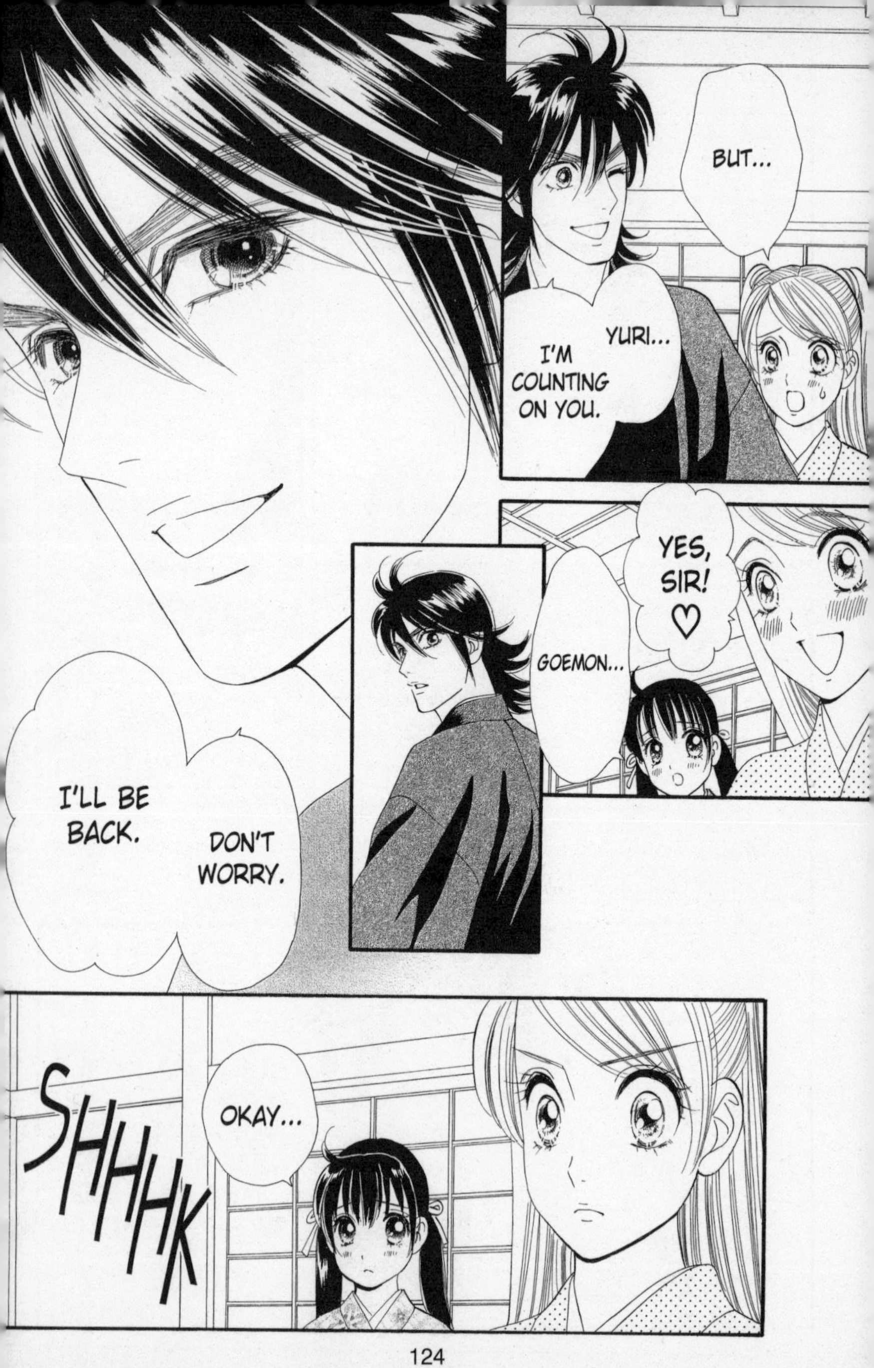
BUT...
YURI... I'M COUNTING ON YOU.
YES, SIR! ♡
GOEMON...
DON'T WORRY.
I'LL BE BACK.
OKAY...
SHHHK

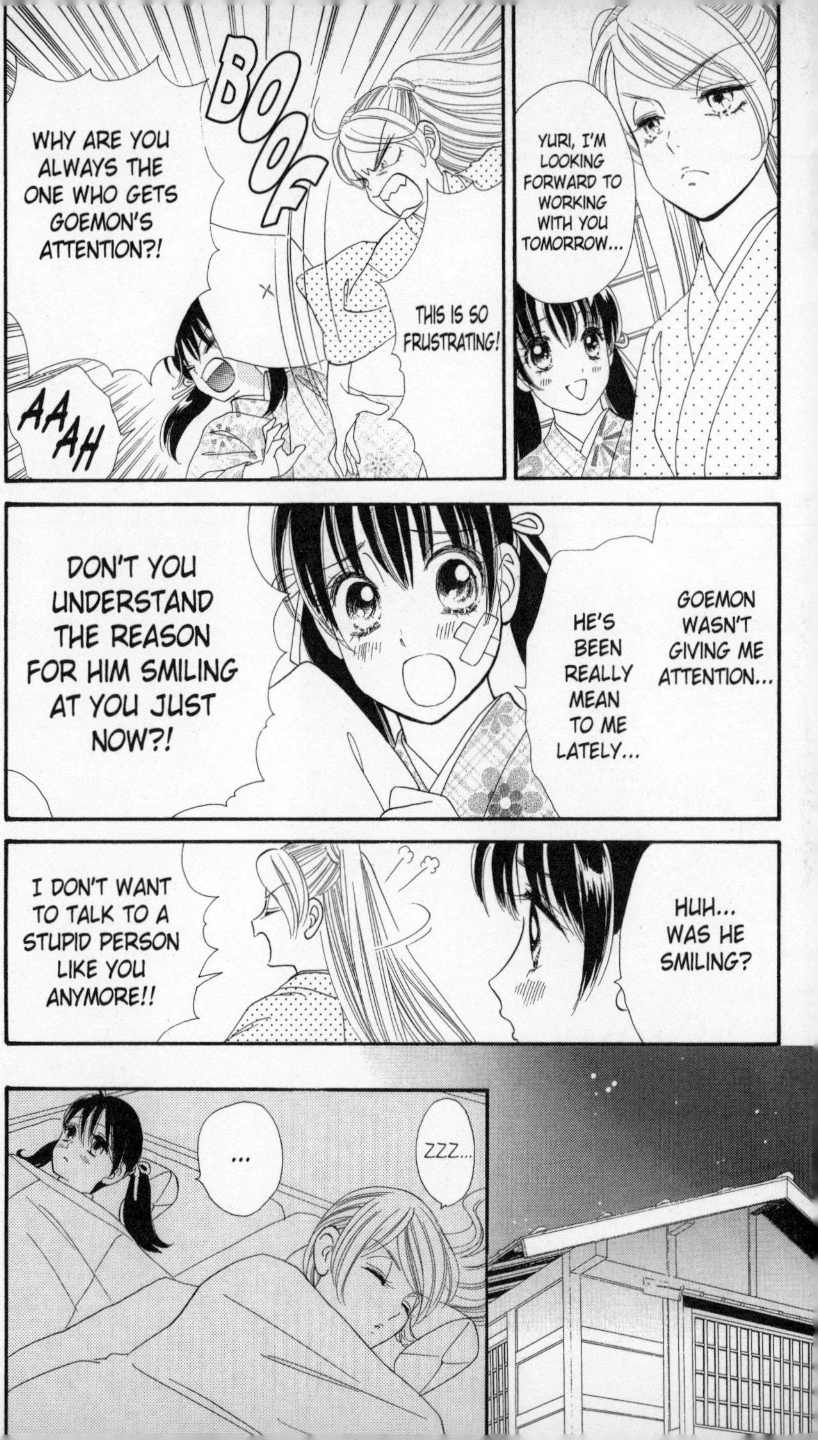
YURI, I'M LOOKING FORWARD TO WORKING WITH YOU TOMORROW...
BOOF
WHY ARE YOU ALWAYS THE ONE WHO GETS GOEMON'S ATTENTION?!
THIS IS SO FRUSTRATING!
AAAH
GOEMON WASN'T GIVING ME ATTENTION...
HE'S BEEN REALLY MEAN TO ME LATELY...
DON'T YOU UNDERSTAND THE REASON FOR HIM SMILING AT YOU JUST NOW?!
HUH... WAS HE SMILING?
I DON'T WANT TO TALK TO A STUPID PERSON LIKE YOU ANYMORE!!
ZZZ...
...

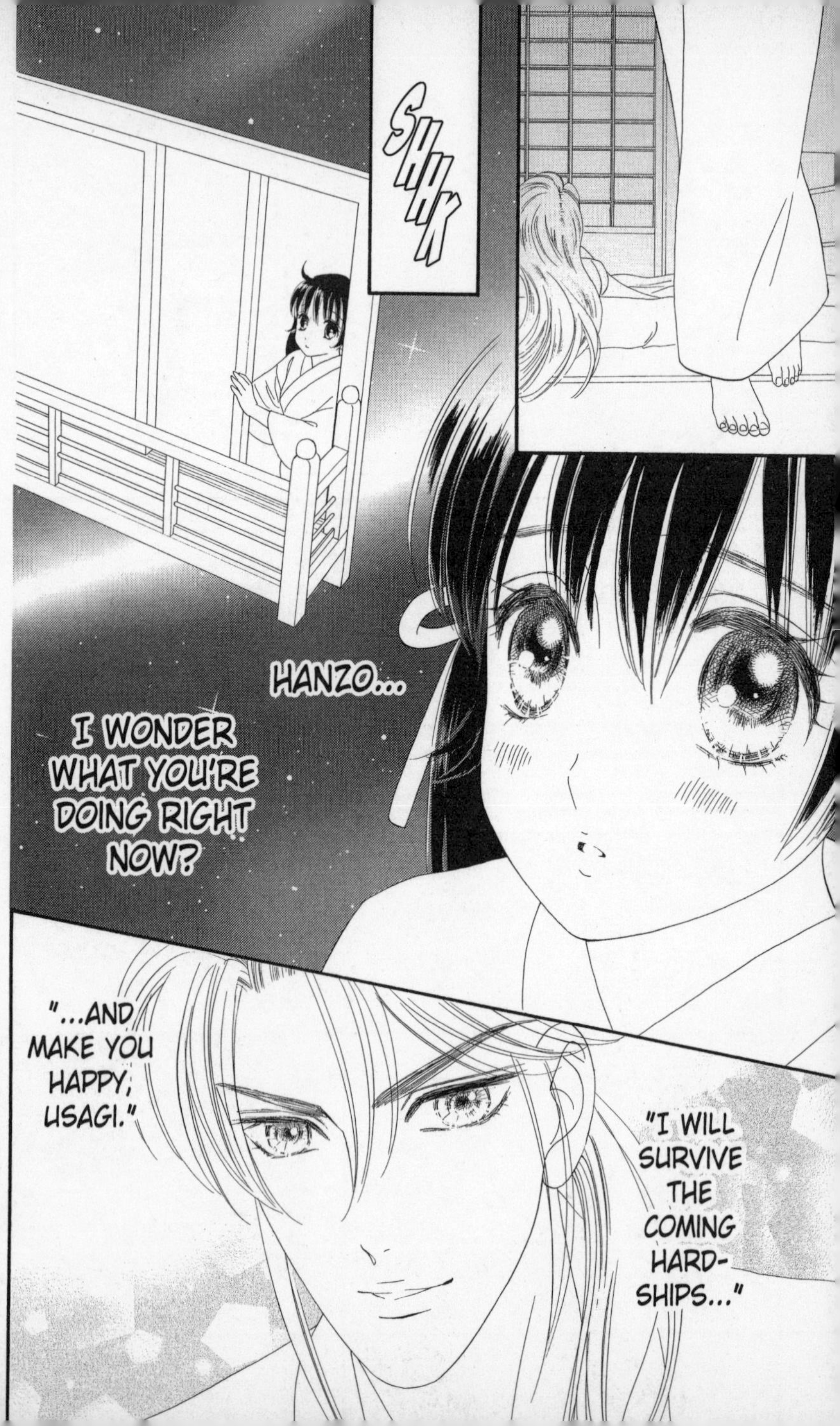
SHHK
HANZO...
I WONDER WHAT YOU'RE DOING RIGHT NOW?
"I WILL SURVIVE THE COMING HARD-SHIPS..."
"...AND MAKE YOU HAPPY, USAGI."

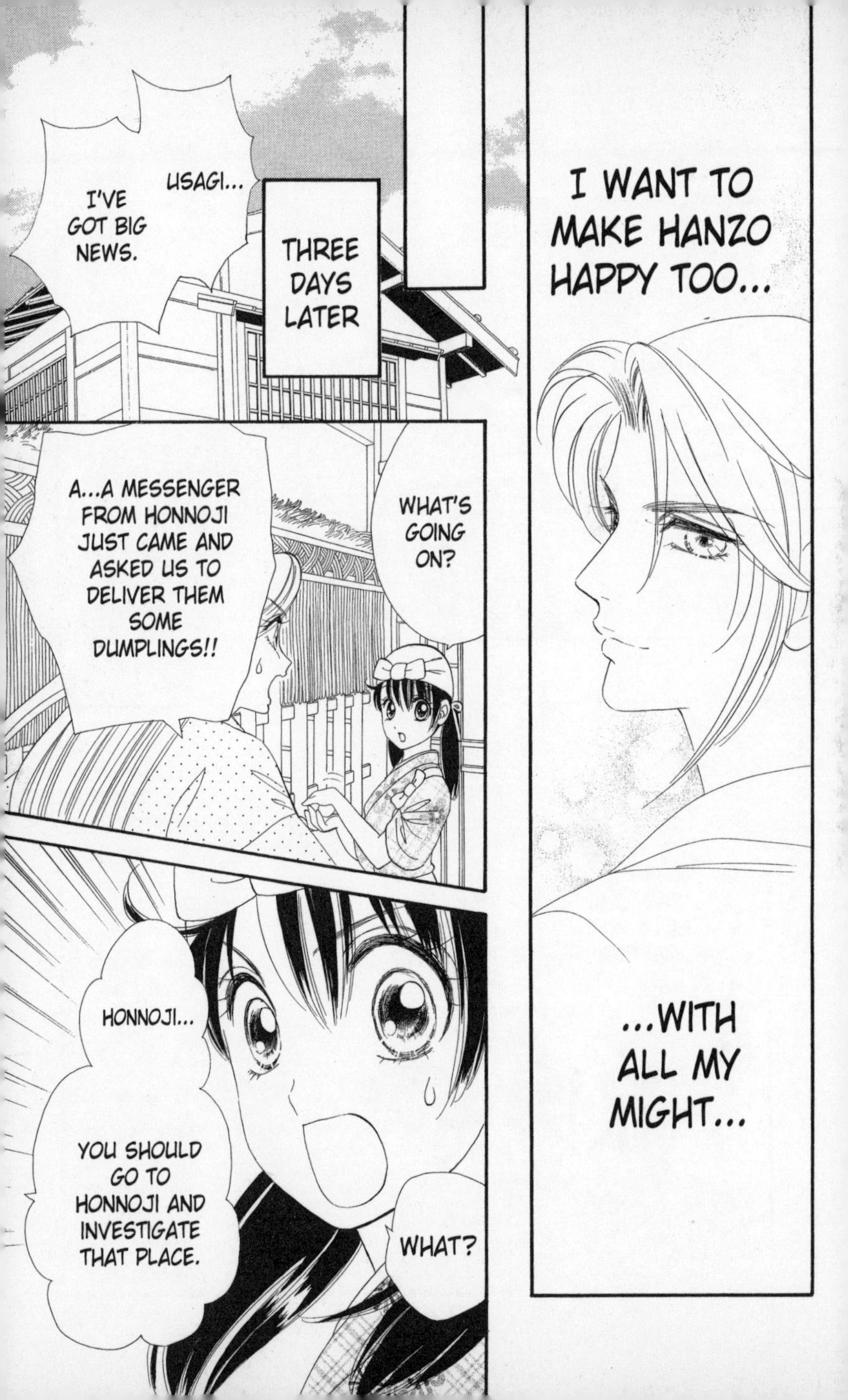
I WANT TO MAKE HANZO HAPPY TOO...
...WITH ALL MY MIGHT...
THREE DAYS LATER
USAGI...
I'VE GOT BIG NEWS.
WHAT'S GOING ON?
A...A MESSENGER FROM HONNOJI JUST CAME AND ASKED US TO DELIVER THEM SOME DUMPLINGS!!
HONNOJI...
WHAT?
YOU SHOULD GO TO HONNOJI AND INVESTIGATE THAT PLACE.

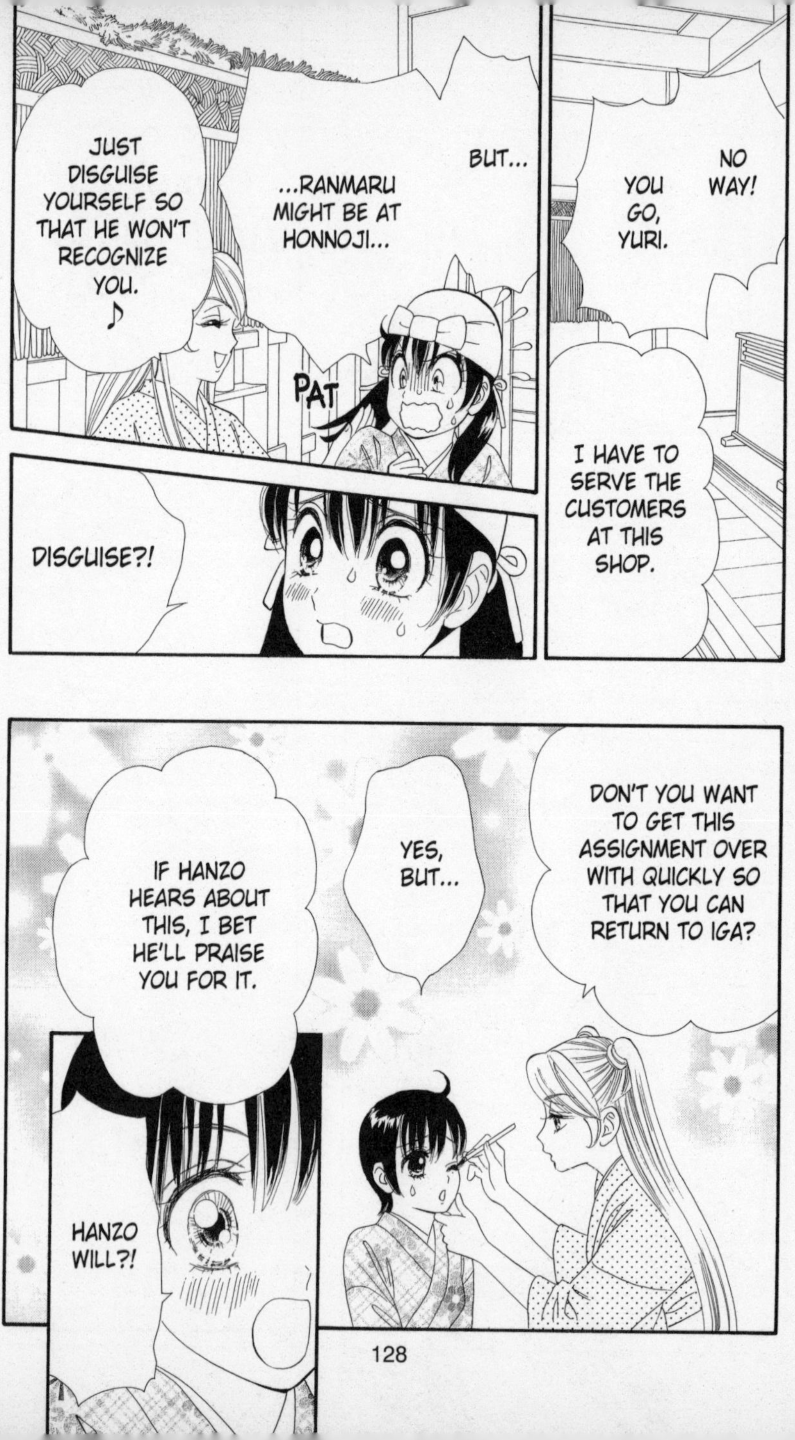
NO WAY!
YOU GO, YURI.
I HAVE TO SERVE THE CUSTOMERS AT THIS SHOP.
BUT...
...RANMARU MIGHT BE AT HONNOJI...
PAT
JUST DISGUISE YOURSELF SO THAT HE WON'T RECOGNIZE YOU. ♪
DISGUISE?!
DON'T YOU WANT TO GET THIS ASSIGNMENT OVER WITH QUICKLY SO THAT YOU CAN RETURN TO IGA?
YES, BUT...
IF HANZO HEARS ABOUT THIS, I BET HE'LL PRAISE YOU FOR IT.
HANZO WILL?!

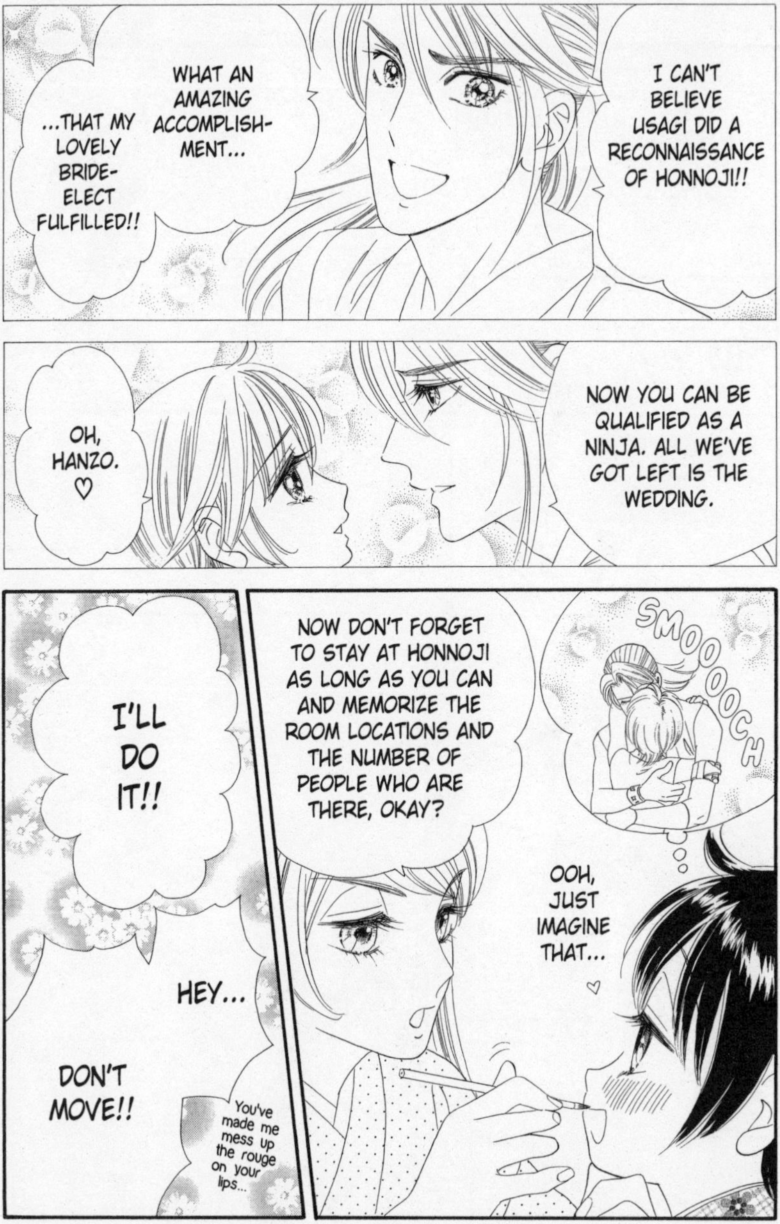
I CAN'T BELIEVE USAGI DID A RECONNAISSANCE OF HONNOJI!!
WHAT AN AMAZING ACCOMPLISHMENT...
...THAT MY LOVELY BRIDE-ELECT FULFILLED!!
NOW YOU CAN BE QUALIFIED AS A NINJA. ALL WE'VE GOT LEFT IS THE WEDDING.
OH, HANZO. ♡
SMOOOOOCH
NOW DON'T FORGET TO STAY AT HONNOJI AS LONG AS YOU CAN AND MEMORIZE THE ROOM LOCATIONS AND THE NUMBER OF PEOPLE WHO ARE THERE, OKAY?
OOH, JUST IMAGINE THAT... ♡
I'LL DO IT!!
HEY...
DON'T MOVE!!
You've made me mess up the rouge on your lips...

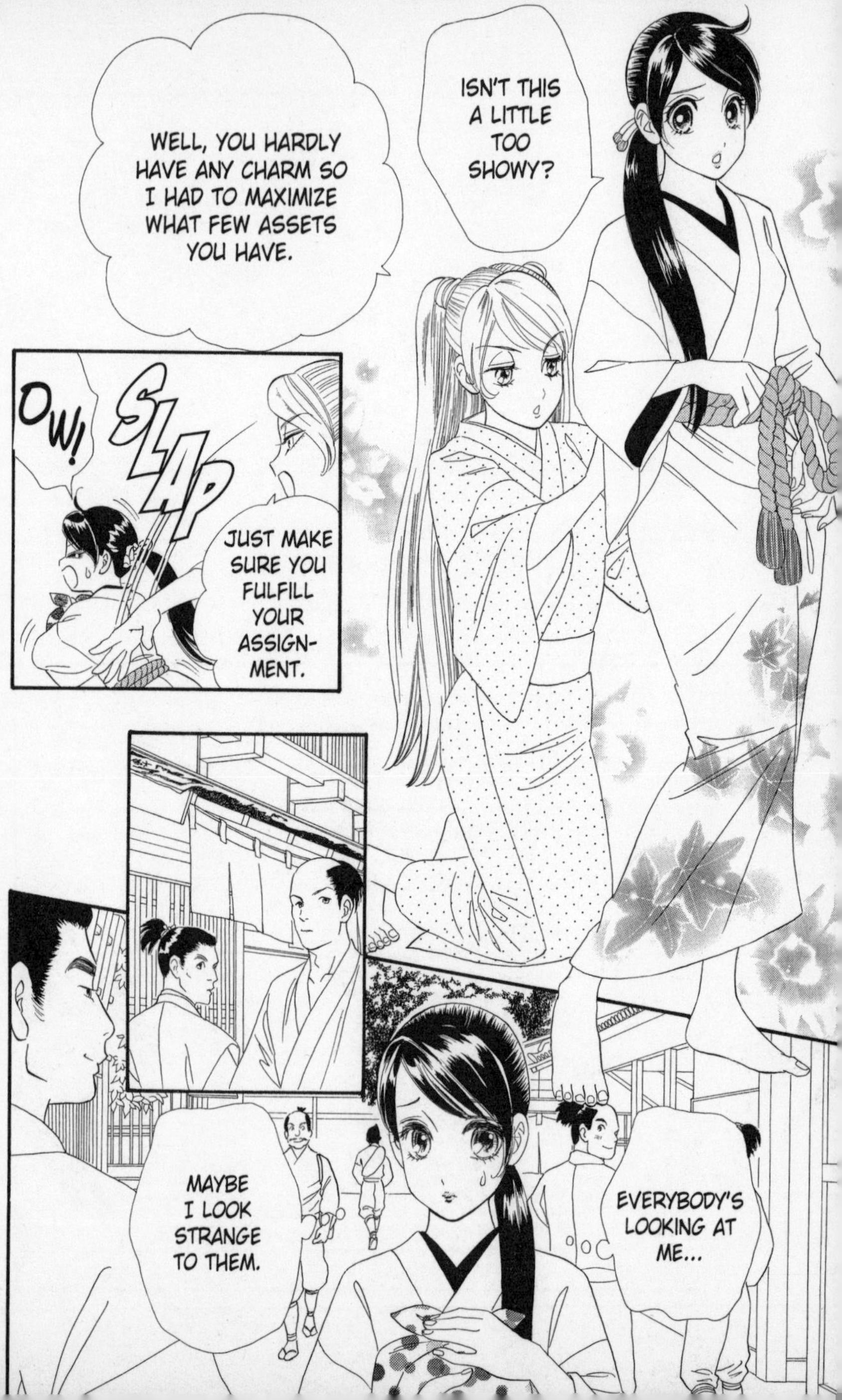
ISN'T THIS A LITTLE TOO SHOWY?
WELL, YOU HARDLY HAVE ANY CHARM SO I HAD TO MAXIMIZE WHAT FEW ASSETS YOU HAVE.
SLAP
OW!
JUST MAKE SURE YOU FULFILL YOUR ASSIGN- MENT.
EVERYBODY'S LOOKING AT ME...
MAYBE I LOOK STRANGE TO THEM.

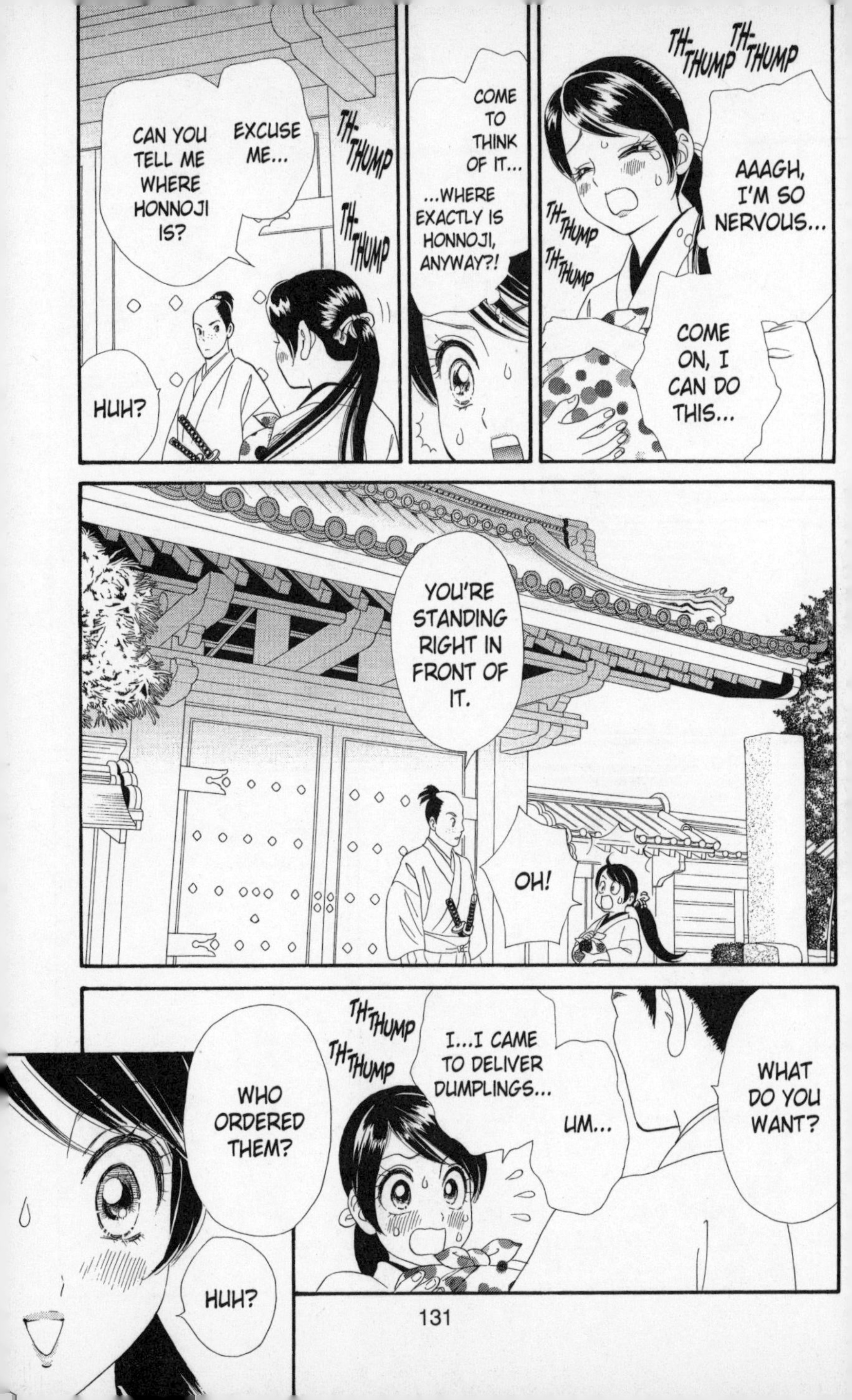
TH-THUMP TH-THUMP
AAAGH, I'M SO NERVOUS...
TH-THUMP TH-THUMP
COME ON, I CAN DO THIS...
COME TO THINK OF IT...
...WHERE EXACTLY IS HONNOJI, ANYWAY?!
TH-THUMP TH-THUMP
EXCUSE ME...
CAN YOU TELL ME WHERE HONNOJI IS?
HUH?
YOU'RE STANDING RIGHT IN FRONT OF IT.
OH!
WHAT DO YOU WANT?
UM...
I...I CAME TO DELIVER DUMPLINGS...
TH-THUMP TH-THUMP
WHO ORDERED THEM?
HUH?

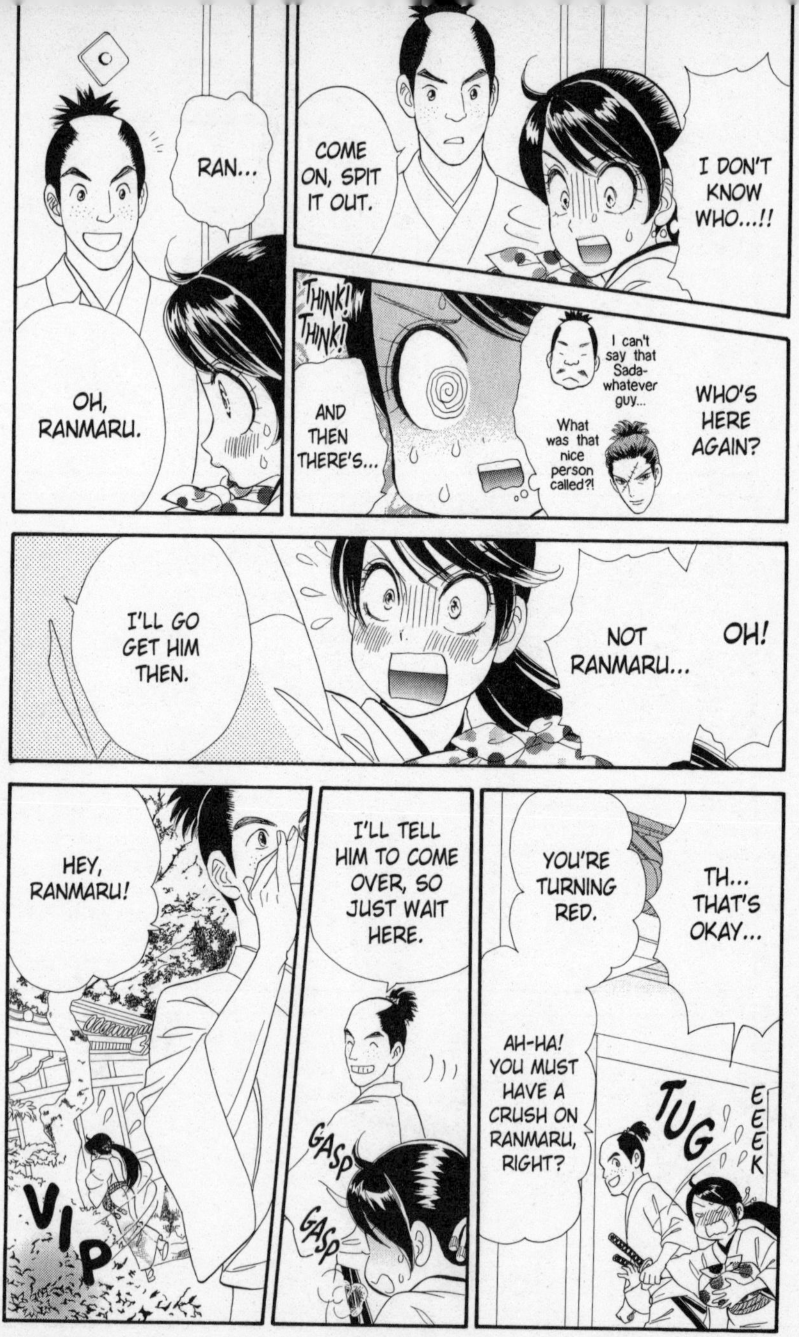
I DON'T KNOW WHO...!!
COME ON, SPIT IT OUT.
WHO'S HERE AGAIN?
I can't say that Sada-whatever guy...
What was that nice person called?!
THINK! THINK!
AND THEN THERE'S...
RAN...
OH, RANMARU.
OH!
NOT RANMARU...
I'LL GO GET HIM THEN.
TH... THAT'S OKAY...
YOU'RE TURNING RED.
EEEK
TUG
AH-HA! YOU MUST HAVE A CRUSH ON RANMARU, RIGHT?
I'LL TELL HIM TO COME OVER, SO JUST WAIT HERE.
GASP
GASP
HEY, RANMARU!
VIP

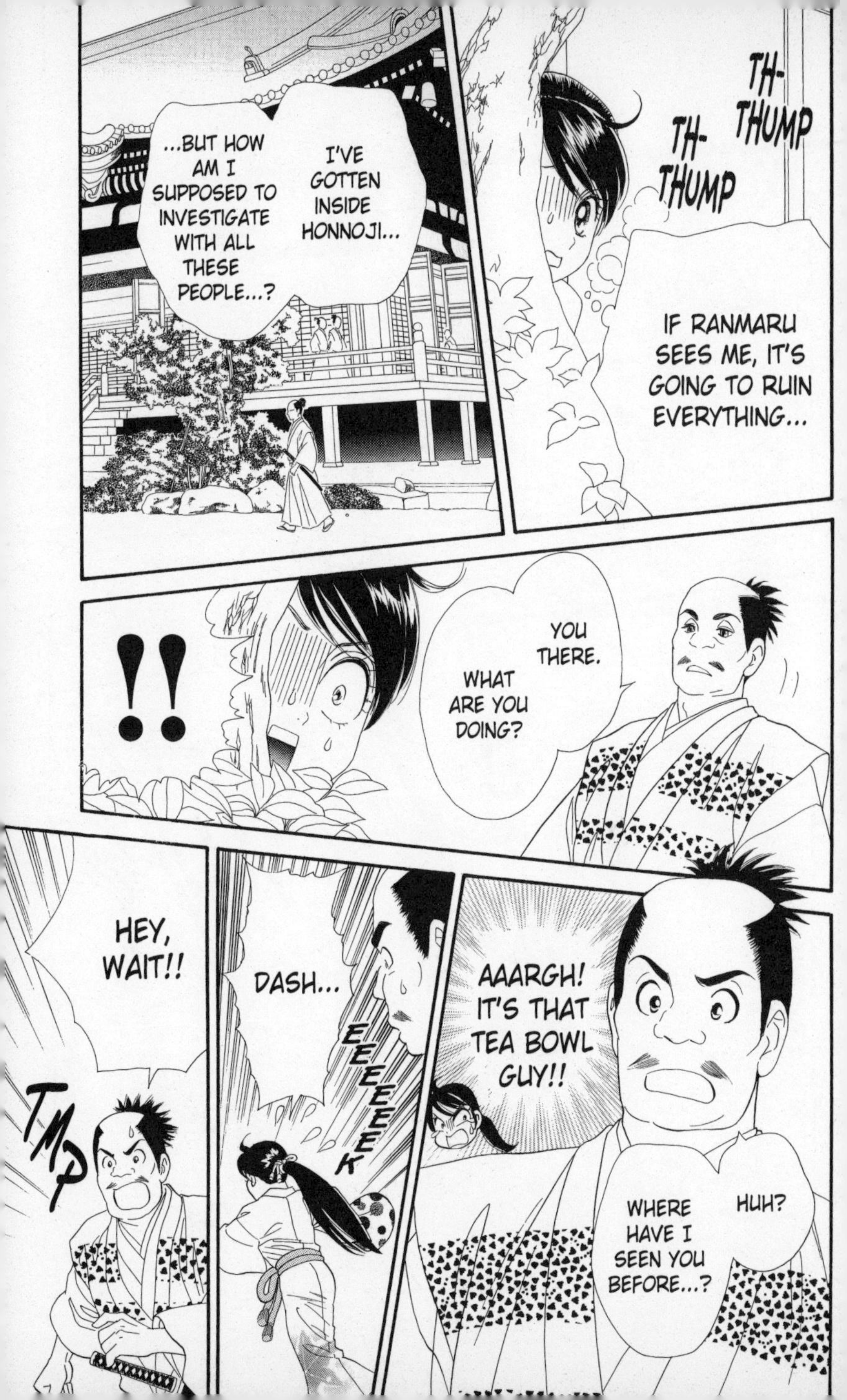
TH-THUMP
TH-THUMP
IF RANMARU SEES ME, IT'S GOING TO RUIN EVERYTHING...
I'VE GOTTEN INSIDE HONNOJI...
...BUT HOW AM I SUPPOSED TO INVESTIGATE WITH ALL THESE PEOPLE...?
YOU THERE.
WHAT ARE YOU DOING?
!!
HUH?
WHERE HAVE I SEEN YOU BEFORE...?
AAARGH! IT'S THAT TEA BOWL GUY!!
DASH...
EEEEEEEEK
HEY, WAIT!!
TMP

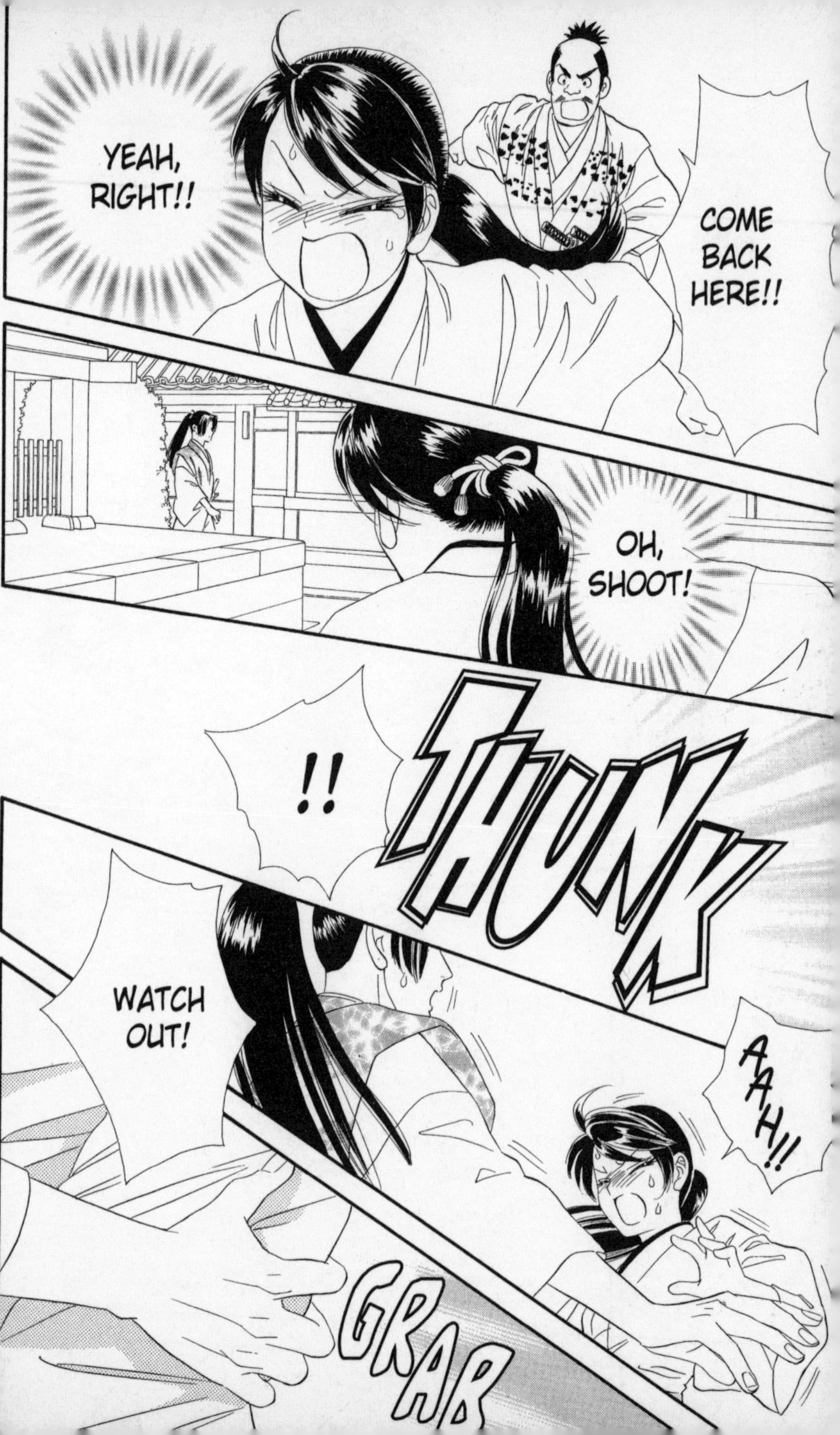
COME BACK HERE!!
YEAH, RIGHT!!
OH, SHOOT!
THUNK
!!
AAAH!!
WATCH OUT!
GRAB

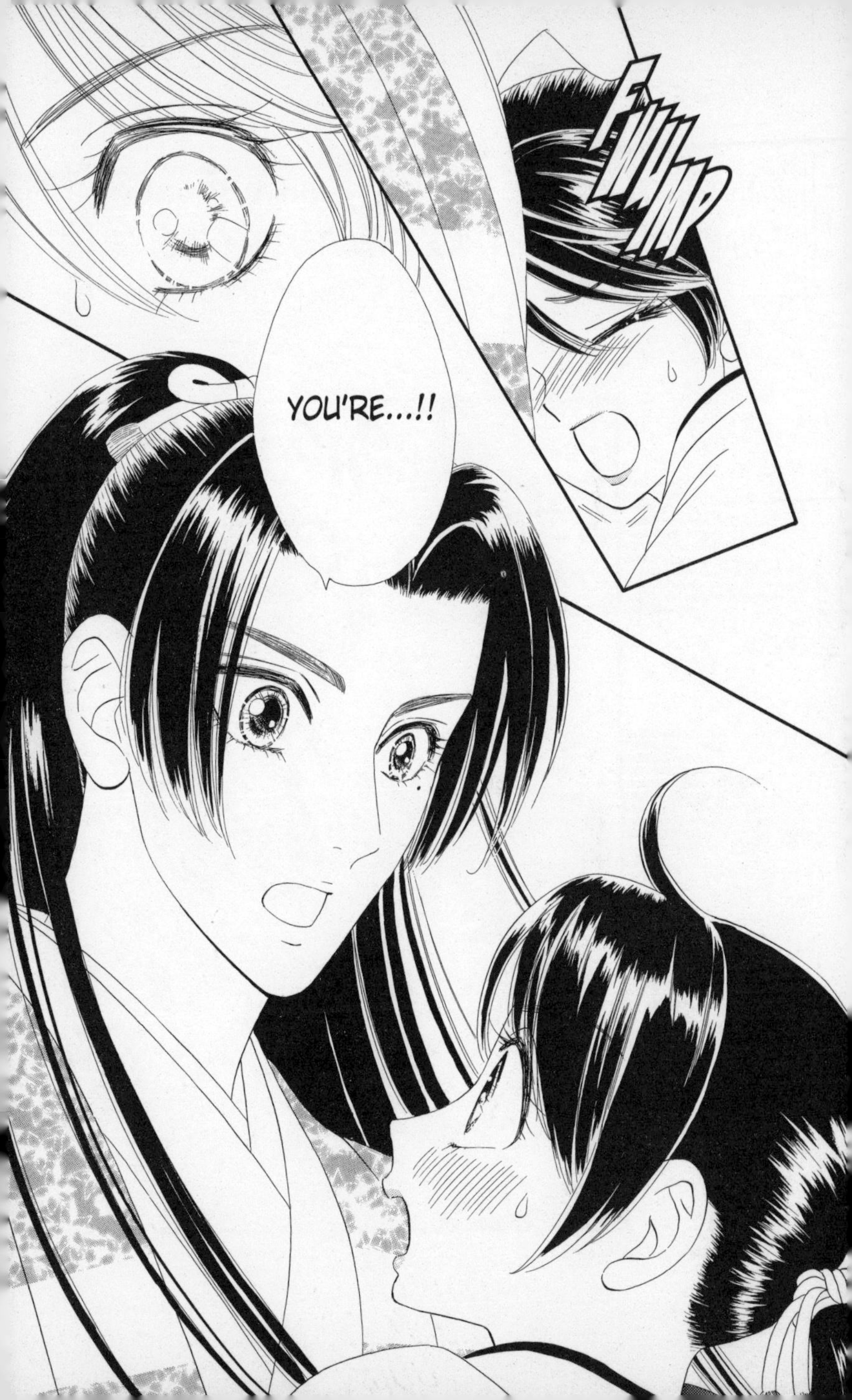
FWUMP
YOU'RE...!!

TAIL OF THE MOON EXTRA: TODAY'S MISSION

"I WANT TO SEE HANZO AS A TEACHER IN SCHOOL!"

-TOMOPYON, HOKKAIDO

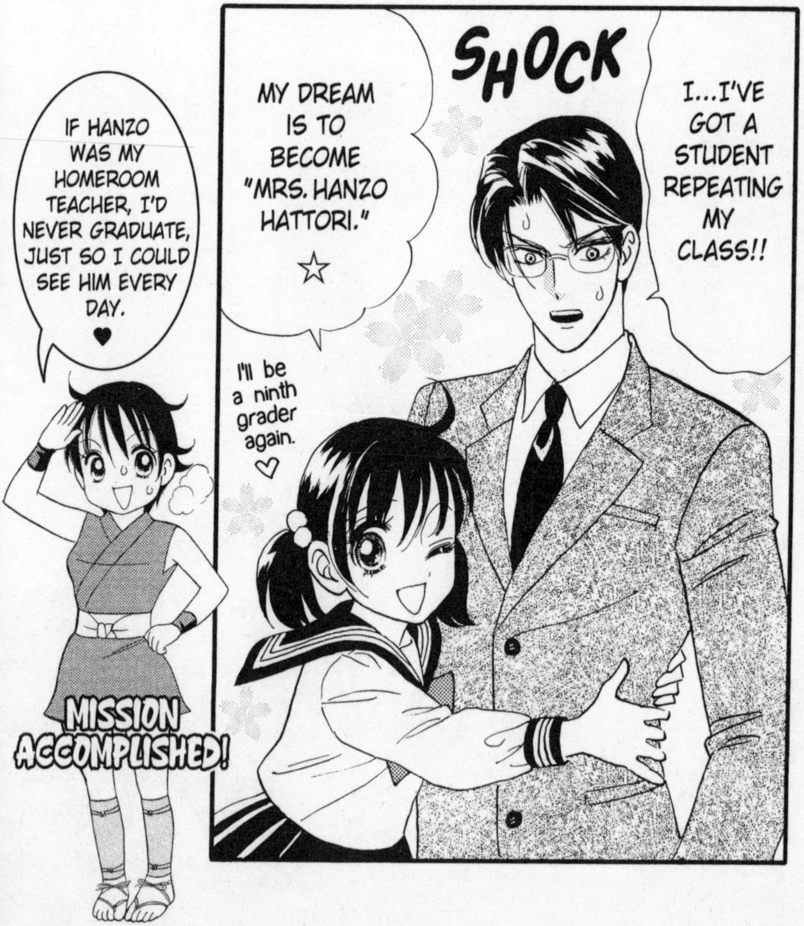
I...I'VE GOT A STUDENT REPEATING MY CLASS!!
SHOCK
MY DREAM IS TO BECOME "MRS. HANZO HATTORI." ☆
I'll be a ninth grader again. ♡
IF HANZO WAS MY HOMEROOM TEACHER, I'D NEVER GRADUATE, JUST SO I COULD SEE HIM EVERY DAY. ♥
MISSION ACCOMPLISHED!

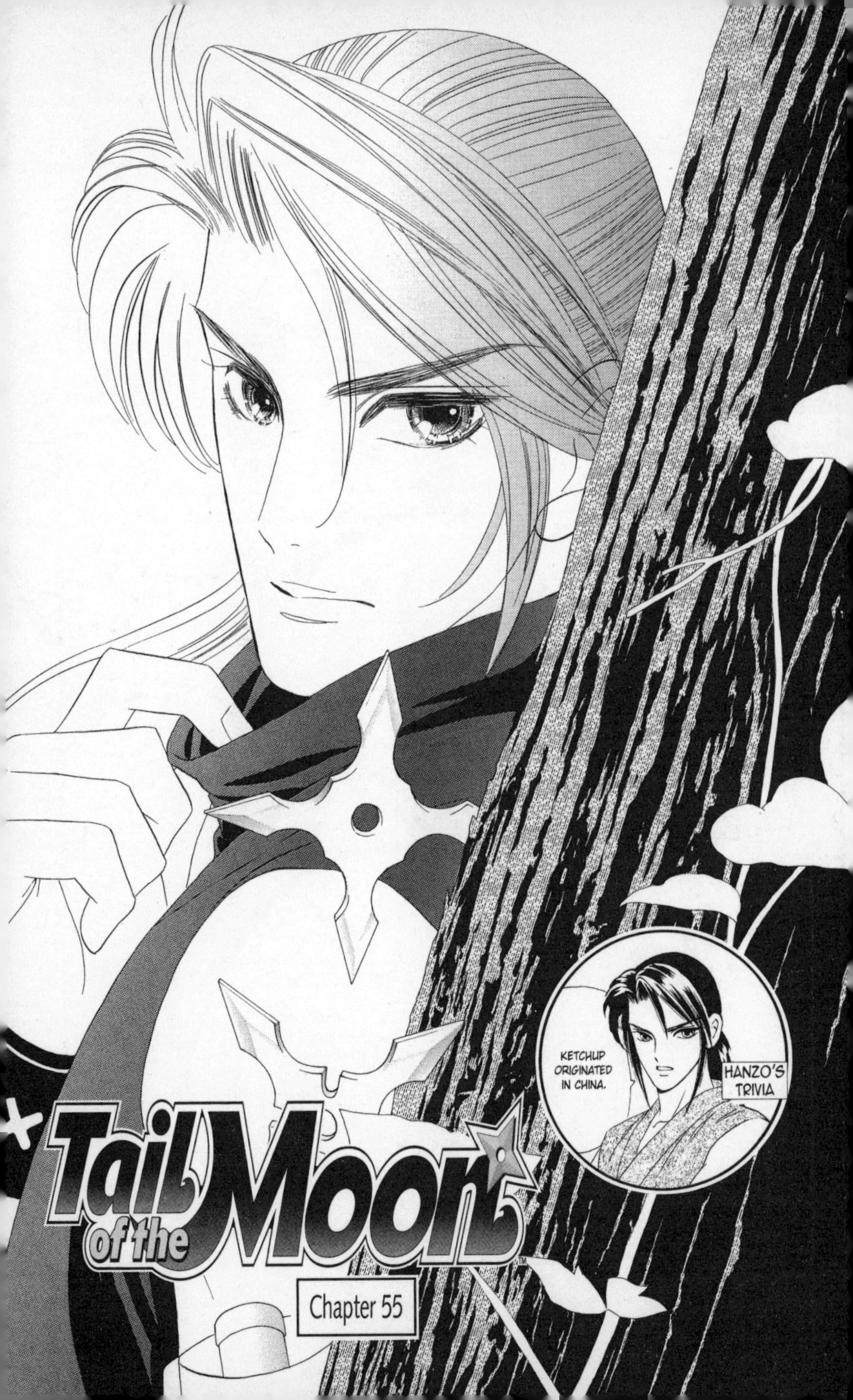
Tail of the Moon
Chapter 55
HANZO'S TRIVIA
KETCHUP ORIGINATED IN CHINA.

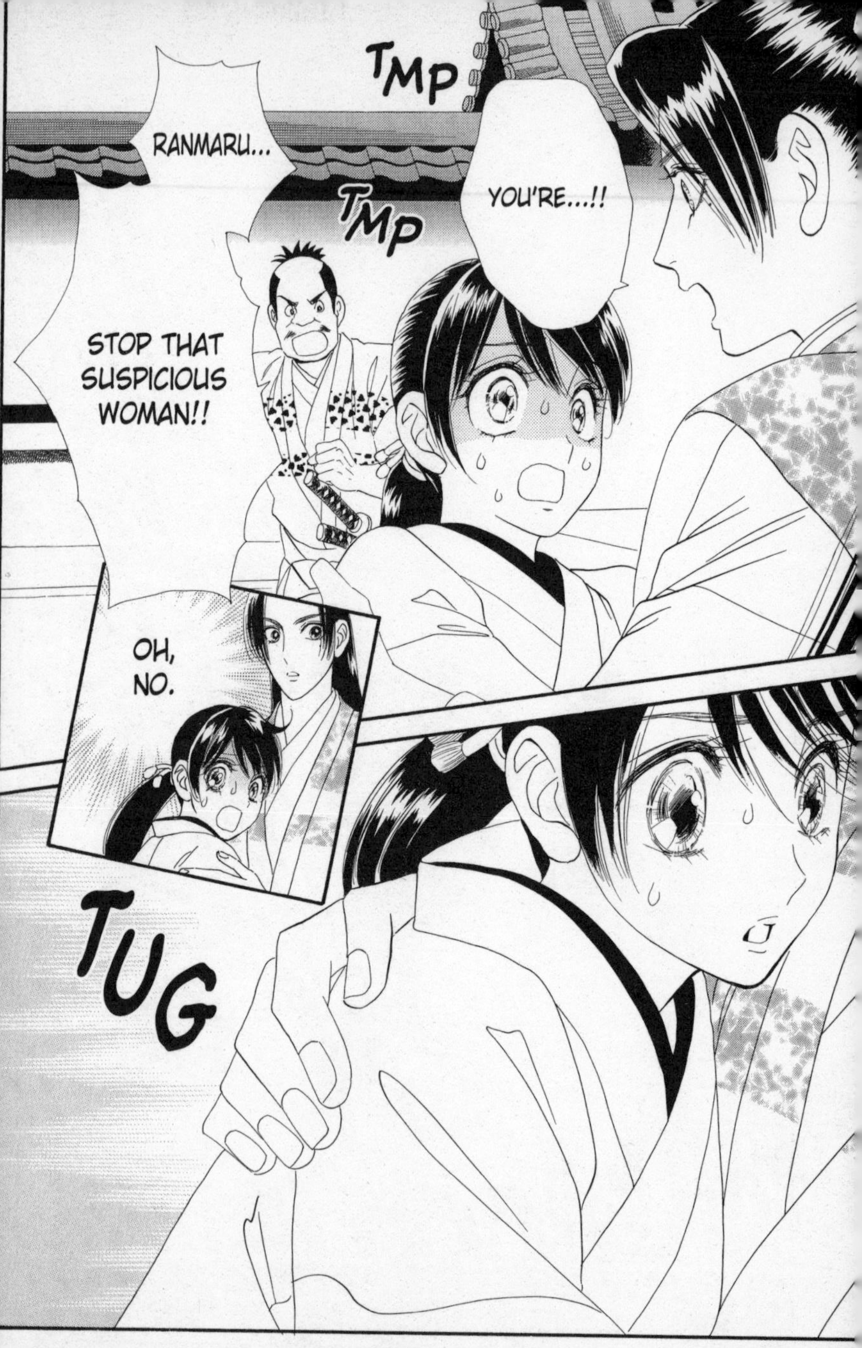
TMP
YOU'RE...!!
TMP
RANMARU...
STOP THAT SUSPICIOUS WOMAN!!
OH, NO.
TUG

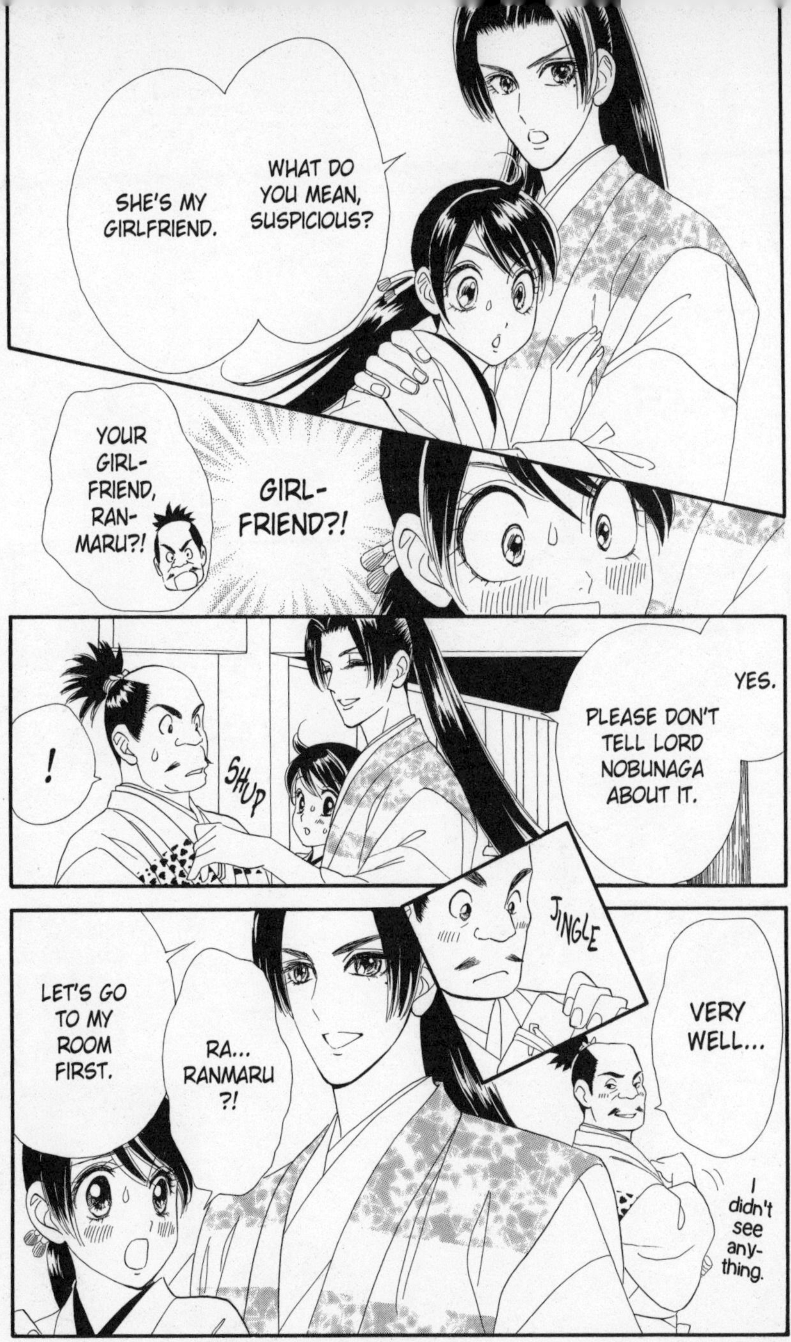
WHAT DO YOU MEAN, SUSPICIOUS?
SHE'S MY GIRLFRIEND.
GIRL-FRIEND?!
YOUR GIRL-FRIEND, RAN-MARU?!
YES.
PLEASE DON'T TELL LORD NOBUNAGA ABOUT IT.
SHUP
!
JINGLE
VERY WELL...
I didn't see any-thing.
RA... RANMARU ?!
LET'S GO TO MY ROOM FIRST.

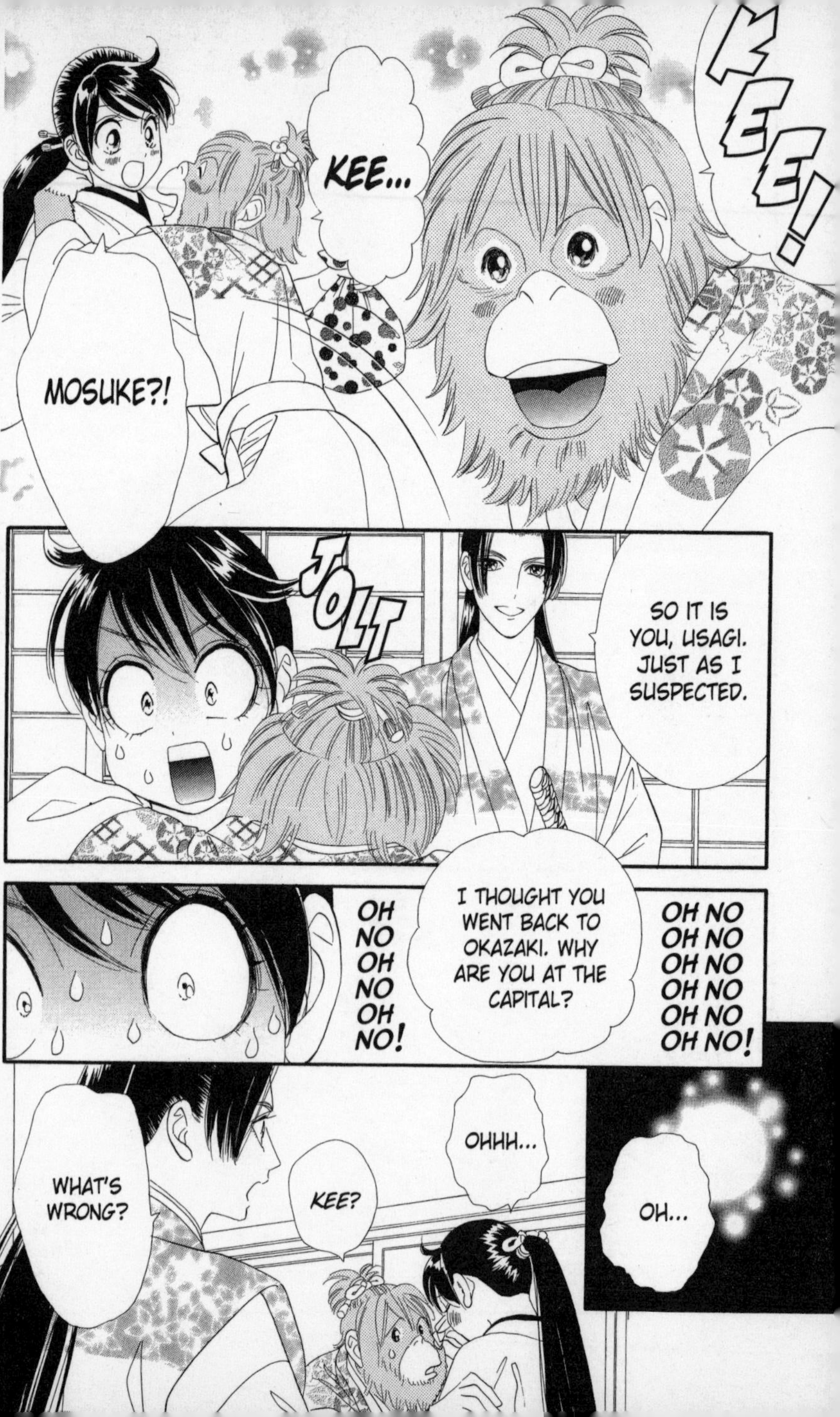
KEE!
KEE...
MOSUKE?!
SO IT IS YOU, USAGI. JUST AS I SUSPECTED.
JOLT
OH NO OH NO OH NO OH NO OH NO OH NO!
I THOUGHT YOU WENT BACK TO OKAZAKI. WHY ARE YOU AT THE CAPITAL?
OH NO OH NO OH NO!
OH...
OHHH...
KEE?
WHAT'S WRONG?

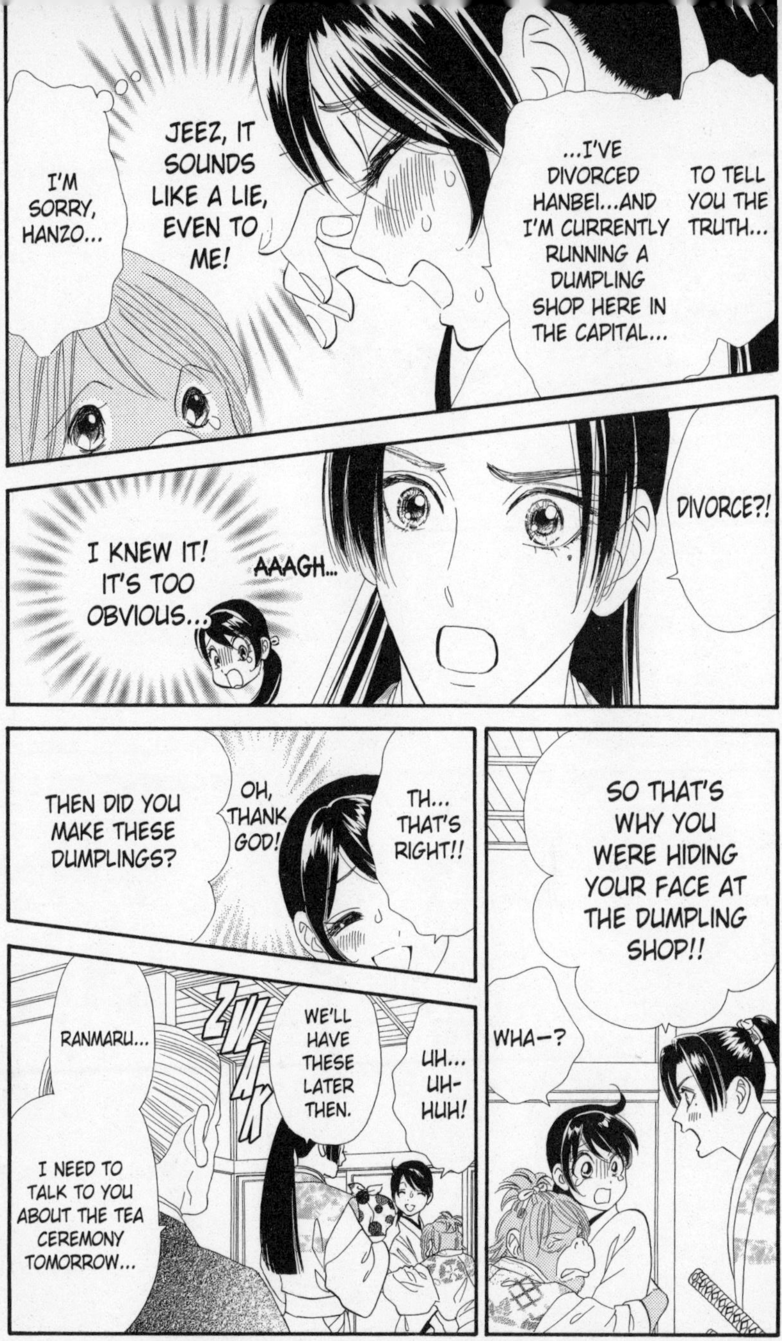
TO TELL YOU THE TRUTH...
...I'VE DIVORCED HANBEI...AND I'M CURRENTLY RUNNING A DUMPLING SHOP HERE IN THE CAPITAL...
JEEZ, IT SOUNDS LIKE A LIE, EVEN TO ME!
I'M SORRY, HANZO...
DIVORCE?!
AAAGH...
I KNEW IT! IT'S TOO OBVIOUS...
SO THAT'S WHY YOU WERE HIDING YOUR FACE AT THE DUMPLING SHOP!!
WHA-?
TH... THAT'S RIGHT!!
OH, THANK GOD!
THEN DID YOU MAKE THESE DUMPLINGS?
UH... UH-HUH!
WE'LL HAVE THESE LATER THEN.
ZWAK
RANMARU...
I NEED TO TALK TO YOU ABOUT THE TEA CEREMONY TOMORROW...

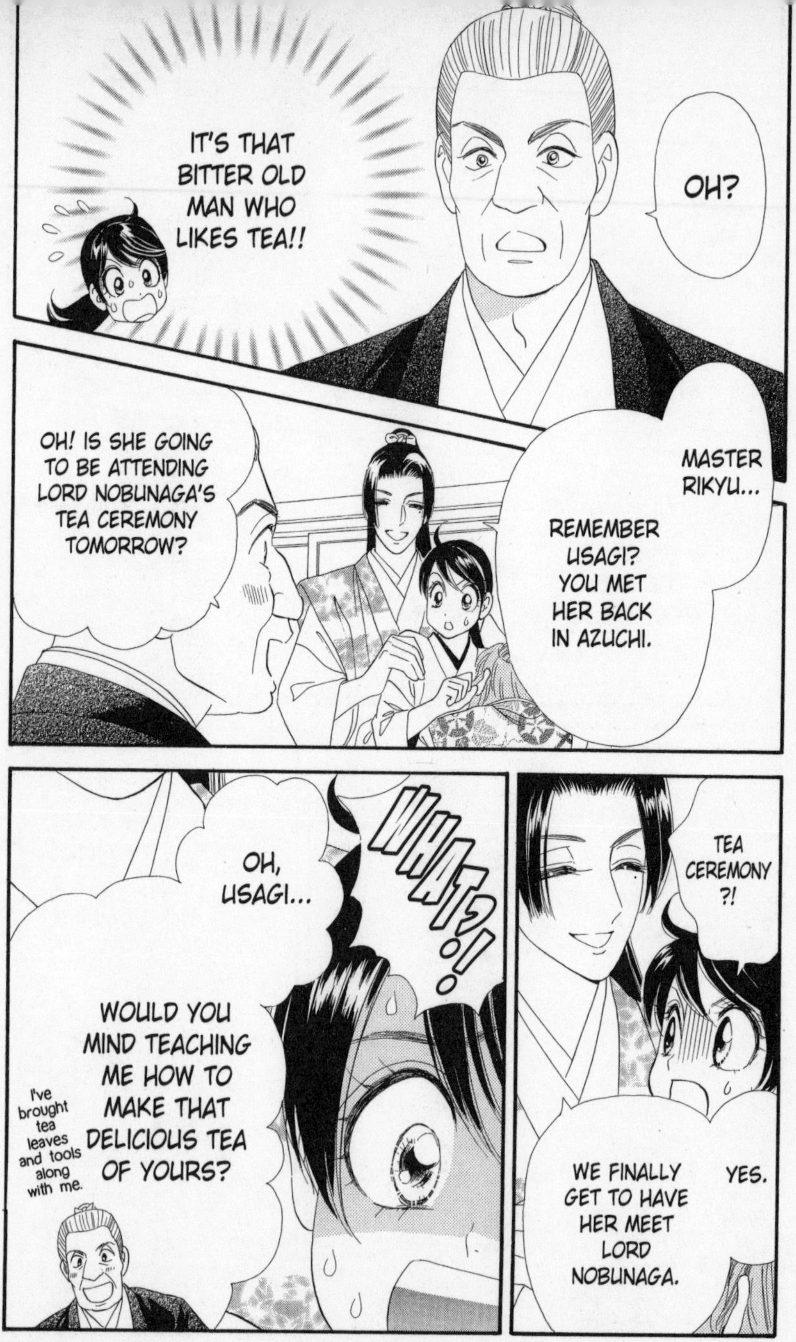
OH?
IT'S THAT BITTER OLD MAN WHO LIKES TEA!!
MASTER RIKYU...
REMEMBER USAGI? YOU MET HER BACK IN AZUCHI.
OH! IS SHE GOING TO BE ATTENDING LORD NOBUNAGA'S TEA CEREMONY TOMORROW?
TEA CEREMONY ?!
YES.
WE FINALLY GET TO HAVE HER MEET LORD NOBUNAGA.
WHAT?!
OH, USAGI...
WOULD YOU MIND TEACHING ME HOW TO MAKE THAT DELICIOUS TEA OF YOURS?
I've brought tea leaves and tools along with me.

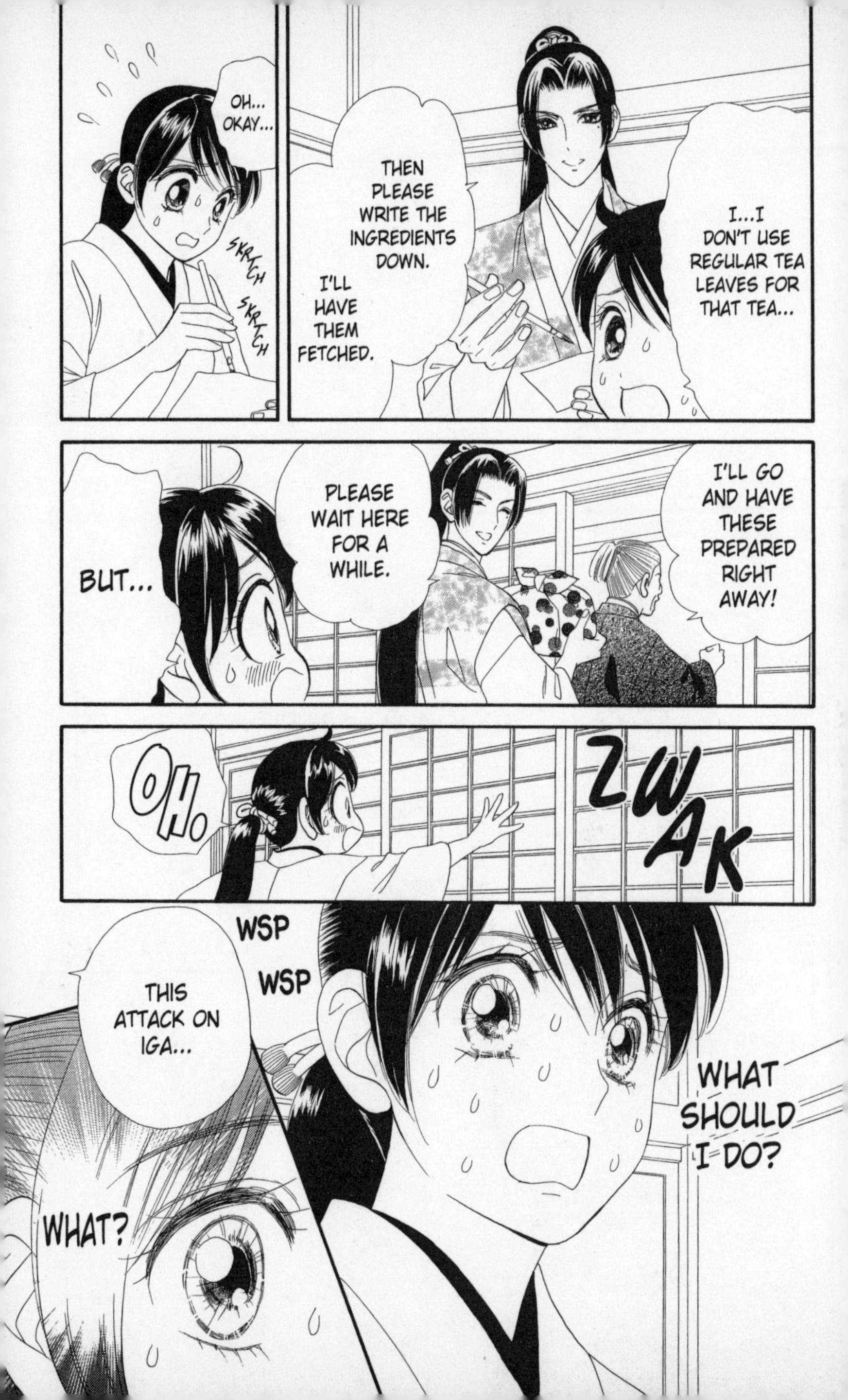
I...I DON'T USE REGULAR TEA LEAVES FOR THAT TEA...
THEN PLEASE WRITE THE INGREDIENTS DOWN.
I'LL HAVE THEM FETCHED.
OH... OKAY...
SKRATCH SKRATCH
I'LL GO AND HAVE THESE PREPARED RIGHT AWAY!
PLEASE WAIT HERE FOR A WHILE.
BUT...
ZWAK
OHO
WHAT SHOULD I DO?
WSP WSP
THIS ATTACK ON IGA...
WHAT?

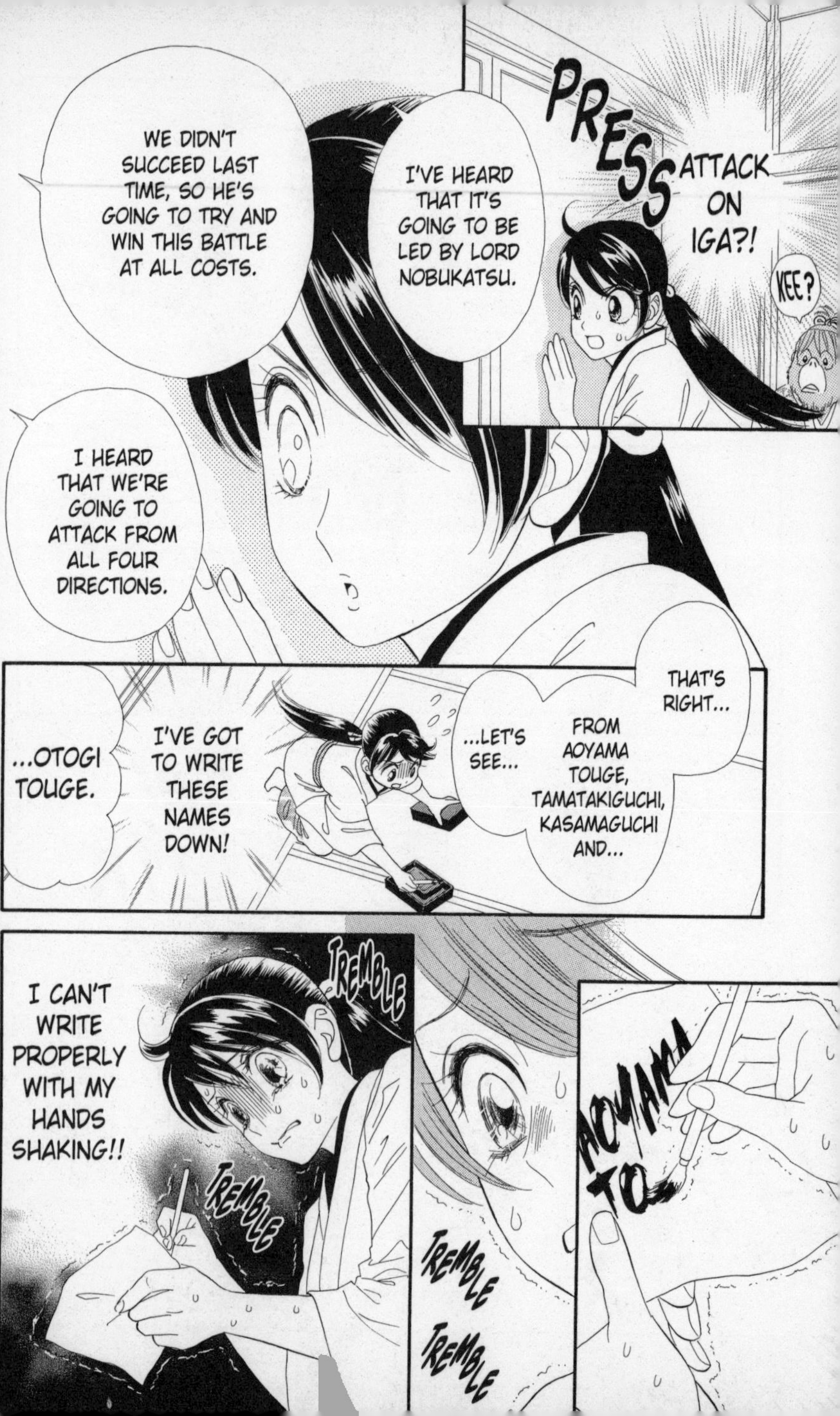
PRESS
ATTACK ON IGA?!
KEE?
I'VE HEARD THAT IT'S GOING TO BE LED BY LORD NOBUKATSU.
WE DIDN'T SUCCEED LAST TIME, SO HE'S GOING TO TRY AND WIN THIS BATTLE AT ALL COSTS.
I HEARD THAT WE'RE GOING TO ATTACK FROM ALL FOUR DIRECTIONS.
THAT'S RIGHT...
FROM AOYAMA TOUGE, TAMATAKIGUCHI, KASAMAGUCHI AND...
...LET'S SEE...
I'VE GOT TO WRITE THESE NAMES DOWN!
...OTOGI TOUGE.
AOYAMA TO
TREMBLE
TREMBLE
TREMBLE
I CAN'T WRITE PROPERLY WITH MY HANDS SHAKING!!
TREMBLE

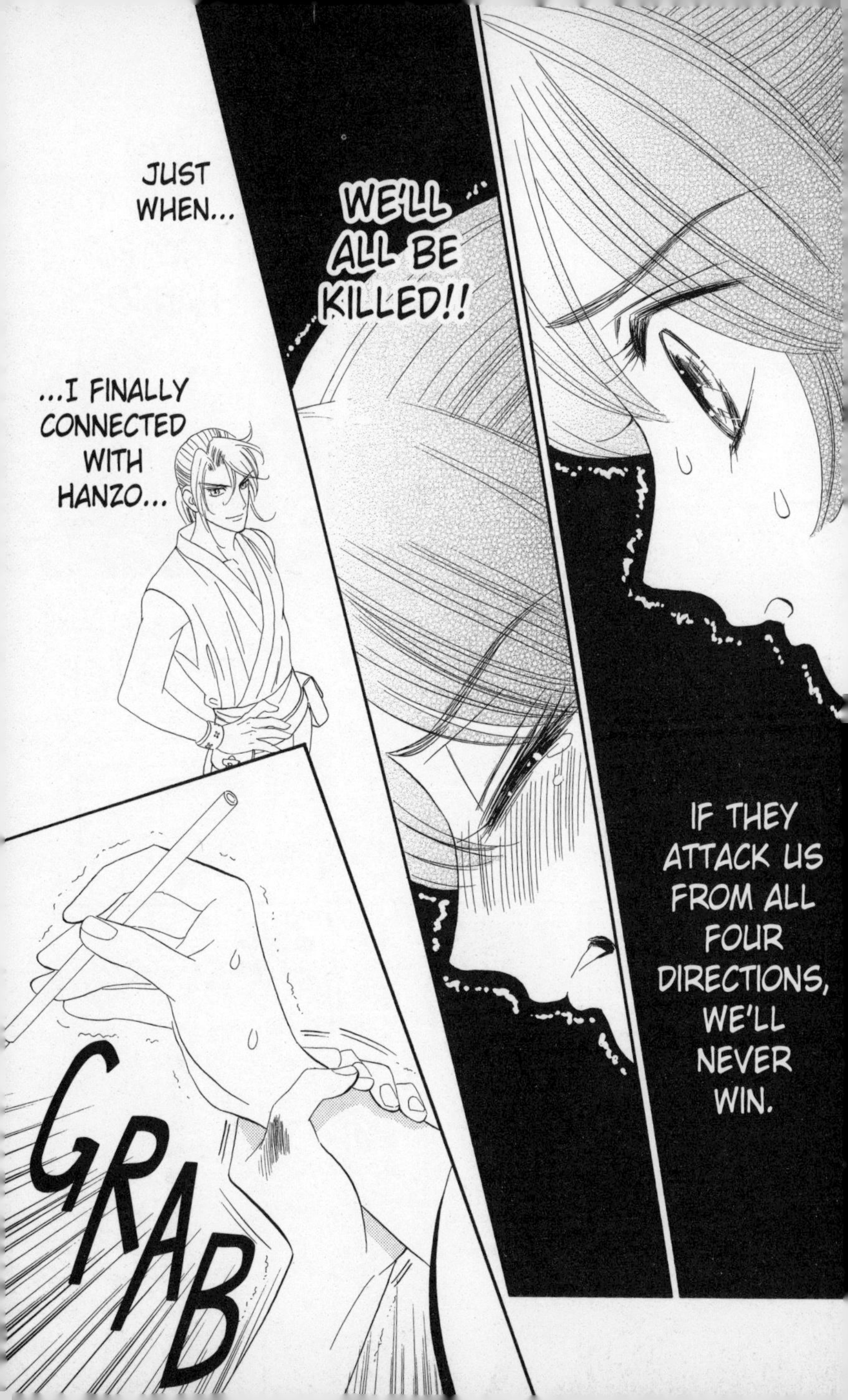
IF THEY ATTACK US FROM ALL FOUR DIRECTIONS, WE'LL NEVER WIN.
WE'LL ALL BE KILLED!!
JUST WHEN...
...I FINALLY CONNECTED WITH HANZO...
GRAB

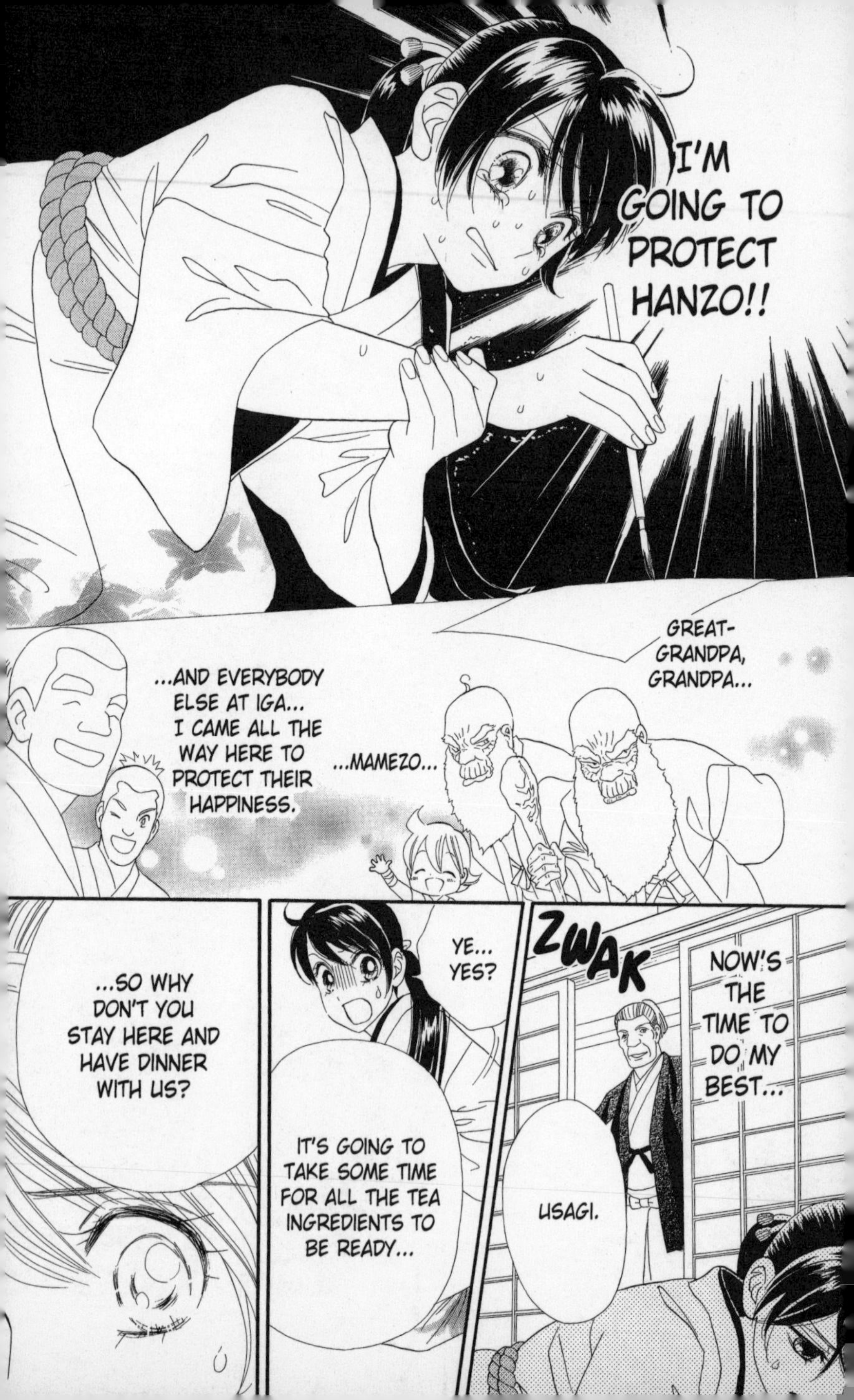
I'M GOING TO PROTECT HANZO!!
GREAT-GRANDPA, GRANDPA...
...MAMEZO...
...AND EVERYBODY ELSE AT IGA... I CAME ALL THE WAY HERE TO PROTECT THEIR HAPPINESS.
NOW'S THE TIME TO DO MY BEST...
ZWAK
USAGI.
YE... YES?
IT'S GOING TO TAKE SOME TIME FOR ALL THE TEA INGREDIENTS TO BE READY...
...SO WHY DON'T YOU STAY HERE AND HAVE DINNER WITH US?

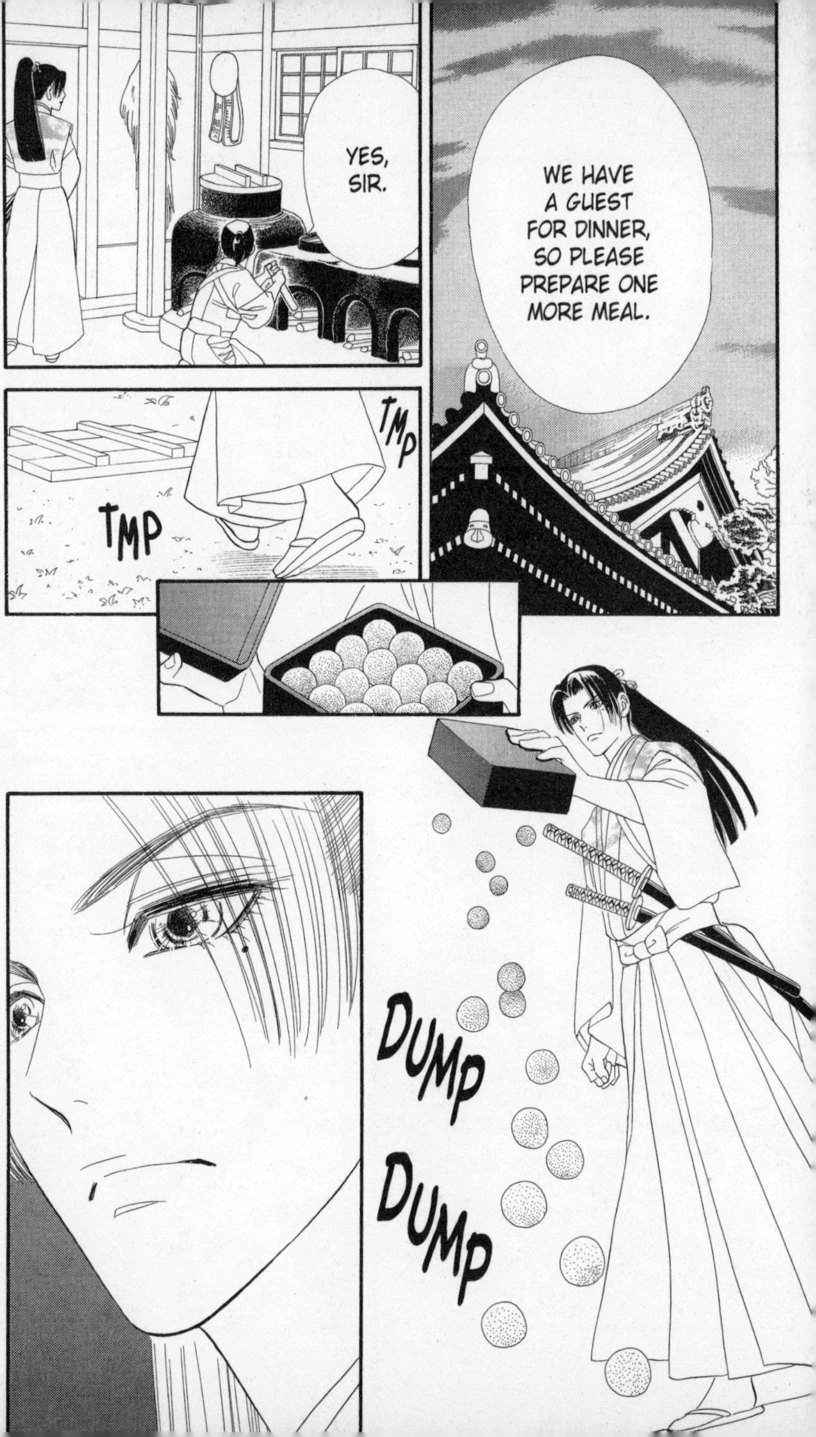
WE HAVE A GUEST FOR DINNER, SO PLEASE PREPARE ONE MORE MEAL.
YES, SIR.
TMP
TMP
DUMP
DUMP

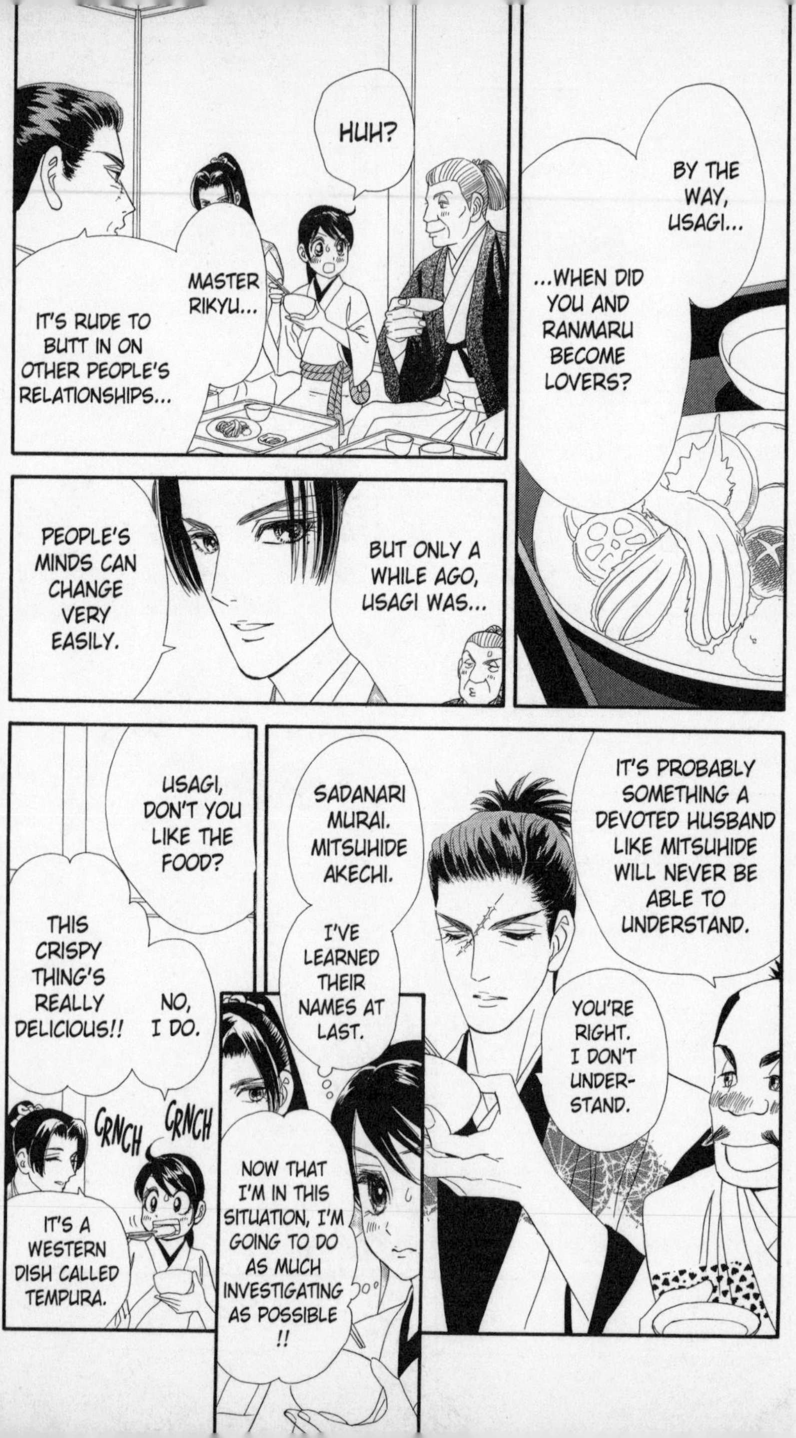
BY THE WAY, USAGI...
...WHEN DID YOU AND RANMARU BECOME LOVERS?
HUH?
MASTER RIKYU...
IT'S RUDE TO BUTT IN ON OTHER PEOPLE'S RELATIONSHIPS...
BUT ONLY A WHILE AGO, USAGI WAS...
PEOPLE'S MINDS CAN CHANGE VERY EASILY.
IT'S PROBABLY SOMETHING A DEVOTED HUSBAND LIKE MITSUHIDE WILL NEVER BE ABLE TO UNDERSTAND.
YOU'RE RIGHT. I DON'T UNDER-STAND.
SADANARI MURAI. MITSUHIDE AKECHI.
I'VE LEARNED THEIR NAMES AT LAST.
NOW THAT I'M IN THIS SITUATION, I'M GOING TO DO AS MUCH INVESTIGATING AS POSSIBLE !!
USAGI, DON'T YOU LIKE THE FOOD?
NO, I DO.
THIS CRISPY THING'S REALLY DELICIOUS!!
CRNCH
CRNCH
IT'S A WESTERN DISH CALLED TEMPURA.

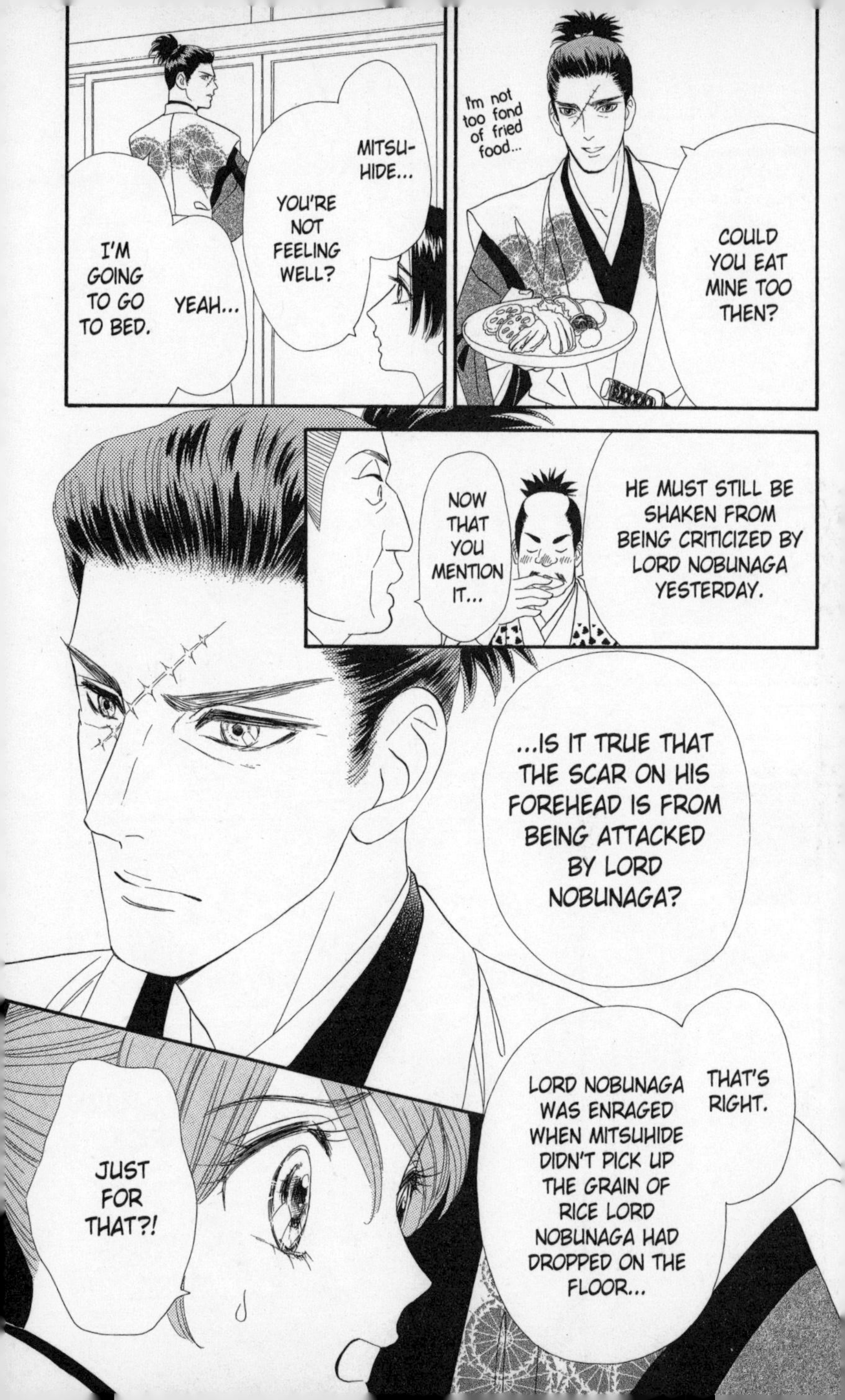

I'm not too fond of fried food...
COULD YOU EAT MINE TOO THEN?
MITSU-HIDE...
YOU'RE NOT FEELING WELL?
YEAH...
I'M GOING TO GO TO BED.
HE MUST STILL BE SHAKEN FROM BEING CRITICIZED BY LORD NOBUNAGA YESTERDAY.
NOW THAT YOU MENTION IT...
...IS IT TRUE THAT THE SCAR ON HIS FOREHEAD IS FROM BEING ATTACKED BY LORD NOBUNAGA?
THAT'S RIGHT.
LORD NOBUNAGA WAS ENRAGED WHEN MITSUHIDE DIDN'T PICK UP THE GRAIN OF RICE LORD NOBUNAGA HAD DROPPED ON THE FLOOR...
JUST FOR THAT?!

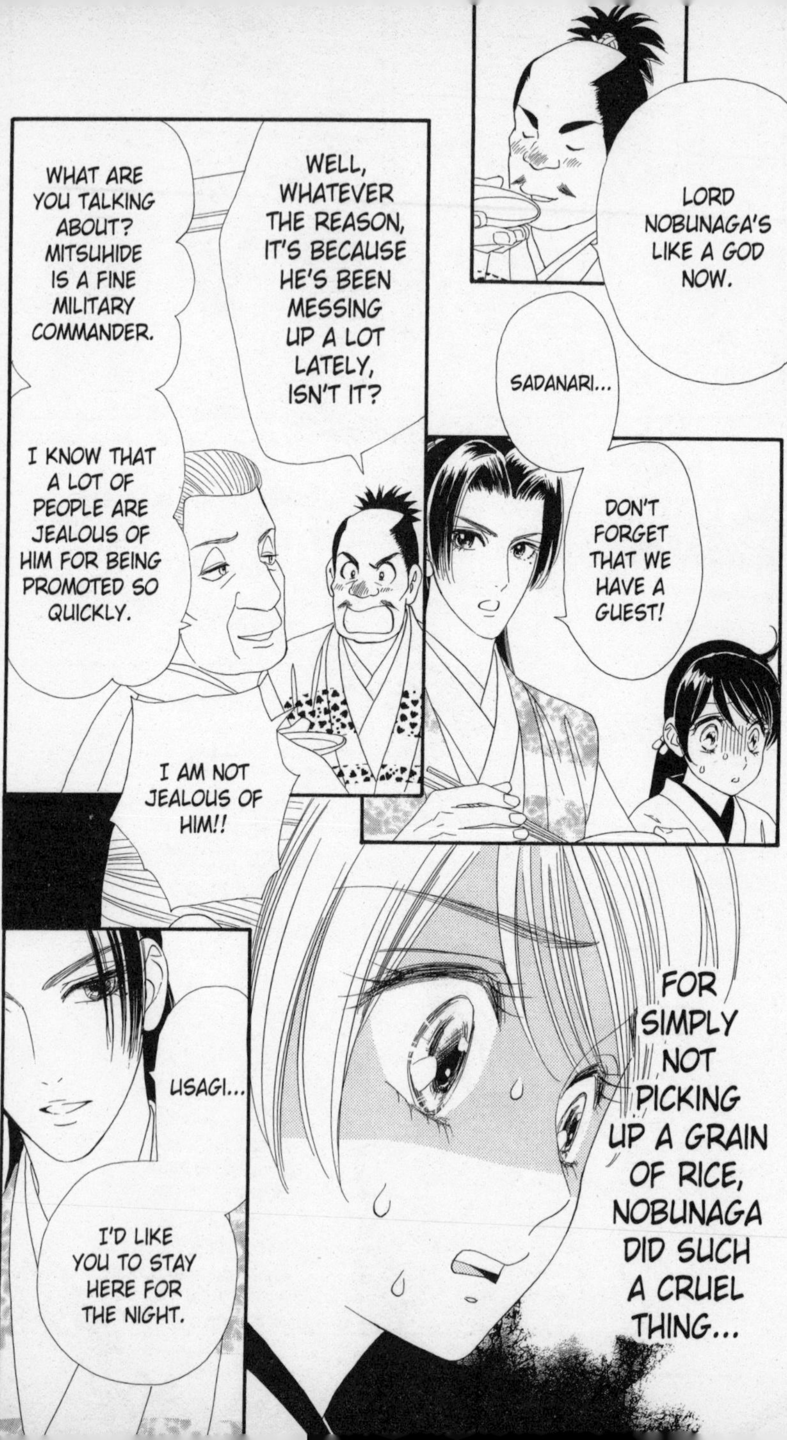
LORD NOBUNAGA'S LIKE A GOD NOW.
WELL, WHATEVER THE REASON, IT'S BECAUSE HE'S BEEN MESSING UP A LOT LATELY, ISN'T IT?
WHAT ARE YOU TALKING ABOUT? MITSUHIDE IS A FINE MILITARY COMMANDER.
I KNOW THAT A LOT OF PEOPLE ARE JEALOUS OF HIM FOR BEING PROMOTED SO QUICKLY.
I AM NOT JEALOUS OF HIM!!
SADANARI...
DON'T FORGET THAT WE HAVE A GUEST!
FOR SIMPLY NOT PICKING UP A GRAIN OF RICE, NOBUNAGA DID SUCH A CRUEL THING...
USAGI...
I'D LIKE YOU TO STAY HERE FOR THE NIGHT.

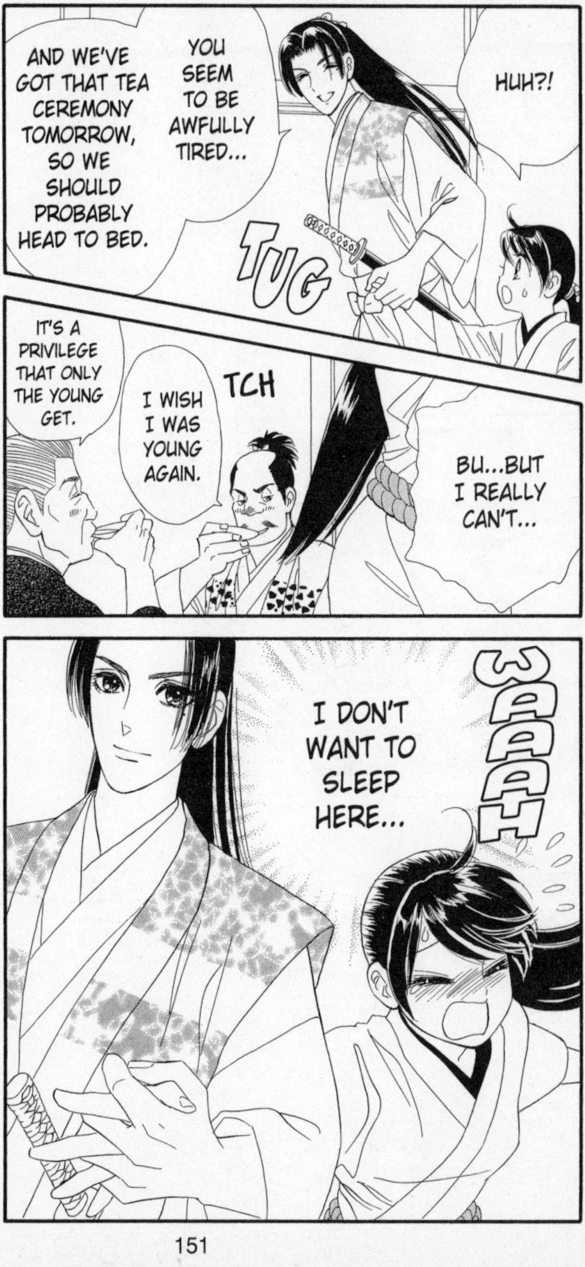
HUH?!
YOU SEEM TO BE AWFULLY TIRED...
AND WE'VE GOT THAT TEA CEREMONY TOMORROW, SO WE SHOULD PROBABLY HEAD TO BED.
TUG
BU...BUT I REALLY CAN'T...
TCH
I WISH I WAS YOUNG AGAIN.
IT'S A PRIVILEGE THAT ONLY THE YOUNG GET.
WAAAAH
I DON'T WANT TO SLEEP HERE...

UE-RIN'S WAY OF THE MANGA ⑮

Back then, household fax machines, convenience stores, and door-to-door delivery service weren't that common. That's why I would photocopy my storyboard at the local stationery (It was expensive!) store for 30 yen per page, send it by express mail, and wait for a reply to come.

Unfortunately, the reply from the editor always took a long time. I kept worrying, thinking things like, "Maybe it didn't reach them because of some accident..." Even though I wanted to call to see if my storyboard got there okay, I was kind of scared and embarrassed...

(I never did call them in the end.)

The long waiting time felt like such a waste of time to me...

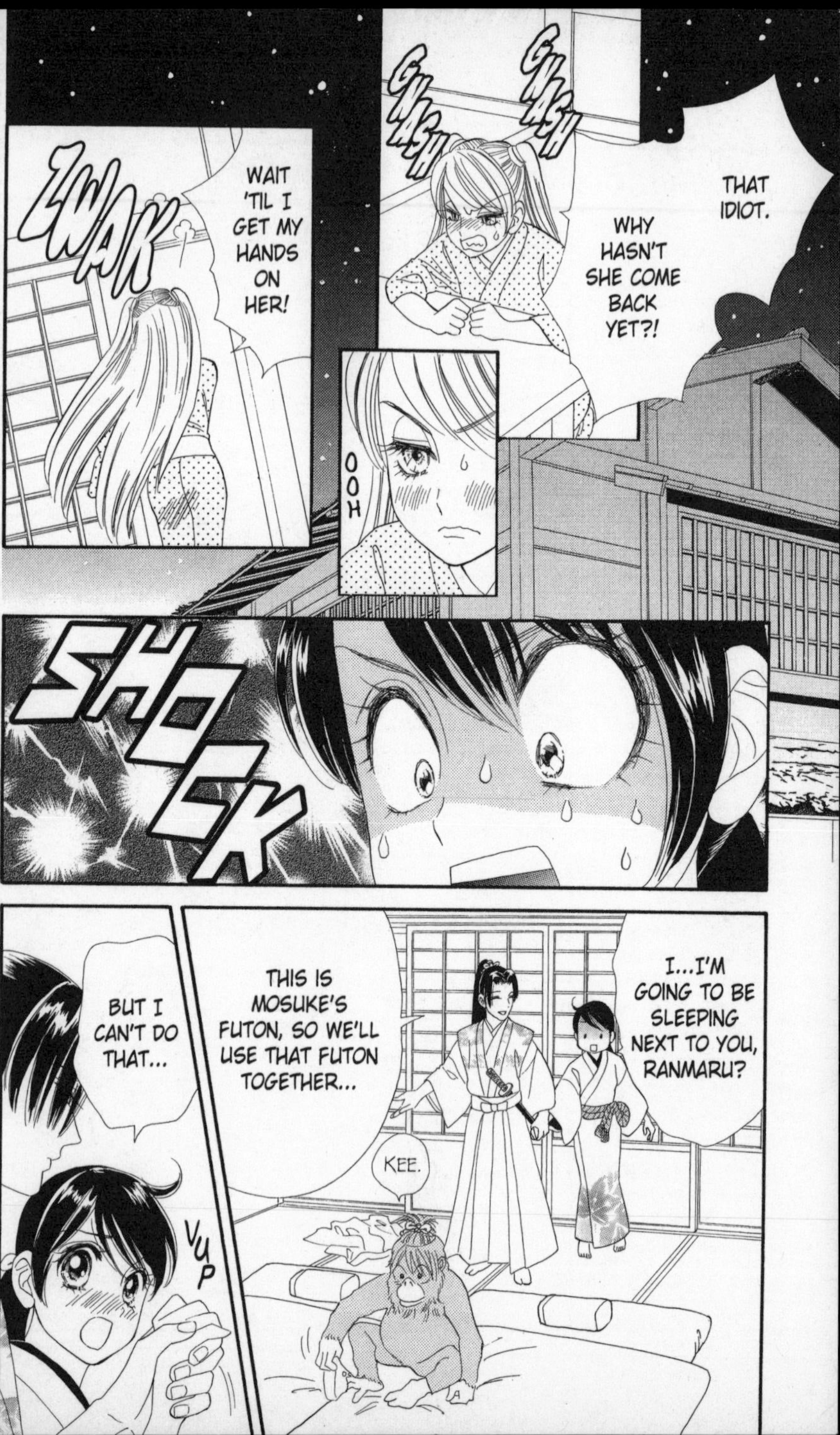
THAT IDIOT.
GNASH
GNASH
WHY HASN'T SHE COME BACK YET?!
OOH
ZWAK
WAIT 'TIL I GET MY HANDS ON HER!
SHOCK
I...I'M GOING TO BE SLEEPING NEXT TO YOU, RANMARU?
THIS IS MOSUKE'S FUTON, SO WE'LL USE THAT FUTON TOGETHER...
KEE.
BUT I CAN'T DO THAT...
VUP

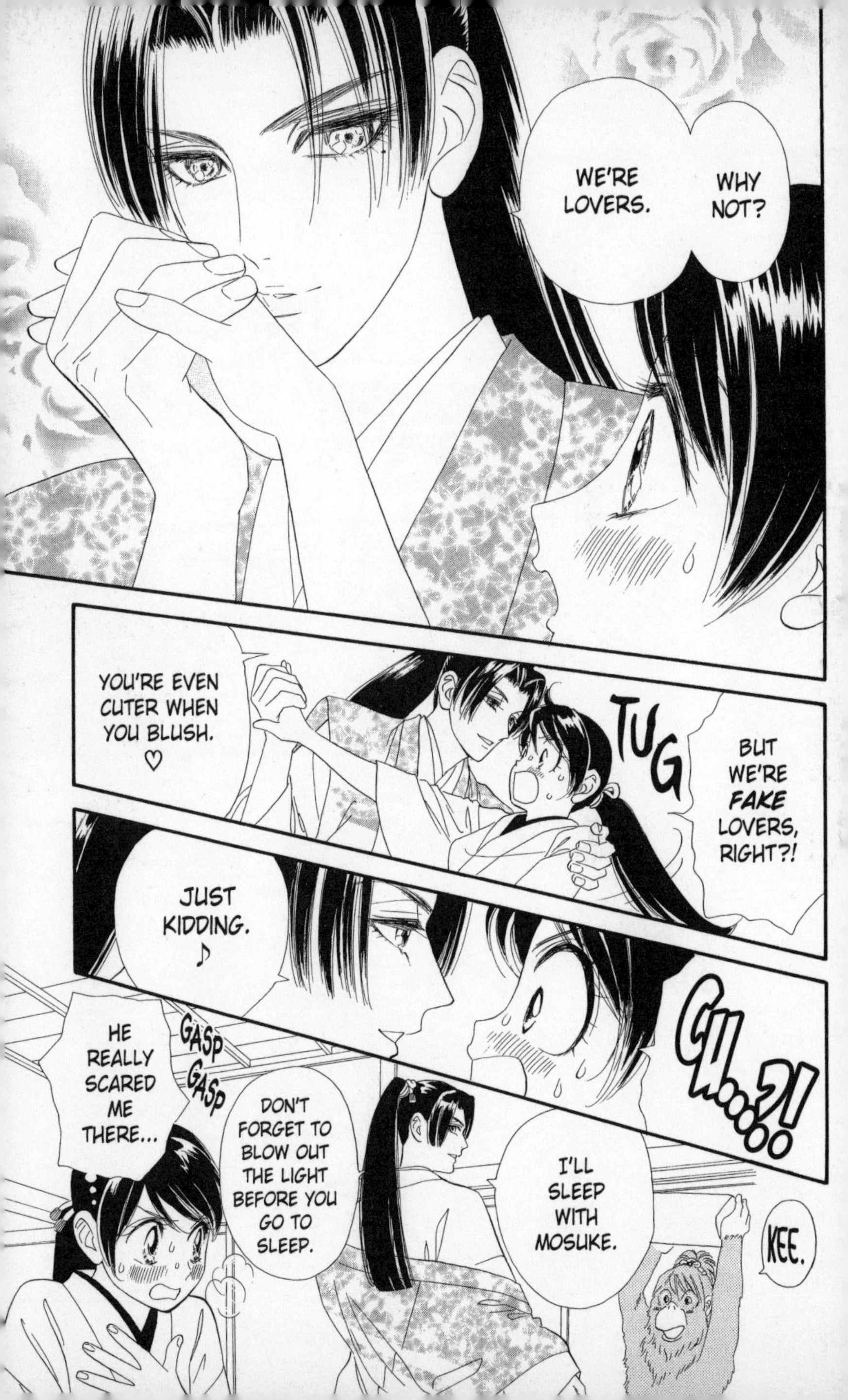
WHY NOT?
WE'RE LOVERS.
BUT WE'RE *FAKE* LOVERS, RIGHT?!
TUG
YOU'RE EVEN CUTER WHEN YOU BLUSH. ♡
GUOOOOO?!
JUST KIDDING. ♪
KEE.
I'LL SLEEP WITH MOSUKE.
DON'T FORGET TO BLOW OUT THE LIGHT BEFORE YOU GO TO SLEEP.
GASP GASP
HE REALLY SCARED ME THERE...

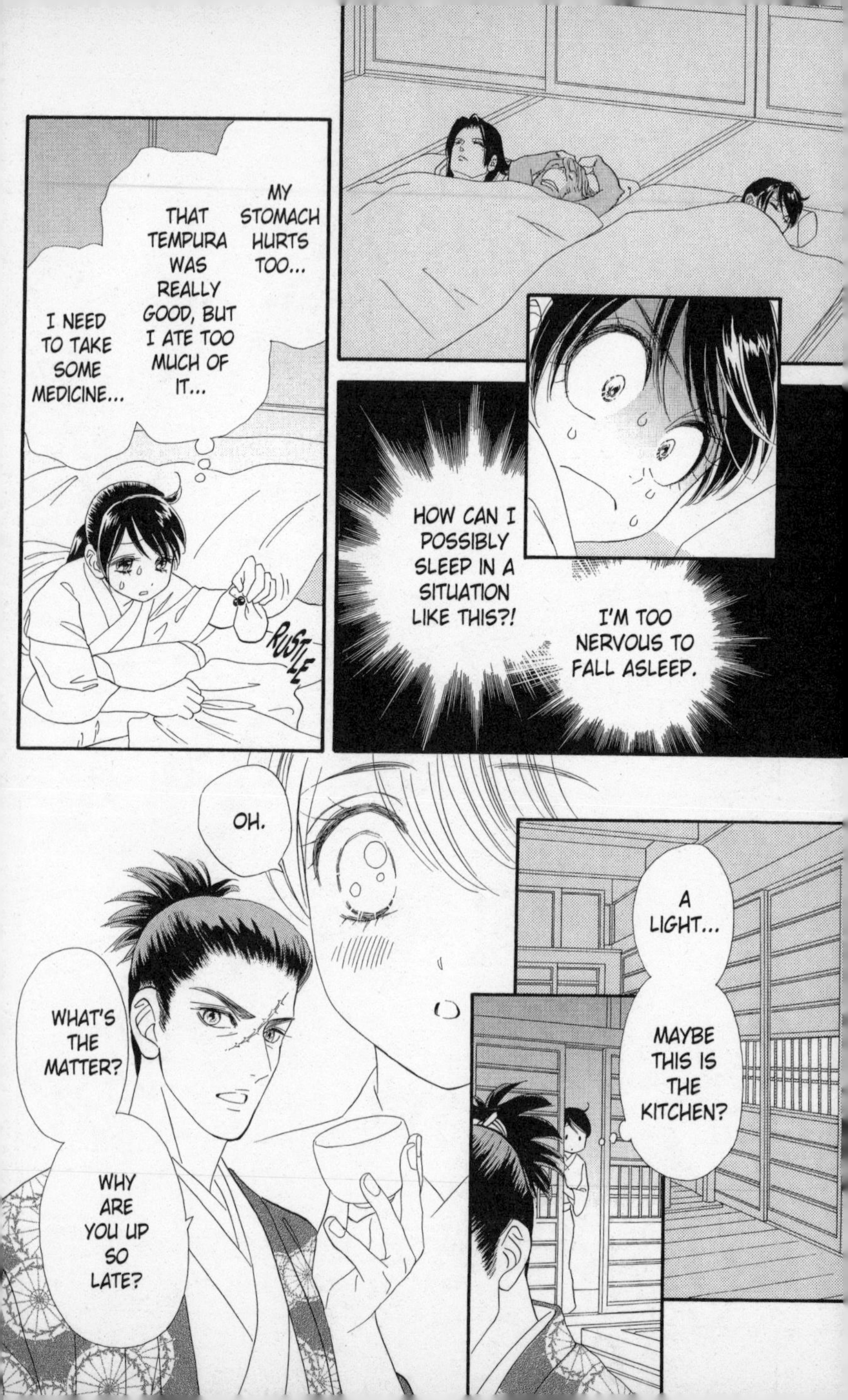
I'M TOO NERVOUS TO FALL ASLEEP.
HOW CAN I POSSIBLY SLEEP IN A SITUATION LIKE THIS?!
MY STOMACH HURTS TOO...
THAT TEMPURA WAS REALLY GOOD, BUT I ATE TOO MUCH OF IT...
I NEED TO TAKE SOME MEDICINE...
RUSTLE
A LIGHT...
MAYBE THIS IS THE KITCHEN?
OH.
WHAT'S THE MATTER?
WHY ARE YOU UP SO LATE?

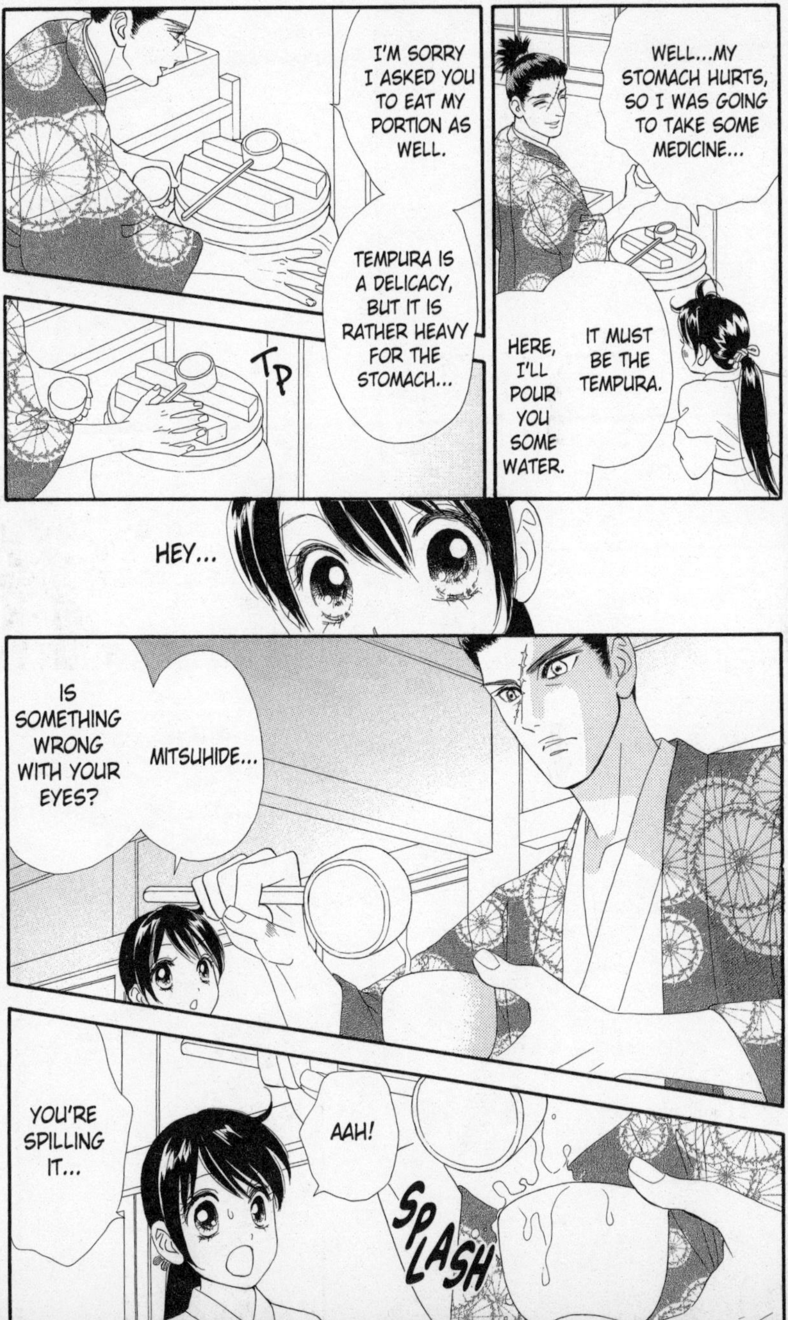
WELL...MY STOMACH HURTS, SO I WAS GOING TO TAKE SOME MEDICINE...
IT MUST BE THE TEMPURA.
HERE, I'LL POUR YOU SOME WATER.
I'M SORRY I ASKED YOU TO EAT MY PORTION AS WELL.
TEMPURA IS A DELICACY, BUT IT IS RATHER HEAVY FOR THE STOMACH...
TP
HEY...
MITSUHIDE...
IS SOMETHING WRONG WITH YOUR EYES?
AAH!
SPLASH
YOU'RE SPILLING IT...

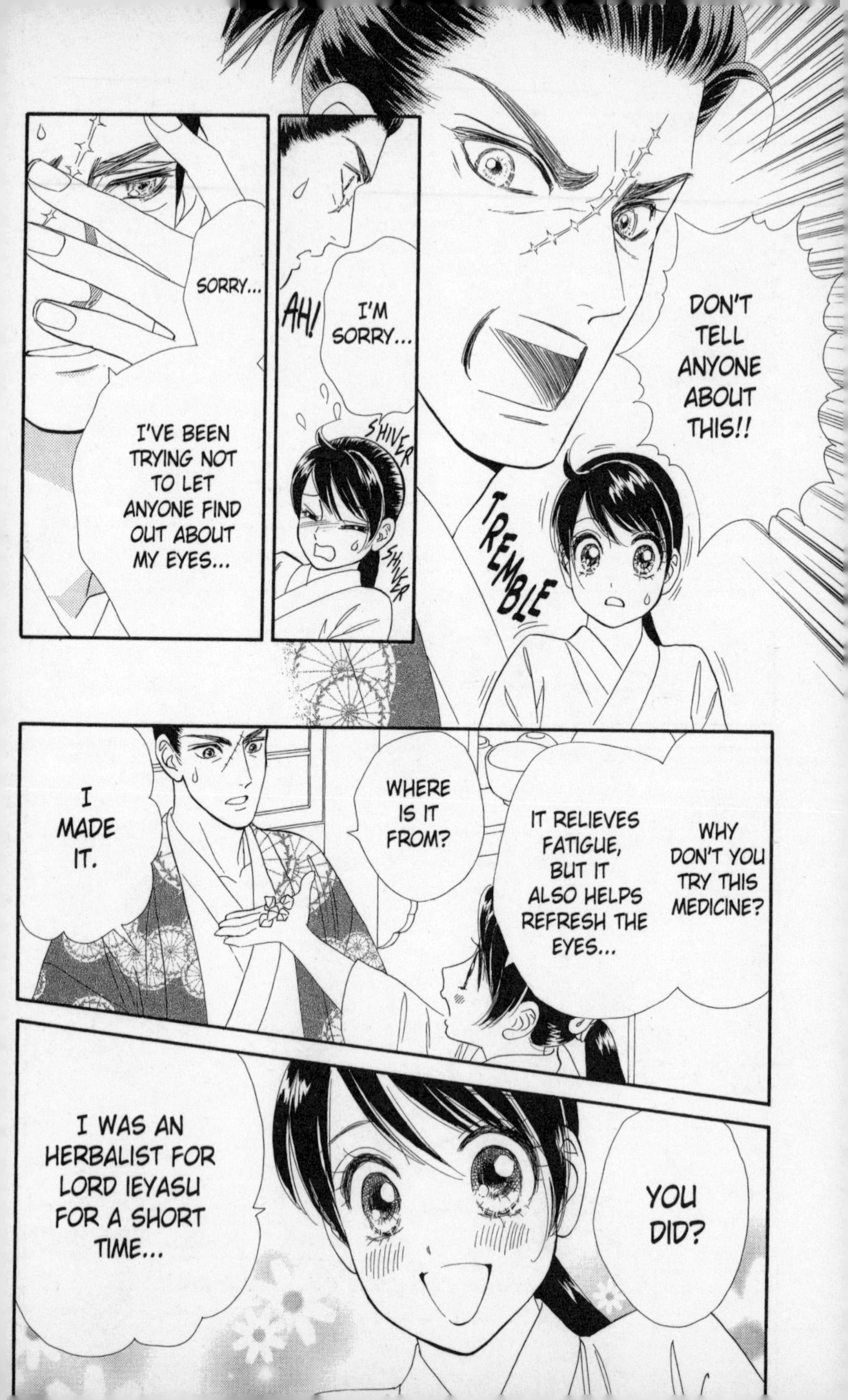
DON'T TELL ANYONE ABOUT THIS!!
TREMBLE
AH!
I'M SORRY...
SHIVER
SHIVER
SORRY...
I'VE BEEN TRYING NOT TO LET ANYONE FIND OUT ABOUT MY EYES...
WHY DON'T YOU TRY THIS MEDICINE?
IT RELIEVES FATIGUE, BUT IT ALSO HELPS REFRESH THE EYES...
WHERE IS IT FROM?
I MADE IT.
YOU DID?
I WAS AN HERBALIST FOR LORD IEYASU FOR A SHORT TIME...

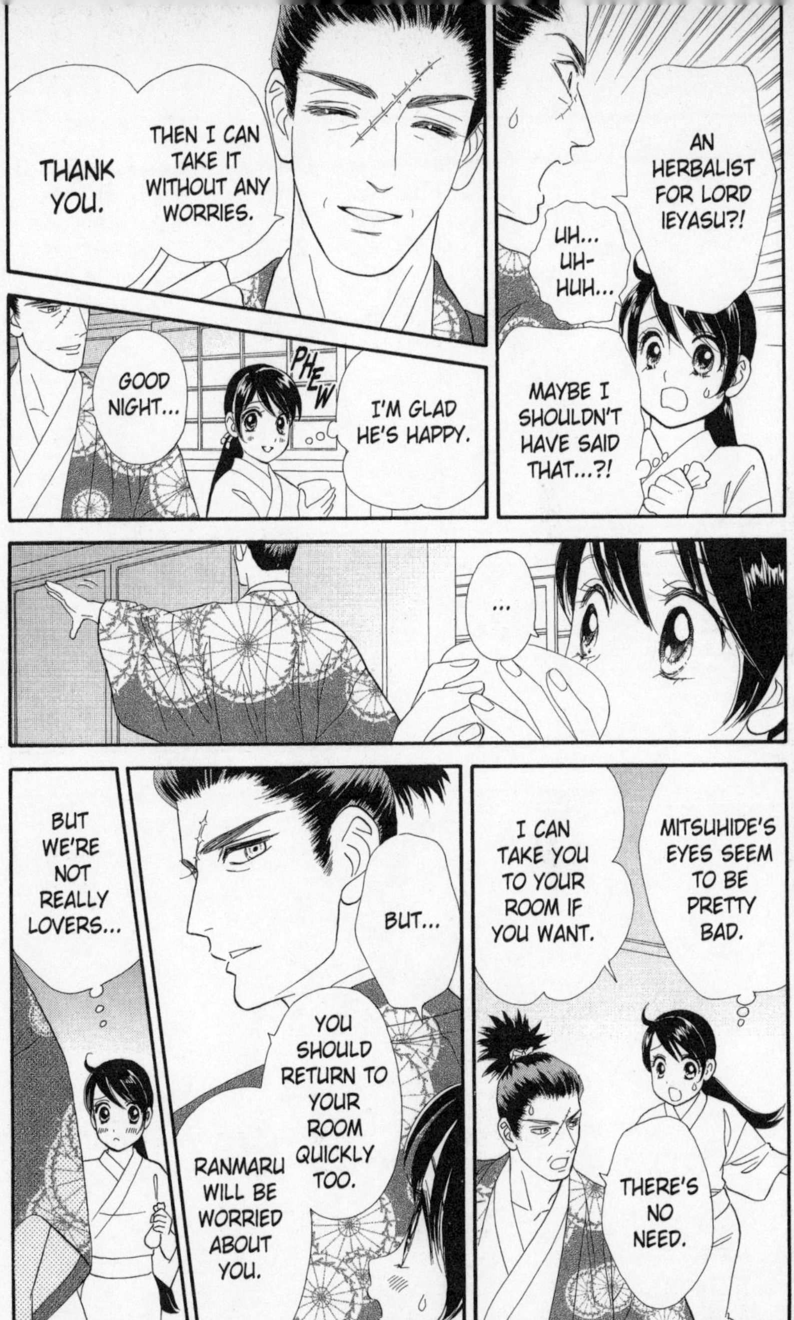

AN HERBALIST FOR LORD IEYASU?!
UH... UH-HUH...
MAYBE I SHOULDN'T HAVE SAID THAT...?!
THEN I CAN TAKE IT WITHOUT ANY WORRIES.
THANK YOU.
PHEW
I'M GLAD HE'S HAPPY.
GOOD NIGHT...
...
MITSUHIDE'S EYES SEEM TO BE PRETTY BAD.
I CAN TAKE YOU TO YOUR ROOM IF YOU WANT.
THERE'S NO NEED.
BUT...
YOU SHOULD RETURN TO YOUR ROOM QUICKLY TOO.
RANMARU WILL BE WORRIED ABOUT YOU.
BUT WE'RE NOT REALLY LOVERS...

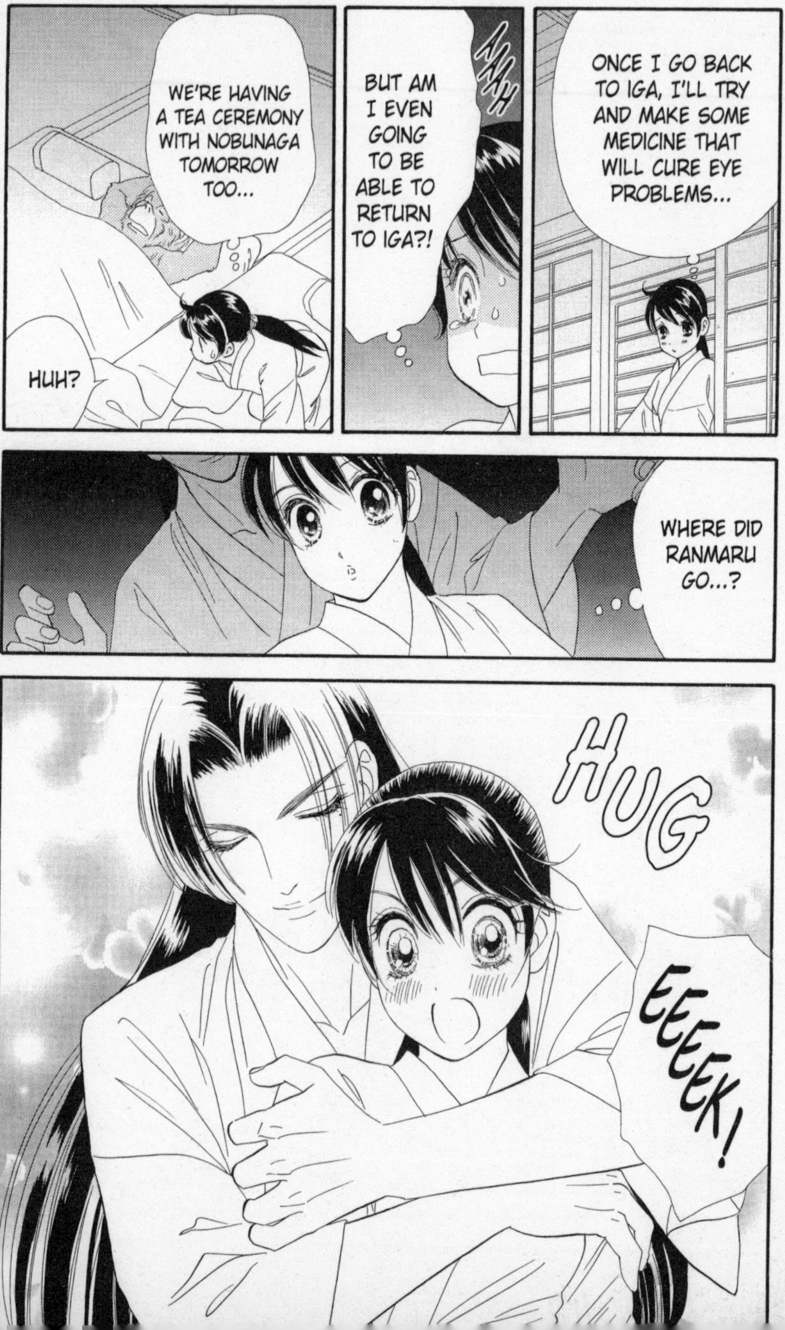
ONCE I GO BACK TO IGA, I'LL TRY AND MAKE SOME MEDICINE THAT WILL CURE EYE PROBLEMS...
BUT AM I EVEN GOING TO BE ABLE TO RETURN TO IGA?!
WE'RE HAVING A TEA CEREMONY WITH NOBUNAGA TOMORROW TOO...
HUH?
WHERE DID RANMARU GO...?
HUG
EEEEK!

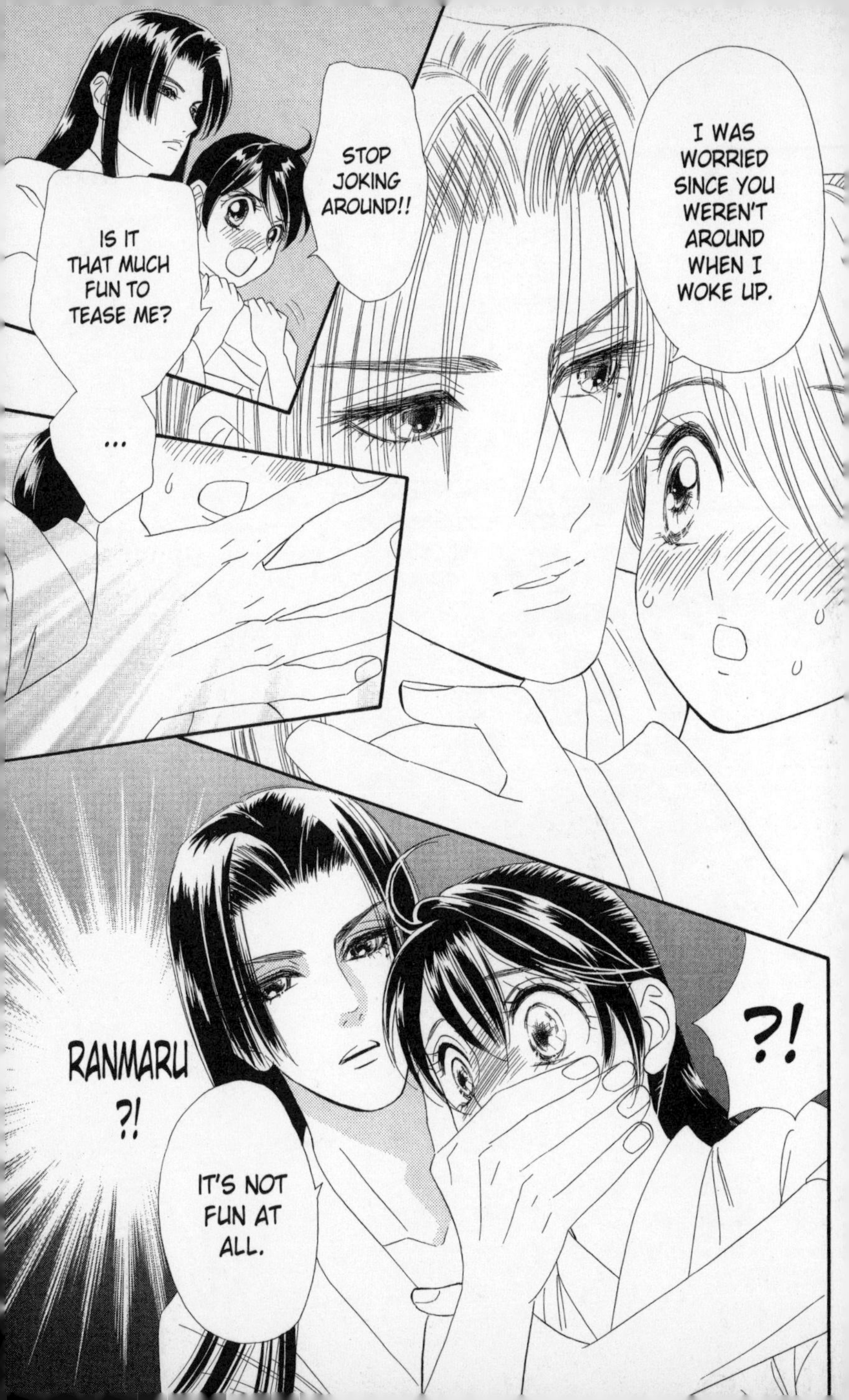

I WAS WORRIED SINCE YOU WEREN'T AROUND WHEN I WOKE UP.
STOP JOKING AROUND!!
IS IT THAT MUCH FUN TO TEASE ME?
...
?!
RANMARU ?!
IT'S NOT FUN AT ALL.

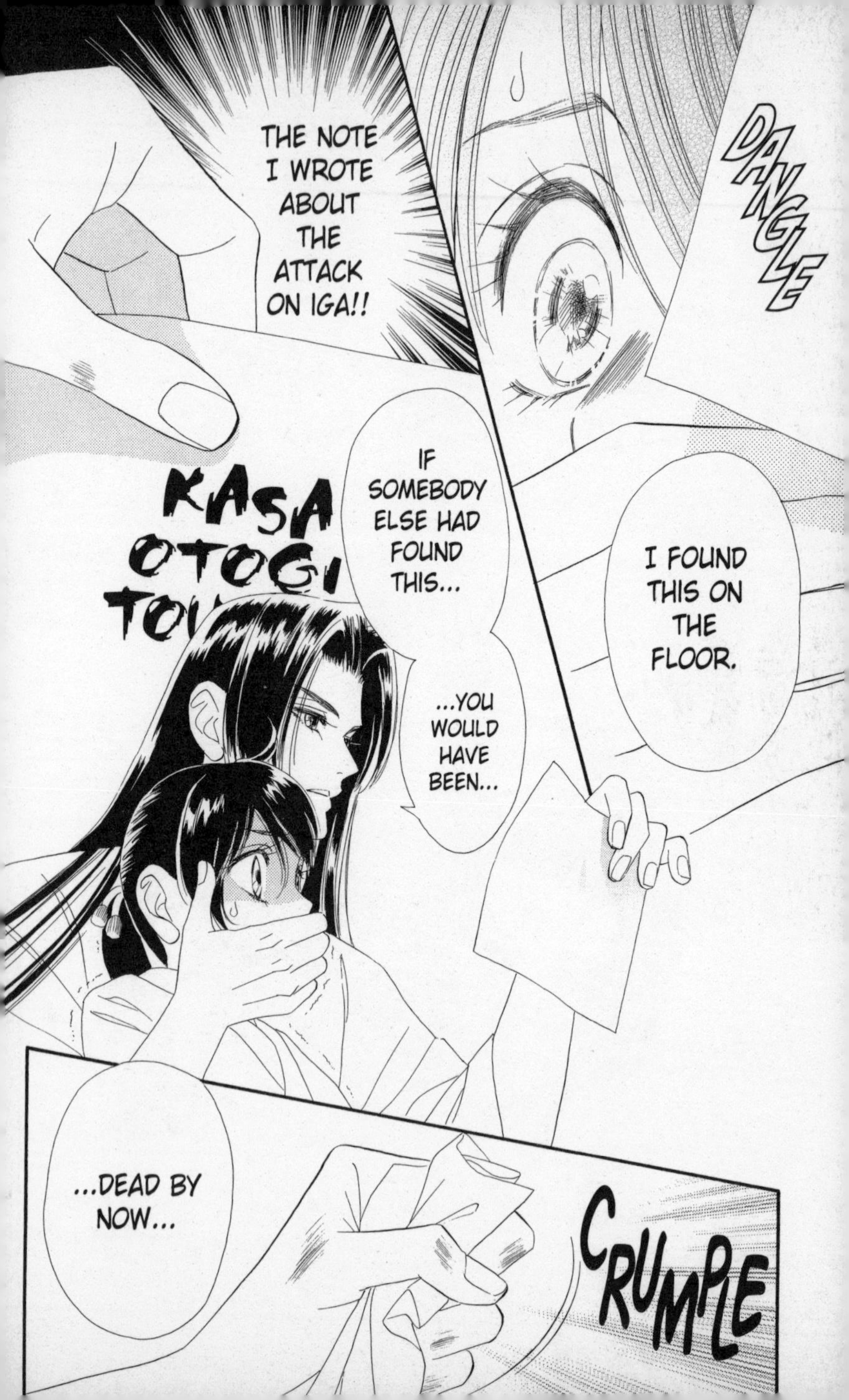
DANGLE
THE NOTE I WROTE ABOUT THE ATTACK ON IGA!!
I FOUND THIS ON THE FLOOR.
IF SOMEBODY ELSE HAD FOUND THIS...
KASA OTOGI
...YOU WOULD HAVE BEEN...
CRUMPLE
...DEAD BY NOW...

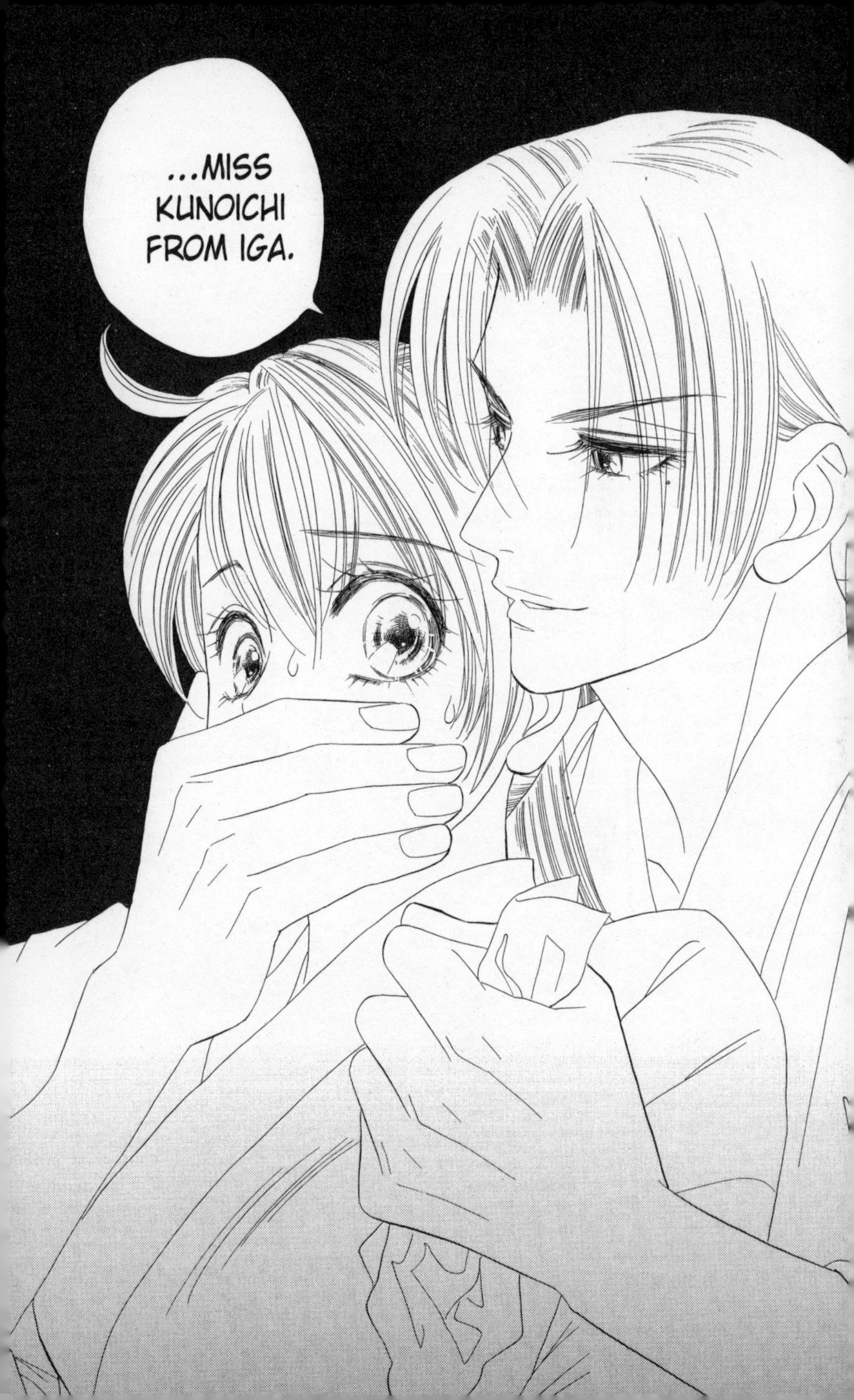
...MISS KUNOICHI FROM IGA.

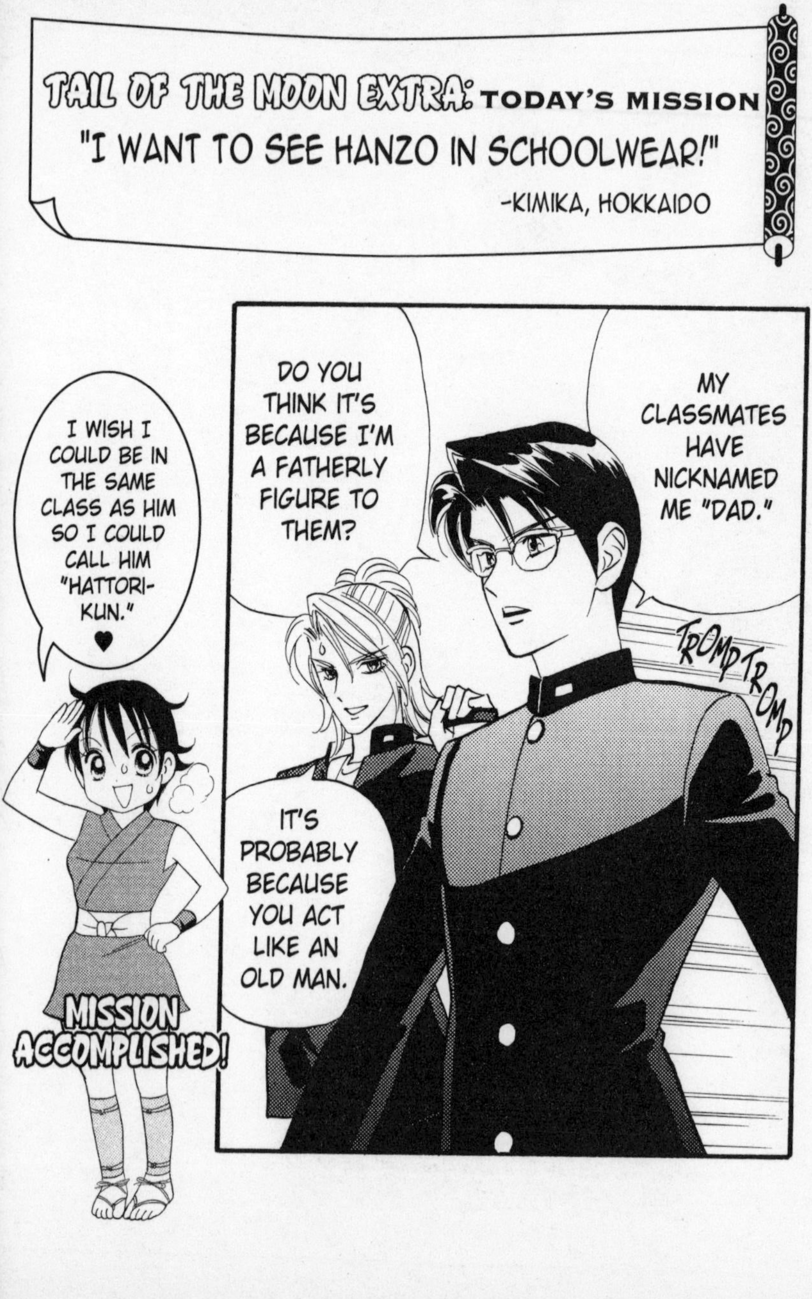
TAIL OF THE MOON EXTRA: TODAY'S MISSION
"I WANT TO SEE HANZO IN SCHOOLWEAR!"
-KIMIKA, HOKKAIDO
MY CLASSMATES HAVE NICKNAMED ME "DAD."
DO YOU THINK IT'S BECAUSE I'M A FATHERLY FIGURE TO THEM?
TROMP TROMP TROMP
IT'S PROBABLY BECAUSE YOU ACT LIKE AN OLD MAN.
I WISH I COULD BE IN THE SAME CLASS AS HIM SO I COULD CALL HIM "HATTORI-KUN." ♥
MISSION ACCOMPLISHED!

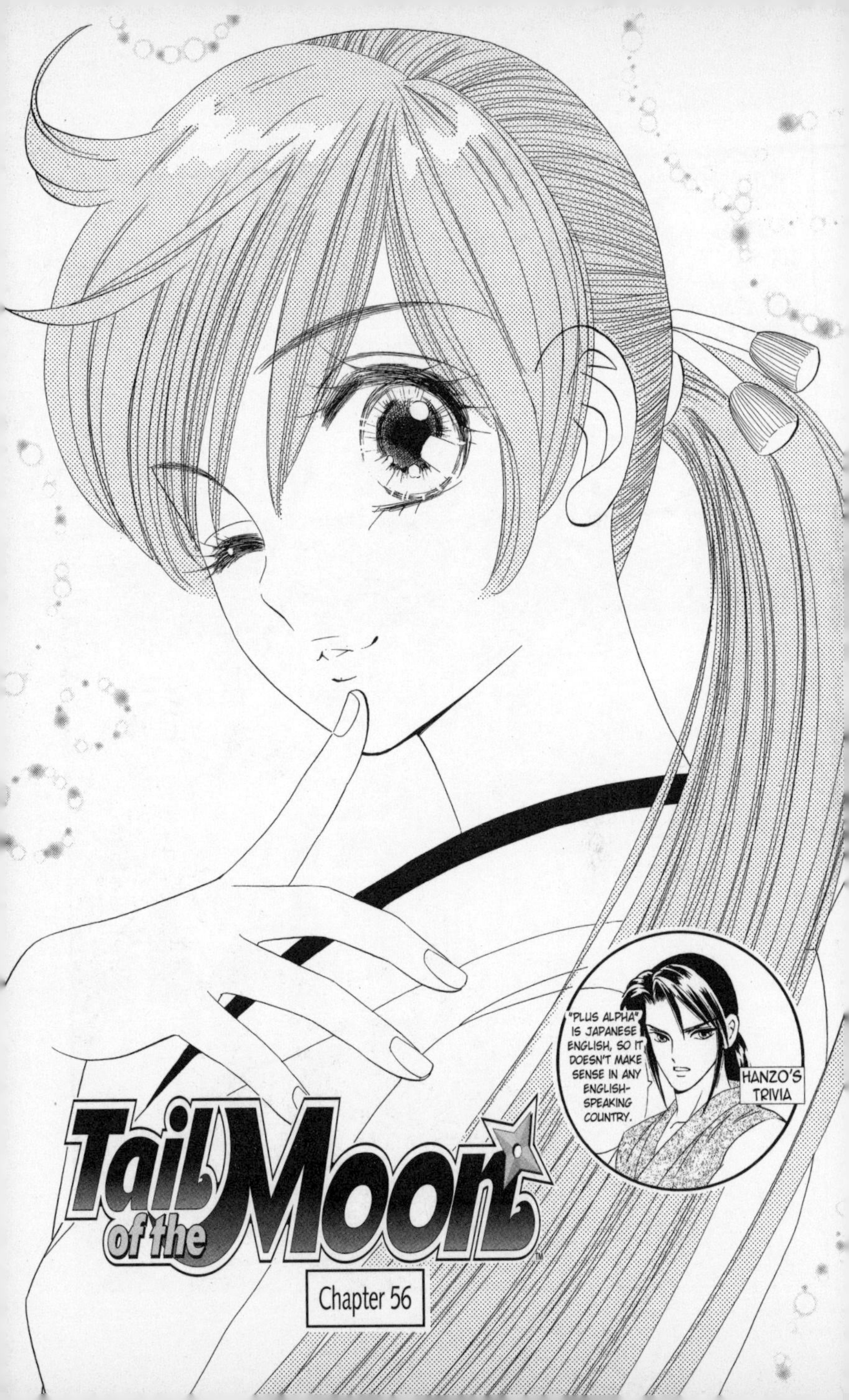
"PLUS ALPHA" IS JAPANESE ENGLISH, SO IT DOESN'T MAKE SENSE IN ANY ENGLISH-SPEAKING COUNTRY.
HANZO'S TRIVIA
Tail of the Moon™
Chapter 56

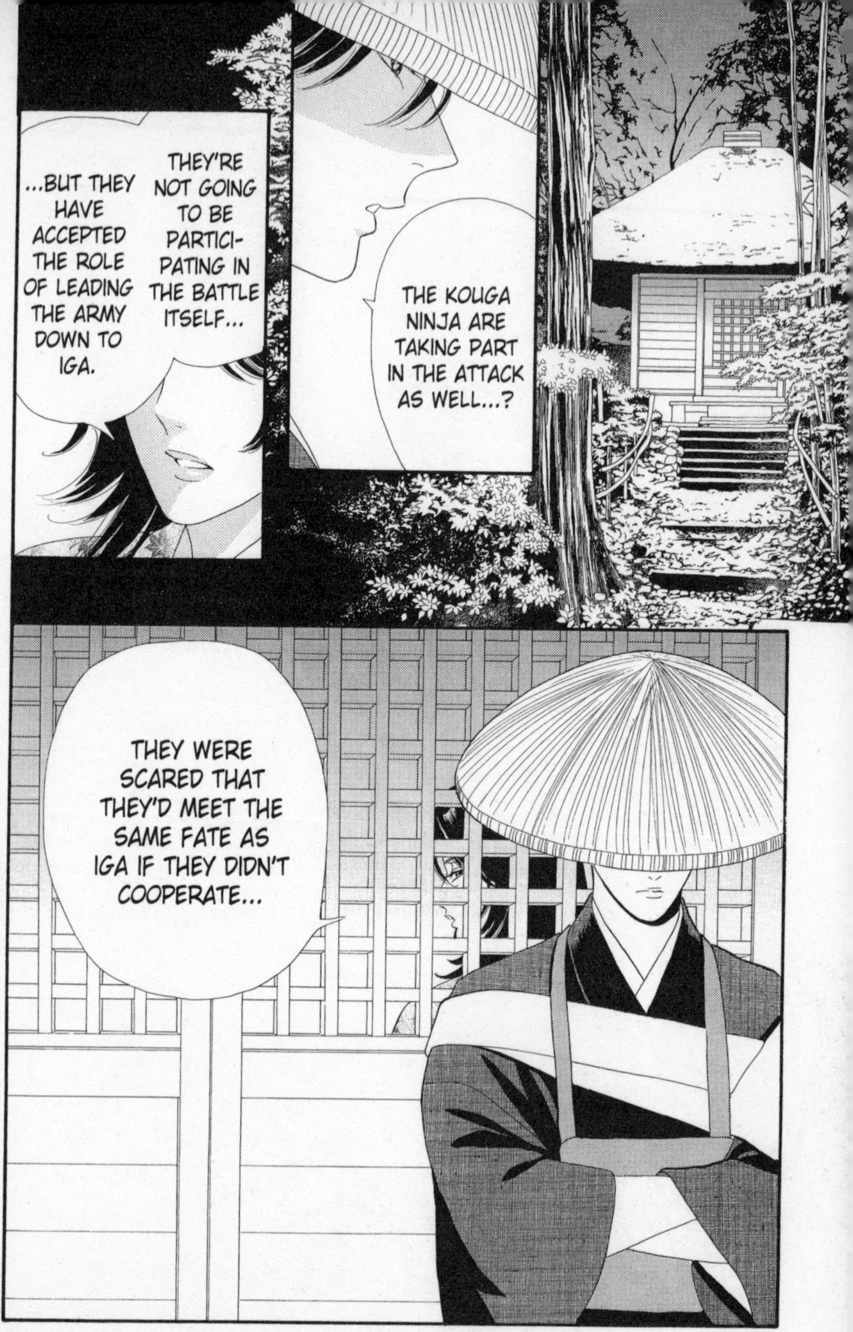
THE KOUGA NINJA ARE TAKING PART IN THE ATTACK AS WELL...?
THEY'RE NOT GOING TO BE PARTICI-PATING IN THE BATTLE ITSELF...
...BUT THEY HAVE ACCEPTED THE ROLE OF LEADING THE ARMY DOWN TO IGA.
THEY WERE SCARED THAT THEY'D MEET THE SAME FATE AS IGA IF THEY DIDN'T COOPERATE...

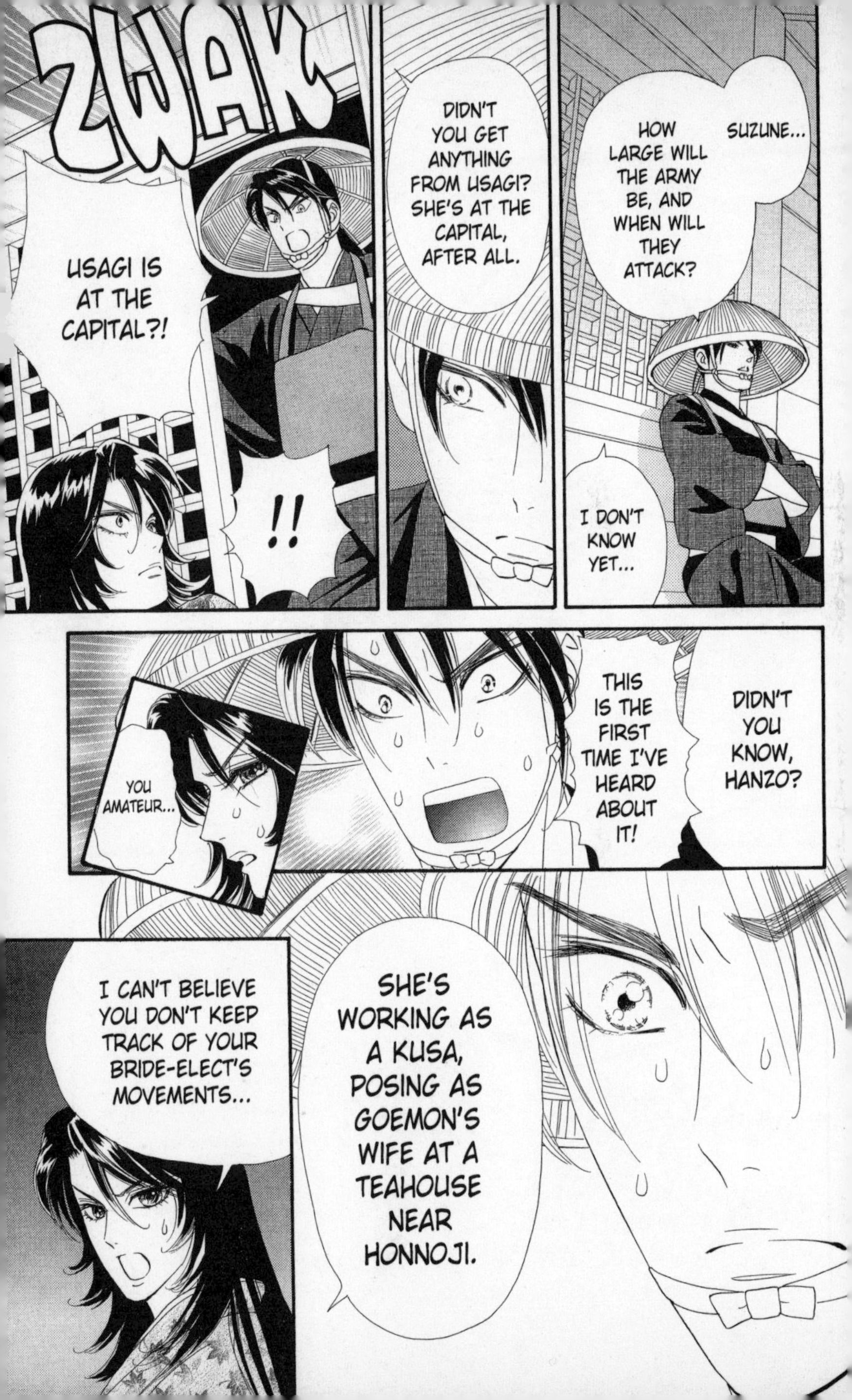
SUZUNE...
HOW LARGE WILL THE ARMY BE, AND WHEN WILL THEY ATTACK?
I DON'T KNOW YET...
DIDN'T YOU GET ANYTHING FROM USAGI? SHE'S AT THE CAPITAL, AFTER ALL.
ZWAK
USAGI IS AT THE CAPITAL?!
!!
DIDN'T YOU KNOW, HANZO?
THIS IS THE FIRST TIME I'VE HEARD ABOUT IT!
YOU AMATEUR...
SHE'S WORKING AS A KUSA, POSING AS GOEMON'S WIFE AT A TEAHOUSE NEAR HONNOJI.
I CAN'T BELIEVE YOU DON'T KEEP TRACK OF YOUR BRIDE-ELECT'S MOVEMENTS...

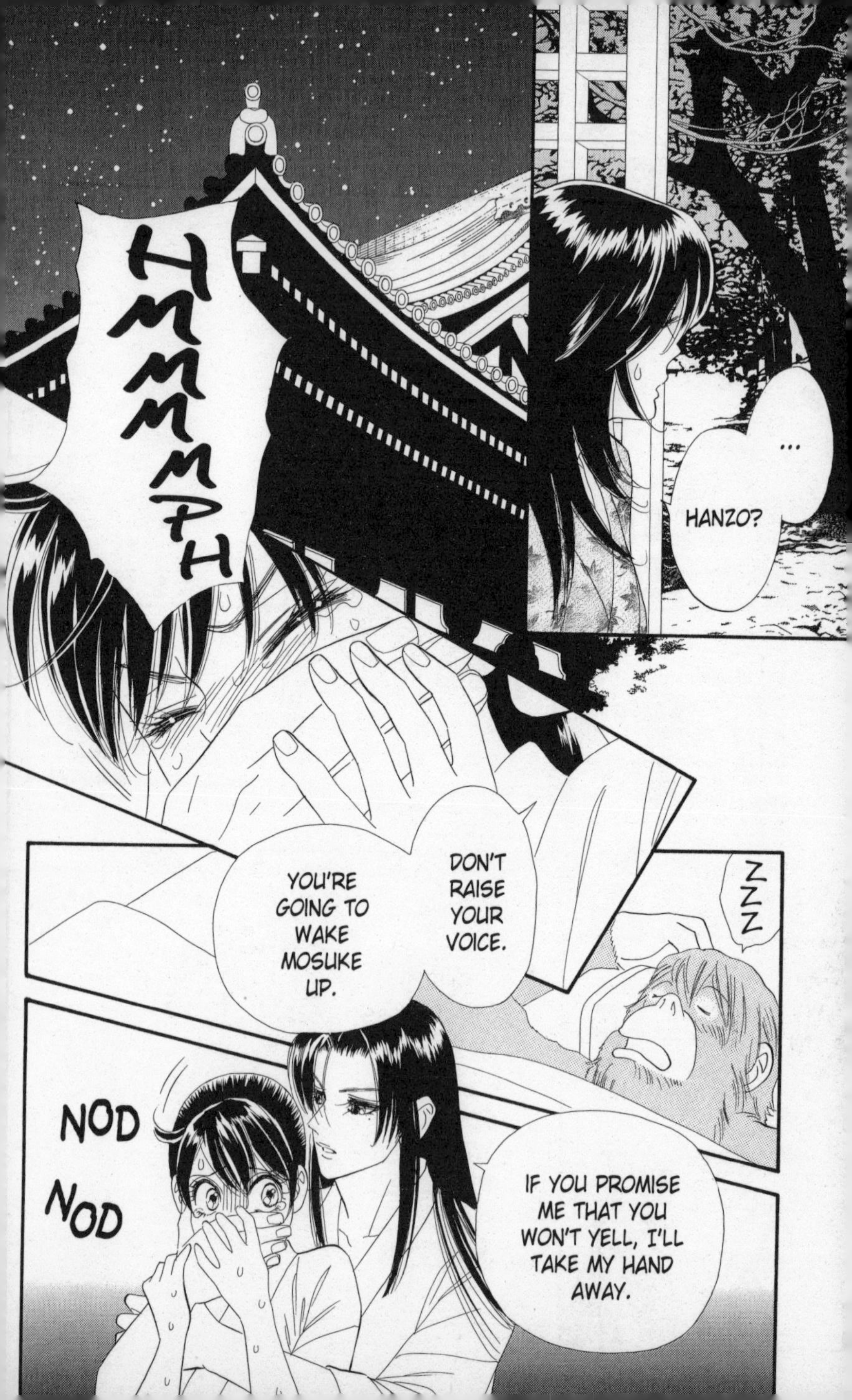
...
HANZO?
HMMMMPH
DON'T RAISE YOUR VOICE.
YOU'RE GOING TO WAKE MOSUKE UP.
ZZZ
IF YOU PROMISE ME THAT YOU WON'T YELL, I'LL TAKE MY HAND AWAY.
NOD NOD

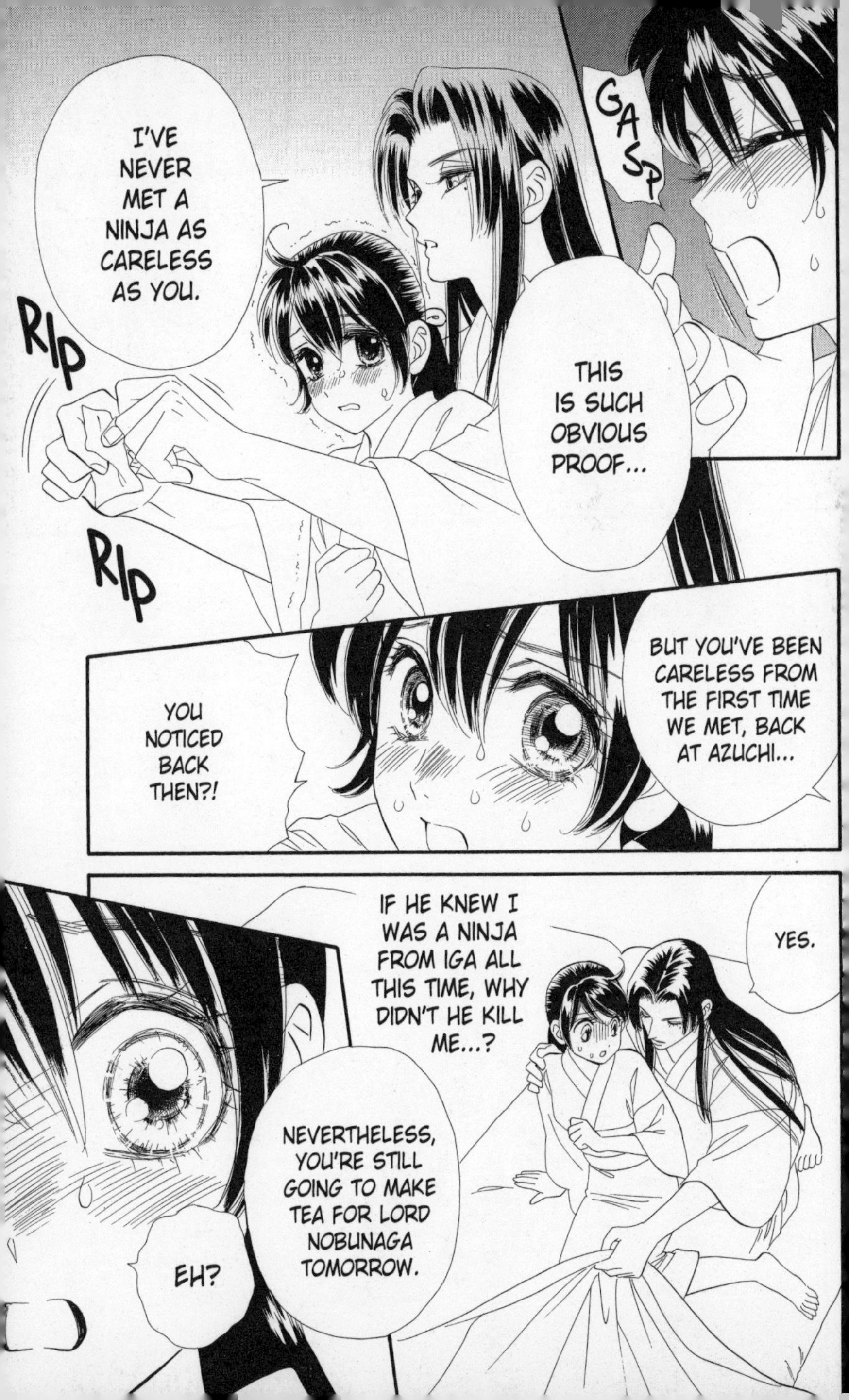
GASP
I'VE NEVER MET A NINJA AS CARELESS AS YOU.
RIP
RIP
THIS IS SUCH OBVIOUS PROOF...
BUT YOU'VE BEEN CARELESS FROM THE FIRST TIME WE MET, BACK AT AZUCHI...
YOU NOTICED BACK THEN?!
YES.
IF HE KNEW I WAS A NINJA FROM IGA ALL THIS TIME, WHY DIDN'T HE KILL ME...?
NEVERTHELESS, YOU'RE STILL GOING TO MAKE TEA FOR LORD NOBUNAGA TOMORROW.
EH?

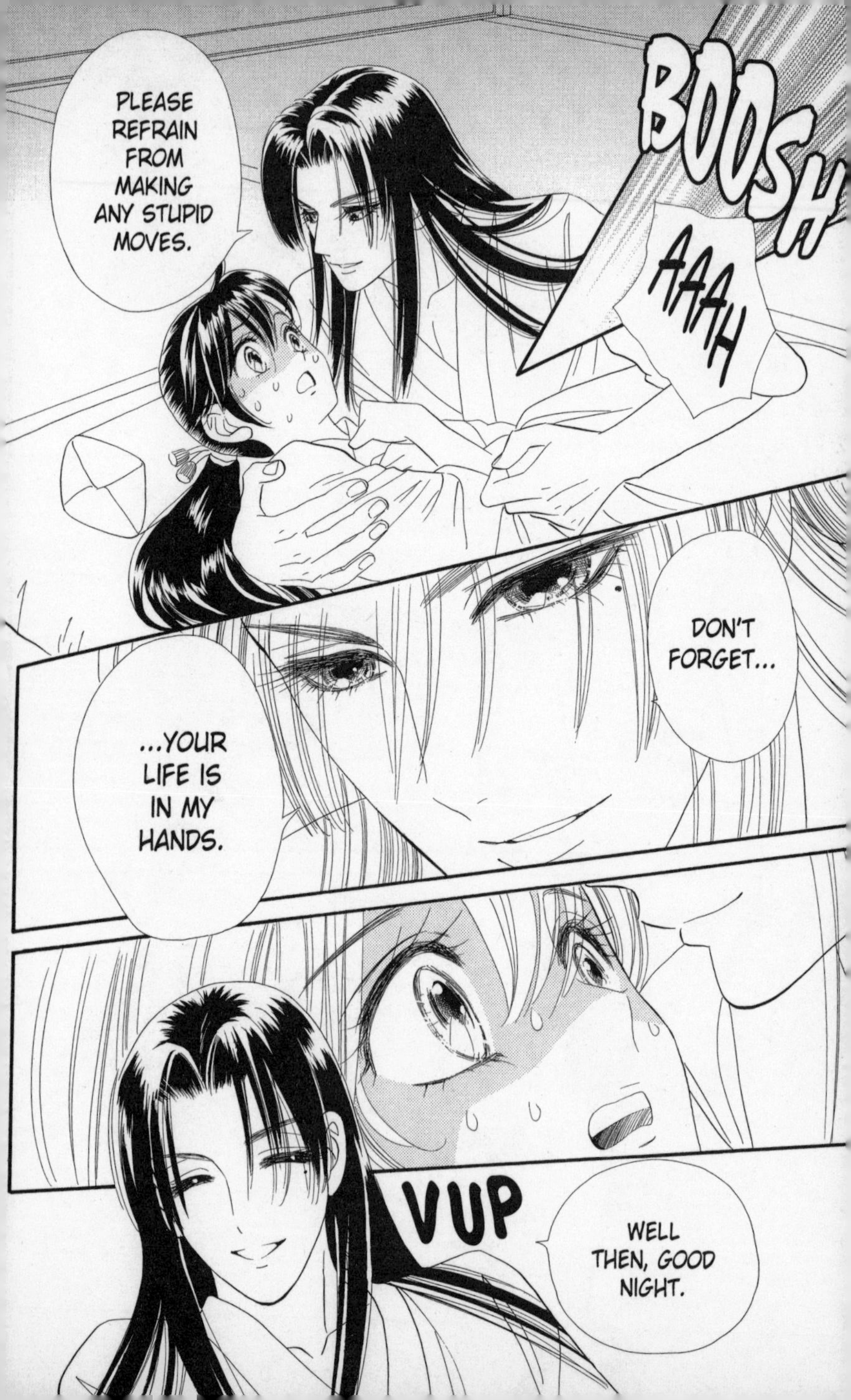
BOOSH
AAAH
PLEASE REFRAIN FROM MAKING ANY STUPID MOVES.
DON'T FORGET...
...YOUR LIFE IS IN MY HANDS.
WELL THEN, GOOD NIGHT.
VUP

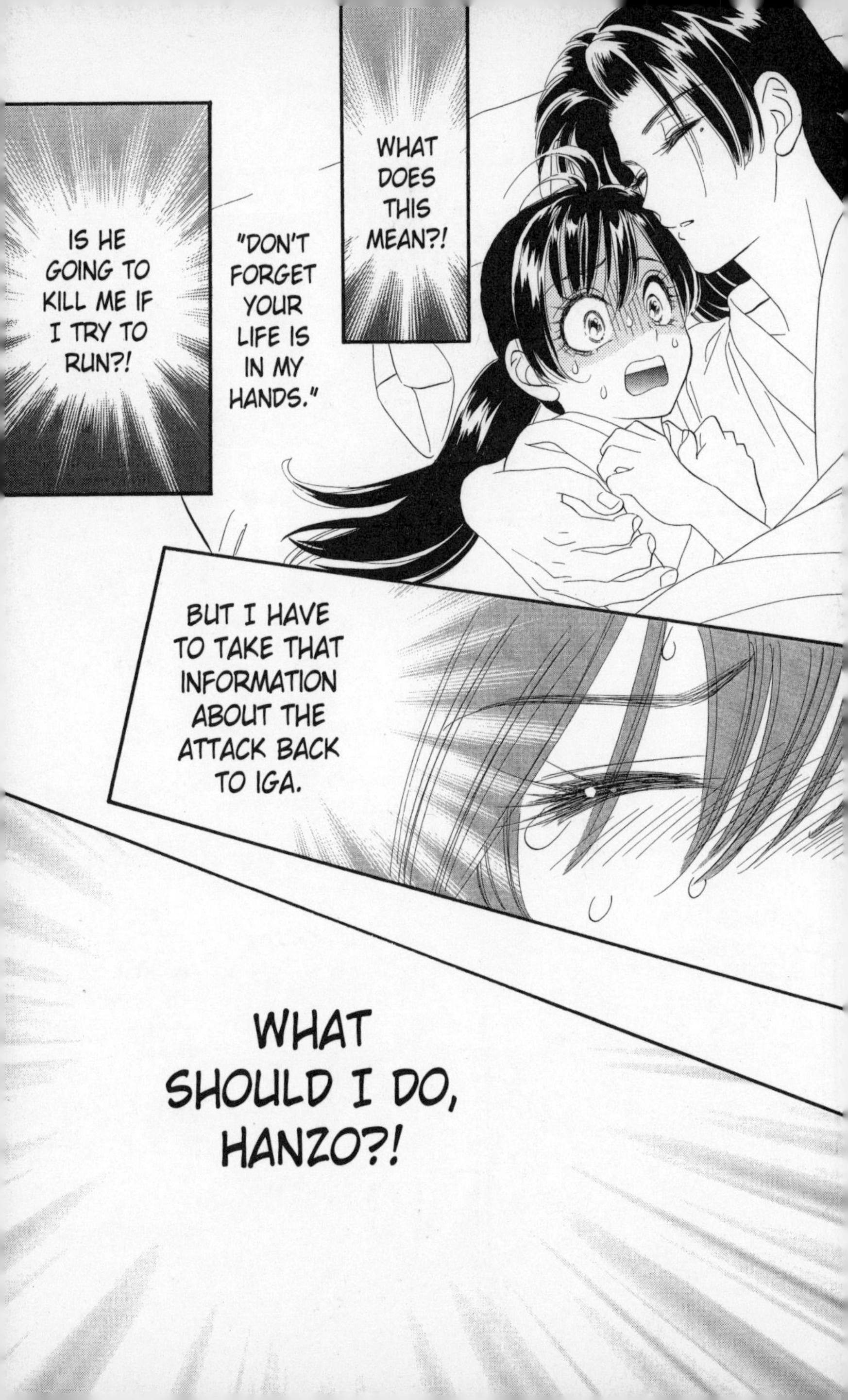

WHAT DOES THIS MEAN?!
"DON'T FORGET YOUR LIFE IS IN MY HANDS."
IS HE GOING TO KILL ME IF I TRY TO RUN?!
BUT I HAVE TO TAKE THAT INFORMATION ABOUT THE ATTACK BACK TO IGA.
WHAT SHOULD I DO, HANZO?!

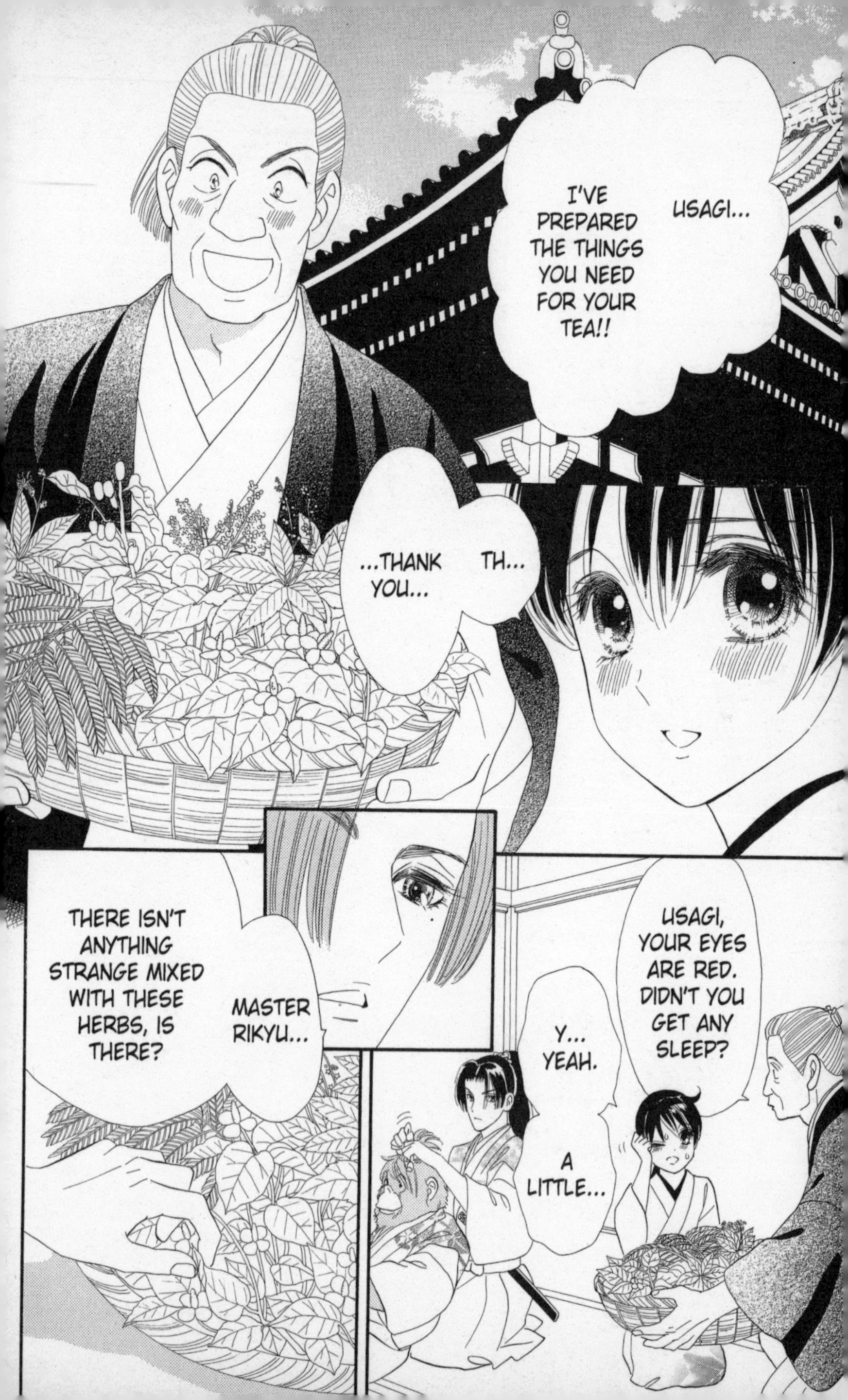
USAGI... I'VE PREPARED THE THINGS YOU NEED FOR YOUR TEA!!
TH... ...THANK YOU...
USAGI, YOUR EYES ARE RED. DIDN'T YOU GET ANY SLEEP?
Y... YEAH.
A LITTLE...
MASTER RIKYU...
THERE ISN'T ANYTHING STRANGE MIXED WITH THESE HERBS, IS THERE?

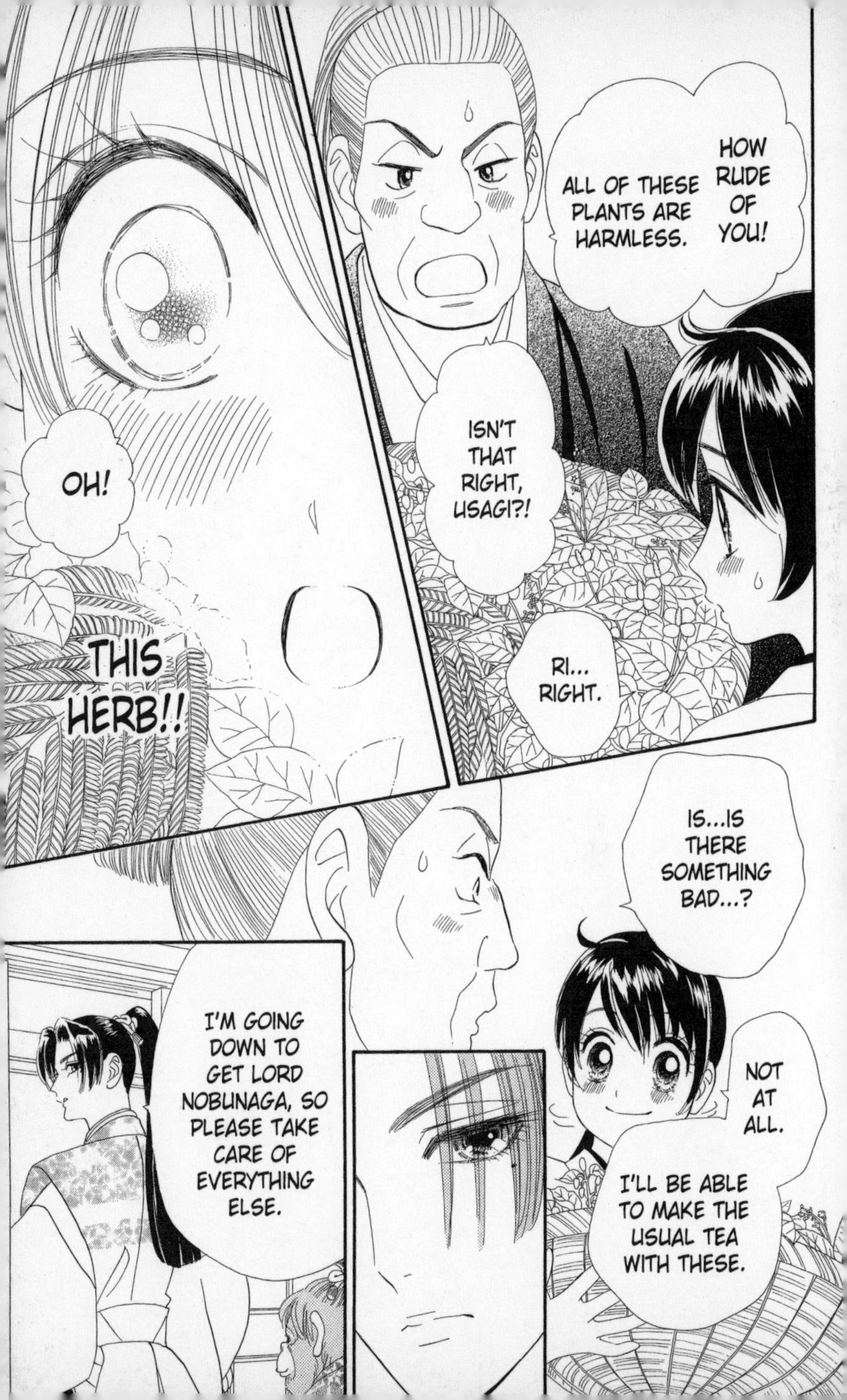
HOW RUDE OF YOU!
ALL OF THESE PLANTS ARE HARMLESS.
ISN'T THAT RIGHT, USAGI?!
RI... RIGHT.
OH!
THIS HERB!!
IS...IS THERE SOMETHING BAD...?
NOT AT ALL.
I'LL BE ABLE TO MAKE THE USUAL TEA WITH THESE.
I'M GOING DOWN TO GET LORD NOBUNAGA, SO PLEASE TAKE CARE OF EVERYTHING ELSE.

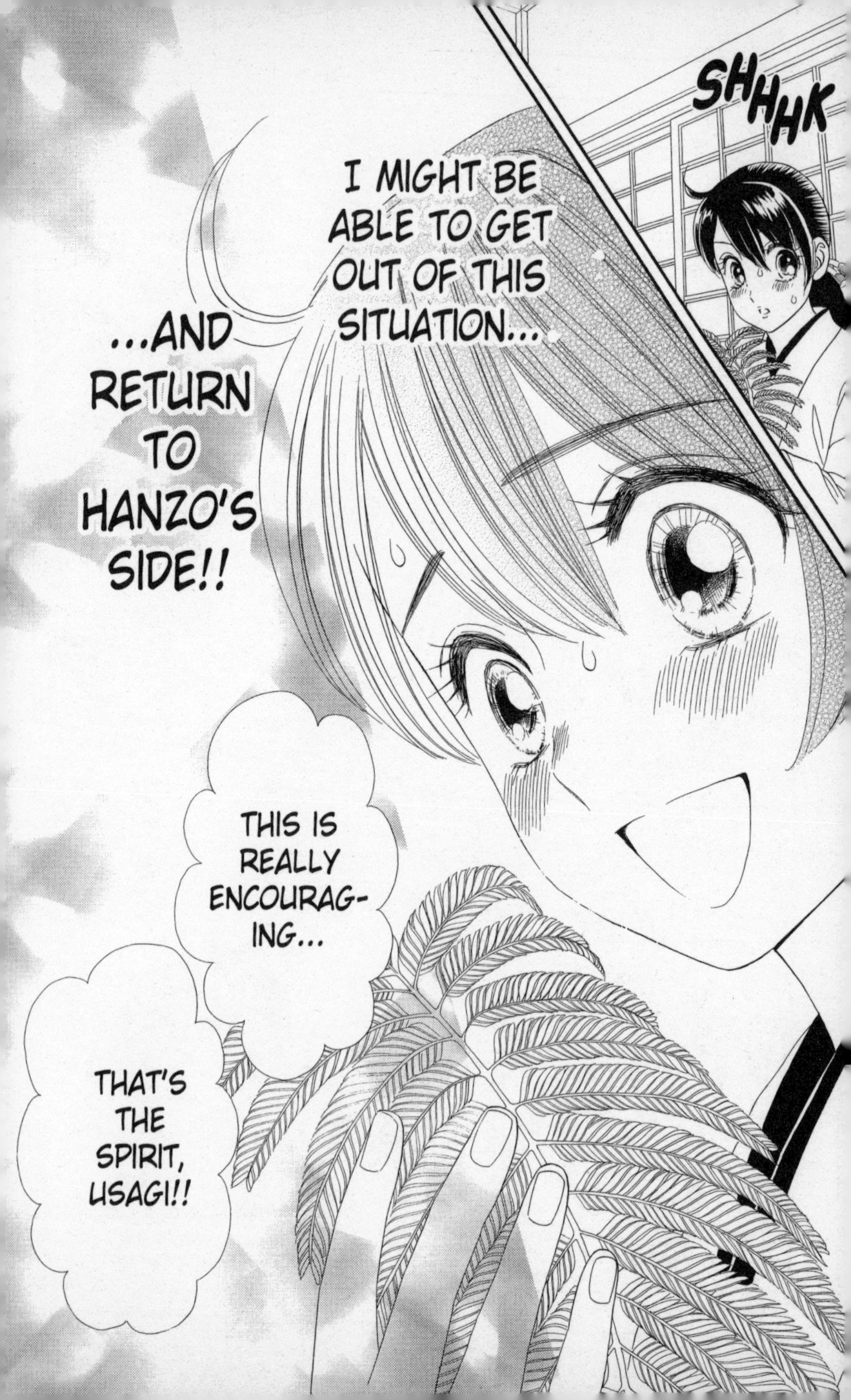
SHHHK
I MIGHT BE ABLE TO GET OUT OF THIS SITUATION...
...AND RETURN TO HANZO'S SIDE!!
THIS IS REALLY ENCOURAG-ING...
THAT'S THE SPIRIT, USAGI!!

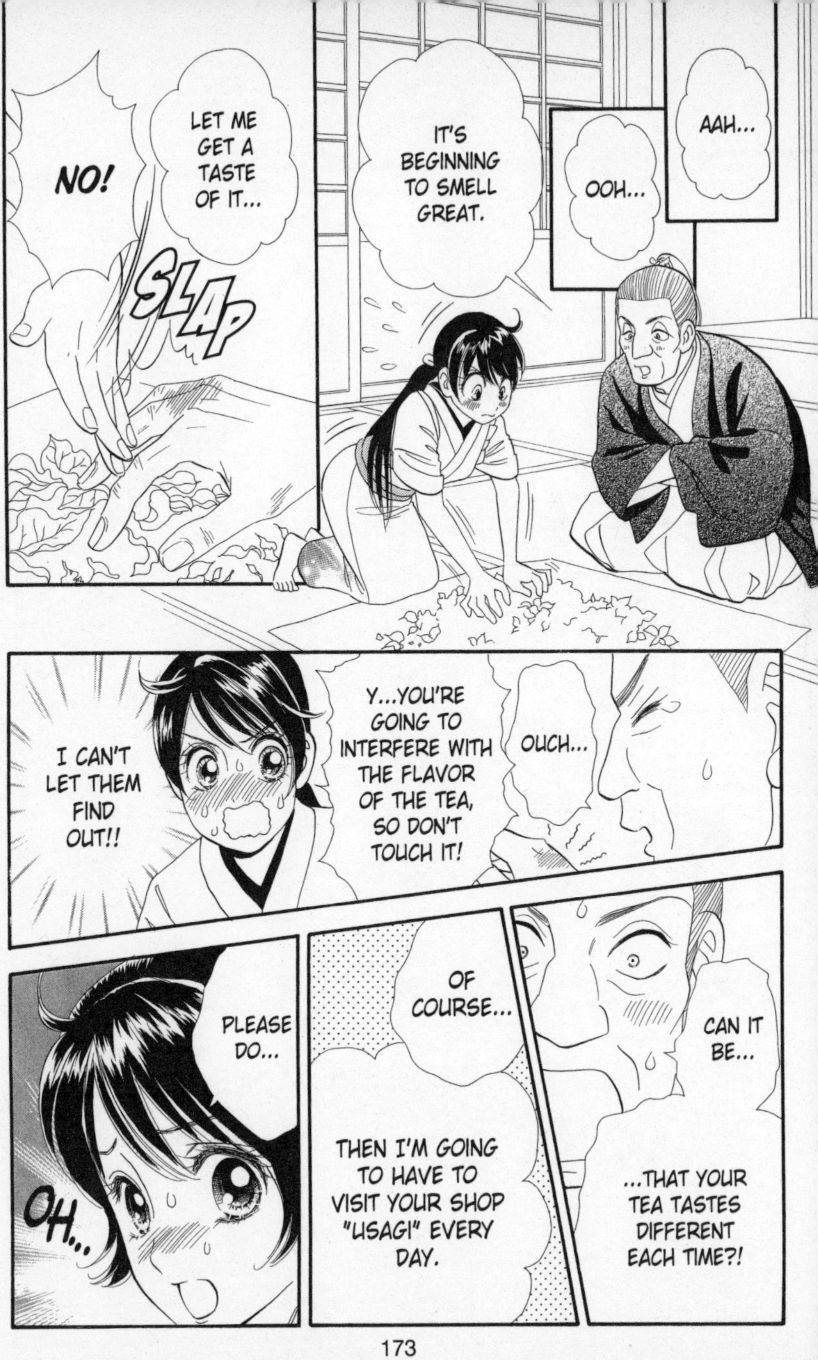
AAH...
OOH...
IT'S BEGINNING TO SMELL GREAT.
LET ME GET A TASTE OF IT...
NO!
SLAP
OUCH...
Y...YOU'RE GOING TO INTERFERE WITH THE FLAVOR OF THE TEA, SO DON'T TOUCH IT!
I CAN'T LET THEM FIND OUT!!
CAN IT BE...
...THAT YOUR TEA TASTES DIFFERENT EACH TIME?!
OF COURSE...
THEN I'M GOING TO HAVE TO VISIT YOUR SHOP "USAGI" EVERY DAY.
PLEASE DO...
OH...

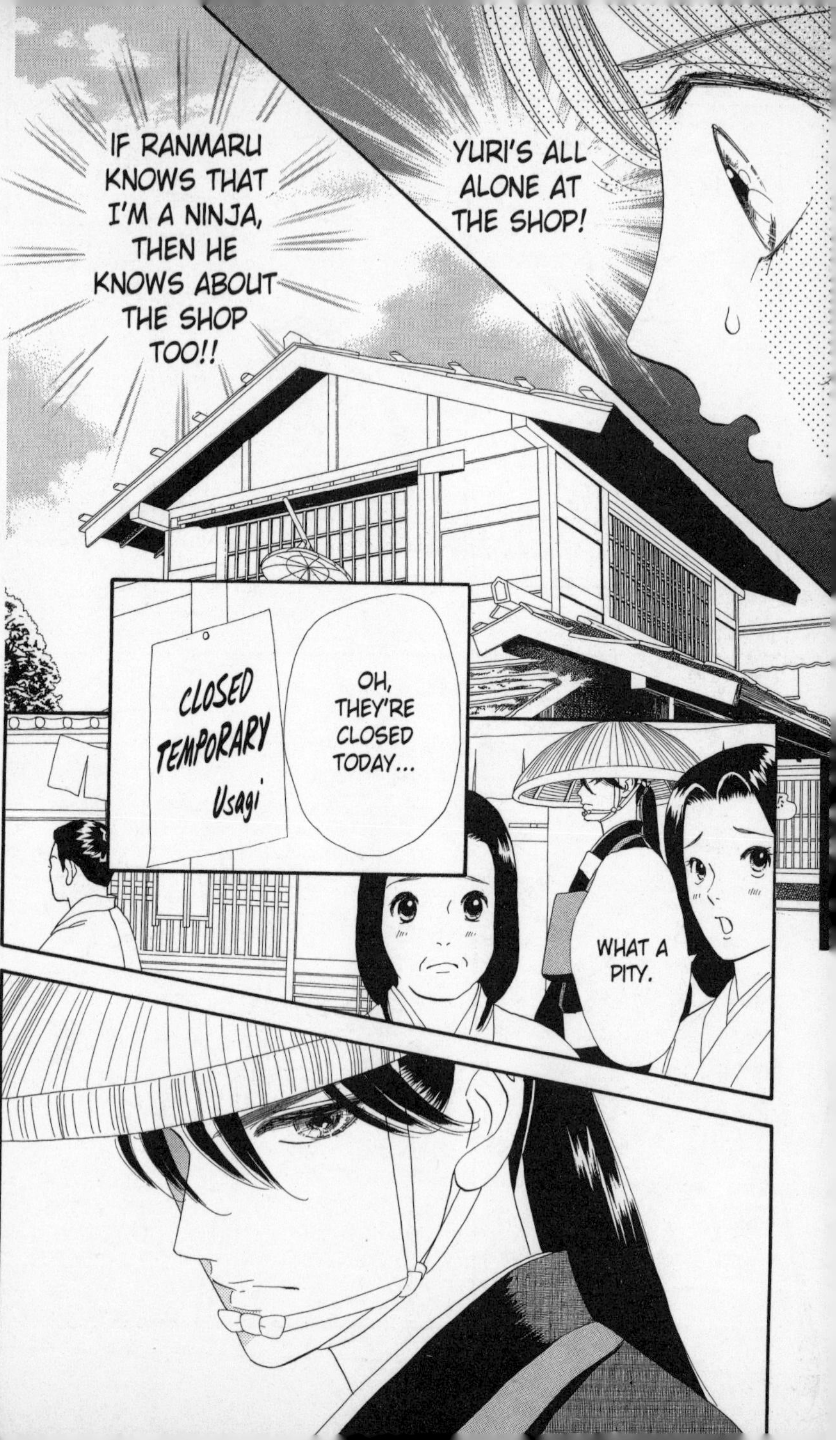
YURI'S ALL ALONE AT THE SHOP!
IF RANMARU KNOWS THAT I'M A NINJA, THEN HE KNOWS ABOUT THE SHOP TOO!!
CLOSED TEMPORARY
Usagi
OH, THEY'RE CLOSED TODAY...
WHAT A PITY.

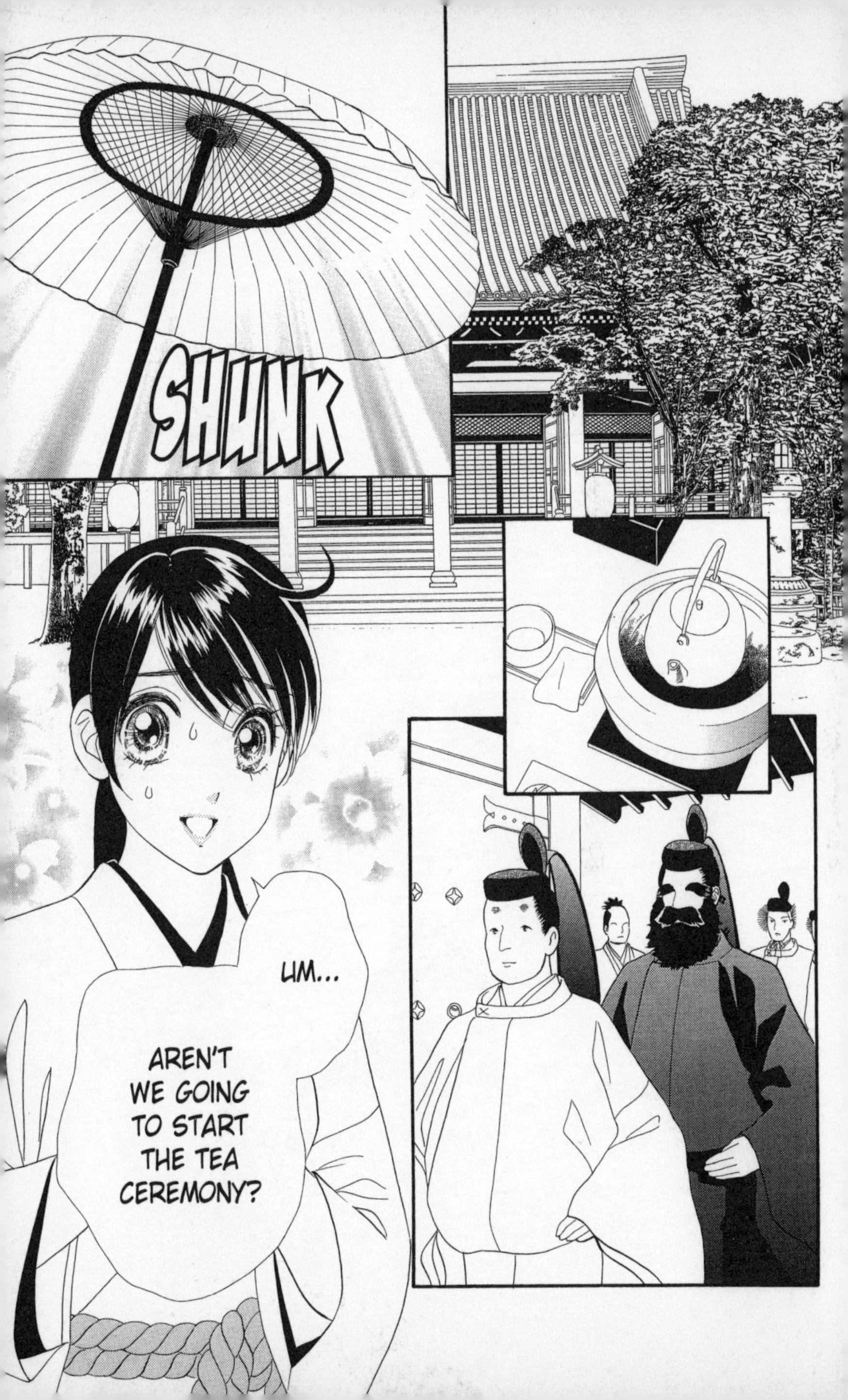
SHUNK
UM...
AREN'T WE GOING TO START THE TEA CEREMONY?

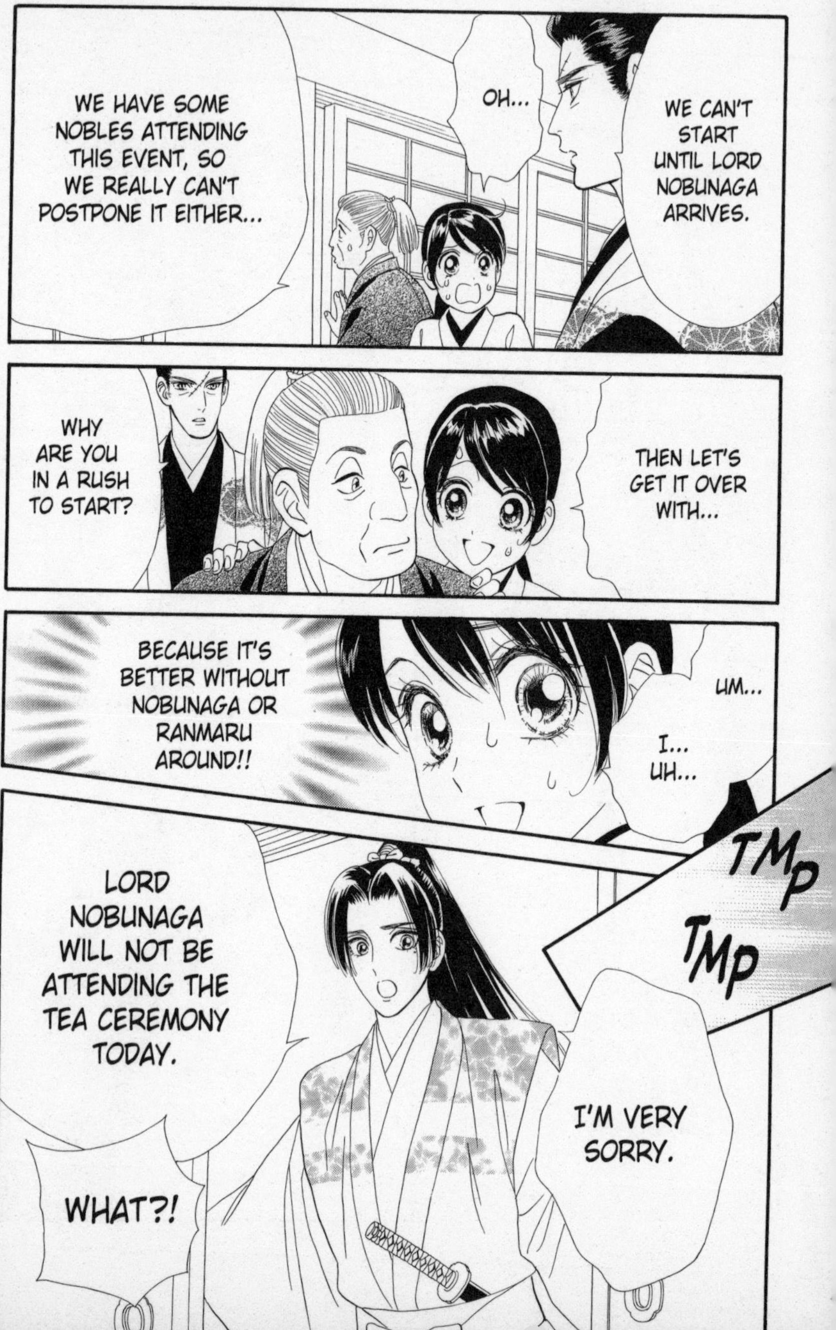
WE CAN'T START UNTIL LORD NOBUNAGA ARRIVES.
OH...
WE HAVE SOME NOBLES ATTENDING THIS EVENT, SO WE REALLY CAN'T POSTPONE IT EITHER...
THEN LET'S GET IT OVER WITH...
WHY ARE YOU IN A RUSH TO START?
UM...
I... UH...
BECAUSE IT'S BETTER WITHOUT NOBUNAGA OR RANMARU AROUND!!
TMP
TMP
LORD NOBUNAGA WILL NOT BE ATTENDING THE TEA CEREMONY TODAY.
I'M VERY SORRY.
WHAT?!

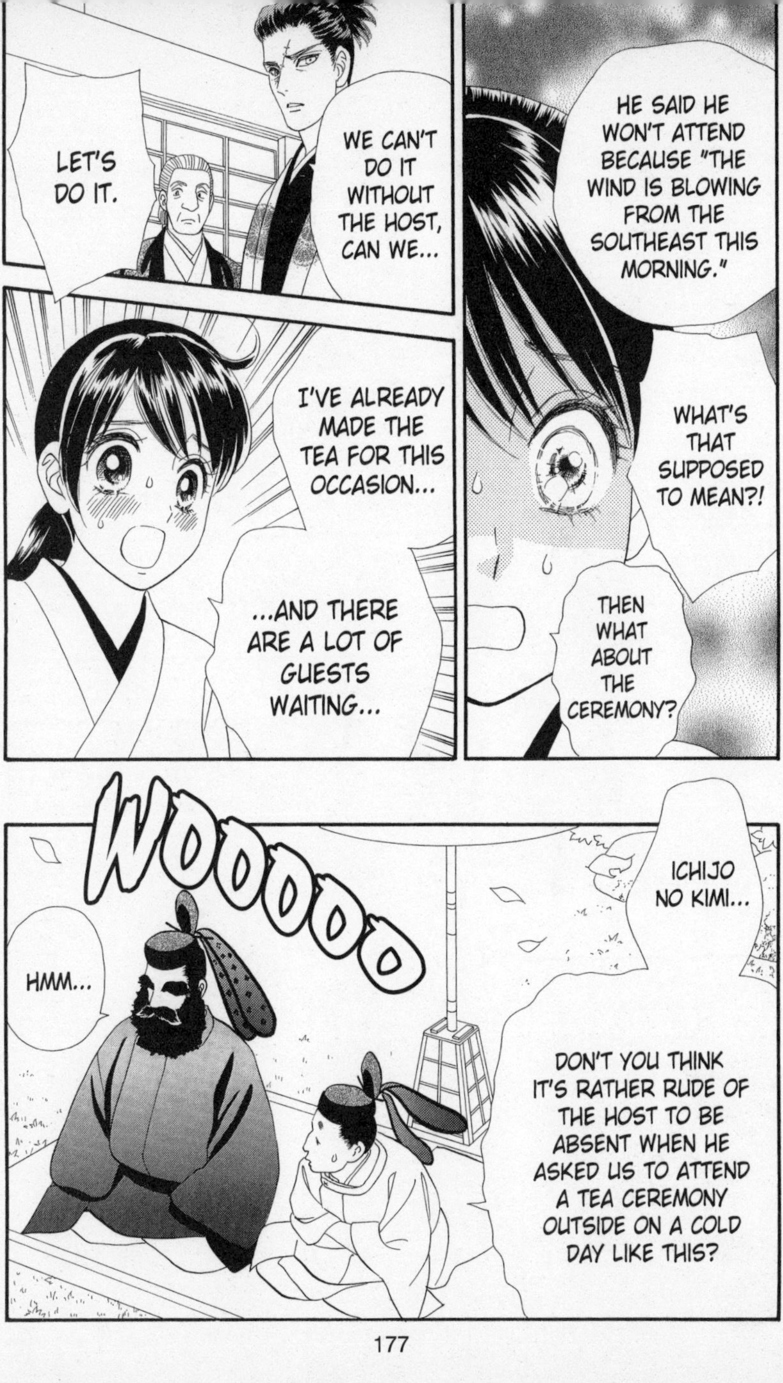
HE SAID HE WON'T ATTEND BECAUSE "THE WIND IS BLOWING FROM THE SOUTHEAST THIS MORNING."
WHAT'S THAT SUPPOSED TO MEAN?!
THEN WHAT ABOUT THE CEREMONY?
WE CAN'T DO IT WITHOUT THE HOST, CAN WE...
LET'S DO IT.
I'VE ALREADY MADE THE TEA FOR THIS OCCASION...
...AND THERE ARE A LOT OF GUESTS WAITING...
ICHIJO NO KIMI...
WOOOOOO
DON'T YOU THINK IT'S RATHER RUDE OF THE HOST TO BE ABSENT WHEN HE ASKED US TO ATTEND A TEA CEREMONY OUTSIDE ON A COLD DAY LIKE THIS?
HMM...

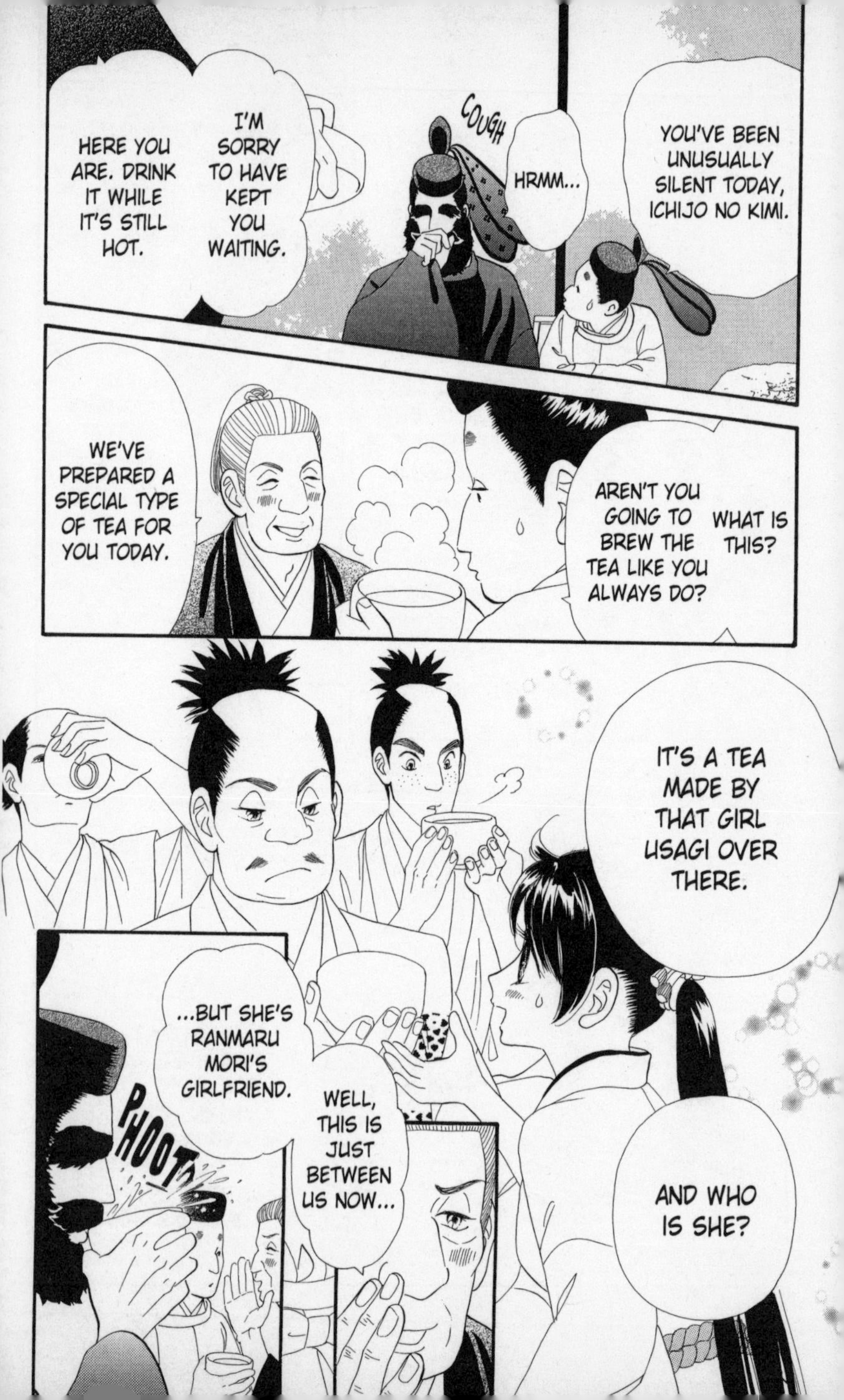
YOU'VE BEEN UNUSUALLY SILENT TODAY, ICHIJO NO KIMI.
COUGH
HRMM...
I'M SORRY TO HAVE KEPT YOU WAITING.
HERE YOU ARE. DRINK IT WHILE IT'S STILL HOT.
WHAT IS THIS?
AREN'T YOU GOING TO BREW THE TEA LIKE YOU ALWAYS DO?
WE'VE PREPARED A SPECIAL TYPE OF TEA FOR YOU TODAY.
IT'S A TEA MADE BY THAT GIRL USAGI OVER THERE.
AND WHO IS SHE?
WELL, THIS IS JUST BETWEEN US NOW...
...BUT SHE'S RANMARU MORI'S GIRLFRIEND.
PHOOT!

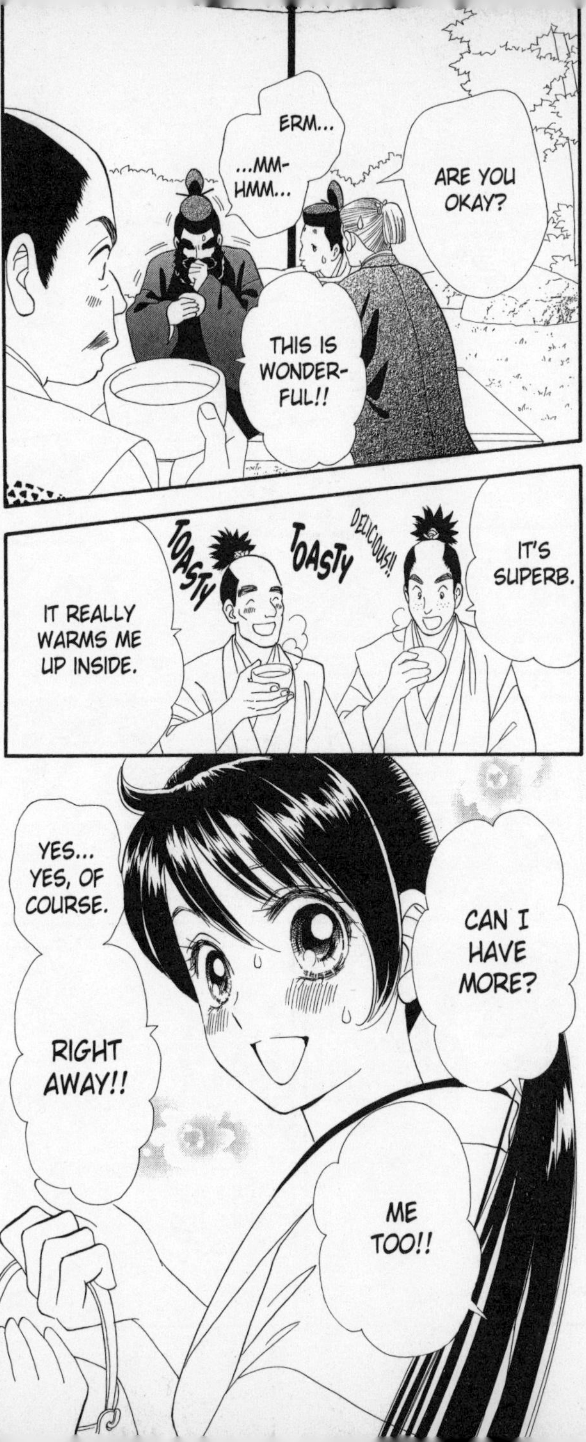
ARE YOU OKAY?
ERM...
...MM-HMM...
THIS IS WONDERFUL!!
IT'S SUPERB.
DELICIOUS!!
TOASTY
TOASTY
IT REALLY WARMS ME UP INSIDE.
CAN I HAVE MORE?
YES... YES, OF COURSE.
RIGHT AWAY!!
ME TOO!!

UE-RIN'S WAY OF THE MANGA ⑯

The reply from the editor came after 2-3 weeks, but all the parts that were pointed out after re-drawing, I had to wait for the next response to come again. I couldn't bear all that waiting anymore, so I decided to send my manga to other publishers.

As for how that turned out...
...check out the next volume!

• • • • • • • • • • • • • • •

Send your messages and letters to the following address. We're looking forward to your requests for the Extra Missions as well!

Rinko Ueda
C/O Shojo Beat
Viz Media
P.O. Box 77010
San Francisco, CA
94107

Rinko Ueda

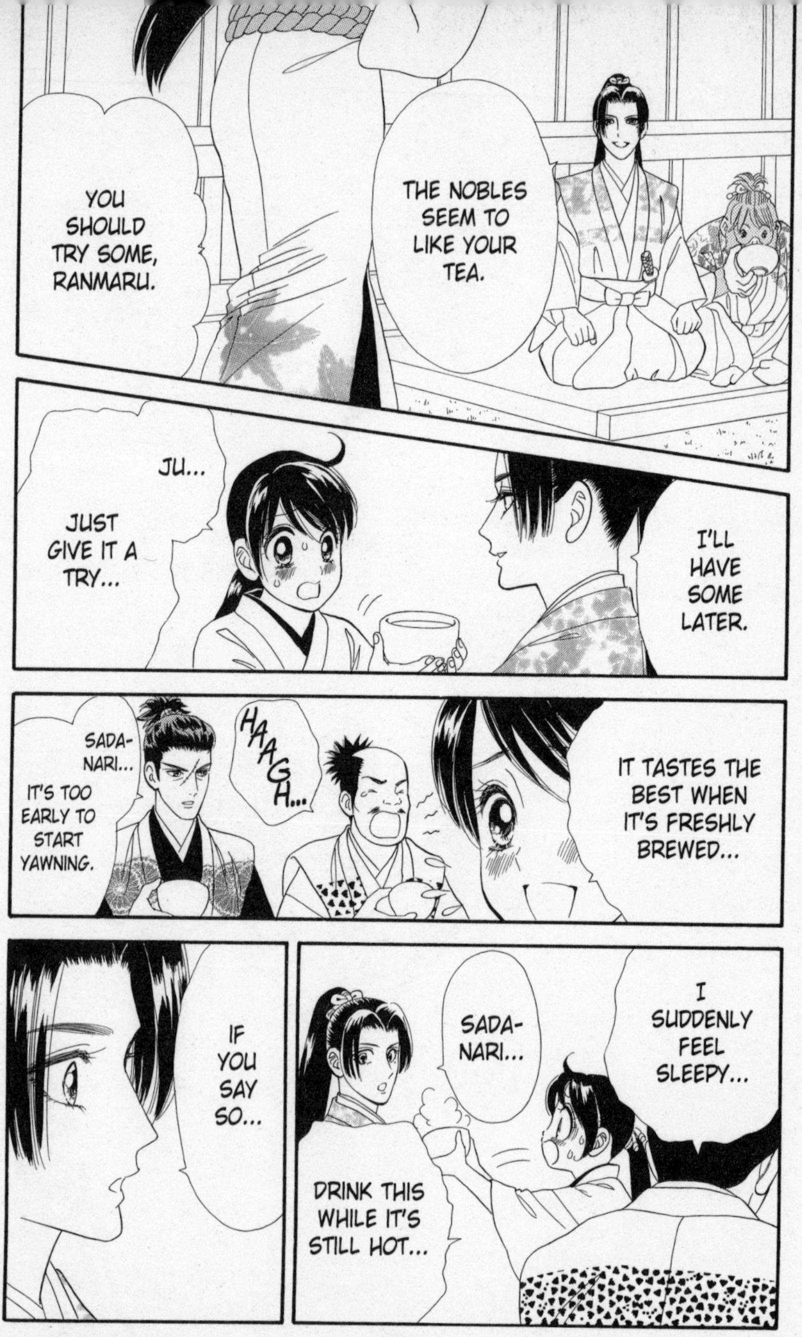
THE NOBLES SEEM TO LIKE YOUR TEA.
YOU SHOULD TRY SOME, RANMARU.
I'LL HAVE SOME LATER.
JU...
JUST GIVE IT A TRY...
IT TASTES THE BEST WHEN IT'S FRESHLY BREWED...
HAAGH...
SADA-NARI...
IT'S TOO EARLY TO START YAWNING.
I SUDDENLY FEEL SLEEPY...
SADA-NARI...
DRINK THIS WHILE IT'S STILL HOT...
IF YOU SAY SO...

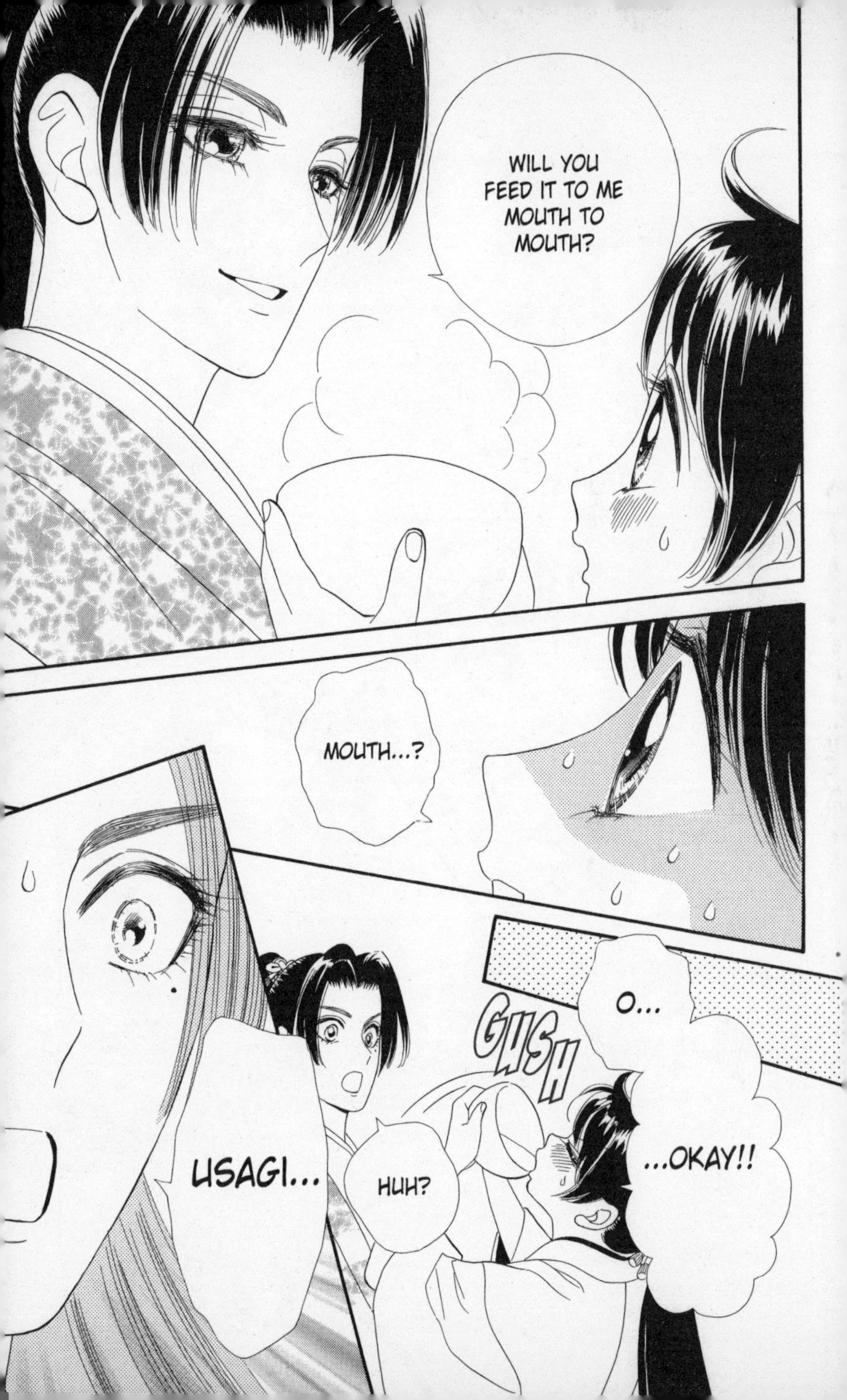
WILL YOU FEED IT TO ME MOUTH TO MOUTH?
MOUTH...?
O...
...OKAY!!
GUSH
HUH?
USAGI...

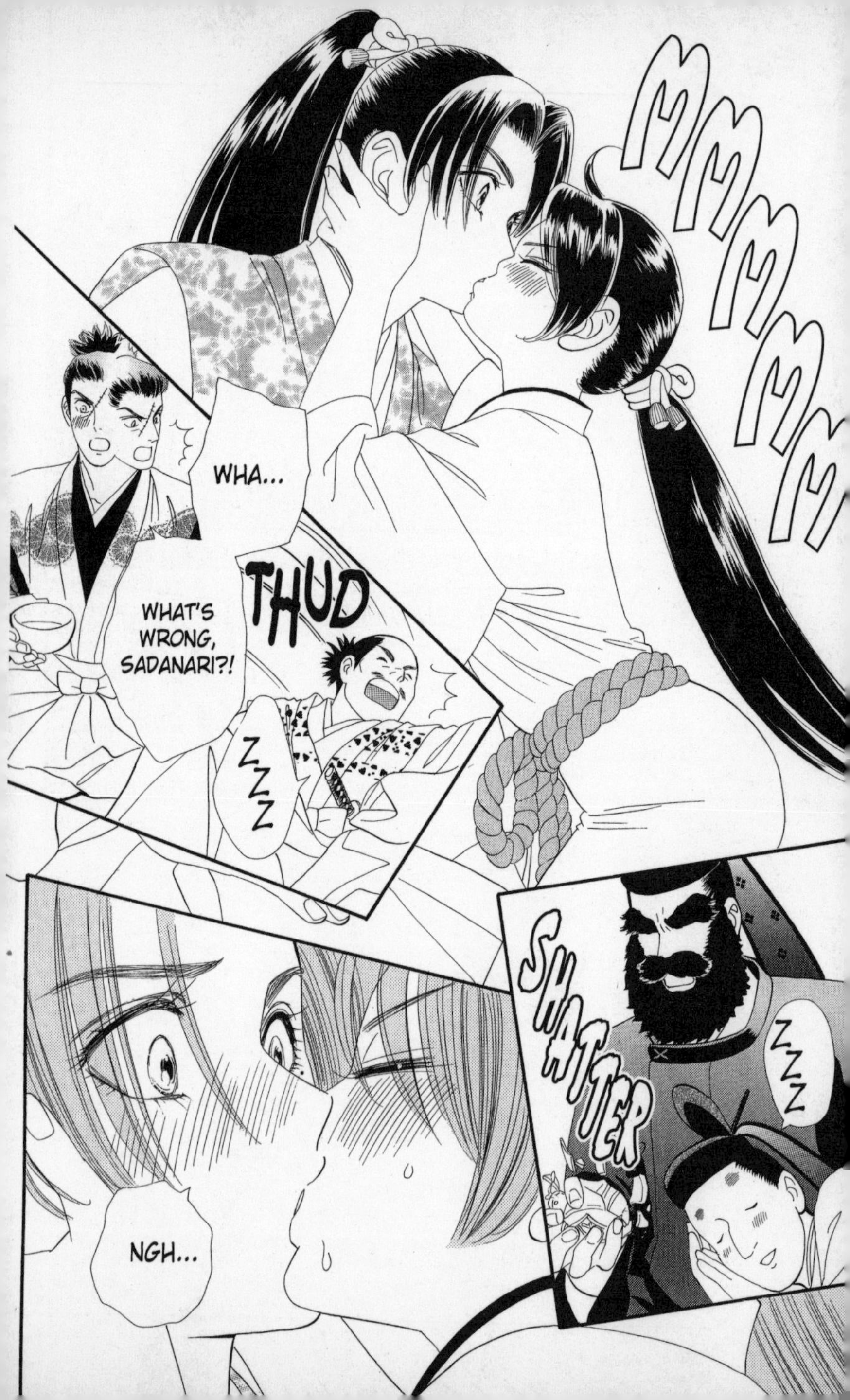
MMMMMMM
WHA...
THUD
ZZZ
WHAT'S WRONG, SADANARI?!
SHATTER
ZZZ
NGH...

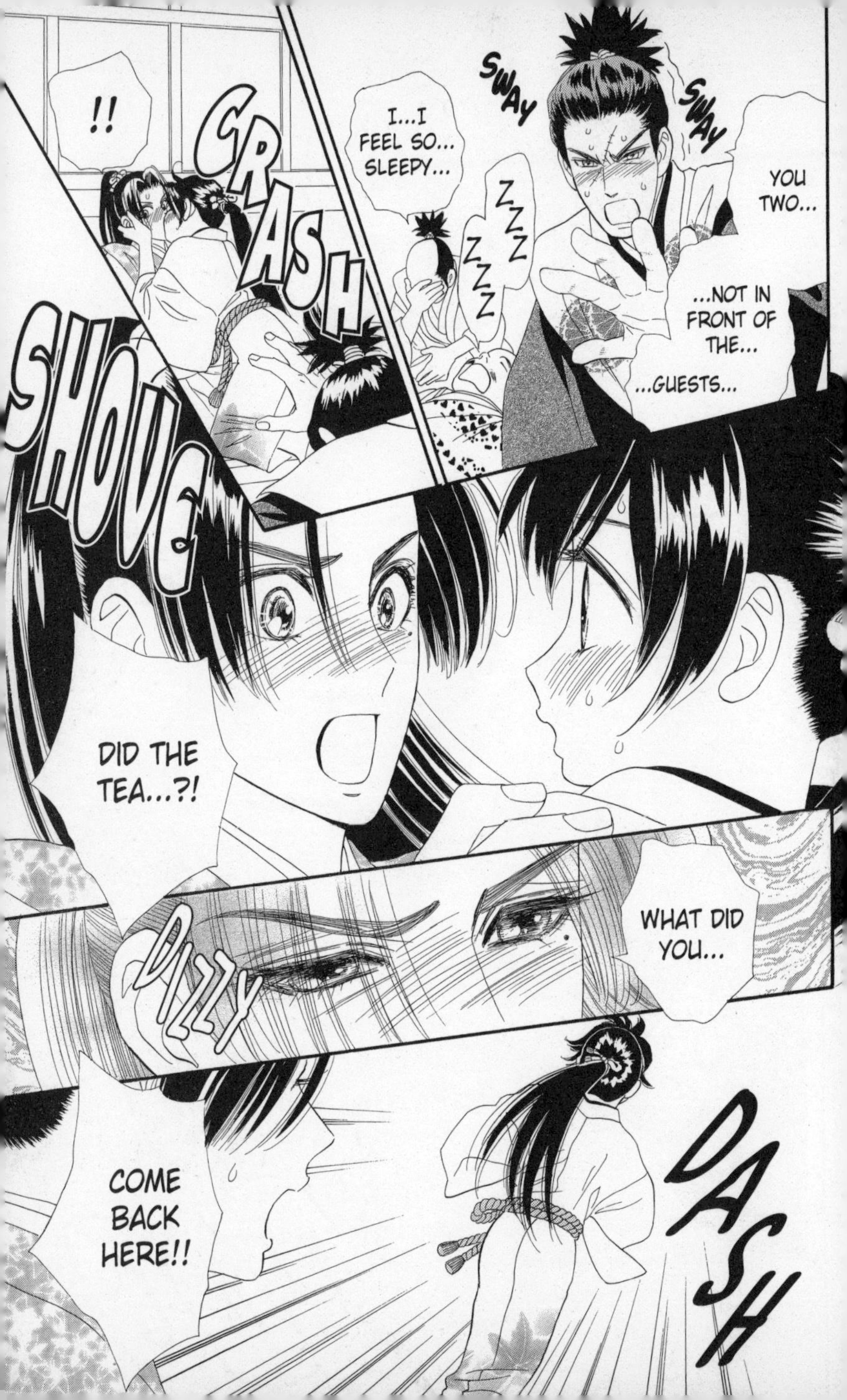
SWAY
SWAY
YOU TWO...
...NOT IN FRONT OF THE...
...GUESTS...
I...I FEEL SO... SLEEPY...
ZZZ
ZZZ
!!
CRASH
SHOVE
DID THE TEA...?!
WHAT DID YOU...
DIZZY
DASH
COME BACK HERE!!

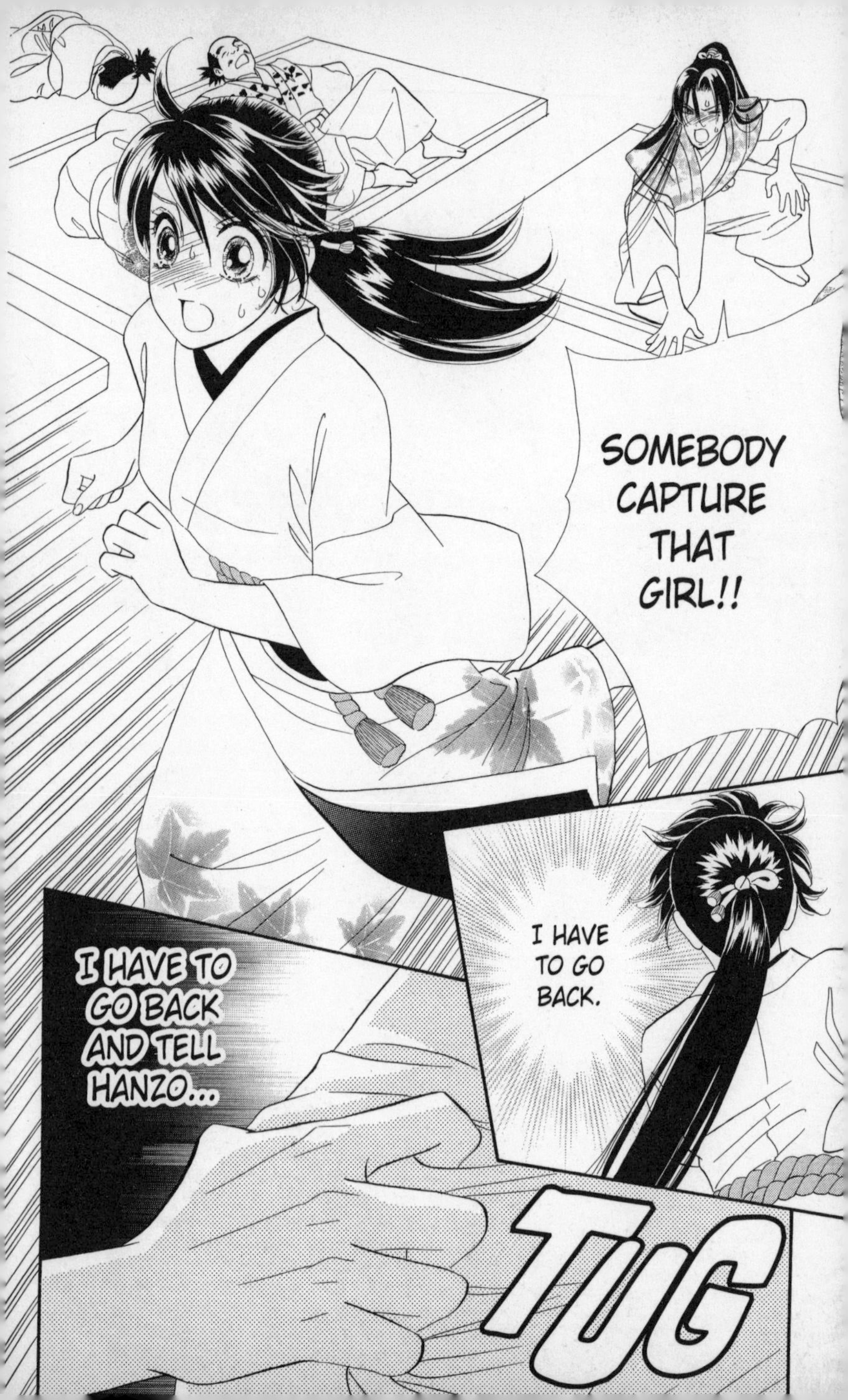
SOMEBODY CAPTURE THAT GIRL!!
I HAVE TO GO BACK.
TUG
I HAVE TO GO BACK AND TELL HANZO...

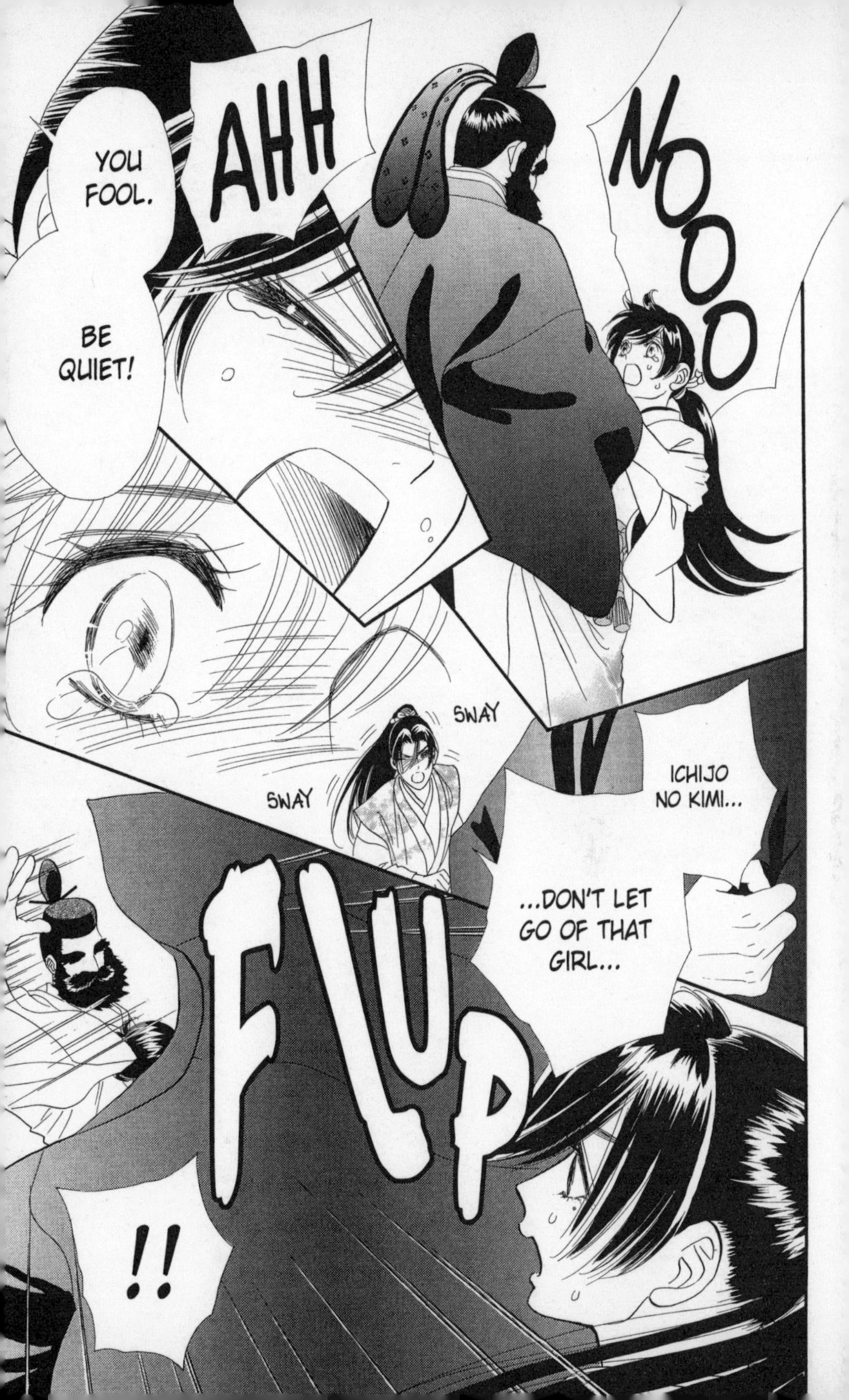
NOOOO
AHH
YOU FOOL.
BE QUIET!
SWAY
SWAY
ICHIJO NO KIMI...
...DON'T LET GO OF THAT GIRL...
FLUP
!!

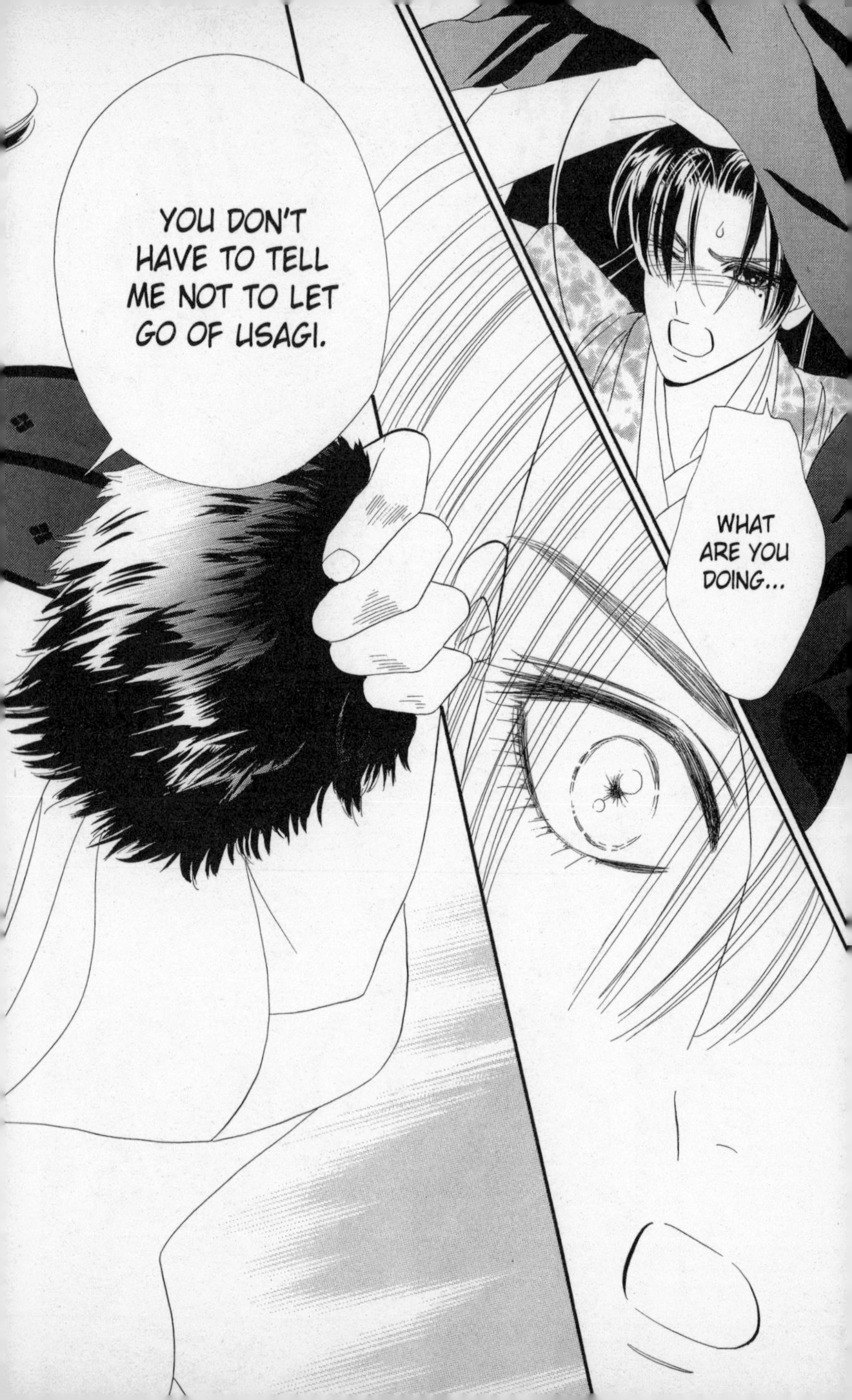
WHAT ARE YOU DOING...
YOU DON'T HAVE TO TELL ME NOT TO LET GO OF USAGI.

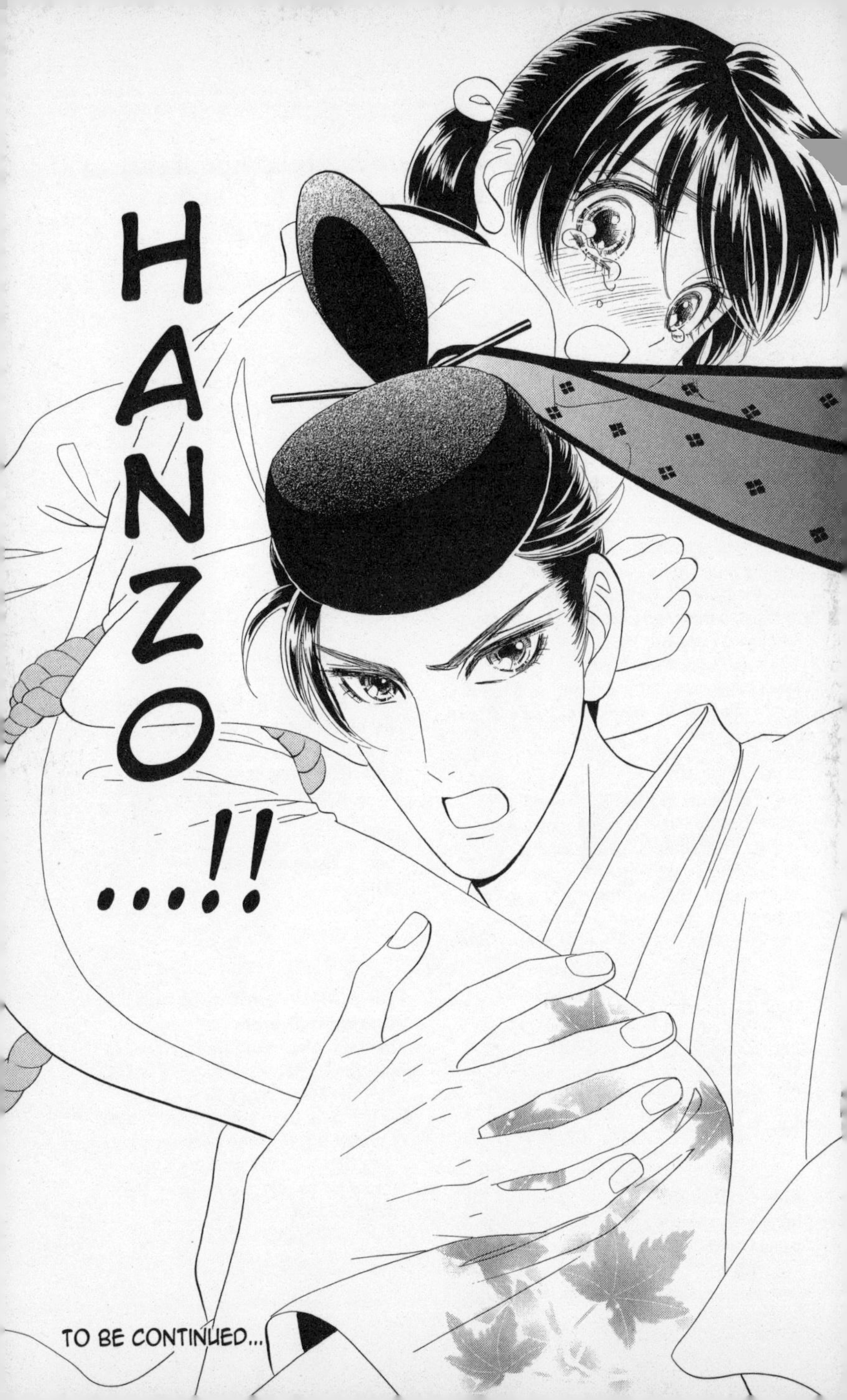
HANZO...!!
TO BE CONTINUED...

The ways of the ninja are mysterious indeed, so here is a glossary of terms to help you navigate the intricacies of their world.

Page 8, panel 4: Tokugawa Ieyasu
Tokugawa Ieyasu (1543-1616) was the first Shogun of the Tokugawa Shogunate. He made a small fishing village named Edo the center of his activities. Edo thrived and became a huge town and was later renamed Tokyo, the present capital.

Page 9, panel 4: Iga
Iga is a region on the island of Honshu and also the name of the famous ninja clan that originated there. Another area famous for its ninja is Kouga, in the Shiga prefecture on Honshu. Many books claim that these two ninja clans were mortal enemies, but in reality inter-ninja relations were not as bad as stories might suggest.

Page 15, panel 5: Manga School
"Manga School" is a section in Japanese manga magazines for people who want to become manga artists. Participants who receive high scores for their sample manga submissions get an award along with a chance to make their debut in the magazine.

Page 23, panel 3: Castella
Castella is a type of sponge cake made from sugar, flour, eggs, and starch syrup. This sweet was brought over to Japan by Portuguese merchants and was originally called "pão de Castella" (meaning "bread from Castile").

Page 32: Benkei
Benkei is a character from Rinko Ueda's manga series *Ryo*. He is based on the Japanese historical figure Saito Musashibo Benkei, who is known for his strength and loyalty.

Page 2: Shimo no Hanzo
Shimo no means "the Lower," and in this case refers to Hanzo's geographic location rather than social status.

Page 2: Azuchi
Azuchi is by Lake Biwa in Shiga Prefecture, where Oda Nobunaga built his castle and the town that were the center of his operations.

Page 2: Oda Nobunaga
Nobunaga lived from 1534 to 1582, and came close to unifying Japan. He is probably one of the most famous Japanese warlords. He was the first warlord to successfully incorporate the gun in battle and is notorious for his ruthlessness.

Page 2: Okazaki
Okazaki is in Aichi Prefecture on the main island of Honshu, about 22 miles from Nagoya.

Page 6: Matsuken Samba and Abarenbo Shogun
The song "Matsuken Samba" was a big hit around 2005; it's sung by Japanese actor Ken Matsudaira ("Matsuken" is derived from combining the first syllable of his last name "Matsu" with his first name "Ken.") Ken Matsudaira is also famous for his role in a TV series called *Abarenbo Shogun*.

Page 96, panel 1: Enryakuji
Enryakuji is a famous temple on Mt. Hiei and was a significant symbol of Buddhism at the time. Because the Buddhists did not obey Nobunaga, he burned the temple to the ground in 1571, killing 20,000-30,000 men, women, and children in the process.

Page 114, panel 3: Mitsuhide Akechi
Mitsuhide Akechi became one of Oda Nobunaga's retainers after Nobunaga's conquest of Mino province (now Gifu prefecture) in 1566. Akechi is known to have been more of an intellectual and a pacifist than a warrior.

Page 123, panel 4: Sakai
Sakai is a city in Osaka prefecture that is one of the largest and most important seaports in Japan. Once known for samurai swords, Sakai is now famous for quality kitchen knives and other cutlery.

Page 142, panel 2: Sen no Rikyu
Sen no Rikyu (1522-1591) is famous for having a huge influence on the Japanese tea ceremony, particularly in wabi-cha (a style that emphasizes simplicity). Rikyu became tea master for Oda Nobunaga when he was 58 years old.

Page 148, panel 6: Tempura
Although tempura is now considered a classic Japanese dish, it was Portuguese missionaries who first introduced this batter-coated deep fried delicacy to Japan during the 16th century.

Page 161: Kunoichi
A term often used for female ninja. The word is spelled くノ一, and when combined, the letters form the kanji for woman, 女。

Page 163: Plus Alpha
In Japanese, "plus alpha" is used to amplify something. For example, if someone asks you how busy your work is, you might reply, "I'm pretty busy right now. I've got my usual stuff to do plus alpha on the side."

Page 38, panel 3: Rubia Akane
Rubia Akane is a plant that can be found in the mountains of Japan. Its root is used in Chinese and Japanese medicine to heal anemia, stop bleeding, etc. It is also used in cloth dyeing, as it has an orange yellow color when the root is dried.

Page 58: Ryo
Ryo is the title character of Rinko Ueda's manga series *Ryo*. The story features Saito Musashibo Benkei and Minamoto no Yoshitsune, two popular characters from Japanese history.

Page 58: Juni-hitoe
A juni-hitoe is a very elegant and complex kimono worn by court ladies in Japan. The name literally translates into "twelve-layer robe," and it can weigh up to 20 kilograms.

Page 68, panel 2: Kami no Hanzou
The term *kami no* means "the Upper," and can refer to social status. However, since Hanzou is a member of a branch family, it is very unlikely that his status is higher than that of the head of the entire clan, Hanzo. The term *kami no* can also refer to geographic location in relation to an important city center, such as the capital. Hanzou is from Okazaki, which is closer to Edo than Hanzo's home in Segachi.

Page 77, panel 1: Ninjutsu
Ninjutsu means the skill or ability of a ninja.

Page 84: Guitar Samurai
Guitar Samurai is a TV character played by Japanese comedian Yoku Hata. He appears in a man's kimono with a guitar and sings a song that usually makes fun of a famous celebrity. After imitating the celebrity, Guitar Samurai finishes by saying, "Slash!" Yoku Hata also uses the phrase "Isn't that what people say?" in his puns.

Usagi wasn't good at anything in the beginning, but lately she's been acting more like a kunoichi (which is something even I never expected to see). In addition, Hanzo seems to be becoming more human. I really enjoy showing these small changes. Usagi's encounter with Ranmaru has brought a big turning point in this story, so please continue to follow the adventures of Usagi and her friends.

–Rinko Ueda

Rinko Ueda is from Nara prefecture. She enjoys listening to the radio, drama CDs, and Rakugo comedy performances. Her works include *Ryo*, a series based on the legend of Gojo Bridge, *Home*, a story about love crossing national boundaries, and *Tail of the Moon (Tsuki no Shippo)*, a romantic ninja comedy.

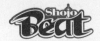

TAIL OF THE MOON

Vol. 8

The Shojo Beat Manga Edition

STORY & ART BY
RINKO UEDA

Translation & Adaptation/Tetsuichiro Miyaki
Touch-up Art & Lettering/Mark McMurray
Design/Izumi Hirayama
Editor/Amy Yu

Editor in Chief, Books/Alvin Lu
Editor in Chief, Magazines/Marc Weidenbaum
Sr. Director of Acquisitions/Rika Inouye
VP of Sales/Gonzalo Ferreyra
Sr. VP of Marketing/Liza Coppola
Publisher/Hyoe Narita

Printed in Canada

Published by VIZ Media, LLC
P.O. Box 77064
San Francisco, CA 94107

Shojo Beat Manga Edition
10 9 8 7 6 5 4 3 2 1
First printing, December 2007

www.viz.com

store.viz.com

PARENTAL ADVISORY
TAIL OF THE MOON is rated T+ for Older Teen and is recommended for ages 16 and up. This volume contains brief nudity and ninja violence.
ratings.viz.com

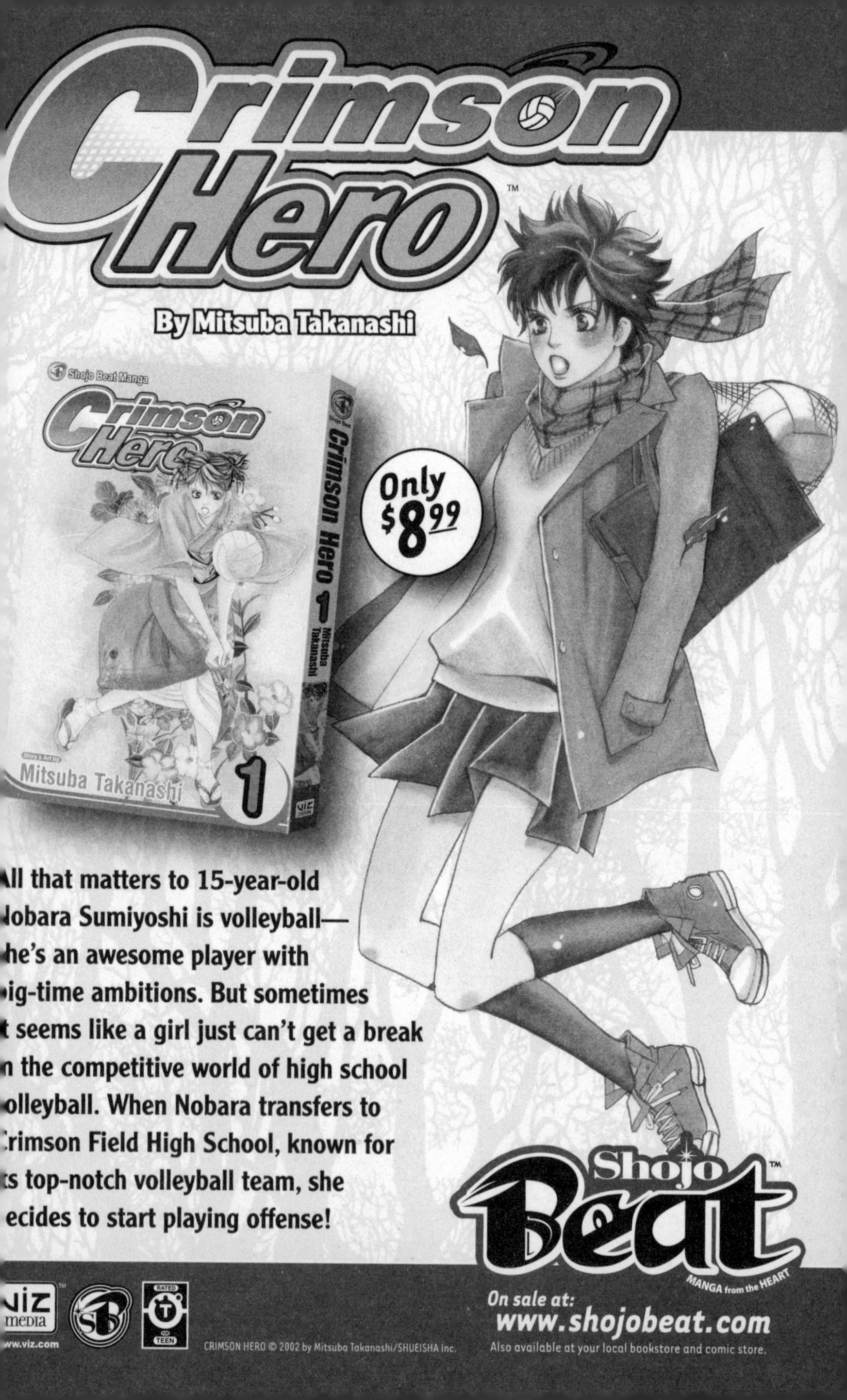
Crimson Hero™
By Mitsuba Takanashi
Shojo Beat Manga
Crimson Hero
Story & Art by
Mitsuba Takanashi
1
Shojo Beat
Crimson Hero 1
Mitsuba Takanashi
Only $8.99
ll that matters to 15-year-old
lobara Sumiyoshi is volleyball—
he's an awesome player with
ig-time ambitions. But sometimes
t seems like a girl just can't get a break
n the competitive world of high school
olleyball. When Nobara transfers to
rimson Field High School, known for
s top-notch volleyball team, she
ecides to start playing offense!
Shojo Beat™
MANGA from the HEART
On sale at:
www.shojobeat.com
Also available at your local bookstore and comic store.
ww.viz.com
RATED T FOR TEEN
CRIMSON HERO © 2002 by Mitsuba Takanashi/SHUEISHA Inc.

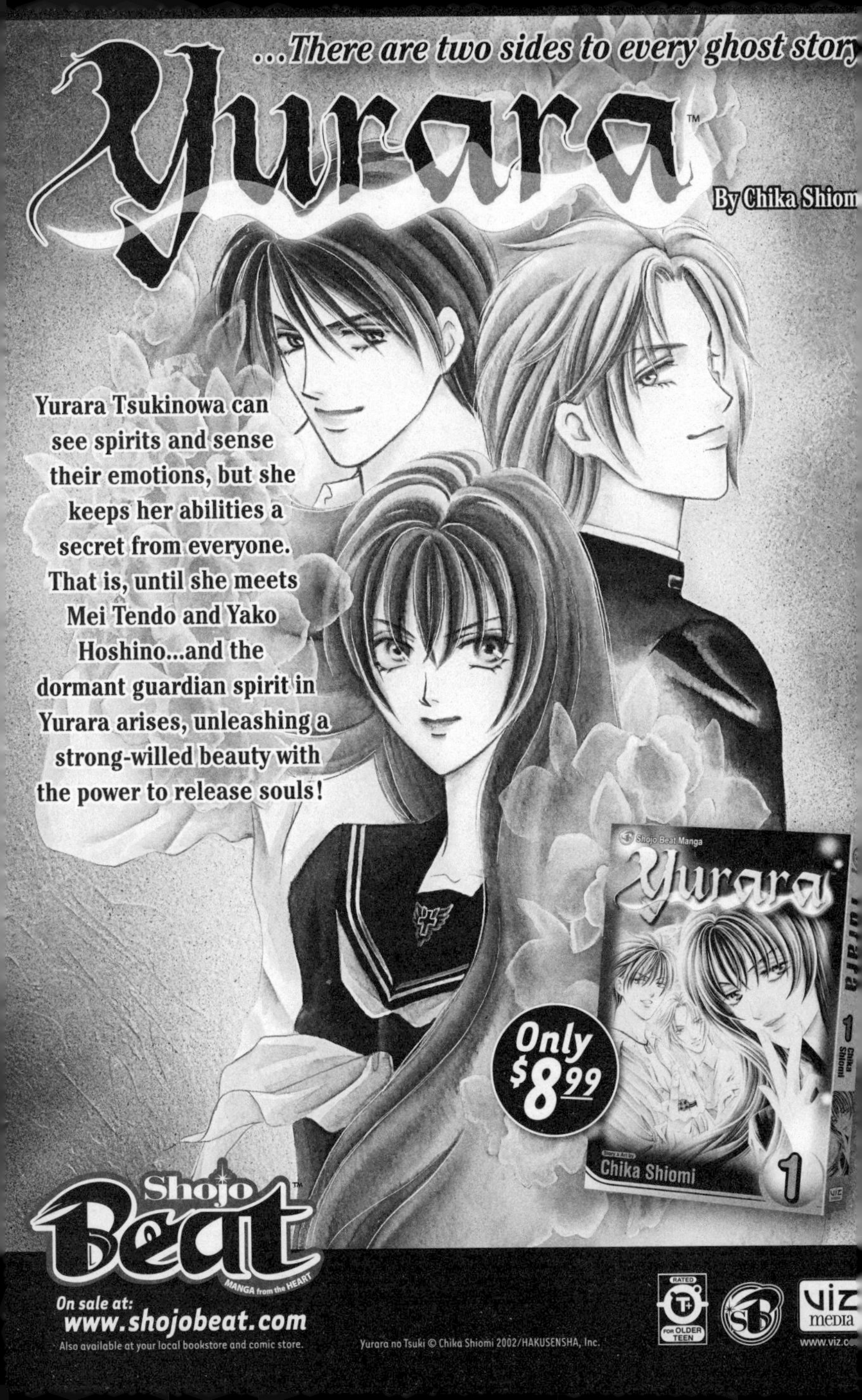
...There are two sides to every ghost story
Yurara™
By Chika Shiom
Yurara Tsukinowa can see spirits and sense their emotions, but she keeps her abilities a secret from everyone. That is, until she meets Mei Tendo and Yako Hoshino...and the dormant guardian spirit in Yurara arises, unleashing a strong-willed beauty with the power to release souls!
Shojo Beat Manga
Yurara
Chika Shiomi
1
Only $8.99
Shojo Beat™
MANGA from the HEART
On sale at:
www.shojobeat.com
Also available at your local bookstore and comic store.
Yurara no Tsuki © Chika Shiomi 2002/HAKUSENSHA, Inc.
RATED T+ FOR OLDER TEEN
VIZ media
www.viz.c

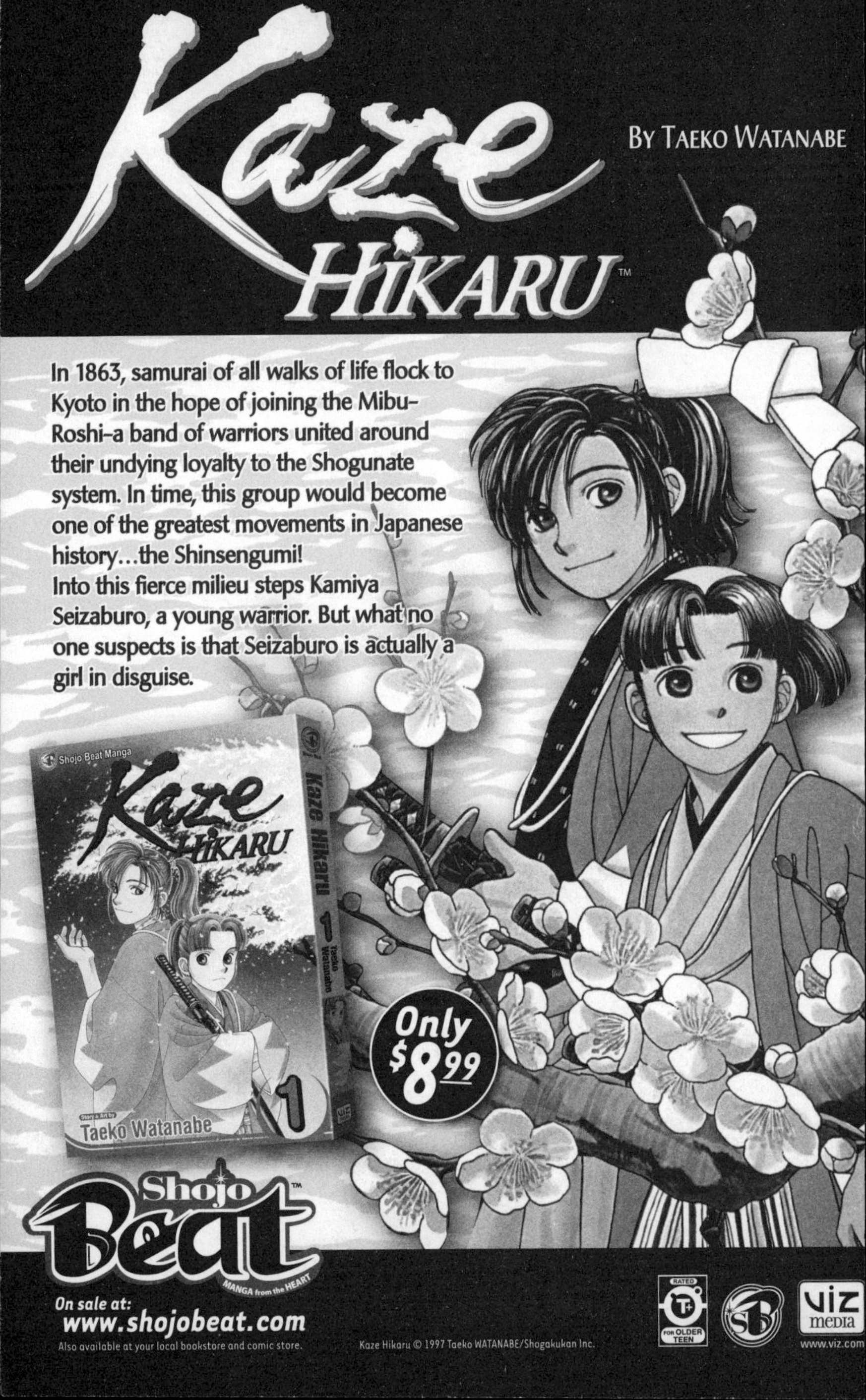
Kaze Hikaru™
By Taeko Watanabe
In 1863, samurai of all walks of life flock to Kyoto in the hope of joining the Mibu-Roshi–a band of warriors united around their undying loyalty to the Shogunate system. In time, this group would become one of the greatest movements in Japanese history…the Shinsengumi!
Into this fierce milieu steps Kamiya Seizaburo, a young warrior. But what no one suspects is that Seizaburo is actually a girl in disguise.
Shojo Beat Manga
Kaze Hikaru
1
Story & Art by
Taeko Watanabe
Only $8.99
Shojo Beat™
MANGA from the HEART
On sale at:
www.shojobeat.com
Also available at your local bookstore and comic store.
Kaze Hikaru © 1997 Taeko WATANABE/Shogakukan Inc.
RATED T+ FOR OLDER TEEN
viz media
www.viz.com

Tell us what you think about Shojo Beat Manga!

Our survey is now available online. Go to:

shojobeat.com/mangasurvey

Help us make our product offerings better!